MONOGRAPH 39

Recent Advances in the Archaeology of the Northern Andes

In Memory of Gerardo Reichel-Dolmatoff

Edited by Augusto Oyuela-Caycedo and J. Scott Raymond

The Institute of Archaeology
University of California, Los Angeles
1998

Edited by Rita Demsetz, Marilyn Gatto, Beverly Godwin, and Brenda Johnson-Grau
Designed by Brenda Johnson-Grau
Production by Linda Tang, Michael Tang, and Amy Chen

LIBRARY OF CONGRESS CATALOGING-IN-PUBLICATION DATA
Recent Advances in the Archaeology of the Northern Andes: in
     memory of Gerardo Reichel-Dolmatoff / edited by A. Oyuela-
     Caycedo and J. Scott Raymond.
          p.   cm. -- (Monograph / Institute of Archaeology, University
     of California, Los Angeles ; 39)
        Includes bibliographical references.
        ISBN 0-917956-90-7
          1. Indians of South America--Andes Region--Antiquities. 2.
     Indians of South America--Andes Region--History. 3. Indians of
     South America--Andes Region--Social life and customs. 4. Excava-
     tions (Archaeology)--Andes Region--Methodology. 5. Andes
     Region--Antiquities. 6. Reichel-Dolmatoff, Gerardo. I. Reichel-
     Dolmatoff, Gerardo. II. Oyuela-Caycedo, Augusto, 1961- III.
     Raymond, J. Scott. IV. Series: Monograph (University of California,
     Los Angeles. Institute of Archaeology); 39.
     F2229.R394   1998
     980'.01--dc21   97-53049
                                                             CIP

Contents

Gerardo Reichel-Dolmatoff with a member of the Kogi

Foreword

Peter T. Furst

COMPOSING a foreword for a volume honoring Gerardo Reichel-Dolmatoff is both an honor and an occasion for reflection and sadness. After a first get-together nearly thirty-five years ago in his office at the Universidad de los Andes in Bogotá, of whose Department of Anthropology he had then just become chair, we met only sporadically. Regrettably this was so especially after 1971, when I moved from Los Angeles to the State University of New York at Albany. Thereafter I missed him almost every time he visited UCLA, where he had become closely associated with the Latin American Center and its longtime director, Johannes Wilbert. But every get-together—including the last one a few months before his untimely death—was over lunch with Wilbert, his good friend and mine (and, incidentally, my mentor in graduate school and since) at the UCLA Faculty Center. Perhaps his death of a heart attack was not untimely but, if death can ever be that, fortunate, for it spared him a more protracted and painful death from cancer of the bladder.

Like many other colleagues in the field of shamanic studies, I owe him more than I can ever express. He was an inspiring scholar and colleague; the depth and breadth of his knowledge and insights never failed to amaze. To me personally the fact that on three occasions—in 1957 in the journal *Folklore America*, in 1972 in *Flesh of the Gods: The Ritual Use of Hallucinogens*, and in 1976 in *Enculturation in Latin America*, an anthology edited by Wilbert—we found ourselves between the covers of the same publication, is a source of personal pleasure and professional satisfaction. For anything to which he contributed his experience and wisdom was enriched.

Let me single out just one example. In 1967 I published an essay, "Huichol Conceptions of the Soul," in the unfortunately now defunct *Folklore Americas*, published for many years by the UCLA Center for Comparative Folklore and Mythology. The essay took up 67 pages, virtually the entire issue, but there was space for just one more short contribution. The editor, Stanley Robe, made a fortunate choice that should by rights

have had a lasting impact on rock art studies, not just in South America but generally. That was a brief paper Reichel-Dolmatoff had sent to Wilbert, as Associate Editor of the journal, entitled "Rock Paintings of the Vaupés: An Essay of Interpretation." Behind that modest, not to say pedestrian, title lay a rare insight into the religious structure of native peoples of the Vaupés region of Amazonian Colombia, and the reciprocal relationships between archaeological rock art, the living present, and the shaman as mediator between people, animals, souls, and the spirit master, or "owner," of human, animal, and plant fertility. In just a few pages it proposes one of the most sophisticated conceptualizations of the human soul and how it fits into the concept of reciprocity I have ever come across in nearly four decades of reading and fieldwork. The religion of the native peoples of the Vaupés, we learned from Reichel-Dolmatoff, is based on the fundamental concept that there exists in the biosphere a limited supply of energy, or life force. Animals and people participate in this energy cycle on an equal basis. When a hunter kills an animal to feed his family, he diminishes the total energy available for fertility and fecundity, human as well as animal. To compensate, the shaman of the Tukanoan-speakers of the Vaupés region enters into a deal with the Master of Animals, here called Wai-maxsë. Places with ancient rock art are his "houses." In his ecstatic trance, the shaman visits these to give the Master of Animals—conceived as a red-colored humpbacked dwarf whose giant erect phallus (reminiscent of the red-colored phallic dwarfs in Western Mexican shaft tomb art) is filled with the seeds of useful plants—a list of people who have committed an offense against the social and religious norms and promises their souls as replacements for those of the animals.

Further, according to Reichel-Dolmatoff, along the courses of the many rivers of the Vaupés region there are rapids whose turbulent waters pass over large rocks covered with ancient abstract designs. These too are conceived as dwellings of Wai-maxsë, here in his capacity of Master of Fish. As close observers of nature and natural cycles, Indian people make careful note of the annual migrations of fish that swim hundreds of kilometers back to their original spawning grounds. But not all the species make the same journey along the entire river, stopping to spawn at certain rapids and eddies that for the Indians have uterine associations. Here the Master of Fish ensures the multiplication of the species. These "Houses of Wai-maxsë," too, the shamans visit in ecstatic trances triggered by inebriating sniff or infusions of the "Vine of the Soul."

In his brief and unfortunately little-known paper Reichel-Dolmatoff pointed the way for those of us who have long been dissatisfied with standard "hunting magic" explanations of Paleolithic rock art, but who have also been struggling to come up with something better—something that, like the recent work of the South African cognitive archaeologist David Lewis-Williams, might more closely correspond to the way people who, like the San of South Africa, were not all that long ago still recording intimate, and reciprocal, relationships with the animals on the walls of caves and rock shelters.

Nearly three decades ago, the late anthropologist of religion Weston La Barre made the then-radical suggestion that the "base religion" of all Native American societies, past and present, was an essentially Mesolithic, or even Paleolithic, Eurasiatic shamanism. Early migrants carried it out of Asia into the Americas, where over the millennia it was reshaped by different cultural, social, and natural environments—without, however, ever losing its essential core. For the rest of us in shamanic studies, it was a real eye-opener, one that we are still digesting today.

I'm not sure how well Gerardo Reichel-Dolmatoff knew La Barre, or even whether they ever met. But I do know that from his own experience in the Colombian Amazon, he fully agreed with La Barre's explanation for the extraordinary proliferation in the religions of Native Americans, especially in Meso- and South America, of what were then called "hallucinogenic" plants and for which some of us now prefer the term "entheogen," a Greek-Latin compound meaning the sacred, or god, within, as more closely corresponding to how native peoples view these extraordinary plants. It was La Barre's contention that because shamanism is by definition inseparable from the ecstatic-visionary experience, the early migrants out of Asian arrived programmed, so to speak, for conscious exploration of their new environments for species that facilitated the ecstatic-visionary trance.

Along with La Barre's colleagues in the comparative and culture-specific study of shamanism, Reichel-Dolmatoff agreed that shamanism, presumably the most ancient form of human spirituality, must have derived some of its basic beliefs about the place of humans and animals and plants in the organization and functioning of the cosmos, and the relationship between them from natural modeling, that is, the close observation of nature and natural processes and their transposition into metaphor. It was in this, and not just in the human imagination, or psychological processes, that we had to seek a logical explanation for the extraordinary persistence,

over vast spans of time and space, not just of shamanism itself but the numerous striking similarities that have been noted in the basic beliefs informing the shamanic world view, its cosmic architecture, its concepts of disease and healing, its techniques of manipulating the sacred, and often even its diverse paraphernalia, over time and space.

In our own studies of the phenomenon of shamanism, there was not one of us who has not benefited over the years from Reichel-Dolmatoff's encyclopedic knowledge and practical experience among traditional peoples of the Colombian Amazon: La Barre in his philosophical searches for the origins of religion in ecstatic shamanism; Richard Evans Schultes, long-time director of Harvard's Botanical Museum, and the world authority on the plant "hallucinogens" of the Americans and their cultural uses; Johannes Wilbert, who in *Flesh of the Gods* published his first exploration of the role of *Nicotiana rustica* tobacco as a shamanic inebrient in South America alongside Reichel-Dolmatoff's essay on the aboriginal cultural contest of *ayahuasca*, and who with his 1987 book, *Tobacco and Shamanism in South America*, was to become the ranking authority on the cultural use and pharmacology of tobacco as, in many places, the preferred, if not sole, ecstatic intoxicant for shamans; and certainly myself.

In 1981, Jill L. Furst and I co-authored a review article of some of Reichel-Dolmatoff's books. We gave that essay the title "Seeing a Culture Without Seams." I'd like to conclude these few words of appreciation by paraphrasing some key passages from that essay:

Reichel-Dolmatoff worked in the great tradition of anthropology. Above all, he appreciated the role of ideology, or mental life. But for him it was not just ideology influencing daily life but a far more complex process of reciprocal interaction between ideology, mental processes (both waking and in ecstatic-visionary trance states), environment, economics, technology, the arts and crafts, conservation of scarce natural resources, the enculturation of the young, and so forth. The implication of his work is that where these essential interrelationships are not recognized and honored culture is distorted.

No doubt, some of Reichel-Dolmatoff's European heritage profoundly influenced his concern and respect for native intellectual attainment. In this he was colleague and heir to a long and honorable list of Americanists of European intellectual heritage or education, deceased or still active, whose major concern has been the ideological universe of indigenous peoples of the so-called New World. Among others, Boas, Kroeber, Lowie, Preuss, Diguet, Hultkrantz, Schultze Jena, Levi-Strauss, Rasmussen, W. Müller, Wilbert, and some of their American students come to mind. In that tradition, the tradition in which Reichel-Dolmatoff was educated and made his major contributions, ideas are important and are capable, like faith, of moving mountains. I venture that long after postmodernism and deconstruction have joined the company of yesterday's fads, the baseline ethnographies of such spiritual ancestors as Reichel-Dolmatoff will continue to be read and followed as honorable examples.

Preface

THE NORTHERN ANDES has had a subdued voice in the literature of American archaeology. Our purpose in putting together this volume has been to provide a published outlet for the recent significant research which has been carried out in the region and at the same time, to pay homage to the Gerardo Reichel-Dolmatoff (1912–1994), a giant among anthropologists and Colombia's most prolific and renowned archaeologist. Much of the research presented here either emerged directly from work initiated by Reichel-Dolmatoff or was inspired by his ideas and interests. Eight of the twelve chapters derive from the invited presentations of a symposium on the northern Andes which we organized in honor of Reichel-Dolmatoff at the Meeting of the Society for American Archaeology in Minneapolis in May of 1995. The papers have been revised and enlarged, and four additional chapters (chapters 1, 3, 7, and 11) have been included to round out and give coherence to the book. The scope of the chapters includes advances in research on the first human colonization of the region, the origins of sedentism and food production, the rise of chiefdoms, and the importance of symbolism and iconography. The lowlands and highlands of the northern Andes (Colombia, Panama, Ecuador, and Venezuela) comprise a pivotal region for understanding many of the social, economic, political, and ideological changes which pre-Columbian cultures experienced. For example, why inventions such as pottery and goldsmithing occurred in this region earlier than in most other places in the Americas looms as an imporant question in New World archaeology. We hope that the discussion of the cultural contexts of these phenomena in this volume will contribute significantly to the more general debate and, as well, awaken a critical interest in the archaeology of this important region.

It is not possible in the scope of a single book to encompass more than part of the breadth of Professor Reichel-Dolmatoff's experiences, interests, and contributions. He was born in Salzburg on 6 March 1912, in what was the Austro-Hungarian Empire and died on 16 May 1994, in Bogotá in his adopted homeland, Colombia. His secondary education was oriented to the classics (Latin and Greek) at the Benedictine school of Kremsmünster in Austria (1923–1931). He graduated in Fine Arts at the Akademie der Bildenden Künste in Munich, Germany (1934–1936). He then moved to Paris where he attended both the Falculté des Lettres of the Sorbonne and the Université de Paris, Ecole du Louvre (1937-1939). During his years in Paris, he attended lectures by Marcel Mauss and the sociologist George Gurvitch. In 1939, on the eve of the Second World War, he immigrated to Colombia, following the advice of the French political scientist André Siegfried. During the war years, he worked in paleontology for petroleum companies in Bogotá (1941-1946) and became involved in ethnological and archaeological research in Bogotá at the Instituto Etnológico Nacional (1941-1946), which was founded by his friend the French ethnologist Paul Rivet, who was in exile in Colombia.

Reichel-Dolmatoff's field research began in 1940 with a trip to the upper Meta River in the Orinoco plains which generated one of the earliest published studies on the material culture of the Guahibo Indians. In 1941, he and Alicia Dussán Maldonado started archaeological research projects in the highlands at the Sabana de Bogotá, and then conducted excavations in Sopó, Soacha, and in the lowlands near the Magdalena River close to the city of Girardot.

Reichel-Dolmatoff became a Colombian citizen in 1942, and the following year he married Alicia Dussán Maldonado, an ethnologist who was part of the first generation of graduate students of the Instituto Etnológico Nacional directed by Paul Rivet. The couple worked as a research team for the rest of his life.

The Reichel-Dolmatoffs were unstoppable researchers, and the diversity of research programs which they undertook was enormous. Gerardo became a research member of the new Instituto Colombiano de Antropología (1953–1960). In 1963, he and Alicia created the first Department of Anthropology in Colombia at the Universidad de Los Andes where he became chairman (1963–1969). In 1974, Gerardo became Adjunct Professor in the Department of Anthropology at the University of California at Los Angeles, where occasionally he gave lectures and taught classes.

The enormous contribution that Gerardo Reichel-Dolmatoff made to science has been recognized internationally on several occasions. In 1976 he was made a Foreign Associate Member of the National Academy of Sciences in the United States; in 1983, a Member of the Academia Real Española de Ciencias; and in 1989, a Fellow of the Linnean Society. He was also awarded, in 1975, the Thomas H. Huxley medal by the Royal Anthropological Institute of Great Britain and Ireland. As well, in 1983 he became a Founding Member of the Third World Academy of Sciences.

The archaeology and anthropology of Colombia and Latin American have lost a brilliant scholar. Gerardo, however, has left behind a rich legacy of academic achievement and inspiration, as this book demonstrates. The imprint of his scholarly influence can be seen not only in his own students and followers in Colombia but also in the students of Donald Lathrap, five of whom are contributors to this volume. Reichel and Lathrap were friends and colleagues, and admired each other's research. Reichel at times sent students to study with Lathrap at the University of Illinois and in turn helped facilitate the field research of Lathrap's students. Lathrap, the Great Caiman, as his students affectionately referred to him, died in 1990. Now Reichel, the Great Jaguar of the neotropics, has followed his friend, the Great Caiman, but their discoveries, ideas, and teachings live on.

Augusto Oyuela-Caycedo
J. Scott Raymond

Bibliography of Gerardo Reichel-Dolmatoff
1943 to 1997

Compiled by Augusto Oyuela-Caycedo

This bibliography is based partly on the bibliography compiled by Alicia Dussán de Reichel (1992) and includes all publications through 9 September 1997.

1943a   Apuntes arqueológicos de Soacha. *Revista del Instituto Etnológico Nacional, Bogotá* 1(1):15–25.

1943b   Las urnas funerarias en la cuenca del río Magdalena. With Alicia Dussán de Reichel.*Revista del Instituto Etnológico Nacional,* 1(1):209–28.

1944a   La cultura material de los indios Guahibo. *Revista del Instituto Etnológico Nacional* 1(2):437–506.

1944b   Grupos sanguíneos entre los indios Pijao del Tolima. With Alicia Dussán de Reichel. *Revista del Instituto Etnológico Nacional* 1(2): 507–520.

1945a   Los indios Motilones (Etnografía y Lingüística). *Revista del Instituto Etnológico Nacional* 2(1):15–115.

1945b   Mitos y cuentos de los indios Chimila. *Boletín de Arqueología* 1(1):4–30.

1945c   La manufactura de cerámica entre los Chami. *Boletín de Arqueología* 1(5):425– 430.

1945d   Bibliografía lingüística del Grupo Chocó. *Boletín de Arqueología* 1(6):625–627.

1946a   Las zonas culturales de Colombia y sus elementos constitutivos. *Boletín de Arqueología* 2(1):3–17.

1946b   Etnografía Chimila. *Boletín de Arqueología* 2(2):95–155.

1946c   Informe sobre las investigaciones preliminares de la Comisión Etnológica al Catatumbo (N. de Santander). *Boletín de Arqueología* 2(4):381–394.

1946d   Toponimia del Tolima y Huila. *Revista del Instituto Etnológico Nacional* 2(2):105–134.

1947a   La Lengua Chiniüa. *Journal de la Société des Américanistes* 31:15–50.

1947b   La cueva funeraria de La Paz (presentación preliminar). *Boletín de Arqueología* 2(5/6):403–412.

1948a   El cultivo del maíz y la etnología en el Norte de Colombia. *Agricultura Tropical* 4(1):7–12.

1948b   La marimba atanquera. *Revista de Folklore* 2:255–258.

1948c   El Instituto Etnológico del Magdalena (Colombia) en 1947. *Boletín Bibliográfico de Antropología Americana* 10:22–24.

1949a   Aspectos económicos entre los indios de la Sierra Nevada. *Boletín de Arqueología* 2(5/6):573–580.

1949b   Tres cerámicas indígenas. *Proa* no. 29.

1949c   Bibliografía etnológica del Departamento del Magdalena. *Divulgación Cultural del Instituto Etnológico del Magdalena* no. 3.

1949d   El Instituto Etnológico del Magdalena (Colombia) en 1948. *Boletín Bibliográfico de Antropología Americana* 11:79–81.

1950a   Los Kogi: Una tribu indígena de la Sierra Nevada de Santa Marta, Colombia. Tomo I. *Revista del Instituto Etnológico Nacional* 4(1/2):1–320.

1950b   El Instituto Etnológico del Magdalena (Colombia) en 1949. *Boletín Bibliográfico de Antropología Americana* 12(1):93–96.

1950c   Colombia. Las ciencias del hombre en el período 1945–1950. *RevistaUniversidad Nacional de Argentina* 3(1–2):278–282.

1950d   Parentela, parentesco y agresión entre los Iroka. With Alexander L. Clark. *Journal de la Société des Américanistes* 39:97–109.

1951a   *Los Kogi: Una tribu indígena de la Sierra Nevada de Santa Marta, Colombia,* Tomo 2. Bogotá: Editorial Iqueima.

1951b   *Datos histórico–culturales sobre las tribus de la antigua Gobernación de Santa Marta.* Bogotá: Banco de la República.

1951c   Notas sobre la alfarería del Bajo Magdalena. *Revista de Folklore* 6:169–176.

1951d   Conceptos biológicos de los indios Kogi de la Sierra Nevada de Santa Marta. *Anales de la Sociedad de*

Biología 4(6): 212–217.

1951e   *Notes on the Present State of Anthropological Research in Northern Colombia.* Bogotá: Editorial Iqueima.

1951f   El Instituto Etnológico del Magdalena (Colombia) en 1950. *Boletín Bibliográfico de Antropología Americana* 13 (1-1950):47–49.

1951g   Notas sobre la estratificación social en Colombia. *Divulgaciones del Instituto de Investigación Etnológica* 2(3):139–143.

1951h   Investigaciones arqueológicas en el Departamento del Magdalena: 1946–1950; Parte l: Arqueología del río Ranchería; Parte II: Arqueología del río Cesar. With Alicia Dussán de Reichel. *Boletín de Arqueología* 3(1–6):1–334.

1952a   Notas sobre la determinación del Carbono 14 para constatar la edad de muestras animales y vegetales. *Anales de la Sociedad de Biología* 5(1):18–20.

1952b   Notas sobre la clase media en Colombia. *Ciencias Sociales* 3(13):1–5.

1953a   Notas sobre la clase media en Colombia. In *Tres estudios sobre la clase media en Colombia,* edited by Luis López de Mesa, 43–54. Bogotá: Banco de la República.

1953b   Actitudes hacia el trabajo en una población mestiza de Colombia. *América Indígena* 13 (3):165–174.

1953c   *Colombia: período indígena.* Programa de Historia de América, México, Instituto Panamericano de Geografía e Historia, 1(6).

1953d   Colombia: período indígena. *Suplemento.* Programa de Historia de América, vol. 1, nos. 4 y 6, México, Instituto Panamericano de Geografía e Historia.

1953e   Colombia, período indígena. Complemento. In *Area Circuncaribe* edited by Miguel Acosta Saignes, 1(5):89–101. Programa de Historia de América (México). Instituto Panamericano de Geografía e Historia.

1953f   Prácticas obstétricas como un factor de control social en una cultura de transición. *Anales de la Sociedad de Biología* 6(1):30–37.

1953g   Contactos y cambios culturales en la Sierra Nevada de Santa Marta. *Revista Colombiana de Antropología* 1(1):15–122.

1953h   Algunos mitos de los Indios Chami, (Colombia). *Revista Colombiana de Folklore,* 2(1):148–165.

1953i   El marco cultural en el estudio de la vivienda: la comunidad rural Magdalenense. *Serie Resúmenes de Clase,* Bogotá, no. 4. Centro Inter-Americano de Vivienda, Servicios de Intercambio Científico, Unión Panamericana.

1953j   Perspectivas de la arqueología en el Norte de Colombia. *Boletín del Instituto de Antropología* 1(1):80–88.

1953k   Reseña de Marius Barbeau: Haida myths illustrated in argyllite carvings. *Revista Colombiana de Folklore* 2:299.

1953l   Reseña de: Robert Wavrin: Chez les indiens de la Colombie. *Revista Colombiana de Folklore* 2:298–299.

1953m   Reseña de Irving Rouse: The circum-Caribbean theory: An archaeological test. *Revista Colombiana de Antropología* 1(1):423–424.

1953n   Investigaciones arqueológicas en el Departamento del Magdalena: 1946–1950; Parte III, Arqueología del Bajo Magdalena. With Alicia Dussán de Reichel. *Divulgaciones Etnológicas* 3(4):1–96.

1954a   A preliminary study of space and time perspective in northern Colombia. *American Antiquity* 19(4):352–365.

1954b   Investigaciones arqueológicas en la Sierra Nevada de Santa Marta, Partes 1 y 2. *Revista Colombiana de Antropología* 2(2):145–206.

1954c   El marco cultural en el estudio de la vivienda. *Economía Colombiana* 1(2):309–318.

1954d   Investigaciones arqueológicas en la Sierra Nevada de Santa Marta, parte 3. Sitios de contacto español en Pueblito. *Revista Colombiana de Antropología* 3:139–170.

1954e   La civilisation Tairona. *La Revue Française* 6(58):67–70.

1954f   Reseña de Miguel Acosta Saignés: Estudios de etnología antigua Venezolana. *Revista Colombiana de Antropología* 3: 394–395.

1954g   Reseña de Wendell C. Bennett: Excavations at Wari, Ayacucho Perú. *Revista Colombiana de Antropología* 3:397.

1954h   Reseña de Juan Comas: Bibliografía selectiva de las culturas indígenas de América. *Revista Colombiana de Antropología* 2:283.

1954i   Reseña de Handbook of Latin American Studies, V.16. *Revista Colombiana de Antropología* 3:397–398.

1954j   Reseña de Emil W. Haury y Julio César Cubillos: Investigaciones Arqueológicas en la Sabana de Bogotá, Colombia (Cultura Chibcha). *Revista Colombiana de Antropología* 2(2):279–281.

1954k   Reseña de Federico Medem: El Cocodrilo: Estudio inicial de las representaciones zoomorfas precolombinas en el arte indígena de Colombia. *Revista Colombiana de Antropología* 3:396–397.

1954l   Actividades antropológicas en Colombia: 1952–1953. *Boletín Bibliográfico de Antropología Americana,* 15–16(1):78–82.

1954m   Documentación afro-colombiana. *Revista Colombiana de Antropología* 3:407.

1954n   Contribuciones a la arqueología del Bajo Magdalena (Plato, Zambrano, Tenerife). With Alicia Dussán de Reichel. *Divulgaciones Etnológicas* 3(5):145–163.

1955a   Excavaciones en los Conchales de la Costa de Barlovento. *Revista Colombiana de Antropología* 4:247–272.

1955b   Conchales de la Costa Caribe de Colombia. *Anais do XXXI Congreso Internacional de Americanistas,* São Paulo, 1954, 2:619–626.

1955c   Algunos aspectos de la medicina popular de una población mestiza de Colombia. *Folklore Americano* 3(3):3–17.

1955d   Actividades antropológicas en Colombia: 1954. *Boletín Bibliográfico de Antropología Americana* 17(1):102–104.

1955e   Reseña de José Pérez de Barradas: Orfebrería prehispánica de Colombia-Estilo Calima. *Revista Colombiana de Antropología* 4:325–327.

1955f   Reseña de Harold S. Colton: Potsherds, an Introduction to the study of prehistoric southwestern ceramics and their use in historic reconstructions. *Revista Colombiana de Antropología* 4:328.

1955g   Reseña del P. Francisco Romero: Llanto sagrado de la América Meridional. *Revista Colombiana de Antropología* 4:332–333.

1955h   Reseña de Gordon R. Willey and Charles R. McGimsey: The Monagrillo Culture of Panamá. *Revista Colombiana de Antropología* 4:328–330.

1955i   Editor, *Diario de viaje del P. Joseph Palacios de la Vega, entre los indios y negros de la provincia de Cartagena en el Nuevo Reino de Granada, 1787–1788*, Bogotá, Editorial A. B. C.

1955j   Investigaciones arqueológicas en la Sierra Nevada de Santa Marta, parte 4. Sitios de habitación del período Tairona II , en Pueblito. With Alicia Dussán de Reichel. *Revista Colombiana de Antropología* 4:191–245.

1956a   Casta, clase y aculturación en una población mestiza de Colombia. In *Estudios antropológicos publicados en homenaje a Manuel Gamio*, 435–446. México City: Universidad Autónoma de México, Sociedad Mexicana de Antropología.

1956b   Múltiple-Stemmed Pipe Bowls. *Man* 56:75.

1956c   Actividades antropológicas en Colombia: 1950–1955. *Revista Universidad Nacional de Argentina* 7(1):143–147.

1956d   Actividades antropológicas en Colombia: 1955. *Boletín Bibliográfico de Antropología Americana*, México, 17(2):70–74.

1956e   Reseña de Julio César Cubillos: Tumaco (Notas Arqueológicas). *Revista Colombiana de Antropología* 5:384–385.

1956f   Reseña de Richard B. Woodbury, Aubrey S. Trick and others: The ruins of Zaculeu. *Revista Colombiana de Antropología* 5:383–384.

1956g   Momil: excavaciones en el río Sinú. With Alicia Dussán de Reichel. *Revista Colombiana de Antropología* 5:109–333.

1956h   La literatura oral de una aldea colombiana. With Alicia Dussán de Reichel. *Divulgaciones Etnológicas* 5:4–125.

1957a   Momil: A formative sequence From the Sinu Valley. *American Antiquity* 22(3):226–234.

1957b   On the discovery of the lkat technique in Colombia. *American Anthropologist* 59(1):133.

1957c   Actividades antropológicas en Colombia 1956. *Revista Universidad Nacional de Argentina* 8(1):134–135.

1957d   Highland South America. *American Antiquity* 22(3):334–335.

1957e   Review of Horst Nachtigall: Tierradentro-Archaelogie und Ethnographie einer Kolumbianischen Landschaft. *American Antiquity* 22(4):429.

1957f   Highland South America. *American Antiquity* 23(1):105–106.

1957g   Reconocimiento arqueológico de la hoya del río Sinú. With Alicia Dussán de Reichel. *Revista Colombiana de Antropología* 6:29–157.

1958a   Notas sobre la metalurgia prehistórica en el litoral Caribe de Colombia. In *Homenaje al Profesor Paul Rivet*, 69–94. Academia Colombiana de Historia, Bogotá: Editorial ABC.

1958b   Highland South America. *American Antiquity* 23(3):343–344.

1958c   Highland South America. *American Antiquity,* 24(1):105–106.

1958d   Actividades antropológicas en Colombia: 1956–1957. *Boletín Bibliográfico de Antropología Americana* 19–20 (1):20–25.

1958e   Review of Betty S. Meggers and Clifford Evans: Archaelogical investigations at the mouth of the Amazon. *American Antiquity* 24(2):199–200.

1958f   Nivel de salud y medicina popular en una aldea mestiza de Colombia. With Alicia Dussán de Reichel. *Revista Colombiana de Antropología,* 7:199–249

1959a   The Formative Stage: An appraisal from the Colombian perspective. *Actas del XXXIII Congreso Internacional de Americanistas,* San José, 1958. Costa Rica 1:152–164.

1959b   Recientes investigaciones arqueológicas en el Norte de Colombia. *Miscelanea Paul Rivet Octogenario Dicata,* Publicaciones del Instituto de Historia, Primera Serie, no. 5(2):471–486. México: Universidad Autónoma de México.

1959c   Indígenas de Colombia. *América Indígena* 19(4):245–253.

1959d   Urgent tasks of research in Colombia. *Bulletin of the International Committee on Urgent Anthropological and Ethnological Research,* 2: 50–61. Vienna: International Union of Anthropological and Ethnological Sciences.

1959e   Highland South America. *American Antiquity* 24(3):347–348.

1959f   Highland South America. *American Antiquity* 25(1):151.

1959g   Review of Horst Nachtigall: Die Alten Amerikanischen Megalithkulturen, *American Anthropologist* 61(1):151–152.

1959h   La Mesa. Un complejo arqueológico de la Sierra Nevada de Santa Marta. With Alicia Dussán de

Reichel. *Revista Colombiana de Antropología* 8:159–214.

1960a   Notas etnográficas sobre los indios del Chocó. *Revista Colombiana de Antropología* 9:73–158.

1960b   Contribuciones al conocimiento de las tribus de la región de Perijá. *Revista Colombiana de Antropología* 9:159–197.

1961a   Puerto Hormiga: Un complejo prehistórico marginal de Colombia (Nota preliminar).*Revista Colombiana de Antropología* 10:347–354.

1961b   *Tlie people of Aritama: the cultural personality of a Colombian mestizo village.* With Alicia Dussán de Reichel. Chicago: The University of Chicago Press.

1961c   The agricultural basis of the sub–Andean chiefdoms of Colombia. In *The evolution of horticultural systems in native South America: causes and consequences,* edited by Johannes Wilbert, Caracas: *Antropológica* (Sociedad de Ciencias Naturales de La Salle). Suplement 2:83–100.

1961d   The archaeology of the northern lowlands. In *Arte colombiano,* edited by Martha Traba, Suplemento especial de la Revista *Lámpara.* Bogotá: Talleres Semana Ltda.

1961e   Anthropomorphic figurines from Colombia: their magic and art.In *Essays in pre- Columbian art and archaelogy,* edited by Samuel K. Lothrop, pp. 229–241. Cambridge, Massachusetts: Harvard University Press.

1961f   Investigaciones arqueológicas en la costa Pacífica de Colombia. l.: El sitio de Cupica. *Revista Colombiana de Antropología* 10:237–330.

1962a   Little red schoolhouse in Latin America. With Alicia Dussán de Reichel. *Midway* 9:114–125.

1962b   Emilio Estrada Ycaza (necrólogo). *Revista Colombiana de Antropología* 10:373– 374.

1962c   Contribuciones a la etnografía de los indios del Chocó. *Revista Colombiana de Antropología* 11:169–188.

1962d   Investigaciones arqueológicas en la costa Pacífica de Colombia II: Una secuencia cultural del bajo río San Juan.. With Alicia Dussán de Reichel. *Revista Colombiana de Antropología* 11:9–70.

1962e   Una nueva fecha de carbono–14 de Colombia. *Revista Colombiana de Antropología* 11:331–332.

1963a   Apuntes etnográficos sobre los indios del alto río Sinú. *Revista de la Academia Colombiana de Ciencias Exactas, Físicas y Naturales* 12(45):29–40.

1963b   Bibliografía de la Sierra Nevada de Santa Marta. *Revista de la Academia Colombiana de Ciencias Exactas, Físicas y Naturales* 11(44):367–374.

1963c   Bibliografía de la Guajira. *Revista de la Academia Colombiana de Ciencias Exactas, Físicas y Naturales* 12(45):47–56.

1963d   Review of Irving Goldman: The Cubeo: Indians of the Northwest Amazon. *American Anthropologist*

65(6):1377–1379.

1964   La antropología y la planificación médica moderna. In *Medicina y Desarrollo social,* edited by José Félix Patiño, 182–188. Bogota: Asociación Colombiana de Facultades de Medicina, Bogotá, Editorial Tercer Mundo.

1965a   *Colombia: Ancient peoples and places,* London: Thames and Hudson.

1965b   *Excavaciones Arqueológicas en Puerto Hormiga (Departamento de Bolívar). Antropología* no. 2, Ediciones de la Universidad de los Andes. Bogotá: Editorial Tercer Mundo.

1966a   Jungle gods of San Agustín. *Natural History* 75(10):42–49.

1966b   Proyecto de investigación etnológica en Colombia dentro de un orden tentativo de prioridades por razón de regiones o grupos tribales por estudiar. In *Congreso de Territorios Nacionales,* no. 8. Bogotá: Instituto Geofísico de los Andes.

1966c   Notas sobre un movimiento apocalíptico en el Chocó, Colombia. With Alicia Dussán de Reichel. *Folklore Americano* 14 (14):110–132.

1967a   Notas sobre el simbolismo religioso de los indios de la Sierra Nevada de Santa Marta. *Razón y fábula* 1:55–72.

1967b   Rock paintings of the Vaupés: An essay of interpretation. *Folklore Americas* 2:107–113.

1967c   Recientes investigaciones arqueológicas en San Agustín. *Razón y Fábula.* 2:35–38.

1967d   A brief report on urgent ethnological research in the Vaupés area, Colombia, South America. *Bulletin of the International Committee on Urgent Anthropological and Ethnological Research* 9:53–61.

1967e   Enquetes ethnographiques á entrependre d'urgence (Río Vaupés, Colombia). *Journal de la Société des Américanistes* 56(2):323–332.

1967f   *Bibliografía antropológica de Gerardo y Alicia Reichel-Dolmatoff, 1943-1967.* With Alicia Dussán de Reichel. Bogotá: Universidad de los Andes, Departamento de Antropología.

1968a   Djungleguder i San Agustín. *Naturens Varld* 10:289–298.

1968b   Junglegudere i San Agustín. *Naturens Verden* 257–266.

1968c   El arte rupestre del Vaupés: un ensayo de interpretación. In *Antigüedad del Hombre Peruano,* edited by Juan Luis Alva P., 22–31, Lima: Colegio Nacional Daniel A. Carrion.

1968d   *Desana: simbolismo de los indios Tukano del Vaupés.* Bogotá: Departamento de Antropología, Universidad de los Andes.

1968e   Chibcha. In *Encyclopedia Universalis* 4: 221–222. Bogotá.

1969a   Puerto Hormiga y los comienzos de la cerámica en Colombia. *Revista del Museo Nacional* 14: 14–19.

1969b El contexto cultural de un alucinógeno aborigen: *Banisteriopsis caapi. Revista de la Academia Colombiana de Ciencias Exactas, Físicas y Naturales* 13(51):327–345.

1969c El misionero ante las culturas indígenas. In *Antropología y evangelización: Un problema de iglesia en América Latina,*147–158, Bogotá: Departamento de Misiones CELAM.

1970 Notes of the cultural extent of the use of Yagé (*Banisteriopsis caapi*) among the indians of the Vaupés, Colombia. *Economic Botany* 24(1):32–33.

1971a Early pottery from Colombia. *Archaeology* 24(4):338–345.

1971b *Amazonian Cosmos: The sexual and religious symbolism of the Tukano Indians,* Chicago and London: University of Chicago Press.

1972a The cultural context of an aboriginal hallucinogen (*Banisteriopsis caapi*). In *Flesh of the gods: The ritual use of hallucinogens,* edited by Peter T. Furst, 84–113. New York: Praeger Publishers.

1972b *San Agustín: a culture of Colombia.* New York and Washington, DC: Praeger.

1972c The feline motif in prehistoric San Agustín sculpture. In *The cult of the feline,* edited by Elizabeth P. Benson, 51–68. Washington DC: Dumbarton Oaks.

1972d El misionero ante las culturas indígenas. *América Indígena* 32(4)1137–1149.

1972e Le missionaire face aux cultures indiennes. In *L'ethnocide á travers les Amériques* edited by Robert Jaulin, 339–355. París, Editions Fayard.

1972f The cultural context of early fiber-tempered pottery in Northern Colombia. In *Fiber-tempered pottery in southeastern United States and northern Colombia: Its origins, context, and, significance,* edited by Ripley Bullen and James B. Stoltman. Gainesville: Florida Anthropological Society Publications 6:1–8.

1972g Formal schooling. With Alicia Dussán de Reichel. In *Education and development: Latin America and the Caribbean,* edited by Thomas J. La Belle, 533–542. Los Angeles: Latin American Center, University of California, Los Angeles.

1973a The cultural context of early fiber-tempered pottery in Northern Colombia. *Revista Dominicana de Antropología e Historia, Santo Domingo* 2:2:4:123–130.

1973b *Desana, le symbolisme universal des indiens Tukano du Vaupés,* Bibliothequé des Sciences Humaines, París, Gallimard.

1973c *Desana* (edición japonesa). Tokyo: Iwanami Shoten.

1973d The agricultural basis of the sub-Andean chiefdoms of Colombia. In *Peoples and cultures of native South America,* edited by Daniel R. Gross, 28–36, Garden City, NY: Doubleday Natural History Press.

1973e La enseñainza formal en Aritama. In *Educación y sociedad* edited by Gonzalo Cataño, 127–142. Bogotá: Universidad Pedagógica.

1974a Le contexte culturel du yagé (*Banisteriopsis caapi*). In *La chair des dieux: l'usage rituel des psychédéliques,* edited by Peter T. Furst, 56–92. París: Editions du Seuil.

1974b Funerary customs and religious symbolism among the Kogi. In *Native South Americans: Ethnology of the least known continent,* edited by Patricia J. Lyon, 289–301. Boston and Toronto: Little, Brown & Company.

1974c Momil: dos fechas de radiocarbono. With Alicia Dussán de Reichel. *Revista Colombiana de Antropología* 17:185–187.

1974d Un sistema de agricultura prehistórica de los Llanos Orientales. With Alicia Dussán de Reichel. *Revista Colombiana de Antropología* 17:188–194.

1975a *The shaman and the jaguar: A study of narcotic drugs among the indians of Colombia.* Philadelphia: Temple University Press.

1975b *Contribuciones al conocimiento de la estratigrafía cerámica de San Agustín, Colombia.* Bogotá: Biblioteca Banco Popular.

1975c Templos Kogi: Introducción al simbolismo y a la astronomía del espacio sagrado. *Revista Colombiana de Antropología* 19:199–245.

1976a O contexto cultural de un alucinógeno aborígene *Banisteriopsis caapi.* In *Os alucinógenos eo mundo simbólico,* edited by Vera Penteado Coelho, 59–103, Sáo Paulo: Universidad de Sáo Paulo.

1976b Training for the priesthood among the Kogi of Colombia. In *Enculturation in Latin America: an anthology,* edited by Johannes Wilbert, 265–288. Los Angeles: Latin American Center, University of California.

1976c Desana curing spells: An analysis of some shamanistic metaphors. *Journal of Latin American Lore* 2(2):157–219.

1976d The Huxley Memorial Lecture: Cosmology as ecological analysis, a view from the rain forest. *Man* 11(3):307–318.

1977a Cosmología como análisis ecológico: Una perspectiva desde la selva pluvial. Lima: *Gaceta* 14:6–14.

1977b La antropología patrocinada por la gobernación del Departamento del Magdalena. In *Primer Congreso Nacional de Historiadores y Antropólogos* (Santa Marta, 1975), 98–102. Medellín: Editorial Argemiro Salazar.

1977c *Estudios Antropológicos.* With Alicia Dussán de Reichel. Biblioteca Básica Colombiana, no. 29. Bogotá: Instituto Colombiano de Cultura.

1977d Cosmology as ecological analysis: A view from the rain forest. *The Ecologist* 7(1): 4–11.

1978a *El chamán y el jaguar: Estudio de las drogas narcóticas entre los indios de Colombia.* México/Barcelona/Buenos Aires/Bogotá: Siglo XXI Editores.

1978b *Beyond the Milky Way: Hallucinatory imagery of the Tukano indians.* UCLA Latin American Studies, vol.

42. Los Angeles: Latin American Center, University of California.

1978c   Colombia indígena: Período prehispánico. In *Manual de historia de Colombia,* vol. 1, edited by J.G. Cobo Borda and Santiago Mutis Durán, 31–115. Bogotá: Instituto Colombiano de Cultura.

1978d   Desana animal categories, food restrictions, and the concept of color energies. *Journal of Latin American Lore* 4(2):243–291.

1978e   The loom of life: A Kogi principle of integration. *Journal of Latin American Lore* 4(1):5–27.

1978f   Drug induced optical sensations and their, relationships to applied art among some Colombian indians. In *Art in society: Studies in style, culture and aesthetics,* edited by Michael Greenhalg and Vicent Megaw, 289–304. London: Duckworth.

1979a   Desana shaman's rock crystals and the hexagonal universe. *Journal of Latin American Lore* 5(1):117–128.

1979b   Conceptos indígenas de enfermedad y de equilibrio ecológico: Los Tukano y los Kogi de Colombia. In *Simposio internazionale sulla medicina indigena e popolare dell'America Latina* (Rome, 1977), 151–162. Rome: Instituto ltalo/Latino Americano-IILA.

1979c   Some source materials on Desana shamanistic initiation. *Antropológica* 51:27–61.

1980   Notas sobre el simbolismo religioso de los indios de la Sierra Nevada de Santa Marta. In *La antropología americanista en la actualidad: homenaje a Rafael Girard,* vol l., 525–540. México: Editores Mexicanos Unidos, .

1981a   Things of beauty replete with meaning: metals and crystals in Colombian indian cosmology. In *Sweat of the sun, tears of the moon: gold and emerald treasures of Colombia,*17–33. Los Angeles: Natural History Museum of Los Angeles County.

1981b   Algunos conceptos de geografía chamanística de los indios Desana de Colombia. In *Contribuções a antropologia em homenagem do Profesor Egon Schaden,* edited by Thekla Hartmann y Vera Penteado Coelho, vol. 4:255–270. São Paulo: Caoleção Museu Paulista, Série Ensaios, Universidades de Sáo Paulo.

1981c   Brain and mind in Desana shamanism. *Journal of Latin American Lore* 7(1):73–98.

1982a   Astronomical models of social behavior among some indians of Colombia. In *Ethnoastronomy and archaeastronomy in the American tropics,* edited by Anthony F. Aveni and Gary Urton. *Annals of the New York Academy of Sciences* 85:165–181.

1982b   Cultural change and environmental awareness: A case study of the Sierra Nevada de Santa Marta. *Mountain Research and Development* 2(3):289–298.

1983   The Kogi indians and the environment: Impending disaster. *The Ecologist* 13(1).

1984a   Some Kogi models of the beyond. *Journal of Latin American Lore* 10(1):63–85.

1984b   Palabras pronunciadas ante la Asamblea de la Academia de Ciencias del Tercer Mundo, reunida en Trieste, Italia. *Noticias Antropológicas* 6–7.

1985a   *Monsú: Un sitio arqueológico.* Bogotá: Biblioteca Banco Popular, Textos Universitarios.

1985b   *Los Kogi: Una tribu de la Sierra Nevada de Santa Marta, Colombia.* 2 vols. Bogotá: Procultura, Nueva Biblioteca Colombiana de Cultura.

1985c   Aspectos chamanísticos y neurofisiológicos del arte indígena. In *Estudios en arte rupestre,* edited by Carlos Aldunate del Solar, José Berenguer, and Victoria Castro R., 291–307. Santiago: Museo Chileno de Arte Precolombino, Primeras Jornadas de Arte y Arqueología.

1985d   *Basketry as metaphor: Arts and crafts of the Desana indians of the northwest Amazon.* Occasional Papers, no. 5. Los Angeles: Museum of Cultural History, University of California, .

1985e   Algunos conceptos de geografía chamanística de los indios Desana de Colombia.In *Myth and the imaginary in the New World,* edited by Eduardo Magaña and Peter Mason, 75–92. Amsterdam: Centre for Latin American Research and Documentation.

1985f   Tapir avoidance in the Colombian northwest Amazon. In *Animal myths and metaphors in South America,* edited by Gary Urton, 107–143. Salt Lake City: University of Utah Press.

1985g   Cambio cultural y conciencia del medio ambiente: Un estudio característico de la Sierra Nevada de Santa Marta, Colombia. In *Informe sobre los conocimientos actuales de los ecosistemas andinos,* vol. 3: *Los Andes Septentrionales-Cambios ambientales y culturales,* 81–96. Montevideo: Unesco, Rostlac.

1986a   *Desana: simbolismo de los indios Tukano del Vaupés.* Segunda edición. Bogotá: Procultura, Nueva Biblioteca Colombiana de Cultura.

1986b   Things of beauty replete with meaning: Metals and crystals in Colombian indian cosmology. In *The gold of El Dorado,*16–23. Tokyo: Seibu Museum of Art.

1986c   A hunter's tale from the Colombian northwest Amazon. *Journal of Latin American Lore* 12(1):65–74.

1986d   *Arqueología de Colombia: Un texto introductorio.* Bogotá: Presidencia de la República, Fundación Segunda Expedición Botánica.

1987a   *Shamanism and art of the eastern Tukanoan indians: Colombian northwest Amazon.* Iconography of Religions, section IX, South America. Leiden: Institute of Religious lconography, State University of Groningen.

1987b   The great mother and the Kogi universe: A concise overview. *Journal of Latin American Lore* 13(1):73–113.

1987c   Análisis de un templo de los indios Ika de la Sierra Nevada de Santa Marta, Colombia. In *Antropológica*

68:3–22.

1988a   Cultural change and environmental awareness: A case study of the Sierra Nevada de Santa Marta, Colombia. *Revista de la Academia Colombiana de Ciencias Exactas, Físicas y Naturales* 16(63):121–130.

1988b   *Orfebrería y chamanismo: Un estudio iconográfico del Museo del Oro.* Medellín: Editorial Colina.

1988c   *Goldwork and shamanism: An iconographic study of the Gold Museu.* Medellín: Editorial Colina.

1989a   *Orfévrerie et chamanisme: Une étude iconographique du Musée de l'or.* Medellín: Editorial Colina.

1989b   Biological and social aspects of the Yurupari complex of the Colombian Vaupés territory. *Journal of Latin American Lore* 15(1):95–135.

1989c   Palabras pronunciadas en la Universidad Nacional de Colombia, al recibir el Doctorado Honoris Causa. *Gradiva-Revista Literaria* 111(7/8):5–6.

1989d   Zur Zerstöhrung des Urwalds aus Indianish-schamanistischer Sicht. In *Amazonas,* edited by Christian Kobau,78–86. Graz: Leykam Verlag.

1989e   Contribuciones al conocimiento del idioma Sanká, Sierra Nevada de Santa Marta. In *Lenguas aborígenes de Colombia; Descripciones 3.* Bogotá: Sierra Nevada de Santa Marta Centro Colombiano de Estudios de Lenguas Aborígenes, Universidad de Los Andes.

1989f   *Desana texts and contexts.* Acta Etnologica et Lingüística, no. 62, Series Americana 12, Vienna-Foehrenau.

1990a   Kosmologie ais kölogishe Analyse: ein Blick aus dem Regenwald. In *Die Zweite Schôpfung: Geist and Ungeist in der Biologie des 20 Jahrhunderts,* edited by Jost Herbig and Rainer Hohlfeld, 257–277. Munich: Carl Hanser Verlag.

1990b   Algunos conceptos de los indios Desana del Vaupés sobre manejo ecológico. *Ecológica* 4: 48–52.

1990c   *The sacred mountain of Colombia's Kogi indians.* Iconography of Religions, section IX, South America, fasc. 2 Leiden: Institute of Religious Iconography, State University Groningen.

1990d   Algunos conceptos de los indios Desana del Vaupés, sobre manejo ecológico.In *La selva humanizada: Ecología alternativa en el trópico húmedo colombiano.* edited by Frangois Correa, 35–41. Bogotá: Instituto Colombiano de Antropología.

1990e   Pasado arqueológico: Legado y desafío. In *Caribe Colombia,* edited by Angel Guarnizo, 3–13. Bogotá: Fondo para la Protección del Medio Ambiente José Celestino Mutis, Financiera Energética Nacional.

1990f   Sierra Nevada: Cambio cultural. In *Caribe Colombia,* edited by Angel Guarnizo, 203–227. Bogotá: Fondo para la Protección del Medio Ambiente José Celestino Mutis, Financiera Energética Nacional.

1990g   El mundo de los Desana. *Iberoamericana* 12(2):31–37.

1990h   A view from the headwaters: A Colombian anthropologist looks at the Amazon and beyond. In *Ethnobiology: Implications and applications,* Proceedings of the First International Congress of Ethnobiology (Belem, 1988), Vol. 1:9–17. Belem: Museo Paraense,

1991a   *Los Ika, Sierra Nevada de Santa Marta, Colombia: Notas etnográficas 1946–1966.* Bogotá: Centro Editorial, Universidad Nacional de Colombia.

1991b   *Indios de Colombia: Momentos vividos-mundos concebidos.* Bogotá: Villegas Editores.

1991c   *Indians of Colombia: Experience and cognition.* Bogotá: Villegas Editores.

1991d   *Arqueología del Bajo Magdalena: Estudio de la cerámica de Zambrano.* With Alicia Dussán de Reichel. Bogotá: Banco Popular-Colcultura.

1991e   Palabras del Profesor Gerardo Reichel-Dolmatoff. In *Premio nacional al mérito científico,* edited by Alicia Dussán de Reichel, 37–40. Bogotá: Granahorrar and Asociación Colombiana para el Avance de la Ciencia.

1991f   Conferencia dictada al recibir la Medalla Thomas Henry Huxley, del Royal Anthropological Institute, London, 1975. In *Premio nacional al mérito científico,* edited by Alicia Dussán de Reichel, 85–102. Bogotá: Granahorrar and Asociación Colombiana para el Avance de la Ciencia.

1991g   Fishing and eating pepper-pot, reading a Desana text. *Journal of Latin American Lore* 17:165–198.

1992a   La Antropología: Toda una actitud ante la vida. In *Doctorado honoris causa,* edited by Constanza de León L, 9–10. Bogotá: Universidad de los Andes.

1992b   Motivaciones. In *Doctorado honoris causa,* edited by Constanza de León L., 11–14. Bogotá: Universidad de los Andes.

1995   Introducción: Koch–Grünberg en Colombia. In *Dos años entre los indios* by Theodor Koch-Grünberg, 11–17. Bogotá: Editorial Universidad Nacional.

1996a   *Los Kogi de Sierra Nevada.* Bitzot: Palma de Mallorca.

1996b   *The forest within: The world-view of the Tukano Amazonian indians.* Devon: Themis Books.

1996c   *Yurupary: Studies of an Amazonian foundation myth.* Cambridge, Massachusetts: Harvard University Center for the Study of World Religions.

1996d   *Das Schamanische Universum: Schamanismus, Bewußtsein und Ökologie in Südamerika.* Munich: Diederichs Gelbe Reihe.

1996e   Anthropologist's debts to Richard Spruce. In *Richard Spruce (1817–1893) Botanist and Explorer,* edited by M.R.D. Seaward and S.M.D. Fitzgerald, 239–243. London: The Royal Botanical Gardens, Kew.

1997a   Rain forest shamans. Dartington, U.K.: Themis Books.

1997b   Chamanes de la Selva Pluvial. Dartington, U.K.: Themis Books.

1997c   *Arquelogía de Colombia.* Bogotá: Biblioteca Familiar Presidencia de la República, Imprenta Nacional de Colombia.

PART I
Foragers and Collectors

Evidence of Late Pleistocene/Early Holocene Occupations in the Tropical Lowlands of the Middle Magdalena Valley

Carlos López

In other countries and places, such as the United States, Mesoamerica and the Southern Cone, projectile points are abundant and are valuable indicators of the strategies of hunting and the changes of technology in lithic manufacture, but in Colombia few artifacts of this type have been found. It is true also that there are large and extended unexplored regions that still may hold great unexpected surprises and their study should take priority in the archaeological research in the country. – Gerardo Reichel-Dolmatoff 1986:37–38, editors' translation.

THE IMPORTANCE of the Magdalena Valley preceramic period was first recognized by Gerardo Reichel-Dolmatoff in the early 1960s. Nonetheless, until recently no preceramic materials had been recovered in stratigraphic contexts. This chapter presents newly discovered evidence of Late Pleistocene/Early Holocene occupations in the middle Magdalena Valley. A preliminary survey, including test excavations, has identified a range of preceramic sites dating between 10,400 and 3,000 BP (uncalibrated radiocarbon dates). The antiquity of the bifacial technology is still uncertain, and my perception of the Paleo-Indian Pleistocenic complex is tentative. An analysis of the lithic collections shows that stemmed, triangular, bifacially flaked points are the most numerous; however, they have not yet been found in primary contexts dating prior to 6000 BP. The middle Magdalena early preceramic tradition contrasts with the Abriense tradition from the highlands (Sabana de Bogotá), the El Jobo tradition

from western Venezuela, and the (fluted) fishtail tradition found in the Cauca Valley, Ecuador, and in Central America. This chapter discusses the evidence for a drier, more open landscape in the middle Magdalena region during the early part of this occupation. The research for this period provides important data concerning the antiquity of early human populations in the tropical environments of northern South America.

In the 1960s, Reichel-Dolmatoff described archaeological sites in the Atlantic coastal plains and in the lower and middle Magdalena Valley that were characterized by high densities of lithics without ceramic associations. He also reported bifacial projectile points from other sites in the country found on the surface without specific archaeological context. He postulated that interior large valleys, ancient Pleistocene lake shores, and areas near obsidian sources had a high potential for containing the ancient remains of early populations (Reichel-Dolmatoff 1965b).

Many sites excavated during the 1970s and 1980s in the highlands of the Sabana de Bogotá by Correal and van der Hammen and their colleagues (Correal and van der Hammen 1977; Correal 1988, 1990; Ardila 1991) confirmed Reichel-Dolmatoff's hypothesis. Furthermore, in the 1980s important archaeological evidence of early occupation, including bifacial points of obsidian, was found in excavations near Popayan (Gnecco and Salgado 1989), corroborating Reichel-Dolmatoff's original hypothesis. Stratigraphic preceramic sites have long been assumed to exist in the Magdalena Valley, although until recently the evidence has been restricted to surface manifestations, as described by Robledo (1954), Reichel-Dolmatoff (1965b, 1986), Correal (1973, 1977), Castaño (1985), Ardila and Politis (1989), and Ardila (1991). The stratigraphic evidence and radiocarbon dates were obtained in the 1990s, as presented in this chapter.

Recent surveys that I conducted along the middle sector of the Magdalena River revealed preceramic occupations in stratified contexts in a dozen Late Pleistocene and Early Holocene sites. These sites were located during the course of two rescue archaeology projects carried out in conjunction with pipeline and power-line construction (López 1989, 1992, 1994; ICAN 1991; Lopez et al. 1994). The sites provide data relevant to questions concerning early human occupation in the region and subsequent changes in the forest and savanna environments of the middle Magdalena (López 1992, 1994; ICAN 1994; Lopez et al. 1994).

Geographic Context

The Magdalena River is the most prominent corridor through the Andean mountains in northern South America. Historically, this wide valley has been the gateway to the interior of the continent. The middle sector is more than 300 km long, located between the towns of La Dorada (Department of Caldas), 200 m above sea level, and Gamarra (Department of Cesar), 50 m above sea level (figure 1.1). Geologically, the middle Magdalena Valley is formed from a large plateau shaped in the Tertiary. The landscape of the Magdalena Valley is characterized by a mosaic of hills, plains, and depressions (IGAC 1980, 1982).

The climate is warm and humid, with temperatures averaging above 24°C throughout the year and rainfall averaging 2500 mm/year, during two distinct seasons. In the absence of human disturbance, the vegetation in the entire region would be Humid Tropical Forest, according to the Holdridge classification. The composition of the forest species varies, however, depending on the nature of the substrate (alluvial plain, piedmont, mountain slopes). Forests still cover large areas of the cordillera slopes (IGAC 1980, 1982). Unfortunately, in the last three decades, deforestation has intensified as a result of the increasing use of land for raising cattle.

The main rivers tributary to the Magdalena in the study area are the Carare, Opón, Oponcito, San Bartolomé, and Nare (figure 2.1). Swamps are very common, especially in the eastern watershed. The slopes of the cordillera are deeply dissected by mountain streams (IGAC 1980, 1982).

Previous Archaeological Research

As stated by Reichel-Dolmatoff (1965b, 1986) and other scholars (Bray 1990; Ardila 1991), the oldest archaeological sites in Colombia are assumed to lie in the Darién area along the border with Panama. This region represents the northwestern

connection with Central America and the obvious migration route for Pleistocene populations. This forested area in the corner of the continent has not been heavily investigated, however. In contrast, on the other side of the Darién Gap, several Late Pleistocene sites in Central Panama have been recorded (Bird and Cooke 1977, 1978; Bray 1990; Ranere and Cooke 1991; Cooke and Ranere 1992b; Ranere 1992). At present, only a few sites with preceramic artifacts have been discovered in the Colombian Darién (Correal 1983, 1988).

Along the Atlantic shore, the Colombian lowlands are extensive. Nonetheless, the proximity of the Andean Cordillera changes the interior landscapes toward the south. Only in the large valleys of the Magdalena and Cauca rivers do the lowlands extend between the Andean ranges. Several lithic industries have been documented in the Atlantic lowlands as preceramic, but no excavations have been carried out (Reichel-Dolmatoff 1965b, 1986; Correal 1977, 1988; Ardila 1991).

All these prehistoric stone industries have common characteristics. All were found on eroded ridges or hilltops, on old river terraces, or in gravel beds. There are no pottery associations, food-grinding implements, or ground or polished stone artifacts. The total tool assemblages consisted mainly of unifacial scrapers and knives, with a few chopping tools and a number of small boring or engraving tools; no projectile points were found. Crude percussion flaking is predominant, with secondary retouch by controlled percussion or pressure flaking occurring only rarely (Reichel-Dolmatoff 1965b:49).

During the late 1960s, the archaeologist Gonzalo Correal and palynologist Thomas van der Hammen began to research Pleistocene and Holocene environments and early human occupations in Colombia. Continued stratigraphic excavations in the Sabana de Bogotá provided information about chronology, technology, and paleoecology, as well as the physical characteristics of the preceramic highland peoples (Correal and van der Hammen 1977; Correal 1988, 1990).

Initially, with W. Hurt's assistance, Correal and van der Hammen excavated the rock-shelter site El Abra, 50 km north of Bogotá (Correal et al. 1969; Hurt et al. 1972). The Late Pleistocene lithic assemblage recovered, identified as Abriense Class, was technologically quite simple. This assemblage has similarities to Late Pleistocene industries at sites in northern South America (Mayer-Oakes 1963; Correal 1988; Ardila and Politis 1989; Ardila 1991; Dillehay et al. 1992) but has very few resemblances to those from early sites in other parts of South America with bifacial artifacts. Later, through excavations in other sites in the Sabana de Bogotá (Tequendama, Tibitó, Sueva, and Aguazuque), Correal and van der Hammen showed that this lithic industry has persisted through more than seven thousand years (Correal 1981, 1988, 1990).

In addition, Correal and van der Hammen identified a second early lithic industry in the Sabana de Bogotá, called Tequendamiense Class, based on five carefully retouched tools

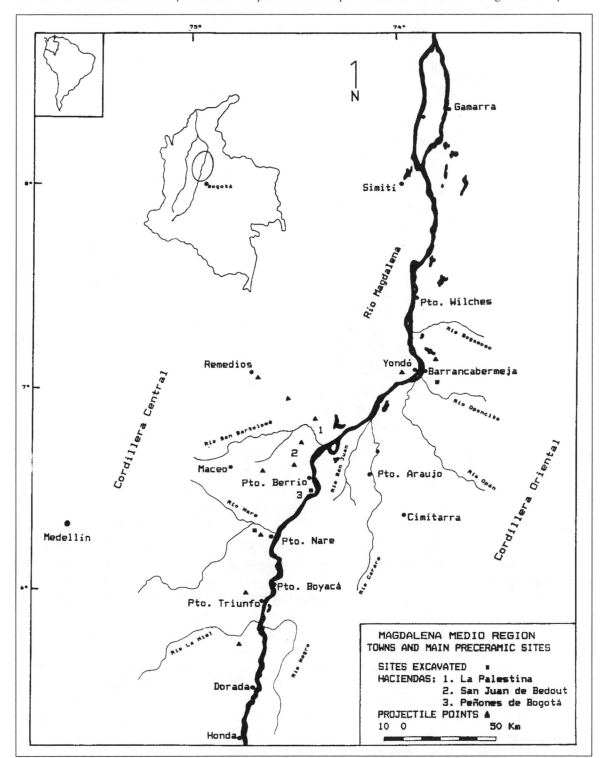

Figure 1.1 Middle Magdalena region, with location of towns and preceramic sites

found in the Tequendama excavations and dated to the eleventh millennium BP. The presence of bifacial reduction and careful edge retouch distinguishes the Tequendamiense from the Abriense technology. Interestingly, the Tequendamiense tools are made from raw materials imported from the Magdalena Valley (Correal and van der Hammen 1977; Correal 1981, 1988; see Wolford 1994).

Correal and van der Hammen suggested that the Magdalena Valley probably was occupied during the Late Pleistocene and Early Holocene by groups taking advantage of the gently rolling terrain, warm climate, and open vegetation that characterized the region (Correal and van der Hammen 1977; Correal 1988; van der Hammen 1988; 1992). Correal (1973, 1977) surveyed the Magdalena Valley where he identified more than twenty preceramic sites, none, unfortunately, with stratified deposits. He described a dense chipped lithic assemblage

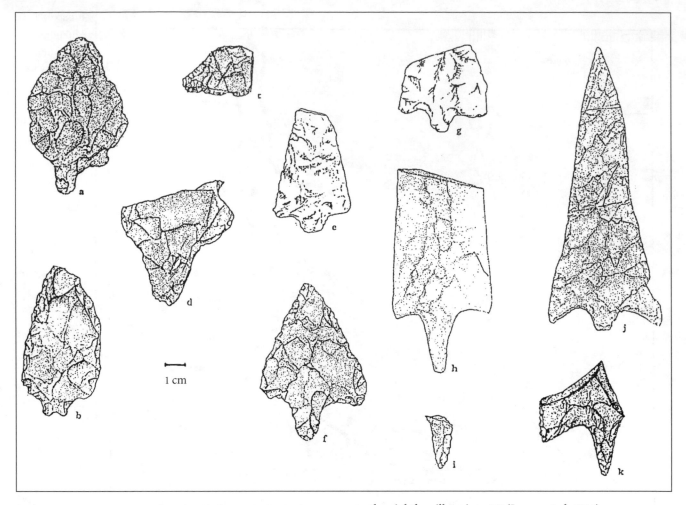

Figure 1.2 Projectile points found in Peñones de Bogotá hacienda. Fragments i, k were excavated.

in chert. Particularly, he noticed a chopper industry and keeled scrapers with characteristics similar to the scrapers found at Tequendama.

In the early 1990s, the project of rescue archaeology for the oil pipeline Vasconia-Coveñas added new data about early human occupation in the region (López 1989; ICAN 1991). Five major preceramic sites were located in the municipalities of Puerto Berrío, Yondó, and Remedios (Department of Antioquia) on the extensive terraces found between the Magdalena River and the Andean foothills (figure 1.1). The lithic assemblages are characterized by small (4 cm long) and large (16 cm long) bifacial projectile points, most of them triangular and stemmed (figure 1.2), and by plano-convex scrapers, thinning flakes, and choppers—rare artifacts in Colombian archaeological sites. Radiocarbon dates on charcoal recovered from stratigraphic test excavations place the earlier occupation in the eleventh millennium BP (López 1989, 1992, 1994; ICAN 1991). A recent transect survey along the western margin of the Magdalena River discovered additional preceramic sites. In the suburbs of the city of Barrancabermeja, a test excavation uncovered a dense lithic concentration dated

to the eighth millennium BP (Lopez et al. 1994).

Main Sites Excavated: Preliminary Results

Five preceramic open-air sites containing surface and buried materials have been examined using small test-pit excavations. The La Palestina site (municipality of Yondó) is located 10 km from the confluence of the San Bartolomé River with the Magdalena, 30 km north of Puerto Berrío, close to the foothills of the cordillera central at 175 msl (figure 1.1). The site is situated on a wide alluvial terrace with a very stable surface (without natural collapses and severe erosion) and extremely acid soils. The terrace is covered with grass, and in an area exceeding 5 km², we found cultural remains, exposed by erosion, scattered on the surface. Soil analysis shows a clear stratigraphic profile (A, E, Bt horizons) and a deposit of fine-grained sand, probably the consequence of diffuse colluvial trickle (*escurrimiento difuso*). According to Pedro Botero (López 1992, 1994; López and Botero 1994), diffuse colluvial trickle is possible only in open grasslands. His analysis suggests that this area may once have been drier and that the large, wide terraces had open savanna vegetation surrounded by tropical mountain and gallery forests.

Two small excavations measuring 3 and 4 m² at La Palestina showed one preceramic cultural component between 18 and

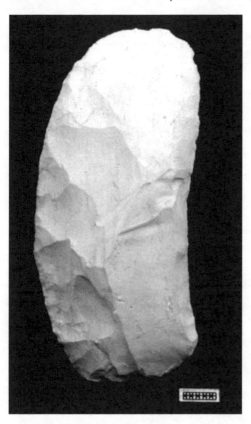

Figure 1.3 Unifacially retouched knife/scraper from La Palestina site, level 35–40 cm

40 cm, with associated radiocarbon dates of 10,400 ± 90 BP (Beta 40855) and 10,230 ± 80 BP, respectively (Beta 40854; López 1992; table 1.1). (*All radiocarbon dates reported in this chapter are uncorrected and uncalibrated.*)

Early cultural material was found in the Bt horizon, 35 to 40 cm below the surface. The assemblage is characterized by a unifacially retouched knife/scraper (figure 1.3), thinning flakes, flake scrapers, cores, choppers, and flaking debris. The predominant lithic material was chert and milky quartz; several quartzite flakes were also found. The chert and quartz were obtained locally from cobbles in the Magdalena River bed and among the materials constituting the terrace (López 1989; ICAN 1991).

Another small test excavation measuring 2 m² was conducted at San Juan de Bedout, located on a colluvial grass-covered terrace near a major stream 20 km north of Puerto Berrío and 5 km west of the Magdalena River (figure 1.1). Its archaeological context is similar to that of the La Palestina site, being located in a Bt horizon at a depth of 30 to 40 cm. The assemblage is also characterized by artifacts similar to Palestina's, most notably a quartz bifacial artifact. A radiocarbon date of 10,350 ± 90 BP (Beta 40852) on charcoal associated with the assemblage indicated that the artifact is contemporary with the La Palestina site occupation (table 1.1; López 1989; ICAN 1991).

Another important archaeological locality is the Peñones de Bogotá site. It is situated on a high Pliocenic terrace 35 m

above the Magdalena River (125 msl) in an area 800 by 100 m, 5 km south of Puerto Berrío. Twenty-five bifacial fragments, some of them projectile points; preforms (table 1.2), and a dozen retouched scrapers (figure 1.2) were found on the surface along eroded pathways. A 2 x 2 m test excavation, carried out to check for buried cultural horizons, revealed a preceramic sequence in a combined AB/Bt horizon 30 to 60 cm below the surface. The cultural level at the bottom of the cut (at 60 cm) could not be dated. Charcoal associated with lithic artifacts in the 35 to 40 cm layer returned a radiocarbon date of 5980 ± 90 BP (Beta 57724). Another charcoal sample, recovered at a depth of 25 to 30 cm, indicated that the materials dated to 3130 ± 70 BP (Beta 53128; table 1.1). The density and variability of artifacts and debris suggest that the site was a lithic workshop. Among other interesting tools, eight associated projectile point fragments were found in both dated layers (table 1.2).

It is possible to establish an interesting correlation between these fragments and an early date obtained many years ago near the city of El Espinal in the Magdalena Valley. At this location, a stemmed projectile point was found 7 m below the surface. According to the information concerning the site and the stratigraphic layers, an associated radiocarbon date of 3780 ± 85 BP was obtained. This date corresponds, however, to the stratum and not to the cultural remains (Correal and van der Hammen 1977).

Twenty-five km south of Puerto Berrío, in the municipality of Nare near the confluence of the Nare and Magdalena rivers at 30 m above the river level (175 msl), another tested colluvial terrace yielded similar archaeological characteristics. A number of lithics were recovered from the surface; fortunately, part of the site remains buried. One small (1 x 0.5 m) test pit held various components, including a ceramic A horizon close to a preceramic layer in the Bt horizon. A single radiocarbon date for the Bt horizon of 10,350 ± 60 BP (Beta 70040) at a depth of 35 to 40 cm confirmed that the oldest occupation was contemporary with those at La Palestina and San Juan de Bedout (Lopez et al. 1994; table 1.1).

On the eastern margin of the Magdalena River in the suburbs of the city of Barrancabermeja (100 msl; figure 1.1), a surface scatter of lithic artifacts, including choppers, plano-convex scrapers, and retouched flakes (figure 1.4), was located in the grass-covered surface of an old dissected erosional terrace (the estimated area of the terrace is 1000 m²). A small cut (1 x 1 m) allowed us to collect an important 200-fragment sample of expedient artifacts, debitage, fire-cracked rocks, and charcoal in a Bt horizon at a depth between 20 to 45 cm. A single radiocarbon determination of 7050 ± 240 BP (Beta 70045) was obtained from a depth of 40 to 50 cm (table 1.1).

Paleoenvironment in the Middle Magdalena

Several scholars have provided data and interpretations con-

Table 1.1 Preceramic dates and general contexts in Middle Magdalena valley sites

	SIZE (m²)	LAB #	DATE (BP)	LAYER (cm)	SOIL HORIZON	ASSOCIATION/CONTEXT[1]
La Palestina 2	3	Beta-40855	10,400 ±90	30–40	B	Knife-scraper in chert; thinning flakes[2,3]
Puerto Nare T-46	0.5	Beta-70040	10,350 ±60	35–40	B	Chert and quartz flakes; quartz scraper[2,3]
San Juan de Bedoit	2	Beta-40852	10,350 ±90	30–40	B	Chert and quartz flakes and tools, biface[3]
La Palestina 2	3	Beta 40854	10,230 ±80	20–30	B	Chert and quartz flakes and tools, thinning flakes
Barranca T-408	1	Beta 70045	7,050 ±240	40–45	B	Chert and quartz flakes and tools, choppers[2,3]
Peñones de Bogotá	4	Beta 57724	5,980 ±90	35–40	B	Projectile point fragments, chert and quartz tools[2,3]
Peñones de Bogotá	4	Beta 53128	3,130 ±70	25–30	AB	Projectile points; chert and quartz tools and chopper

1. All radiocarbon dates reported in this chapter are uncalibrated.
2. Projectile points were found in the surface.
3. Plano-convex scrapers were found in the surface.

Table 1.2 Projectile points found in Peñones de Bogotá

	UNIT	LEVEL (cm)	MATERIAL	WT. (g)	LGTH (mm)	MW (mm)	MT (mm)	LS (mm)	WS (mm)	L/MW
01	X-100	30–35	Chert	19.8	66	49	8	31	15	1.35
02	Y-100	25–30	Quartz	11.7	30	42	9	?	?	0.71
03	Y-99	40–45	Chert	0.5	9	12	4.5	?	?	0.75
04	X-100	30–35	Chert	11.9	34	47	9	15	24	1.72
05	X-100	30–35	Chert	44.5	58	57	14	?	?	1.02
06	Y-99	40–45	Quartz	3.2	28	13	9	28	13	2.15
07	X-100	30–35	Quartz	1.0	19	12.5	7	?	?	1.52
08	Y-100	35–40	Chert	10.2	40	26	12	?	?	1.54
09	Surface		Chert	79.4	163	65	10	11	18	2.51
10	Surface		Chert	12.1	48	33	7	?	?	1.45
11	Surface		Chert	75.4	58	68	26	34	35	0.85
12	Surface		Chert	68.8	99	61	13	10	30	1.62
13	Surface		Chert	54.0	86	60	16	18	17	1.43
14	Surface		Chert	110.0	90	63	24	13	17	1.43
15	Surface		Chert	41.2	85	45	10	9.5	18	1.89
16	Surface		Chert	23.6	67	44	8	7.5	18	1.52
17	Surface		Chert	17.9	45	38	10	11	14	1.18
18	Surface		Quartz	89.0	114	58	18	34	20	1.96
19	Surface		Chert	34.3	49	57	10	0.8	30	0.86
20	Surface		Quartz	23.4	48	49	9	14	13	0.98
21	Surface		Chert	45.4	90	37	16	0	0	2.43
22	Surface		Chert	27.0	64	36	0	0	0	1.78
23	Surface		Chert	17.1	59	30	9	0	0	1.97
24	Surface		Chert	14.9	72	23	10	0	0	3.13
25	Surface		Quartz	18.4	56	35	12.5	0	0	1.60
26	Surface		Quartz	9.3	57	20	9	0	0	2.85
27	Surface		Chert	22.8	65	36	12	?	?	1.80
28	Surface		Chert	13.1	42	42	10.5	?	?	1.00
29	Surface		Chert	11.0	38	40	7	?	?	0.95
30	Surface		Chert	25.8	45	35	13	?	?	1.28
31	Surface		Chert	2.4	28.5	16	6	?	?	1.78
32	Surface		Chert	8.3	40	20	9	?	?	2.00
33	Surface		Quartz	70.0	63	59	11	?	?	1.07

L=length; MW=maximum width; MT=maximum thickness; LS=length of stem; WS=width of stem

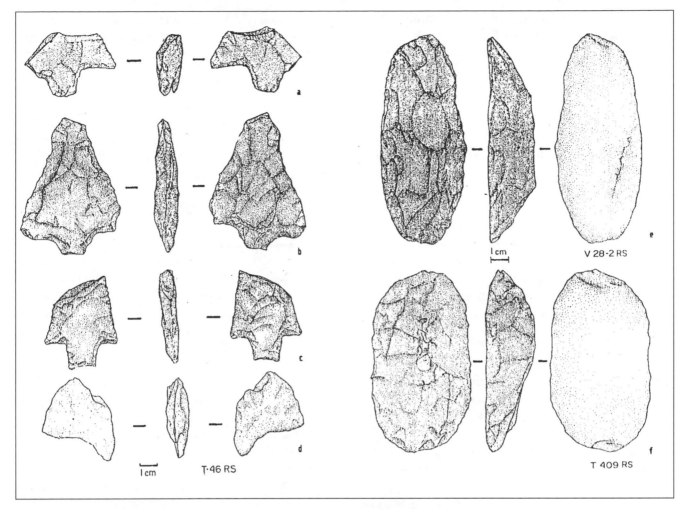

Figure 1.4 Fragments of projectile points and plano-convex scrapers: *a–d,* from surface collection at Nare; *e, f,* from surface collection at Barrancabermeja

cerning the nature of Late Pleistocene environments and climatic changes in northern South America (Vanzolini 1973; Colinvaux and Bush 1991; van der Hammen 1992; van der Hammen and Ortiz-Troncoso 1992; Ranere 1992: Dillehay et al. 1992). Short- and long-term human impact has also been investigated (Cooke and Ranere 1992a). A substantial controversy has centered around the question of tropical forest use for human subsistence (see Bailey et al. 1989, 1991; Colinvaux and Bush 1991). Despite recent work, as noted by Cooke and Ranere, "Archaeological inferences about the history and nature of human occupation of tropical forests (especially before 3000 to 2000 BP) remain, in many regions subservient to definitions, points of view and even guesses" (1992a:114).

For specific references to the middle Magdalena region, only the documentation given by van der Hammen (1988, 1992) is useful. His paleoclimatic regional interpretation was based on comparative pollen analysis from various sites in the Sabana de Bogotá, from Laguna de Pedro Pablo (located on the slopes above the Magdalena) and from the lower

Magdalena River. Van der Hammen provides evidence from the swampy area north of the town of El Banco for climatic change in the Magdalena Valley. He states that there were strong dry phases between circa 2600 and 2000 BP, 4100 and 3800 BP, around 4000 BP, and between 5500 and 7000 BP (van der Hammen 1992:29).

According to van der Hammen (1992), during the Late Pleistocene/Early Holocene, sectors of the Magdalena Valley and the cordilleran foothills could have been open areas, forming grassland corridors during specific dry intervals. Open areas characterized by gentle topography could have supported a diverse community of species, including large mammals that could not have subsisted on forest vegetation (Bombin and Huertas 1981; van der Hammen 1988, 1992). Identifying past environments and the faunal communities associated with them has a direct bearing on our interpretations of the subsistence strategies of early migrants entering South America (Linares and Ranere 1980; Ardila and Politis 1989; Lynch 1990; Dillehay et al. 1992).

The recent archaeological research, and especially the soil analyses done in the middle Magdalena, provide field data that favor the hypothesis concerning the past existence of open formations on the wide terraces in the region. Field observations and soil analyses conducted on terraces around Puerto Berrío and Barrancabermeja enabled the identification of an important aeolic influence that occurred during the preceramic cultural occupation. In fact, the cultural materials were recovered in predominantly wind-blown sediments and colluvial diffuse trickle sediments (López and Botero 1994).

The research has shown that, during the dry periods that predated 3000 BP, the chemically poor soils formed on the ancient terraces would not have supported forests, except on the slopes of the more heavily dissected margins. Soils with similar characteristics exist today in the Llanos Orientales (eastern plains of Colombia) in areas with aeolian influence due to the dry season and savanna vegetation. A granulometric analysis confirmed the similar texture of the soils. The middle Magdalena terrace soils have extremely acidic pH levels and high levels of aluminum, more similar to the current soils in the Amazonian forest than to the savanna soils. This is not an unexpected result given that the vegetation of the terraces changed from savanna to forest when climatic conditions became wetter about three thousand years ago (López and Botero 1994). Forests would have covered the piedmont and slopes of the cordillera even during the dry periods. Soils on the alluvial plains, unlike those on the terraces, are generally poorly drained and quite young, between two hundred and three thousand years old. Before 3,000 BP, plains like those between the Colorada and Opón rivers on the eastern margin of the Magdalena Valley (figure 1.1) were covered with water and swamp vegetation.

The terraces, then, represent areas that were well drained and open between a complex of swamps and gallery forests along the Magdalena River and the forests of the piedmont and cordillera. They provided favorable campsites and easy access to a wide range of open and closed habitats (Lopez and Botero 1994).

Significance of Lithic Assemblages

Raw material (chert and quartz) was abundant in the middle Magdalena, and its availability may have been a cultural consideration in occupying the area. Unifacial tools obtained on large flakes, such as plano-convex scrapers and knives with retouched edges were recovered from among the thousands of chipped waste and expedient tools collected. The regularity of sizes and shapes noticeable among the plano-convex scrapers may demonstrate predetermination in production.

The earliest lithic industry discovered in the middle Magdalena shows an important stylistic variety in projectile point size and shape (López 1989, 1992; ICAN 1991; Lopez et al. 1994; figure 1.2). The twenty-five projectile points recovered from a path in Peñones de Bogotá (table 1.2) constitute the largest assemblage found in Colombia. Their edges were reduced using controlled percussion and, in many cases, were retouched using pressure techniques. Although triangular stemmed points with different sizes and angles predominated, lanceolate and foliate points were also found. It is important to emphasize that eight fragments were excavated and located stratigraphically. Various bifacial preforms were also recovered; some of their edges do not present a complete reduction (López 1992).

All the lithic assemblages found in the middle Magdalena permit comparative studies with other early industries in northern South America. The current studies do not, however, explain variability of the assemblage. The Abriense tradition from the neighboring highlands of the Sabana de Bogotá, with its simple edge-trimmed tools and lack of bifacial flaking, is quite unlike the early tradition from the middle Magdalena. On the other hand, it shares the characteristics of bifacial reduction and careful edge retouch with those of the early middle Magdalena tradition. The small sample of Tequendamiense tools (N = 5) from the Tequendama rock shelter in the Altiplano of Bogotá (Correal and van der Hammen 1977) makes any comparisons unproductive (Wolford 1994:163-164).

The middle Magdalena stemmed points share similarities with the Restrepo type found in the southwest of Colombia; however, none of the Magdalena specimens exhibit fluting or basal thinning (Ardila 1991). There are apparent differences when the assemblage is compared to El Jobo from western Venezuela (Bryan et al. 1978; Cruxent 1970) and the (fluted) fishtail tradition from the upper Cauca River (Gnecco and Salgado 1989), Ecuador (Mayer-Oakes 1963), and Central America (Bird and Cooke 1977, 1978; Ranere and Cooke 1991; Cooke and Ranere 1992a; Ranere 1992). It is possible, however, to find similarities in materials recovered in Costa Rica (Acuña 1975), Venezuela (Barse 1990), and Brazil (Roosevelt et al. 1996), and in the Paijanense tradition in Perú (Chauchat 1977). The middle Magdalena materials seem to represent an identifiable regional tradition that shares only general characteristics with other areas.

Most of the information we have on the variability of early lithic traditions in northern South America is the product of work carried out over the last decade, for example, in Calima (Gnecco and Salgado 1989), the Upper Cauca drainage (Gnecco and Salgado 1989; Gnecco 1990), the Central Cordillera (Rodríguez 1991), the lowlands of eastern Colombia (Correal et al. 1990; Mora et al. 1991), and the Orinoco plains in Venezuela (Barse 1990). As the research in these and other areas is published in more detail over the next few years, our understanding of the relationships among regions will certainly change.

Conclusion

The preceramic sequence found must be viewed as preliminary, based as it is on only seven radiocarbon dates and small test excavations in only a handful of sites. Nonetheless, this initial formulation is useful in comparing the middle Magdalena materials and developments to those in other Colombian regions and neighboring countries (Reichel-Dolmatoff 1986; Correal 1988; Ardila and Politis 1989; Gnecco and Salgado 1989; Dillehay et al. 1992; Ranere 1992).

Research conducted to date suggests that human groups have been living in the lowland forest and savanna environments of the middle Magdalena Valley since at least the Late Pleistocene/Holocene boundary. From the limited evidence, it seems reasonable to speculate that a series of small campsites was established and used to exploit specific food and raw materials. Such camps would almost certainly have been linked to a complex system of mobility, with varying sizes and functions of settlements distributed strategically across the region. The main and more permanent settlements may have been located on the remnants of the wide Plio-Pleistocene terraces and situated in areas of open vegetation. Such settlements would correspond to the larger sites with higher artifact densities, such as La Palestina, San Juan de Bedout, and Peñones de Bogotá. The smaller sites with low artifact densities, situated in the forest terrain of the rolling hills, probably represent the remnants of temporary resource-specific camps.

All the sites are open air, and the collections recovered suggest that most of them included workshop activities. The question concerning the cultural continuity of the hunter-gatherers in the Magdalena Valley throughout the preceramic sequence remains open, as does the question of when bifacial flaking and the manufacture of projectile points became common. More intensive research in the area is clearly required.

With a number of stratified sites with deposits dated from ca. 10,500 to 3,000 BP already identified, there is every reason to believe that further research in the middle Magdalena region will significantly contribute to resolving questions of early human adaptations.

Finally, the evidence from the middle Magdalena Valley does not contradict Reichel-Dolmatoff's (1978d:46) observation that the few projectile points found in Colombia clearly cannot be linked to a stage of very ancient specialized hunters. Rather, they comprise very diverse types of points that were very likely distributed over thousands of years.

Acknowledgments. I extend my sincere gratitude to Dr. Anthony Ranere of Temple University for his guidance, help, and encouragement to pursue my studies in the USA I also thank the various institutions (particularly the Instituto Colombiano de Antropología, Fundación de Investigaciones Arqueológicas Nacionales, Interconexión Eléctrica S.A., and Universidad de Antioquia) as well as the archaeologists and other persons in Colombia who made possible the various middle Magdalena Valley projects between 1989 and 1993. Special thanks go to the Wenner-Gren Foundation for Anthropological Research and Temple University for funding my graduate studies. I also thank Anthony Ranere for not only reviewing this chapter but also helping to edit it and to David Mudge for his help in improving an earlier draft. I want to recognize the permanent support of my wife Martha Cecilia Cano. I am also grateful to the reviewers and the editors for their editorial work.

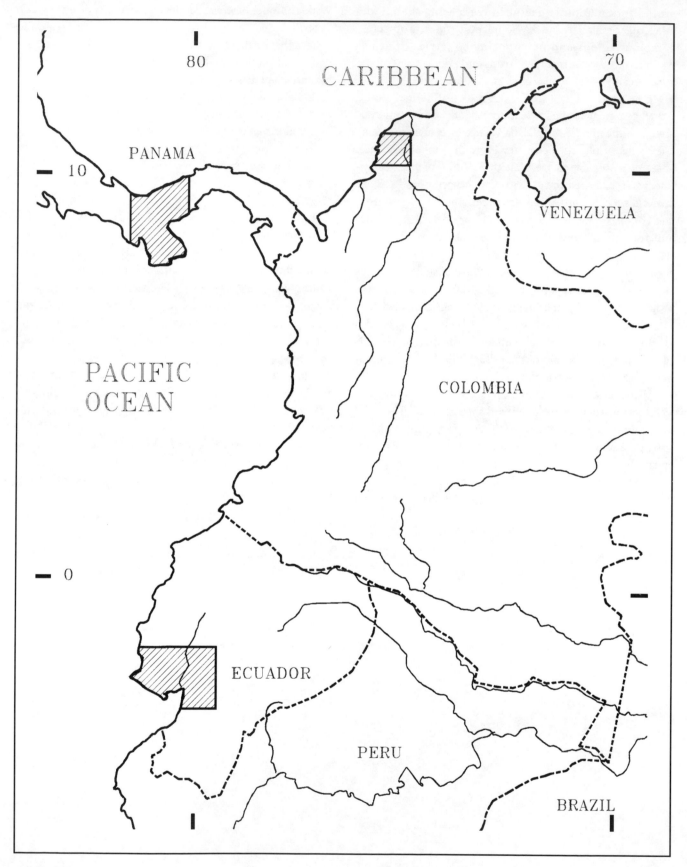

Figure 2.1 Locations of the three research areas in
northwestern South America

2

Beginnings of Sedentism in the Lowlands of Northwestern South America

J. Scott Raymond

IN 1965, Gerardo Reichel-Dolmatoff published the report of his excavations at Puerto Hormiga in northern Colombia (1965a). In the same year, Meggers, Evans, and Estrada's (1965) lengthy report on the Valdivia culture of southwest Ecuador appeared. These two works fueled a debate concerning the antiquity and origins of pottery and sedentism in the New World. The discovery of pottery dating to circa 3000 BC in the tropical lowlands of Colombia and Ecuador did not fit the models of cultural development for South America that were then current. Consequently, much of the early debate centered on arguments about dating and the origins and dispersal of pottery. The fact that the sites were situated near the sea popularized an interpretation that associated the pottery with a maritime seafaring culture.

Since these first discoveries, research in the lowlands flanking the northern Andes has progressed unevenly. Although there is still a comparative paucity of evidence, the record of human presence has been extended back to the Late Pleistocene, and the earliest secure dates for pottery have been pushed back a millennium to circa 4000 BC. (*All dates referred to in this chapter are uncalibrated.*) It is clear that a simple model cannot account for the beginnings of sedentism in the lowlands of northwestern South America.

Three regions—southwestern Ecuador, the northern alluvial plain of Colombia, and the Santa Maria drainage of Pacific Panama—provide fairly detailed records for the analysis and comparison of changing social and economic conditions in the tropics from the seventh through the second millennia BC (figure 2.1). Research has proceeded independently in each of these areas, and the data are not completely comparable. Here, I will draw comparisons in an attempt to identify parallels and differences in the processes that led to sedentism and in its association with particular social, economic, and environmental conditions.

Background and Biases

Before reviewing the results of recent research from each of the three regions, it is important to put that research into a broader intellectual and historical context. In the 1960s and early 1970s, few archaeologists regarded the tropical lowlands of South America as a promising setting for investigating human sedentism. All significant developments, including ceramics, agriculture, and settled village life, were assumed to have begun in the Central Andean region and spread through migration and diffusion to the "less civilized" peoples elsewhere in South America The similarity to diffusionary schemes that derived most prehistoric European culture from the Middle Eastern civilizations is obvious and is certainly not coincidental. South American archaeologists thus had a ready-made model which they adjusted to fit the geography of the continent. This model began to crumble in 1965, however, from the weight of the archaeological evidence from the lowlands of Colombia and Ecuador. It has now fallen apart completely from the force of a growing body of archaeological, ethnological, ethnohistorical, ecological, and paleobotanical evidence from the lowland American tropics.

A residual influence of the diffusionary model can still be seen to some extent, however, in the archaeological data available from each of the three regions in question. In all three, the initial surveys and excavations were carried out on or near the coast, giving the false impression that all of the early settlements were oriented to the sea or to the estuaries. This surmise was a result of research strategies and did not fully reflect the ancient settlement patterns. Shell mounds are easily spotted, and the coastal areas are, from a logistic standpoint, relatively easy to survey. The assumption that the earliest settlers of the tropical lowlands were a fishing, seafaring people became a self-fulfilling prophecy.

A dearth of investigation along lowland rivers and streams

Figure 2.2 Photograph of cut-bank on Daule River, Ecuador, showing buried archaeological occupation 7 m below surface. *Photograph by J. S. Raymond*

accounts for a second significant bias in the data. Not only do the high rates of deposition and erosion in such areas and the high densities of vegetation between the rivers significantly reduce the probability of site survival and discovery but the great effort required to conduct such research with little promise of return has also discouraged investigation.

Over the past two decades, investigators have made a concerted effort to design research strategies that reduce these biases. Recent research in both Colombia and Ecuador has shown, for example, that evidence of deeply buried settlements can be recovered, and sites in high-rate depositional environments may preserve contextual information that rarely survives elsewhere in the tropics (Raymond et al. 1980; Oyuela 1995; figures 2.2, 2.3). The legacy of earlier research still skews the data sets, and of course, the statistical bias will, without doubt, always favor proportional overrepresentation of sites in areas where the chances

of preservation are greater. Estimating the magnitude of the missing data without corrupting the integrity of the research will continue to be a humbling challenge to archaeologists working in the tropical lowlands.

Ecuador

Great strides have been made in documenting the evidence for Archaic and early Formative settlement in southwestern Ecuador; however, the record is still very spotty. The first discoveries of Valdivia sites in the 1950s and 1960s resulted from surveys carried out along the arid shores of the Santa Elena peninsula (Estrada 1956; Meggers et al. 1965). The settlement pattern was interpreted as favoring mangrove lagoons and beaches, which fostered the empirical generalization that the food economy was based on the sea. Recent surveys have encompassed the hinterland, however, showing that the majority of Valdivia sites are situated in the small coastal valleys 2 to 30 km from the sea (figure 2.4). The settlement patterns are complex and suggest a subsistence economy based on intensive use of the resources in small valley flood plains, possibly swidden agriculture along the valley slopes, and utilization of both game and fish (Lathrap et al. 1975; Marcos et al. 1976; Norton 1977, 1982; Raymond 1988, 1989, 1993; Zeidler 1986). Residues of sea fauna in the inland sites indicate regional interchange of food; however, stable isotope values from the human skeletal remains indicate only moderate reliance on seafoods (van der Merwe et al. 1993).

Valdivia is preceded in southwestern Ecuador by the preceramic Las Vegas culture, dated between 8000 and 4600 BC. Las Vegas regional settlement patterns are distinctly different from those of Valdivia, a fact that does not detract from Stothert's (1985) cogent argument that there is a cultural-historical connection between the two, one that indicates significant social and economic changes (figure 2.5). Las Vegas sites are found almost exclusively in the driest, westernmost part of the Santa Elena peninsula, an area only lightly settled by the early Valdivia populations. No Las Vegas sites have been found in the coastal valleys. With the exception of OGSE-80, the Las Vegas sites are shallow, small, and probably associated with transient occupations, contrasting with the deep, large (approximately 3-ha) Early Valdivia sites (Stothert 1985, 1988; Raymond 1993).

The absence of Vegas sites in the valleys may be more apparent than real. It is hard to believe that the Vegas populations, which used a wide range of land and seafood resources, would not have exploited plants and animals in the valleys, at least periodically if not continuously. A possible explanation is that small concentrations of unifacial stone flakes, which are the most distinguishable surficial evidence of a Vegas site, are less visible in the valleys for several reasons: higher vegetation densities, higher subsequent human occupation densities, and higher sedimentation and erosion rates. Further-

Figure 2.3
Photograph of
cut-bank on San
Jacinto Stream,
Colombia,
showing buried
archaeological
occupation 4 m
below surface.
*Photograph by A.
Oyuela-Caycedo*

more, because most Vegas stone tools were expedient, perhaps used to make wooden and bone tools, they would have tended to cluster near rock sources. These sources occur mainly in the valley riverbeds that become inundated during rainy periods. Thus, camps would have been very vulnerable to immediate erosion or burial.

Stothert (1985:614) has suggested that the largest of the Las Vegas sites, OGSE-80, was continuously occupied during the 3400-year span, which is a reasonable interpretation given the homogeneity of the midden. Periodicity of settlement during that span is difficult to determine from the available evidence, so it is possible, I would say probable, that it was occupied repeatedly at regular but short intervals (Raymond 1993) and served as a base camp for logistically mobile populations. A variety of wild resources could have been exploited within a 5 km radius of the base camp, and the 30 small sites may have been special-purpose camps. More research effort is needed to model the seasonality of wild plant and animal resources in the region. It seems evident that grasses, chenopodia, acacia, and cattail, all of which are present in the pollen from OGSE-80, are potential food resources that would have been abundant during the wet and early dry seasons. During much of the dry season, a portion of the Vegas population may have found foraging and hunting more profitable in the wetter middle and upper sections of the valleys. Moreover, if the Santa Elena Peninsula was subject to periods of prolonged drought, as it is today, most of the population may have retreated at times to the inner valleys for most of the year. The presence of horticulture about 6000 BC, as phytoliths indicate (Stothert

1985; 1988; Piperno 1988), suggests increased sedentism but does not preclude a high degree of mobility in the dry season.

The question whether maize was among the crops cultivated by the populations of Las Vegas and Valdivia has been controversial (Lippi et al. 1984; Fritz 1994; Piperno 1994a; Smith 1995:157–160). The principal archaeobotanists responsible for the research have mounted cogent arguments in support of its presence (Pearsall and Piperno 1990). It is beyond the scope of this chapter to enter into the debate; however, bone chemistry of human skeletal remains indicates that maize did not become a staple food until circa 500 BC (van der Merwe et al. 1993).

The human populations of southwestern Ecuador seem to have experienced a dramatic demographic change between Las Vegas and Valdivia. Following a hiatus in the nearly 1000 year record, there was a punctuated change in settlement at 3500 to 3000 BC, from the semi-arid savannas to the wetter, more forested river valleys. The change was also associated with evidence of a greater degree of sedentism. Larger planned settlements were established on river terraces and hillocks safely above flood waters; the middens contain grinding stones, stone axes, and high densities of broken pottery. Small ephemeral sites decreased dramatically in frequency (Raymond 1988, 1989, 1993; Schwarz 1987; Schwarz and Raymond 1996).

Panama

Along the estuary of the Santa Maria river on the Pacific coast of Panama, two shell midden sites, Cerro Mangote and Monagrillo, dating respectively to the fifth and third millennia BC, were discovered in the 1950s (McGimsey 1956; Willey

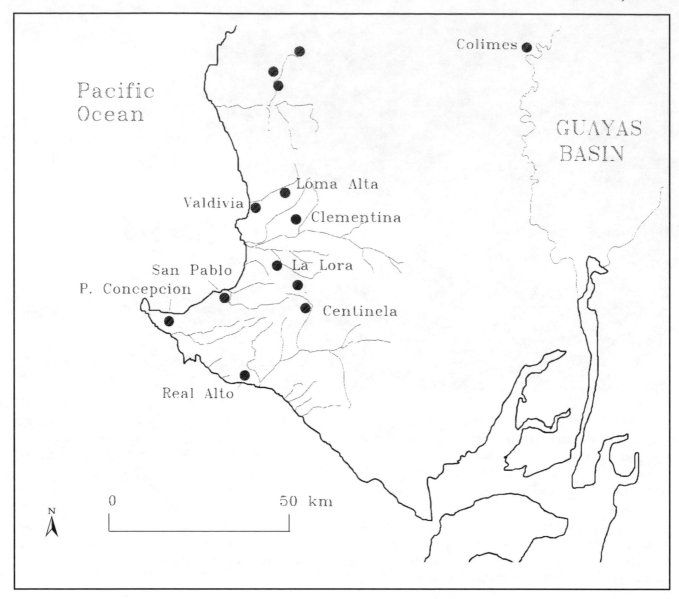

Figure 2.4 Locations of principal Valdivia sites in
southwestern Ecuador

and McGimsey 1954; figure 2.6). Because the testing of these
sites was not followed by further systematic research in the
area, it was believed that a marine-based economy, relying
mainly on shellfish, accounted for early settlement (Willey
1971:263–277). In the past two decades, however, a long-term
multidisciplinary project has defined a regionally balanced
record of settlement, subsistence, and environmental changes
(Cooke and Ranere 1984, 1992a, 1992b; Cooke et al. 1995).

Analysis of microbotanical remains from lake cores and
middens has provided a record of human presence that is
partly independent of the archaeological record. The two
records are not, however, always in clear agreement. Stable
isotope geochemistry of human bone from Cerro Mangote
and Sitio Sierra provides a further assessment of the prehistoric food economy.

By the fifth millennium BC, a wide range of marine and
terrestrial animal resources was being used at such sites as
Cerro Mangote (Ranere and Hansell 1978; Norr 1995; Cooke
et al. 1995). The estuarine sites were complemented by inland
sites situated in the Santa Maria watershed. The occurrence
of pottery after 2500 BC was associated with an increase in site
size. Monagrillo, for example, at 1.4 ha is eight times larger
than Cerro Mangote. It is unclear whether these sites were occupied seasonally or continuously, and investigators are ad-
mirably cautious on this point. The significant increase in site
size after 2500 BC and the identification of at least one probable residential structure (Cooke and Ranere 1992a:126) suggest a trend toward sedentism in settlements near the estuary.

The paleobotanical records of the region indicate that humans began burning areas in the cordillera and hillsides early
in the Holocene. Between 5000 and 2000 BC, the clearing and
burning of the forest intensified, possibly an indirect indica-
tion of swidden horticulture, and there was further intensifi-

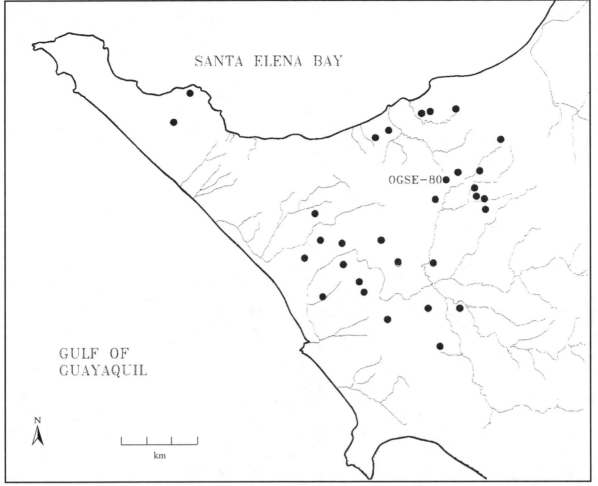

SANTA ELENA BAY

OGSE-80

GULF OF
GUAYAQUIL

N

km

Figure 2.5
Locations
of Las
Vegas sites
in south-
western
Ecuador

cation between 2000 and 1600 BC (Cooke and Ranere 1992a:123; Cooke et al. 1995; Piperno et al. 1991). A significant increase in the number of sites after 5000 BC (more than 260 recorded in the watershed) corresponds well with earlier indications of forest burning, but the intensification at 2000 BC is not noticeably reflected in the archaeological record. Because the sites are small, investigators have interpreted them as short-term settlements of people practicing swidden horticulture, hunting, and gathering. Maize pollen and phytoliths have been recorded from rock shelter deposits dating to 5000 BC, and are present in lake core sediments by 2000 to 1500 BC (Piperno et al. 1991). The earliest macrobotanical remains of maize do not occur, however, until circa 500 BC and are found abundantly at large nucleated settlements that were apparently associated with a drastic shift in settlement away from the hillslopes to the colluvial lowlands (figure 2.7).

A comparative analysis of the archaeofaunal record and the human bone biochemistry from Cerro Mangote suggests that the site was occupied each year for short periods of time by populations that spent most of the year in the hinterland. The absence of known sites in the flood plain and the discovery of numerous small sites along the hillslopes support the inference that people resided in ephemeral hamlets, practicing swidden horticulture (possibly cultivating maize) and hunting. Dried and salted fish may have been taken from the estuary back to sites in the foothills (Norr 1995:219-222; Cooke et al. 1995).

As mentioned previously, the degree of sedentism may have increased during the third millennium BC as evidenced by the establishment of larger settlements such as Monagrillo and the occurrence of pottery. A change in fishing strategies, reflecting the use of fine-mesh nets and watercraft, occurred at the same time (Cooke and Ranere 1992a:125), suggesting that Monagrillo may have been a specialized fishing settlement. Comparable coeval nucleated settlements have not been recorded from the watershed; however, if they were situated in the colluvial lowlands, they may possibly have been buried by flood sediments.

Colombia

The late Archaic and Formative sites of Colombia are found on the broad Caribbean plain near Cartagena (figure 2.8). This region comprises the alluvial lands and estuaries of the Magdalena, Cauca, and Sinu rivers and low hilly country extending from the Andes. Beginning in the 1950s with the research of Gerardo Reichel-Dolmatoff and Alicia Dusan de

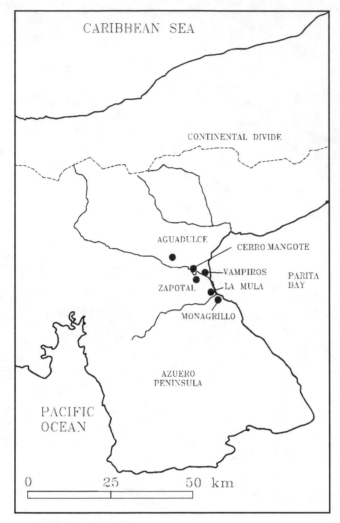

Figure 2.6 Map of Santa Maria Valley, Panama, showing locations of settlements before 1600 BC

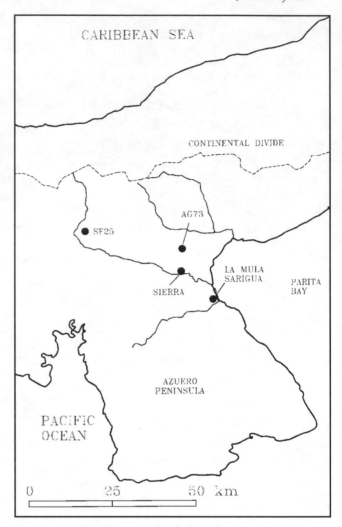

Figure 2.7 Map of Santa Maria Valley, Panama, showing locations of settlements circa 500 BC

Reichel, archaeological investigations have concentrated on locating and excavating shell middens (Reichel-Dolmatoff 1955, 1965a, 1965b, 1985a). Research since then has concentrated on defining chronological sequences, and consequently the data for defining regional settlement patterns is less complete than that for Ecuador or Panama.

Recent research inland, in the hills and savannas bordering the lower Magdalena, has significantly broadened the scope of the data relating to the social and economic antecedents of sedentism. As in Panama, the archaeological record is supplemented by a palaeoenvironmental sequence derived from pollen cores. The pollen record has not yet been used to infer the effects of humans on the Archaic plant communities of the lower Magdalena.

With the establishment of settlements such as Puerto Hormiga near the coast and their association with high frequencies of pottery at circa 3100 BC, Reichel-Dolmatoff (1965a, 1965b) saw the beginning of a pattern in which sedentary settlement was linked to the exploitation of the rich sea and estuary environments, supplemented by resources from the nearby savannas and forests. This pattern persisted for several millennia, as attested by later shell mounds such as those at Canapote and Barlovento (circa 2000 to 1000 BC), and according to the model, gradually included a dependency on domesticated plants such as manioc.

Recent surveys in the vicinity of Puerto Hormiga and excavations at the nearby site of Puerto Chacho confirm the pattern of settlement of groups of pottery-using fisher-collectors inhabiting the Magdalena estuary from late in the fourth millennium BC to at least midway through the third. Based on data derived from palaeoenvironmental and geomorphological studies that show the Colombian estuarine environments have been very changeable, Oyuela and Rodriguez (1990; Oyuela 1996) have questioned whether such estuarine adaptations could have been very stable or long-lasting. Wet periods and rising sea levels enlarged estuaries and enhanced their productivity; falling sea levels and dry periods had the reverse effect. The shell middens of Puerto Chacho and Puerto Hormiga accumulated during a high stand of the sea. Monsú (Reichel-Dolmatoff 1985a), a site situated nearby

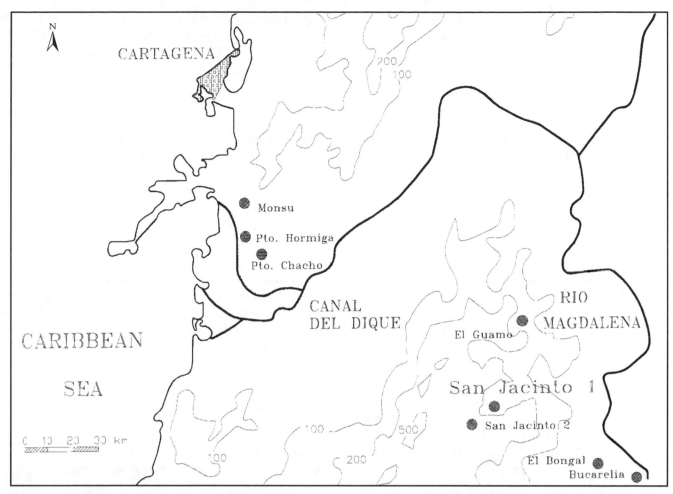

Figure 2.8 Map of Lower Magdalena Valley, Colombia, showing locations of Late Archaic/Early Formative sites

that did not have a shell midden, was occupied afterward when the sea level was lower and foods characteristic of a riverine environment were exploited (Oyuela 1996). Oyuela (1996) has argued that coastal resources encouraged the development of specialized fishing strategies and technologies for effectively exploiting a rich but changeable environment, and that conditions were not conducive to the development of sedentism or horticulture.

As long ago as 1932, Gladys Ayer Nomland (Reichel-Dolmatoff 1985a:179) collected fiber-tempered pottery sherds, similar in style to Puerto Hormiga, from sites along the shores of the lower Magdalena river more than 180 km from the sea. Except for Lathrap's (1970) suggestion that these sites attest to early flood plain settlement, they had not figured in a synthesis of early sedentism until Oyuela's and Bonzani's recent work in the adjacent serrania of San Jacinto (Oyuela 1993; figure 3.1). Their research indicates that by 4000 BC, a thousand years before the first shell middens were occupied on the coast, hunter-collectors, with well-made, elaborately decorated, fiber-tempered pottery, were moving seasonally between base camps and smaller special-purpose camps. The most com-

pelling evidence comes from excavations at the site of San Jacinto 1, which revealed repeated seasonal occupations of a point bar over a period of possibly 700 years. Earth ovens, processing tools, and macrobotanical remains indicate that the occupations were associated with the harvesting, preparation, and storage of localized wild plant resources, especially grasses.

The Serranía de San Jacinto is a transitional forest/savanna environment with marked seasonal precipitation. The patchy distribution of plant foods in this setting, such as grasses found on point bars, and their periodic availability, may have intensified human reliance on predictable resources. Oyuela (1993, 1995) suggests that such a subsistence strategy would have been associated with territorially restricted group mobility and that it plausibly could have been antecedent to the development of horticulture.

Larger sites associated with San Jacinto pottery have been found in contexts that were not subject to annual flooding. Only one of these, San Jacinto 2, has been test excavated, so we are not yet able to understand the role of these sites in the settlement system. They were occupied by at least 3000 BC and may well have been the main residential camps or villages for seasonally mobile populations. The low density of pottery at San Jacinto 1, the dissociation with food preparation loci, and the high frequency of decoration suggest that pottery played more a social than a utilitarian role (Oyuela 1995; Raymond et al. 1994).

Comparisons and Conclusions

Human settlement clearly has a long history in the northwestern tropical lowlands of South America, extending back to the Late Pleistocene in Panama and to at least the Early Holocene in Ecuador and Colombia. While the data available from the three areas are not completely comparable, it is possible to observe both similarities and differences in the sequences:

- The paleoenvironmental record in Panama suggests that, from the first, humans had a noticeable effect on plant communities, initially through burning and later through clearing and burning. Although it seems reasonable to suppose that similar activities were occurring in Ecuador and Colombia, we do not yet have comparable records, highlighting a research priority, especially in Ecuador.

- Trends toward sendentism are evident in all three areas by the late fifth or early fourth millennium BC. Groups began gathering at sites such as Las Vegas and Cerro Mangote for what were probably interrelated social and economic objectives. The large number of burials found at each site (McGimsey 1956; Stothert 1985, 1988) suggests that communal funerary rites were one of the social activities that helped to define group identity (Raymond 1993). Neither the periodicity of these gatherings nor their duration is known; however, as mentioned earlier, the bone chemistry of the Cerro Mangote burials suggests that the individuals spent most of the year in the hinterland.

- Although the exploitation of maritime resources was economically important in all three regions, there is earlier evidence of reliance on the inland resources of savanna, forest, and riverine settings in Colombia and Panama. The Las Vegas economy in Ecuador relied more on terrestrial resources than on seafood. In Panama, coastal and estuarine fishing intensified about 2500 BC and seems to have been linked with increased settlement size and probably with greater sedentism. In Ecuador, although fishing seems to have been an important part of the economy from the time of Vegas, there is no noticeable intensification until about 1500 BC, when fishing communities were established along the coast. In Colombia, the economic pattern represented by coastal shell middens was established by 3000 BC and continued through the first millennium BC, waxing and waning with fluctuating sea levels and precipitation patterns.

- In Colombia, by the early fourth millennium BC, inland populations were harvesting wild seeds in a strategy that anticipated horticulture and may well have been combined with the management and artificial concentration of plant communities. In Ecuador, phytolithic evidence of maize has been interpreted as evidence of horticulture by the sixth millennium BC. In Panama, maize and indications of extensive forest clearing in paleobotanical records of the fifth millennium BC have been interpreted as evidence of swidden agriculture. In neither area is there evidence that maize became a staple food until about 500 BC. The situation of Early Valdivia settlements adjacent to the arable flood plains of the coastal valleys is, however, an additional powerful indicator of horticulture, which may have included a wide range of tropical cultigens, with root crops perhaps constituting the main staples.

- In Ecuador, Valdivia pottery is associated mainly with what seems to be sedentary settlements. In Panama, settlements associated with Monagrillo pottery, such as the Monagrillo site itself, are less clearly fully sedentary. In Colombia, the earliest pottery is clearly associated with a seasonally occupied settlement. Pottery, then, may be associated with a trend toward sedentism but cannot alone be interpreted as its indicator.

The generalizations made here will have a short shelf life. Researchers must set a high priority on making the data from these regions more comparable. In all three areas, but especially in Panama, greater effort must be spent on investigating colluvial areas where ancient occupation may have been deeply buried. Ecuador's deficiency in paleoenvironmental research must be repaired so that meaningful comparisons can be made about the relative impact of human settlement on the natural setting. Human skeletal remains need to be excavated from Colombian sites so that dietary indicators derived from bone chemistry can be used to supplement the archaeobotanical and archaeofaunal evidence.

It is an exciting time to be working in the South American tropics. Archaeological research is advancing quickly, and we are no longer bound by narrow diffusionist models that saw tropical forest cultures as diffused relics of Andean civilization, or by narrow questions such as when and where pottery was invented. The process of sedentation may have been precocious in the tropics; however, it is clear that sedentism and mobility must be treated as variables within a continuum and modeled in relation to what was clearly a highly variable lowland environment.

Acknowledgments. My research in Ecuador has been supported by several grants from the Canada Council and from the Social Sciences and Humanities Research Council of Canada. The assistance, collaboration, criticism, and support of many colleagues and friends have been crucial to the success of the research. Most notable among these are the late Presley Norton, Jorge Marcos, the late Olaf Holm, the late Donald Lathrap, Peter Stahl, Jim Zeidler, Judy Kreid, Michael Muse, Juan Orala, Claire Allum, and Fred Schwarz. I particularly want to acknowledge Karen Stothert, who on numerous occasions has given logistic and moral support as well as the hospitality of her family to me and my graduate students.

It would not have been possible to write this chapter without the excellent published results of the several scholars who, over the past two decades, have collaborated in the investigation of the Santa Maria Valley, Panama. I hope I have not misrepresented or misinterpreted their findings. Augusto Oyuela-Caycedo, who spent two years at Calgary as a postdoctoral fellow, encouraged me to write this chapter. For me, those were two pleasurable years of intellectual growth, stimulated by numerous discussions and debates with Augusto, who always required me to defend my ideas as effectively as possible. Finally, I thank my late mentor and supervisor, Donald Lathrap, who instilled an appreciation of the work of Gerardo Reichel-Dolmatoff in me and in his other students.

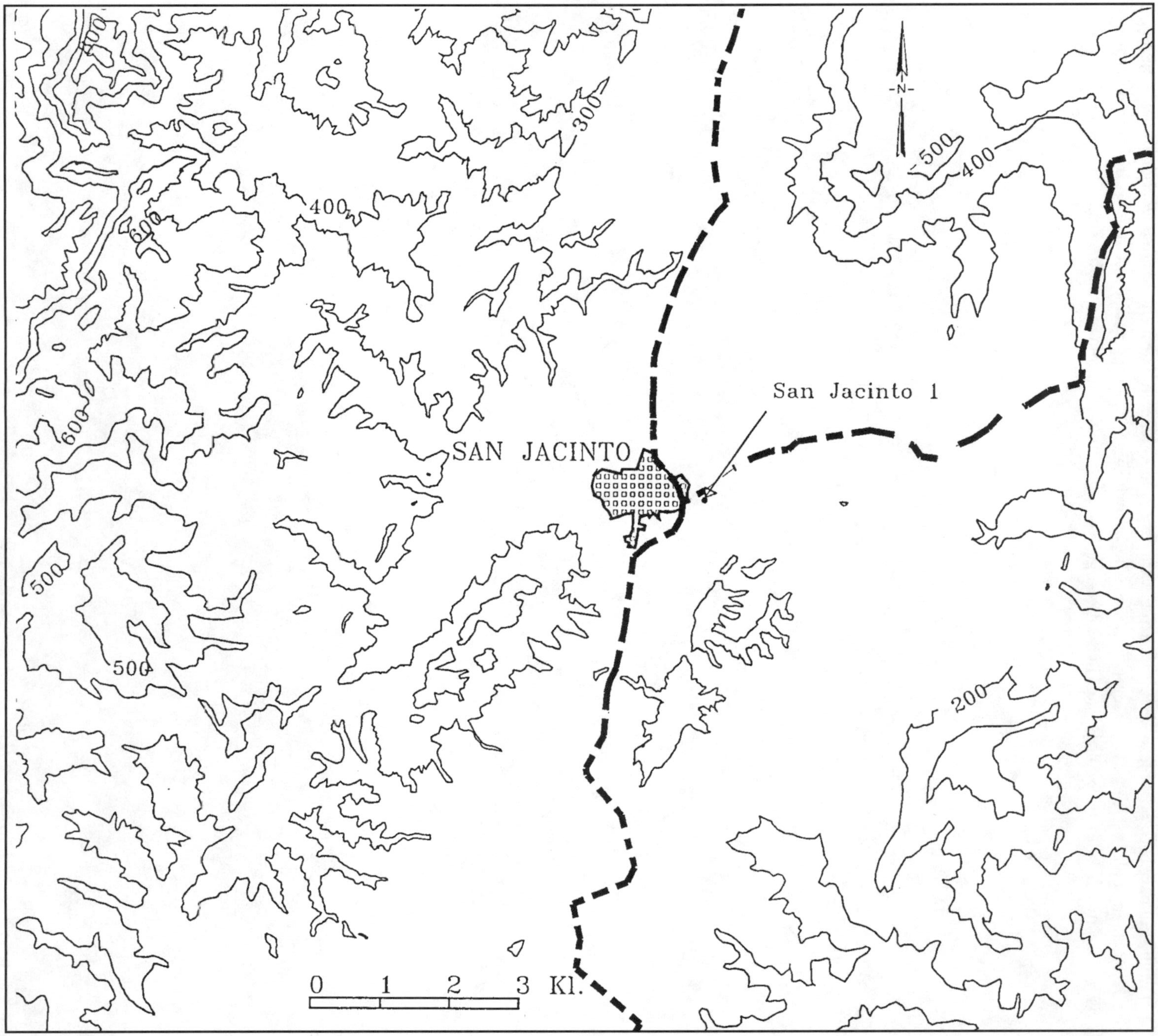

Figure 3.1 Location of
San Jacinto 1 and town

3

Learning from the Present
Constraints of Plant Seasonality on Foragers and Collectors

Renee M. Bonzani

THROUGHOUT Gerardo Reichel-Dolmatoff's works, the importance of present-day inhabitants' information about their environment and its relation to the social and spiritual aspects of their lives is stressed and tied to the archaeological past. Reichel's discussion of contemporary uses and the importance of plants in the Caribbean coastal region of Colombia was integral to the presentation of his and Alicia Dussan's archaeological excavations at Monsú and gave impetus to the current work (Reichel-Dolmatoff 1985a). The collection of information on plant use and seasonality by persons living in and intimately familiar with that environment, whether indigenous or *campesinos*, is extremely important for developing ideas about how past inhabitants may have developed strategies to deal with similar stresses and risks.

This chapter outlines how strategies of mobility are tied to the seasonal availability of resources, how resources produce seasonality in the San Jacinto region of the savanna of Bolívar, and, given this information, what one might expect to recover archaeologically concerning foraging and collecting populations. An archaeological case study, that of San Jacinto 1, is then analyzed with the following developed expectations in mind.

This chapter reviews generalized hunter-gatherer mobility strategies based on plant availability. Data on the current seasonality of useful plants native to Colombia or northern South America are then presented. The seasonality of 20 cultivated plant genera and species and 46 wild plant genera and species are presented. The seasonality of these plant taxa are then tied to hunter-gatherer mobility strategies and resultant site types. Expectations for the associations between site type and plant use are discussed using data from San Jacinto 1, an Archaic/early Formative site (6000 to 5300 BP) located in northern Colombia.

Hunter-Gatherer Mobility Strategies

If hunter-gatherer mobility strategies are viewed as means of obtaining food (this does not preclude strategies for obtaining mates, for instance), then such strategies should be closely tied to the availability of resources both in time and space. Binford (1980, 1983:213-386) found a continuum of mobility strategies dependent on food availability. At one extreme, he defined residential mobility where the whole group moved to the food resource. In this case, the food resource was enough to satisfy the group for a few days to a few weeks. Then the group moved on to the next available resource.

Two aspects of food availability are necessary to practice residential mobility. First, the resource must provide enough food to justify the group's moving to a location and staying there for a certain, though relatively short, time. In other words, a single member of a plant species would have to produce a large volume of food, or several members of a species would have to have fruits available in the same general area and at the same general time. Second, other species would have to be in fruit at times different from those of the first species. This situation would allow the group to move to a new resource following consumption of the first resource. In this case, different plant remains would be recovered archaeologically from the residential base camps. The fruiting time of plants may overlap, and remains of these plants might therefore be expected to occur at a residential site type at the same time. Diversity of macrobotanical remains would be low to medium (<0.75 using Simpson's index of diversity). Thus, residential mobility strategies tend to be tied to food resources that are spread out or evenly available usually over both space and time (Cashdan 1992).

On the other hand, in seasonal environments with yearly periods of stress (that is, water deficits), plant food resources

21

would not occur evenly in space or time and residential mobility geared toward evenly spaced food availability would not always be effective. Resource availability would be patchy in space and time, clustered during times of rainfall or in areas where water is more abundant. In this case, during seasons of abundance (rainy seasons) residential mobility might continue to be practiced. In the stressful less abundant times (dry seasons), other mobility and foraging strategies would be necessary.

Binford (1980) defines logistic mobility as that type of mobility which is more efficient in dealing with patchy resource availability. In this case, a base camp is established from which groups of various sizes and composition are sent out to obtain a resource and bring it back to the base camp. The base camp is generally located between resource zones so groups can be sent out to various locations at various times to collect resources as they become available. The logistic base camp would be more permanent than that for residential mobility and would probably have macrobotanical remains of resources from different seasons of availability and potentially different ecological zones. Diversity of macrobotanical remains would be high (>0.75 using Simpson's index of diversity).

An associated type of site found in logistic mobility is the special-purpose site (Binford 1980, 1983:325-336). This type would be any site associated with a base camp where the activities performed are limited and generally well defined. Special-purpose sites include those where a specific food resource is processed for return to the base camp. The macrobotanical remains would come mainly from the food being processed, as well as food eaten during processing. Diversity of macrobotanical remains would be low (<0.25 using Simpson's index of diversity). Further, the resource would be seasonal and abundant, seasonal in that processing is necessary before the resource disappears and abundant in that it would pay for the effort and time spent in processing. Consequently, a logistic mobility strategy is more likely to be favored in seasonal environments, potentially during periods of food scarcity. Thus, foraging would occur at the same time in different resource zones when food is abundant and can be processed into storable goods to compensate for scarcity of food in a dry period.

Present-day Plant Seasonality in the San Jacinto Region
Cultural and Environmental Setting
The town of San Jacinto was founded in 1776. Le Roy Gordon (1983:126) indicates that many of the towns in the savanna of Bolívar near the town of Colosó, including San Jacinto, were founded by practically pure descendants of the indigenous groups of the Sinú. These towns were founded as part of the mobilization of native persons for labor by the Spanish colonialists. In particular, persons from Morroa were relocated

to what became San Jacinto. Morroa specialized in hammock making, and this practice was brought to San Jacinto. Le Roy Gordon (1983:138) notes that many of the indigenous crafts are still practiced in the region, and includes Morroa and San Jacinto in this group. Indeed, today hammocks are made and sold by individual families in San Jacinto and are displayed for sale by numerous stores that line the Pan-American Highway which cuts through the outskirts of the town.

Through the years, these groups maintained traditional crafts and land management practices. In recent years, however, a dichotomy in knowledge of the uses and management of plants has arisen between those living in the town and those living on the outskirts who work the land. As expected, the campesinos of the area who work the land for food and cash crops know more about plant uses, seasonality, insect pests, and so forth. Compared to general urban/suburban residents' knowledge of plant use, the differences are profound. Knowledge of plant uses disappears as people become less autonomous in obtaining food, medicine, and so forth, from the land and become more tied to institutionalized venues (supermarkets or drugstores).

Seasonal Climate and Periods of Stress
The Serranía de San Jacinto and the Savanna de Bolívar, where the town and archaeological site of San Jacinto are located, have been broadly defined in ecological terms as savanna (IGAC 1975; figure 3.1): that is, they are comprised of a "type of tropical vegetation where certain forms of grasses dominate and where seasonal droughts and frequent fires are normal ecological factors" (Sarmiento 1984:6). From a vegetative survey of the San Jacinto area, 33 percent of the ground cover was grasses, 6 percent trees, and the rest (57 percent) was shrub or herbaceous cover (Bonzani 1995, 1997). A more succinct definition is wooded savanna, where 5 to 15 percent of the ground cover is trees. Wooded savannas range from 500 to 1000 trees per hectare, with San Jacinto falling into the lower part of this range based on percentages at about 500 to 600 trees per hectare, located mainly along stream banks.

The present-day climate of the northwest of Colombia and the Serranía de San Jacinto is marked by "sharply contrasting wet and dry seasons" (Parsons 1980:284) and characterized by a bimodal precipitation pattern (figure 3.2, taken from Oyuela 1993; Walsh 1981). The wettest month is October, followed by a long dry season from December to March/April when water deficits occur. A shorter rainy season occurs in April/May/June, with a short dry season or *veranillo* in July/August. Annual precipitation is 1030 mm, as recorded for a 46-year period from 1931 to 1941 and 1953 to 1987 at the weather station in Carmen de Bolívar, located approximately 12 km south of San Jacinto. Annual mean temperature, as measured at this station, is 27.5° C, with little yearly variation. By looking at these general climatic indicators, the area of San Jacinto falls just outside a subhumid savanna type, with 1000 to 500 mm/yr and a medium dry season of 5 to 7.5 months (Harris 1980).

The past climate in the region is known to have fluctuated between wetter and drier periods. This information is available mainly from palynological studies conducted on the north coast of Colombia and in Central America and northern South America. Van der Hammen (1984) has done palynological work in the area of the Sierra Nevada of Santa Marta and the Cienaga Grande of Santa Marta located on the Caribbean coast approximately 150 km from San Jacinto. Van der Hammen (1974, 1983) and van der Hammen et al. (1991) have also conducted palynological and sediment studies in the Llanos of Colombia, the savanna of Bogotá, and the Colombian Amazon which contain information about the Holocene. Their work indicates that the area around Santa Marta had less precipitation and higher temperatures between 6000 and 5500 BP and that generally in northern South America a dry period occurred at 5500 BP and again at 4700 BP Around 6000 BP, the climate was becoming drier and, by at least this time, savanna existed in the Llanos of Colombia. Further, changing ratios of trees to grasses indicate an alternation between savanna woodland and grass savanna in the Llanos of Colombia and the Rupununi savannas of southern Guyana (Harris 1980:22). Other information based on pollen analysis and changes in lake levels from the Peten, Panama Canal, Lake Valencia in Guyana, and Lake Moriru in Brazil, leads to paleoenvironmental reconstructions of a drier period after 8000 BP until 5500 BP or 3500 BP (Lake Moriru), with the seasonally dry interval becoming more prominent (Markgraf 1989:8).

Oyuela (1996) and Oyuela and Rodrígues (1990) further indicate that at about 5800 to 5400 BP lowering of the sea level correlated with lower river and water table levels and a climatic dry period occurred. These findings might indicate drier conditions than today and point to downcutting of stream channels and a possible increase in savannas (Oyuela 1993:32-33).

Further evidence of potentially drier conditions during the occupation of San Jacinto 1 comes from the recovery of two tree snail species at the site (*Drymaeus* spp. possible *virgulatus* [Férussac] and *Orthalicus maracaibensis* [Pfeifere 1856], reported also as *Orthalicus undatus* [Bruguiére]), which are ecologically indicative of dry xerophytic vegetation or thorn woodlands and arid conditions (Oyuela 1993:152-164). Rainfall amounts of less than 500 mm per year are found in association with the conditions in which these snails generally live. These data indicate that the climate during the occupation of San Jacinto 1 was becoming drier. In general, drier conditions would have made the seasonality of plants more pronounced (Servant et al. 1993). Thus, the seasonality or period of fruiting and flowering of plants would not have occurred at different times of the year but may have been more abrupt in their occurrence and disappearance or more restricted to the middle ranges of the seasonality defined herein.

Methodology

Two hundred and seventy specimens of the modern-day vegetation from the region of San Jacinto, Department of Bolívar, Colombia, were collected from October 1991 to April 1992. Of these, 249 were scientifically identified. The specimens cover 55 different families, 138 genera, and 118 species (Bonzani 1995). Voucher specimens are on file at the Fundación Jardín Botánico "Guillermo Piñeres" (JBGP) in Cartagena, Department of Bolívar, Colombia, and at the Colombian National Herbaria (COL) of the Instituto de Ciencias Naturales, Museo de Historia Natural, Universidad Nacional de Colombia in Bogotá.

During the collection of modern-day plants, informants were asked to name the plant; give its uses, parts utilized, and preparation; whether it was indicative of drier or wetter climate or habitat; and seasonality. If the plant was an important food resource, information was obtained on when it was planted (*epoca de siembra*) and its season of availability (harvest or *cosecha*). Availability or fruiting of food plants was also noted by date.

A survey was also made of the seasonality of 50 plant taxa used for food or other purposes by questioning six campesinos, both men and women, who collaborated in the excavation of San Jacinto. The age of the informants ranged from 20 to 48. Informants were given the name of each plant and asked whether they knew the plant. They were also asked the month of the year the plant was planted if a cultivar, the month the plant had flowers, and the month the fruit was ready to be picked if wild or harvested if planted. Information on cultivated plants included those from both the New and Old Worlds, while information on wild plants and fruit trees focused only on those that originated in the New World, specifically in northern Colombia or lowland tropical regions. Table 3A.1 lists the areas known to be origins of domestication or of native distribution of cultivated and wild plants utilized for food in the San Jacinto region of Colombia.

Results

The information the author obtained concerning plant seasonality in the region of San Jacinto is presented in tables 3A.2 through 3A.8. The seasonality documented runs from the beginning of the wet season in September through the dry season from December to March and to the shorter wet and dry periods from April to August. The information is based on informant surveys, dates for the collection of fruits by the author (listed in footnotes at the end of each table), and a literature review of plant seasonality (Bartholomaus et al. 1990; Castañeda 1965; García Barriga 1992 I, II, III; Gentry 1993; Perez-Arbelaez 1978; Schultes and Raffauf 1990).

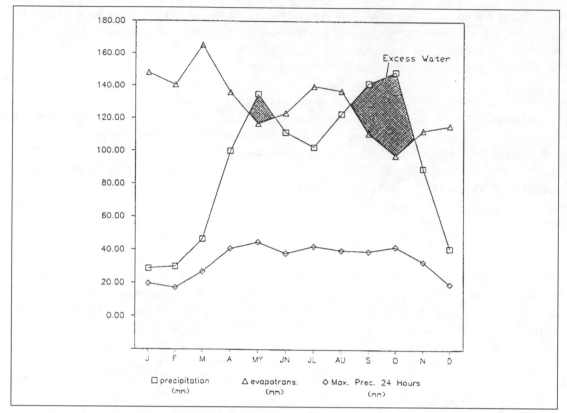

Figure 3.2 Mean annual precipitation and water deficit in millimeters. Lower distribution is maximum monthly precipitation in 24-hour period, mean values. *After Oyuela-Caycedo 1993*

Several observations can be made based on the seasonality data gathered from modern-day plant use at San Jacinto. Not surprisingly, the cultivation of plants in the region where seasonality is based on a bimodal distribution of rainfall requires that plants be planted before the rains and collected following the rainy seasons. This schedule of cultivation occurs both over the major rainy period of September through November and the shorter rainy period of May-June. Planting tends to occur in September and in March through May (tables 3A.2 through 3A.8). Harvesting occurs from October to January. Crops planted in September are ready for harvest (*la cosecha*) in January, as with maize when the grass has dried. Crops planted in March through May are ready for harvest in June to August, as with pepper, squash, or a second crop of maize, or in October as with sweet potato, manioc, and beans (*Phaseolus lunatus*). Achiote (a perennial), bottle gourd, and cotton are also planted in April through May and harvested in the December-January dry season. Tobacco harvests can run from August through December, with a concentration in December. Some cultivated plants such as passion fruit and papaya have become available all year round.

Second, fruiting of different families of trees tends to be seasonal, as indicated for individual species in the literature on this subject from Colombia (Castañeda 1965; Bartholomaus et al. 1990; Perez-Arbelaez 1978; Gentry 1993). The majority of the genera and species of trees fruit in May, however, during the shorter rainy season that occurs after the major dry period in the area. These trees include members of the families of Anacardiaceae, Annonaceae, Guttiferae, Polygonaceae, and *Persea americana* of the Lauraceae.

The major fruiting period of other families occurs during the major rainy season in October and into November. These families may also fruit in May, though informant information and collections of fruits in the field by the author show a clear concentration of fruiting times in October and November. These plants include members of the family Myrtaceae and *Ocotea* of the Lauraceae.

Other families having a more extended fruiting period are the Mimosaceae, with *Inga densiflora* fruiting from October to February and *Prosopis juliflora*, fruiting from August to November. Fruits from *Inga densiflora*, found in Colombia from 800 to 1700 msl, may not have been available in this region (at 210 msl) in Archaic and Formative times (Bartholomäus et al. 1990).

Fruits from trees of other families appear to fall more into the beginning or early part of the major dry season which begins in December and runs until March or April. These families include the Sapotaceae, Sterculiaceae, and *Phyllanthus acidus* of the Euphorbiaceae that fruit in December and January, and the *Cassia grandis* of the Caesalpiniaceae that fruits from December to March.

Although native to Colombia or northern South America, three fruiting trees were either unknown to local informants or, if known, the season of fruiting or flowering was not known. These include *Chlorophora tinctoria* of the Moraceae, *Chysobalanus icaco* of the Rosaceae, and *Genipa americana* of the Rubiaceae.

In summary, the major fruiting period of trees occurs in the short rainy season around May. Fruiting in the major rainy period around October is found in the Lauraceae, Myrtaceae, and Mimosaceae. Dry season fruiting occurs in the Sapotaceae, Sterculiaceae, Euphorbiaceae, and Caesalpiniaceae. The seasonality of more individuals of a species in different locations and other species from each family need to be studied to make these statements more conclusive.

The third observation from these data is that the availability of palm fruits is not as highly seasonal as that of other plant families. Fruiting of palms in seasonal environments of the Amazon runs from the dry season in December through the wet season around May. Data indicate that palms may not be as useful in defining site seasonality as other fruit tree families, though more information on the seasonality of palms in the region of San Jacinto is clearly needed.

As well, the seasonal use of tubers in this region of Colombia may be hard to determine because tubers can be left in the ground for several months and collected as needed. In general, tuberous plants (*Manihot esculenta, Ipomoea* spp., *Dioscorea* spp.) are planted vegetatively in April and collected during the major wet period in September to October, a potentially important point when considering adaptive strategies of plant collection during the dry season. Collection in the wet season may be a matter of taste preference, however, as indicated by informants for manioc; tubers of these same genera are also collected in January.

The fourth observation deals with the availability of grasses. This resource is known to be used archaeologically and ethnographically (Cane 1989; Harlan 1989; Jones and Meehan 1989; Oyuela 1993:209-213; Tindale 1977; Wetterstrom 1993). In the savanna of Bolívar, grasses are highly seasonal, with seed and other reproductive structures available at the end of the rainy season (end of November) and the beginning of the dry season (December). If the collection of other grasses like that of maize is best done when the plants are dry, then collection of seeds or other reproductive structures would occur in December and into January. By the middle of December, the plants in the region are drying up and dying. Further, these resources are r-selected (MacArthur 1972:229-230), having abundant offspring (that is, seeds, cobs) that can be processed as a storable food (that is, flour) for the end of the dry season when food resources become more scarce and less predictable.

Plant Seasonality, Site Type, and Expected Botanical Remains

From these data, associations among plant seasonality, expected botanical remains and site type, and time of occupation can be addressed. Given the seasonal bimodal precipitation pattern in the Colombian savanna of Bolívar, both logis-

tic and residential mobility patterns might be expected. Residential mobility strategies are expected to occur during wet periods and times of food abundance. More logistic strategies are expected in the dry seasons or periods of resource scarcity. Sites of residentially mobile groups focused on the seasonal availability of plants would be expected to have remains of various fruit trees, depending on the time of occupation. For instance, residential base camps occupied in the rainy season around October would be expected to have remains of *Psidium guayaba* (Myrtaceae), *Ocotea* sp. (Lauraceae), *Inga densifolia*, or *Prosopis juliflora* (Mimosaceae). A residential site occupied later in the rainy season and at the beginning of the dry season might have remains also of *Inga densifolia, Cassia grandis* (Caesalpiniaceae), *Manilkara sapota* and *Chrysophillum caimito* (both of the family Sapotaceae), potentially *Phyllanthus acidus* (Euphorbiaceae), or fruits of *Matisia cordata* and *Guazuma ulmifolia* (Sterculiaceae). Most of these food sources would be gone by January or February, leaving several months of scarcity, especially if the climate in the region was drier and the dry season more extensive.

An option to overcome these periods of resource scarcity would be to practice logistic mobility strategies by having a centralized base camp located either where other resource zones could be exploited or where highly abundant seasonal resources could be processed for future use. In this second instance, the base camp would not be expected to be located directly over the resource area. A special-purpose site for resource processing would be required. At least two site types would be necessary because daily living activities would be expected to destroy any surrounding vegetation to a certain degree and because many of these highly seasonal resources in the region are located along waterways that flood and would not be ideal locations for longer term base camps (Oyuela 1996, 1993:133-134).

Given this, a logistic base camp in the region located to best obtain resources from different ecological zones with occupation beginning in the dry season around December and extending through May might have remains from *Psidium guajaba* (Myrtaceae). This fruit is available in February about 10 km away in Cerro Maco, an area of higher altitude (850 msl) and greater rainfall (2000 mm/yr) than San Jacinto. Other fruits that may come from other resource zones at the middle and end of the dry season include *Cassia grandis* (Caesalpiniaceae), *Mammea americana* (Guttiferae) from more inland and higher elevations in Colombia, *Persea americana* (Lauraceae) from the coast, *Inga densifolia* (Mimosaceae) originating in the Colombian cordilleras and found at elevations from 800 to 1700 msl, and potentially *Chrysophillum cainito* (Sapotaceae) found along the dry zones of the Magdalena River about 30 km to the west of San Jacinto (table 3A.1).

If, however, resource extraction from territorial ranges as

Table 3.1 San Jacinto 1 radiocarbon dating

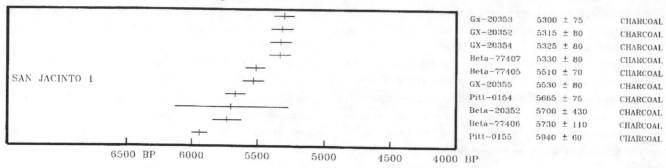

Gx–20353	5300	± 75	CHARCOAL
GX–20352	5315	± 80	CHARCOAL
GX–20354	5325	± 80	CHARCOAL
Beta–77407	5330	± 80	CHARCOAL
Beta–77405	5510	± 70	CHARCOAL
GX–20355	5530	± 80	CHARCOAL
Pitt–0154	5665	± 75	CHARCOAL
Beta–20352	5700	± 430	CHARCOAL
Beta–77406	5730	± 110	CHARCOAL
Pitt–0155	5940	± 60	CHARCOAL

great as these is not practiced for various reasons (for example, restricted territorial ranges, lack of extensive trade networks), then a second option for logistically mobile hunter-gatherers would be to focus on an abundant seasonal resource for processing. Thus, the special-purpose site would have macrobotanical remains indicating a focus on a resource that must undergo processing and transportation back to the base camp. The resource would be seasonal and probably useful as a stress management adaptation to buffer resource scarcity and unpredictability (Cashdan 1990, 1992; Winterhalder 1990, 1986). Such a resource in the savanna of Bolívar would be the highly seasonal grasses available at the beginning of the dry season (December and into January). A special-purpose site of logistically mobile groups in the region would thus be expected to have remains of grasses, as one risk management option. Because a logistic special-purpose site's function is to process a particular resource, this resource should appear to the near exclusion of other plant remains. A site occupied at this time of year might also have remains of the fruit trees or other plants available for consumption at the beginning of the dry season. The plant families with fruits available in the dry season would include Euphorbiaceae, Sapotaceae, Sterculiaceae, and Caesalpiniaceae. Other plants known to have food uses for humans and animals, and which were collected around San Jacinto at the end of October to the middle of December, were the Cyperaceae and Portulacaceae.

Residential mobility strategies would again be practical in the shorter wet season around May. A residential camp occupied in May might have remains of *Spondias mombin* (Anacardiaceae), the various members of the genus *Annona* (Annonaceae), *Mammea americana* (Guttiferae) if found locally, *Coccoloba uvifera* (Polygonaceae), or other trees or plants with fruits at this time. The residential base camps of hunter-gatherers in the savanna of Bolívar would not be expected to have remains of fruits which are available at very different times of the year. For instance, it would be unlikely to find seed remains of *Psidium guajaba, Inga densifolia,* and *Prosopis juliflora* with that of *Manilkara sapota, Annona squamosa,* or *Annona muricata* occurring at a single occupation of a residentially mobile site.

On the other hand, a base camp of a logistically mobile

group occupied in the dry season and short wet season of May-June would be expected to have seed and fruit remains from various seasons of the year. *Manilkara sapota, Guazuma ulmifolia, Annona squamosa, Psidium guajaba,* and so forth, might appear during the same occupation of a logistic base camp. These associations are due to the fact that logistic base camps are occupied for longer periods and can have access to resources available in different seasons.

If the cultivation of plants occurs at a special-purpose site, then macrobotanical remains of plants available both during the time of planting and the time of harvesting are expected. For instance, a special-purpose site could be utilized for plant cultivation with a growth period from September, to December. In this case, macrobotanical remains of plants available during the planting season in August-September and during the time of harvesting in December-January are expected to occur during the same occupation or level of occupation of a site. For August and September, such remains might include *Capsicum* and *Nicotiana tabacum* (both of the Solanaceae), if available. Though more seasonality information is needed for this time of year, it does appear to be correct that few fruit tree resources are available, and plants of other habit need to be studied for seasonal occurrence at this time and for food use.

Fruits available in June and July and which might extend into August include *Spondias mombin* (Anacardiaceae) and *Persea americana* (Lauraceae). For December and January, macrobotanical remains include the plant being cultivated or harvested, such as the grasses, and other fruit trees, including *Cassia grandis* (Caesalpiniaceae), *Phyllanthus acidus* (Euphorbiaceae), *Manilkara sapota* (Sapotaceae), and *Matisia cordata* and *Guazuma ulmifolia* (both of the Sterculiaceae). Wild plants of *Aechmea veitchii* (Bromeliaceae), and *Cucurbita* and possibly *Melothria pendula* (both of the Cucurbitaceae) also have fruits in December. Thus, if available, peppers, squash, grasses, and remains from trees fruiting in August-September and in December-January should be found together at a special-purpose site if cultivation is occurring.

On the other hand, if cultivation or the active planting, tending, and harvesting of plants is not occurring and only the collection of a resource after its edible parts are available is taking place, then only the macrobotanical remains of the required resource and those plants available during collection should be found at the site. Plant remains that are expected for the time of planting are not expected to be found in this case. For instance, in the savanna of Bolívar one might expect to find only the grasses and remains of fruit trees from the families Caesalpiniaceae, Euphorbiaceae, Sapotaceae, and Sterculiaceae. As well, remains from Cyperaceae and Portulacaceae, which have seeds and bulbs in December, might occur. Other wild plants available in December might also be recovered, but plants whose season of fruiting is in August, September, and even into October should not be recovered.

Correspondence of Plant Seasonality and Site Type to Data Collected from San Jacinto 1
Site of San Jacinto 1

In 1986, Oyuela (1987c) investigated two archaeological sites near the town of San Jacinto, located in the savanna of Bolívar, Serrania of San Jacinto, northern Colombia. Because both sites were located near this town, they were called San Jacinto 1 and San Jacinto 2. The older of the two sites, San Jacinto 1 (figures 2.8, 3.3) is located in the northern foothills of the Cordillera Occidental of the Andes approximately 220 m above sea level on a small plain surrounded by low hills. The cultural strata at San Jacinto 1 were formed by human occupation and reoccupation, and were exposed in profile by a meandering stream, the *quebrada San Jacinto*. Approximately 4 m of earth are above the cultural strata. Ten radiocarbon determinations on the charcoal found in association with the fiber-tempered pottery date to between 6000 and 5300 BP (table 3.1; Oyuela 1987c; Bonzani 1995).

Oyuela (1993) indicates that the site, a favored point bar location along a stream or river, was occupied numerous times within a season and year after year. The occupations correspond to the dry season when the site was not in danger of flooding. Flooding occurred after occupations as evidenced by each cultural layer being separated from the next by sterile fluvial depositions. Numerous fire-pit features used for cooking and a ground stone lithic technology of manos and metates indicate that the site was used as a special-purpose location for processing a plant food resource for sustenance during the dry season (Oyuela 1995).

To recover macrobotanical remains from the archaeological site of San Jacinto 1, random samples of soils from each stratum and feature were collected and floated using the generalized procedures outlined in Pearsall (1989; Watson 1976). In total, 77 samples were floated and analyzed for seeds, wood, rind, nutshell, or unidentified parenchyme. From these samples, 4377 seeds, 949 seed clusters, and 37 fragments of fruits were recovered from strata 9 through 20. The macrobotanical remains have been determined to represent 52 seed and 6 fruit types (distinct taxa). Of the recovered seeds and fruits (3988 individual seeds, 945 seed clusters, and 4 cob-like structures),

Figure 3.3 San Jacinto 1 excavation. *Photograph by A. Oyuela-Caycedo*

92 percent are from the grass family (Poaceae) as represented by three of the seed types. Four other seed types represent 5.1 percent (272 seeds) of the recovered macrobotanical seed and fruit remains, while the other 2.9 percent (154 seeds and fruit fragments) represent the remaining unidentified seed and fruit types defined to date. Many of these remaining seed types are represented by only one seed each.

The grass seeds are ubiquitous throughout the site, having been found in all but one of the units and features analyzed (see Hastorf and Popper 1988 for a definition of ubiquity). The seeds are elliptic in longitudinal section and elliptic to ovate in cross section. They average approximately 0.47 mm in length, 0.75 mm in width, and 0.5 mm in height. The surface is smooth to furrowed, with the majority of the seeds having six grooves or transverse indentations per seed (figure 3.4). One of the interesting aspects of these seed remains is that they have also been recovered together, forming a cob-like structure and various other fragments. The most complete, though fragmented, structure of this type measures only 3.6 mm in length and 1.4 mm in diameter and appears to have a spiral configuration to the seed alignment (figures 3.5, 3.6).

Figure 3.4 Carbonized remains of grass seeds (tentatively identified as Poaceae, seed type 2 [Bonzani 1995]) from San Jacinto 1. Provenience: E25N27, stratum 10, level 0-10. *Photograph by G. Newlands*

ABOVE: Figure 3.5 Unidentified carbonized structure (seed type 2) from San Jacinto 1. Provenience: E27N36, E27N37, stratum 12, level 9-28, feature 63. (dated to 5730 ± 110 BP, uncalibrated [Beta-77406]). *Photograph by G. Newlands*

As indicated, the other four major seed types represent 5.3 percent of the recovered seeds. Two of these types have been identified as *Malvastrum* sp. (Malvaceae; 104 seeds) and *Portulaca* sp. (Portulacaceae; 22 seeds). The other two types cannot be definitively identified until further analyses are completed. Other specimens identified from the remaining seed and fruit types include *Eupatorium* sp. (Asteraceae; 1 seed), tentative determination as *Cyperus* sp. (1 seed) and tentative determination as *Eleocharis* sp. (3 seeds; both Cyperaceae), tentative determination as *Sida* sp. (Malvaceae; 3 seeds and 1 fragment), *Polygonum* (Polygonaceae; 1 seed), and members of the Leguminosae (3 seeds).

Uses for members of *Malvastrum* are obscure, except that the plant has useful fibers (specific applications are not indicated), may be used to make brooms, and is mucilaginous with potential medicinal properties. Perez-Arbelaez (1978:476) notes that the seeds may have certain domestic applications but does not present them. He does indicate that such a utilization of the seeds is suspect.

Seeds of the genus *Malvastrum* have also been found at

Pachamachay Cave, a hunting base camp in Peru. The use of *Malvastrum* there is unknown (Pearsall 1980). No specific medicinal or food uses of the genus have been cited, though other members of the Malvaceae are used medicinally (Castañeda 1965; García Barriga 1992; Perez-Arbelaez 1978; Schultes and Raffauf 1990).

Archaeologically, in Colombia at the site of Monsú located on the Dique Canal, an old branch of the Magdalena River on the Caribbean coast, four seeds identified to the family Portulacaceae (Caryophyllaceae) were recovered for the Macaví Period in contexts dating to between 3750 and 3550 BP (Reichel-Dolmatoff 1985a:171). Members of the genus *Portulaca* have been recovered in early contexts (7000 BP) from nine Early Holocene sites in North America, allowing it to be grouped with "early successional floodplain plant species" and adaptations to collect such plants (Smith 1992:102). Later, *Portulaca* is part of the "river valley plant husbandry systems" occurring sometime after AD 1100 in North America (Smith 1992:113).

Discussion

If one ties these identifications to that of the present-day seasonality of plants in the savanna of Bolívar and to the associated site types of mobility, the data should give an idea of the type of site and time of use of San Jacinto 1 by its inhabitants some 6000 to 5000 years ago.

From the data of the plant remains recovered from San Jacinto 1 and the seasonality data associated with mobility site type, a few observations can be made. First, the focus upon grasses at the site, indicated both by their being the majority of the remains recovered (92 percent) and by the ubiquity of their recovery, links the site type to the special purpose of processing a seasonally available resource. This statement is strengthened by the large amount of ground stone lithics and earth oven features recovered at the site to which the grass remains have direct associations. The small recovery of other seed and fruit types (8 percent of the total) indicates that these

Figure 3.6 A second view of Figure 3.5: unidentified carbonized structure (seed type 2) from San Jacinto 1. *Photograph by G. Newlands*

plants were part of the natural surroundings (*Eupatorium*, Cyperaceae, Leguminosae, tentative determination as *Sida*) or were being used as part of occasional meals or snacks (*Portulaca*, possibly *Polygonum*) while the processing of the grasses took place. The seeds of *Malvastrum* were probably part of the natural background vegetation or were accidental inclusions in hearths and earth ovens, if the wood of this shrub can be determined to have been used as firewood (study in progress). The conclusion that the site was a special-purpose one occupied to process a seasonally available resource confirms similar observations made by Oyuela (1993; Castro 1994; Raymond et al. 1994; Pratt 1995) based on the analysis of the material culture at the site. Future survey and excavations of related sites from this time period in the region and elsewhere in Central and South America should yield further data against which these conclusions can be accepted or modified.

Second, the site is tied to a time of occupation at the beginning of the dry season in December and possibly into January when seeds from grasses in the region were available, plants were dry, and seeds more easily collected (table 3A.5). The other identified seed types of the genus *Portulaca* and the families Leguminosae and Cyperaceae indicate a period of availability at the beginning of the dry season. Modern-day samples of *Portulaca meracioides* seeds were collected in December, as were bulbs and reproductive structures of *Cyperus odoratus* from the town of San Jacinto and from near the archaeological site (table 3A.7). Most of the herbaceous plants in the region die back by the middle to the end of December.

No macrobotanical remains from the site have been identified to date that indicate occupation before the rainy season in August or September. These data point to the fact that it is very unlikely that these grasses were being planted or cultivated before the rainy season at San Jacinto 1. Instead, they were probably monitored for availability (see Oyuela 1993:172-173, N.D., and Holldobler and Wilson 1990 for a definition of spacio-temporal territoriality) and the seeds and possible cob-like structures collected when they were available and dry in December and possibly into January. These grasses do not appear to have been cultivated at San Jacinto 1, given the identified plant remains to date and the morphology of the seeds and cob-like structures recovered.

In conclusion, the collection of information on the current seasonality of plants in a region can greatly add to the predictive value and understanding of site use and occupation as recovered in archaeological contexts. The methodologies of modern plant collection and the gathering of information concerning uses and seasonality are particularly important for understanding people's current and past uses of the environment, plants, and animals in a region. With questions in mind, we can develop methodologies that allow us to have productive interactions with people that can be tied to data collected from archaeological sites.

Further investigations in the region concerning different site types occupied at various times of the year should add to the knowledge of the links among plant use, seasonality, and site type. Investigations into the identification of the grass remains may also lead to extremely exciting and unexpected changes in our views of human and plant interactions and of botanical evolutionary relationships.

Acknowledgments. I thank the late Gerardo Reichel-Dolmatoff, Alicia Dussán de Reichel, and their daughters Helena, Ines, and Elizabeth for help and support on the work of my dissertation which generated this chapter. I was very fortunate to be able to meet the Reichels during my year of fieldwork in Colombia in 1991–1992. The field research was supported by a doctoral dissertation grant of the Fulbright Commission. Laboratory analyses were conducted with support from the Dissertation Improvement Grant of the National Science Foundation and a Grants-in-Aid of Research from Sigma Xi, The Scientific Research Society. Modern-day plant collections were identified by Hermes Cuadros Villalobos of the Fundación Jardín Botánico "Guillermo Piñeres" in Cartagena and Daniel Debouck and Alba Marina Torres of CIAT in Cali. Thanks also to Santiago Madriñan, a graduate student in botany at Harvard University, for information on plant collection techniques. Special thanks are also extended to Dr. J. Scott Raymond and the members of the Department of Archaeology, University of Calgary, for the opportunity to complete the laboratory analyses of the macrobotanical remains from San Jacinto 1 and to write this chapter.

Dr. Walton C. Galinat, professor emeritus, Department of Plant and Soil Sciences, University of Massachusetts-Amherst; Dr. C. C. Chinnappa, Department of Botany, University of Calgary; Dr. Robert McK. Bird, associate scientist, CIMMYT Applied Biotechnology; Dr. Paul M. Peterson, associate curator of grasses, Smithsonian Institution; Dr. Mary Eubanks, Department of Botany, Duke University; Dr. Frances King, CCRR, University of Pittsburgh; Dr. Dolores Piperno, Smithsonian Tropical Research Institute; and Drs. Arlene and Steve Rosen, Ben Gurion University, Israel, offered comments on the macrobotanical remains. Dr. Walter Carson, Department of Biological Sciences, University of Pittsburgh, made useful comments on the chapter, which I have tried to incorporate. Finally, I would like to especially thank Augusto Oyuela-Caycedo as husband and co-director of the San Jacinto project without whom none of this research would have been initiated or possible.

Table 3A.1 Origins of plants utilized as food at San Jacinto

BOTANICAL NAME	COMMON NAME	ORIGINS
Cultivated plants		
Convolvulaceae		
Ipomoea	Batatilla	New World (Brücher 1989)
Cucurbitaceae		
Cucurbita spp.	Ahuyama	New World (Smith 1995)
Cucurbita maxima	Ahuyama criolla	South America, potentially Uruguay and Argentina (Smith 1995)
Sicana odorifera	Pepino morado	Grows wild in Venezuela (Brücher 1989)
Dioscoreaceae		
Dioscorea alata	Ñame criollo	Old World (Perez-Arbelaez 1978)
Dioscorea bulbifera	Ñame espina	Old World (Perez-Arbelaez 1978)
Euphorbiaceae		
Manihot sp.	Yuca, Yuca Venezolana amarilla	New World (Perez-Arbelaez, 1978)
Fabaceae		
Cajanus indicus	Wandul, guandul, Wandul pintada	Asiatic (Debouck 1992)
Phaseolus sp.	Caraota	New World (Pickersgill and Heiser 1977)
Phaseolus lunatus	Caraota, Cabeza de Santo Garbanzo frijoles	Northern South America (Pearsall 1992)
Phaseolus vulgaris	Frijol	Central Andes, northern Argentina/ Bolivia/ western Brazil (Pearsall 1992; Pickersgill and Heiser 1977)
Vigna unguiculata	Frijol soya, Frijol blanca, Frijol negra, Frijol	West Africa (Hancock 1992)
Passifloraceae		
Passiflora edulis	Maracuya, var. *flavicarpa*	South America (Perez-Arbelaez 1978; Schultes and Raffauf 1990)
Passiflora quadrangularis	Badea	South America (Perez-Arbelaez 1978; Schultes and Raffauf 1990)
Poaceae		
Zea mays	Maíz	Middle America (Doebley 1990; Johannessen and Hastorf 1994)
Solanaceae		
Capsicum spp.	Aji, Aji dulce	Middle and South America (Brücher 1989)
Wild plants		
Apocynaceae		
Rauvolfia tetraphylla	Cerecillo	New World (Castañeda 1965)
Bromeliaceae		
Aechmea veitchii	Piñuela	New World (Perez-Arbelaez 1978)

continued

Table 3A.1 Origins of plants utilized as food at San Jacinto, *continued*

BOTANICAL NAME	COMMON NAME	ORIGINS
Cucurbitaceae		
Cucurbita spp.	Ahuyama	New World (Smith 1995)
Melothria pendula	Toporotopo	No information found
Solanaceae		
Capsicum spp.	Aji silvestre	Middle and South America (Brücher 1989)
Cultivated fruit trees		
Caricaceae		
Carica papaya	Papaya	Northern Andes/Venezuela (see Pearsall 1992); the foothills and lower mountain slopes of the eastern Andes, in the northwestern Amazon basin, and in Peru, Ecuador, and Colombia (FAO 1986)
Lauraceae		
Ocotea sp.	Avocado	Tropical and subtropical America (Schultes and Raffauf 1990)
Persea americana	Avocado	Caribbean coastal area from Central to South America; in Colombia from 0–2700 msl (Bartholomäus et al. 1990)
Uncultivated fruit trees		
Anacardiaceae		
Anacardium occidentale	Marañón	Coastal strip of northern and northeastern Brasil (FAO 1986)
Spondias spp.	Jobo	Tropical America, southeast Asia, and Indo-Malaysia (Schultes and Raffauf 1990)
Annonaceae		
Annona cherimolia	Chirimoya	Ecuadorian/Peruvian Andes (Pearsall 1992)
Annona muricata	Guanábana	Humid tropics of the Caribbean and northern South America (FAO 1986)
Annona reticulata	Mamón	Tropical America (Schultes and Raffauf 1990)
Annona squamosa	Anón	Tropical America (Schultes and Raffauf 1990)
Bombacaceae		
Ceiba pentandra	Ceiba	Tropical America (Schultes and Raffauf 1990)
Caesalpiniaceae		
Cassia grandis	Cañandonga	Central America; in Colombia from 0–1100 msl (Bartholomäus et al. 1990)
Euphorbiaceae		
Phyllanthus acidus	Grossella	Tropical and subtropical regions of both hemispheres (Schultes and Raffauf 1990); common in Antioquía, Caldas, and the Valley of Cauca in Colombia (Perez-Arbelaez 1978)
Guttiferae		
Mammea americana	Mamey	New World (Schultes and Raffuaf 1990); cultivated in hot climates in the center of Colombia up to 1400 msl (García Barriga 1992, II)
Mimosaceae		
Inga densiflora	Guamo	Colombian cordilleras; in Colombia from 800–1700 msl (Bartholomäus et al. 1990)
Prosopis juliflora	Algarrobo	Central America; in Colombia from 0–1000 msl (Bartholomäus et al. 1990)
Moraceae		
Chlorophora tinctoria	Mora	Found throughout Colombia (García Barriga 1992, I)
Myrtaceae		
Psidium guajaba	Guayaba	Tropical America and the West Indies (Schultes and Raffuaf 1990); open areas like savanna-shrub transitional zones (FAO 1986)
Palmae		
Elaeis melanococca	Corozo	Tropical American, probably Colombian (García Barriga 1992, I)
Polygonaceae		
Coccoloba uvifera	Juan Garrote	West Indian (Schultes and Raffauf 1990); various species of the genus are native to Colombia (Perez-Arbelaez 1978)
Rosaceae		
Chrysobalanus icaco	Icaco	Grows wild in Colombia (Perez-Arbelaez 1978)
Rubiaceae		
Genipa americana	Jugua, bonga	Tropical, family well-represented in northwest Amazon (Schultes and Raffauf 1990); species abundant in Magdalena, Colombia (Perez-Arbelaez 1978)
Sapotaceae		
Chrysophyllum cainito	Caimito	Central America and potentially the West Indian Islands (Brücher 1989); also along the dry zones of

continued

Table 3A.1 Origins of plants utilized as food at San Jacinto, continued

BOTANICAL NAME	COMMON NAME	ORIGINS
		the Magdalena River in Colombia. It grows in Colombia from 0 to 1000 msl (Bartholomäus et al. 1990)
Manilkara sapota	Níspero	South America, grows in hottest climates in Colombia (Perez-Arbelaez 1978)
Sterculiaceae		
Matisia cordata	Zapote	Tropical areas of the Colombian Andes, growing from sea level to 1200 msl (Perez-Arbelaez 1978)
Theobroma spp.	Cacao	Upper Orinoco-Amazonas, with Central America a secondary region of diversification and domestication (Brücher 1989; FAO 1986)
Other		
Bixaceae		
Bixa orellana	Achiote	Lowlands of South America (Pearsall 1992)
Malvaceae		
Gossypium sp.	Algodón	Southwestern Ecuador/ northern coastal Peru (Pearsall 1992)

Table 3A.2 Seasonality of cultivated plants from San Jacinto

	VERY WET		LONG DRY					WET			SHORT DRY	
	S	O	N	D	J	F	M	A	M	J	J	A
Convolvulaceae												
Ipomoea[1] sp.					X							
Ipomoea batatas		X						P				
Cucurbitaceae												
Cucurbita sp.												
First planting							P					X
Second planting				X	X							P
Curcurbita maxima		X	X									
Sicana odorifera[1]					X							
Dioscoreaceae												
Dioscorea alata						X		P				
Dioscorea bulbifera	X							P				
Euphorbiaceae												
Manihot sp.												
Yuca venezolana[1] (4 months)	X	X	X			F		P	P	P		
Other yuca types (8 months)					X			P				
Fabaceae												
Cajanus indicus						X	X	X			P	
Phaseolus lunatus			X							P		
in street[1]		X	X									
Phaseolus vulgaris[1]								X				
Vigna unguiculata[1]	P		X	X	X	X	X	X				
Passifloraceae												
Passiflora edulis[1]	X	X	X	XX	X	X	X	X	X	X	X	X
Passiflora quadrangularis												
in Cartagena[1]						X						
Poaceae												
Zea mays[2]												
Major planting	P			X	X							
Second planting								P				X
Solanaceae												
Capsicum spp.								P	P	X	X	X

P = planting; X = time of fruiting

1. Fruit collected: *Ipomoea* on January 2; *Sicana odorifera* on January 28; *Phaseolus lunatus* beans sold in street on October 20 and November 2; *Phaseolus vulgaris* beans bought from store in San Jacinto on April 22; *Vigna unguiculata* subsp. *unguiculata* beans (frijol soya) ready 40 days from planting in September and produces until April, other types planted in April ready in October; *Passiflora edulis* var. *flavicarpa* available year round but abundant in December; *Passiflora quadrangularis* fruit bought in Cartagena on Febuary 21. Flowers noted: *Manihot* sp., yuca venezolana on January 6.
2. See description of indigenous groups close to Tenerife, a town on the Magdalana River, Colombia, for a near identical planting cycle of maize noted in 1580 (Tovar n.d.:321).

Table 3A.3 Seasonality of fruit trees from San Jacinto

	VERY WET			LONG DRY					WET		SHORT DRY	
	S	O	N	D	J	F	M	A	M	J	J	A
Anacardiaceae												
Anacardium occidentale[1]								X				
Spondias mombin								X	X	X		
Annonaceae									X			
Annona cherimolia									X			
Annona muricata[1]								X				
Annona reticulata									X			
Annona squamosa								F	X			
Caesalpiniaceae												
Cassia grandis[1,2]							X					
					X	X	X	X				
Caricaceae												
Carica papaya	X	X	X	X	X	X	X	X	X	X	X	X
cultivated												
Guttiferae												
Mammea americana									X			
in Cartagena[1]						X						
center of Colombia[3]				X						X		
Euphorbiaceae												
Phyllanthus acidus[1]				X								
Lauraceae												
Ocotea sp.		X	X									
Persea americana[2]							X	X	X	X	X	
Mimosaceae												
Inga densifolia[2]		X	X	X	X	X						
in Cartagena[1]								X				
Prosopis juliflora[2]	X	X	X									X
Moraceae												
Chlorophora tinctoria[4]												
Myrtaceae												
Psidium guajaba		X	X									
immature[1]		X										
Cerro Maco						X						
Polygonaceae												
Coccoloba uvifera									X	X		
Rosaceae												
Chysobalanus icaco[4]												
Rubiaceae												
Genipa americana[4]												
Sapotaceae												
Chrysophyllum cainito												
in Cartagena[1]						X						
Manilkara sapota[1]					X	X						
Sterculiaceae												
Matisia cordata												
in Mariquita[3]				X								
and Cartagena[1]					X							
Guazuma ulmifolia[1]				X	X							

1. Fruits collected: *Anacardium occidentale* from street vendor in Cartagena on April 13; *Annona muricata* on April 17; *Cassia* cf. *grandis* on March 12; *Mammea americana* from supermarket in Cartagena on February 21; *Phyllanthus acidus* on December 26; *Inga* sp. on April 6; *Psidium guajaba* immature fruits collected on October 19 and fruits received as a gift from Cerro Maco on February 7; *Manilkara sapota* on December 27; *Chrysophyllum cainito* from supermarket in Cartagena on February 14; *Guazuma ulmifolia* collected over mature on January 20, fruits noted by author since the end of December; *Matisia cordata* from supermarket in Cartagena on January 7.
2. Data from Bartholomäus et al. 1990.
3. Data from Perez-Arbelaez 1978.
4. Tree not known by the informants questioned.

Table 3A.4 Seasonality and density of palms in tropical regions

	VERY WET			LONG DRY					WET		SHORT DRY	
	S	O	N	D	J	F	M	A	M	J	J	A
Acrocomia sp.												
Amazon savanna (20 trees/ha to 100)[1]				X	X	X	X	X	X			
Bactris gasipaes												
Amazon, 2-3 dry months (considerable density)[1]				X	X	X	X					
Bactris maraja												
Amazon, 4-6 dry months (20-50 clumps/ha												
but usually 0.1 clump/ha)[1]						X	X	X				
Elaeis oleifera				X	X	X	X	X	X	X		
Amazon, wet lowland tropics or transitional forest,												
3-5 dry months (individual or groves)[1]												
Scheelea martiana												
Amazon, occasional flooding (10-20 trees/ha)[1]				X	X	X	X	X	X	X		

X = time of fruiting
1. Data from FAO 1986.

Table 3A.5 Seasonality of grasses from San Jacinto[1]

	VERY WET			LONG DRY					WET		SHORT DRY	
	S	O	N	D	J	F	M	A	M	J	J	A
Axonopus sp.			X	X								
Cenchrus sp.			X	X								
Digitaria insularis		X	X	X								
Paspalum plicatum		X	X	X								
Paspalum virgatum			X	X								
Sporobulus indicus			X	X	X							
Lasiacis sorghoidea[2]		X										
in cultivated field				X								

X = time of fruiting
1. Inflorescences and pollen of grasses were collected between October 27 and November 20. Grasses continued to be available in December and the beginning of the dry season. Eighteen samples were collected from the site area; nine (50%) are introduced from Africa and naturalized in the Americas, five (28 %) are tropical American in origin, and two (11%) are Pantropic in origin.
2. Origin uncertain (11%).

Table 3A.6 Seasonality of wild plants utilized for food at San Jacinto

	VERY WET			LONG DRY					WET		SHORT DRY	
	S	O	N	D	J	F	M	A	M	J	J	A
Apocynaceae												
Rauvolfia tetraphylla[1]		X	X									
Bombacaceae												
Ceiba pentandra[1]					X	X						
Bromeliaceae												
Aechmea veitchii[1]				X								
Cucurbitaceae												
Cucurbita[1] sp.			F	X	X							
Melothria pendula[1]				X								
Solanaceae												
Capsicum sp.												X

F = time of flowering; X = time of fruiting
1. Fruits ready: *Rauvolfia tetraphylla* mature in late October, specimens collected October 24, 29, 30; *Ceiba pentandra* seeds collected on February 27; *Aechmea veitchii* on December 11, beginning of dry season; *Cucurbita* sp. on December 31; *Melothria pendula* on December 9, beginning of dry season.

Table 3A.7 Seasonality of wild plants not utilized for food at San Jacinto

	VERY WET				LONG DRY				WET		SHORT DRY	
	S	O	N	D	J	F	M	A	M	J	J	A
Acanthaceae												
Ruellia[1]					X							
Bignoniaceae												
Crescentia sp.	X	X	X	X	X	X	X	X	X	X	X	X
Tabebuia chrysea[1]				F	F							
Cucurbitaceae												
Luffa cylindrica				X	X							
Cyperaceae												
Cyperus odoratus[1]		X		X								
Cyperus rotundus[1]		X	X									
Malvaceae												
Gossypium[1] sp.			X									
Portulacaceae												
Portulaca meracioides[1]				X								
Sapindaceae												
Serjania[1]						X						
Scrophulariaceae												
Scoparia dulcis[1]			X	X								

F = time of flowering; X = time of fruiting

1. Plant collected: *Ruellia* on December 9, growing late for rainy season; *Tabebuia chrysea* on December 27, informant information indicates that it flowers only in December, beginning of January; *Cyperus odoratus* on October 29 and bulbs collected December 9; *Cyperus rotundus* on October 27 and November 15; *Gossypium* fruits just opening November 15; *Portulaca meracioides* on December 6; *Serjania* on February 19, noted growing only during summer months; *Scoparia dulcis* flowers and fruits collected on October 29 and November 21.

Table 3A.8 Seasonality of cultivated plants not utilized for food at San Jacinto

	VERY WET				LONG DRY				WET		SHORT DRY	
	S	O	N	D	J	F	M	A	M	J	J	A
Bixaceae												
Bixa orellana					X			P	P			
Cucurbitaceae												
Lagenaria sp.				X				P				
Malvaceae												
Gossypium sp.				X			P					
Solanaceae												
Nicotiana tabacum	X	X	X	X				P	P			X

P = time for planting; X = time of fruiting

PART II
Chiefdoms

4

Ideology, Temples, and Priests
Change and Continuity in House Societies in the Sierra Nevada de Santa Marta

Augusto Oyuela-Caycedo

RANKING AS A FORM OF SOCIAL INEQUALITY is not related to the control of the means of production (land) but rather to ideology. This position has been persuasively argued by Drennan (1976, 1995); Wilson (1992); Grove and Gillespie (1992); Rappaport (1990). Even in some instances, the importance of ideology is overstated in materialist approaches and considered as esoteric wealth (Earle 1991:7, also refer to the concept of symbolic capital in Bordieu 1977:179). Is it possible that ideology is the driving force behind the rise of social inequality? If so, then one of the extreme forms to expect in the broad spectrum of chiefdoms is theocratic chiefdom. This is not a new idea. The existence of theocratic chiefdoms was postulated very early in the literature and defined as a society consolidated into a chiefdom for religious reasons rather than for warfare or commerce (Steward and Faron 1959:240).

Even if we verify the existence of theocratic chiefdoms and the role of ideology within them, we next have to ask how such entities operate within the enormous variation of chiefdoms. It is not clear how ideology is tied to social organization, a problem compounded by using the household or community level of analysis. This variation in social organization seems to be missing in the approaches to the study of chiefdoms; here, I attempt to link social organization and ideology by considering the concept of house society.

Recently, Elsa Redmond and Charles Spencer found an old definition of a *cacique*, derived from the Arawak term *kassiquan*, meaning "owner of a house (*ussequa*) or houses"(1994:190). I think that if we pay more attention to the classificatory system of the Indians and to what they recognize as a *cacicazgo* (chiefdom), we may be able to obtain a clearer picture of the social organization of societies.

The significance of kassiquan as an indigenous category of owner of a house or houses was revealed some time ago by Claude Lévi-Strauss (1981:140–162) when he analyzed the social organization of the Kwakiutl. The definition of a kassiquan (chiefdom) makes sense when it is considered in relation to social organization and not just to economic relationships upon which most studies of chiefdoms have focused. Leví-Strauss refers to the social organization of the Kwakiutl as *sociétés à maison* (house societies). What is a house society? Lévi-Strauss defined it as "a moral person holding an estate made up of material and immaterial wealth which perpetuates itself through the transmission of its name down a real or imaginary line, considered legitimate as long as this continuity can express itself in the language of kinship or of affinity, and, most often, of both" (taken from a translation by Carsten and Hugh-Jones 1995:6–7; see Lévi-Strauss 1981:150).

The holistic perspective of house, as it is defined, makes the social organization of chiefdoms appealing to consider in contrast to the economic notion of household or the North American view of house as just a dwelling or building (see Blanton 1994). The concept of house societies clarifies the Arawak definition of what a kassiquan is. As it is expressed, the house as a ritualistic property guarantees its survival through time by renewing human resources and by maintaining the material (for example, land, architecture, emblems, symbols, and ritual paraphernalia) and immaterial (rituals, specialized esoteric knowledge, titles, and prerogatives) wealth of a house (Carsten and Hugh-Jones 1995).

What distinguishes a house as a social institution? First, houses are necessarily hierarchically ranked, and they are vehicles for obtaining rank (Carsten and Hugh-Jones 1995:8). Second, while descent is important, houses are centralized around alliances, and it is through these alliances that unity is achieved. As a consequence, a house-based society is a hybrid between kin-based and class-based social forms (Lévi-Strauss 1981:151). Third, a house acts as a vehicle for the naturalization of rank differences by means of architectural elaboration of the houses of high-ranking groups. This means that there is a high correlation between rank and architectural elaboration. This elaboration occurs also within the buildings of the high-ranking groups in relation to the commoners and gives ranking a sense of being natural (Carsten and Hugh-Jones 1995:10; Hugh-Jones 1995). Fourth, in house societies, continuity of the *lignage* is important, a factor never forgotten when new lignages are formed or even when a temporary alliance results between different lignages. (For a discussion of the problem of translation between lignage and lineages, see Carsten and Hugh-Jones 1995:18.)

The objective of this chapter is to analyze what the rise of the priest-temple institution may have meant and how it is related and articulated in the existence of houses as a form of social organization. Furthermore, it is by analyzing how a house operates that we may understand how theocratic chiefdoms develop. As a case study, one of the last surviving indigenous Andean societies is investigated where the priest-temple persists and seems to have been the center of a society organized around the house as an institution. This society is the Kogi or Kaggaba, and it is analyzed from the AD 1500s to the present. (Kogi refers to the language, and Kaggaba is the term the people use to refer to themselves. Hereafter, I use Kaggaba when referring to the people.)

The Kaggaba live mainly in the northern drainage of the Sierra Nevada de Santa Marta, a geologically independent part of the Andean foldbelt (figures 4.1, 4.2). The Kaggaba are organized around the lignage, which seems to operate mainly within the parameters of alliances. In this case, membership of a house is manipulated for alliance-making (Uribe 1993:99–100, 119–128). Kaggaba houses still maintain enormous autonomy in their social, political, and ideological organization and are even in an irreversible process of revitalization.

Gerardo Reichel-Dolmatoff was the first scholar to consider the transformation of the Kaggaba in time and space, as indicated very clearly in his 1953 article "Contact and Cultural Change in the Sierra Nevada de Santa Marta." In his numerous articles and books on the Kaggaba (1949, 1950, 1951a, 1951b, 1953, 1974, 1976b, 1977, 1978d, 1979, 1982a, 1982b, 1984, 1985c, 1988, 1990, 1991a), Reichel-Dolmatoff proposed a continual transformation of this ethnic group, beginning with the Tairona chiefdoms, showing that the Kaggaba are not a society encapsulated in time. Nor can it be denied that their roots and some basic patterns from the past, such as the authority figure of the priest and the temple, have persisted through time. Also, several scholars have observed the relationship between the Kaggaba and past chiefdoms since the nineteenth century (Brettes 1898, 1903; Reclus 1881; Issacs 1884; Celedon 1886).

Bearing in mind that the Kaggaba are not a pure unchanged society and that they have suffered a series of cultural transformations, I hope to persuade the reader about the heuristic value of the concept of house societies in understanding the variability of chiefdoms—when a chiefdom can be composed of at least two to several houses. These houses can be integrated into a town or group of settlements in a region and joined around a chief as the head of a high ranking house with alliances created by marriage. Houses have sacred temples that give a natural sense of membership in the house by maintaining a cult of the ancestral fathers. The priest of the sacred temple is also the chief or head of the house. The spatial arrangement with the house corresponds to a hierarchy in which the manipulation of kinship terms and alliances plays a significant role.

The Kaggaba or Kogi as a Theocratic Chiefdom Comprised of Houses

The Kaggaba can be defined as a type of theocratic chiefdom for several reasons that have been well described by Preuss (1967) and Reichel-Dolmatoff (1950, 1951a, 1953, 1975b, 1976b, 1978c, 1982a, 1984, 1990). My own field experience with the Kaggaba has led me to confirm Preuss's and Reichel-Dolmatoff's ethnographic observations (Oyuela 1986a, 1991; see also Fischer 1989). Some of the main points that led to classifying the Kaggaba as a living theocratic chiefdom are:

- The Kaggaba are a society in which religion is the source of power (Reichel-Dolmatoff 1987:82) concentrated under the authority of the house priest. The civil authority among the Kaggaba is the *Makú*. This figure has almost disappeared as an institution of power (Reichel-Dolmatoff 1950:135–141); the position is ascribed (the only Makú alive is in San Miguel, the largest present-day village of the Kaggaba).

- Religious knowledge is transmitted by ascribed educational programs of training for the priesthood. In general, the priest's sister's son is preferred for these programs (Reichel-Dolmatoff 1976b, 1990:3–10).

- Specialized sacred areas of religious activities are manifest in the forms of male priests' temples (Reichel-Dolmatoff 1976b, 1977) and female priests' temples, areas of divination, and sacred spots of ritual importance (ancient archaeological ruins, rock shelters, mountain peaks, and rocks; see Reichel-Dolmatoff 1950:154–157). These features are the landmarks of different houses as well, and form a part of the material patrimony of a house. The temples have a vertical spatial hierarchy (Oyuela 1991). Social access to the most prestigious temples and those used for training is restricted. In general, these temples are isolated from the common people by location in the highlands on farms or in temple hamlets (Takina, Makotáma, Noaváka, and Seyua; see Reichel-Dolmatoff 1990:24–25, 26). Low ranking house temples are located in the lowlands or in towns

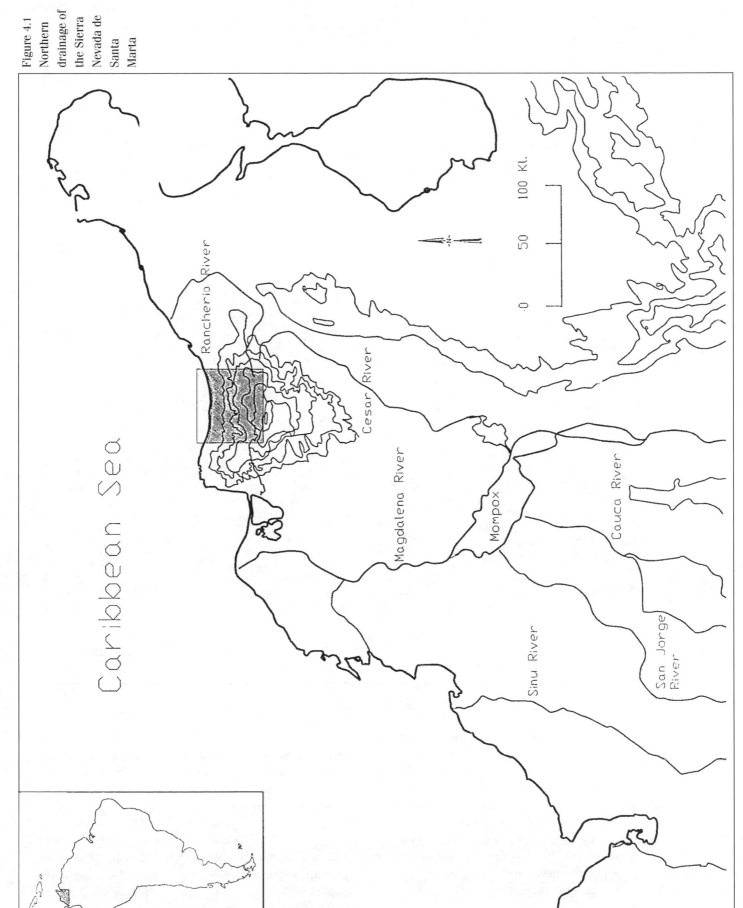

Figure 4.1
Northern
drainage of
the Sierra
Nevada de
Santa
Marta

Caribbean Sea

Rancheria River

Cesar River

Magdalena River

Mompox

Sinu River

Cauca River

San Jorge River

100 Kl.

50

0

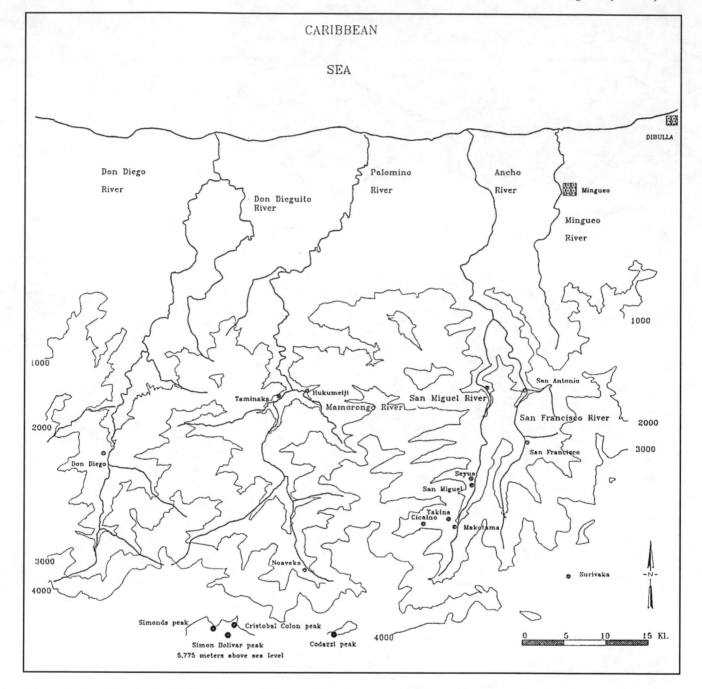

Figure 4.2 Location of main Kogi settlements in the northern drainage of the Sierra Nevada de Santa Marta

with a large indigenous population founded by the Catholic church (San Miguel, San Antonio, San Francisco).

- Religious knowledge is specialized for every aspect of the individual's life, as for example astronomical and agriculture practice and ritual, rites of passage (birth, puberty, sexual initiation, marriage, death), and divination rituals, all of which are controlled by the priest. The nature of this knowledge is a ritualization of the universe and of everyday life activities (Reichel-Dolmatoff 1950:117, 239–276).

- Priestly ranking is the result of contests held about reli-

gious knowledge. This knowledge is achieved by studying in prestigious religious hamlets or houses (where more than one priest lives) or with prestigious priests who have religious temples in the countryside (Reichel-Dolmatoff 1976b, 1977). Commoners occasionally participate in this competition, though generally access to it is restricted.

- Material accumulation of wealth is discouraged by social pressure, with low prestige given to those who accumulate goods (Reichel-Dolmatoff 1978c:8–10). Trade exists at the personal level of obtaining basic goods, such as machetes, cotton, batteries for tape recorders, gun powder, aluminum cooking pots, salt, fish and sea shells for lime, and alcohol (Uribe 1990). Trade is not under centralized control.

- Conflicts are resolved by a third party, the local priest (Reichel-Dolmatoff 1950:131, 241–242). Depending on the complexity of the problem, conflict resolution can also be managed by higher order priests, the order ascending from the country house priest to the town priest to the priest's counsel of the priestly hamlet in the valley. Intervalley conflicts are resolved by the highest priest of the Kaggaba. During my fieldwork, the highest ranking priest was Pedro Awiguí of Noaváka, Palomino River.

- The priest has the authority to punish, as well as to be punished by, a higher ranking priest (Reichel-Dolmatoff 1950:144–151). Punishment can range from authorizing the death of an individual to social ostracism. Other forms of punishment involve removing the clothes and torturing the individual in public at the male temple. This punishment is done with the help of other public officers (*comisario* and *cabos*, which are socially achieved positions; see Reichel-Dolmatoff 1950:138–141).

In summary, the Kaggaba are a society of temples, priests, sacred hamlets, sacred spaces, complex cosmology, and seasonal festivities of rituals, where religious recitation and esoteric knowledge are the bases of power. Such knowledge is the immaterial property of the houses. The power of the priest's knowledge controls individual activities including agricultural practices, rites of passage, individual disputes, cooperative labor of a house, and the location of dwellings. This aspect of a priest's knowledge does not mean that the Catholic church, the government, and other factors have no influence. By studying the changes that occurred in Kaggaba society in relation to Euro-American influences, we may gain a full understanding of how this society operates and how a theocratic chiefdom may have arisen.

Let us now define who the priest is, how he holds power, and what the bases are of the inequality of power and of his relationship to the house. (The following observations are based on my own interpretations and compilation of field data collected between 1982 and 1984 during fieldwork in the upper Buritaca river and in the course of travel to the Don Diego, Palomino, and San Miguel river drainages.)

The Kaggaba priest (*Máma*) is the transmitter of the knowledge of a house; he is the living figure in charge of a temple that belongs to a house. At the same time, the temple building is the landmark of the house. The Máma is the only one who can learn the "Mother Laws" (the ultimate sacred propositions, Rappaport 1971). The word Máma has a definite association with the sun; his wife is called Saxa, which means moon or wife of the sun (Preuss 1967:79; Reichel-

Dolmatoff 1985c:137). The Máma is thinker and philosopher.

Knowledge is the main factor in the prestige and rank given to an individual in relation to his position in a house and between houses. Sacred knowledge is acquired mainly by avuncular descent, but common individuals can achieve status through the payment of goods, work, or cash to the Máma in exchange for knowledge. If an individual wishes to be competent in knowledge, he must study throughout his life with different priests of houses that have alliances with his own. Each main house temple, with the figure of the Máma at the head, specializes in some aspect of knowledge, be it astronomy, mortuary practice, cosmology, or the practical world (flora, fauna, dances, music), but no one master or temple controls the total domain of knowledge. This differential access and domain of knowledge accounts for the competitions and ranking between the priests and temples, as well as between the houses to which they belong.

Sacred knowledge has important links to lignages. These connections were probably more strongly emphasized in the past by the Kaggaba and were probably strongly manipulated according to the political needs of the house. Descent is traced independently through a gender classificatory system, called *Tuxe* for males and *Dake* for females. The Tuxe and Dake have a territorial definition that is related to the birthplaces of the sons and grandsons of the Universal Mother as well as to their altitudinal locations in the steppe environment of the Sierra Nevada de Santa Marta. The status differences of the lignages are determined by how closely the individuals are related to the lines of important mythical fathers (Reichel-Dolmatoff 1950:157–223). Uribe (1993) noted that such a system of Tuxe and Dake cannot work as a kinship system; however, the system does not work according to kinship rules but rather as an alliance system where kinship terminology is manipulated in favor of the house. As Lévi-Strauss (1981:146–147) recognized, the ambivalence created when both patrilineal and matrilineal descent systems or bilateral descent systems are present (Reichel-Dolmatoff 1975a:58; Gawthorne 1985) is part of the reason for the significance of houses and the role of alliances.

The classificatory systems of Tuxe and Dake do not follow a rigid pattern of kinship rules. If this were the case, incestual marriages would occur. It is through the incorporation of new members and the acceptance of new alliances by marriage that the terms of kinship are manipulated in favor of the alliances needed for a house. This process creates a marriage system that appears to fluctuate between endogamy and exogamy, depending on the requirement of the house. Here, as with the Kwakiutl, the emblems are transmitted in similar form (Lévi-Strauss 1981:141–144).

The flexibility of the houses is observed in dress, bag, and temple or dwelling designs. The Indians refer in Spanish to such designs as *las marcas* (the marks) of the houses to which they belong. As Uribe discovered, sometimes lower ranking individuals complain that x or y person has been incorporated into another house by stealing the marks of the other house (as the Kaggaba themselves say, "The vassals are stealing the marks...they are becoming members of castes that are not their own" ["los vasallos se estan robando las marcas....se estan volviendo miembros de castas (clanes) que no son las suyas"]; Uribe 1993:124). From the perspective developed here, it is through creation of significant alliances that such an incorporation of new individuals, or *vasallos,* into a house is tolerated, even if the house gives the impression of being strongly endogamic.

Land Tenure and Food Production

Surprisingly, private land ownership exists in the Kaggaba world where the goal of life according to the religious principles is to know the Mother Laws and where there is powerful criticism of material accumulation. These lands—according to Preuss (1967:83,199), Brettes (1903:28), and my observations, as well as information obtained from different Indians—are in great part the property of the Máma's house.

The concept of private land is strongly developed, even covering areas that have not been exploited agriculturally for many generations or that had been occupied in mythical times. All of the unexploited forest zones in the Sierra Nevada belong to specific houses, and the person who knows who has the right to exploit them is the main priest of the house who controls the territory in question. The basis for the distribution of land tenure is imbedded in mythology, beginning with partitioning of valleys to the sons of the Universal Mother and with the relations of the individual through his or her kinship and alliances to a house. It is only in the last century that it has become possible for an individual who does not have land, or not enough land, to obtain it by purchasing it from *colonos* (nonindigenous peoples).

The mechanism of land rights inheritance among the Kaggaba is not clear, but it does exist. Circumstantial evidence indicates that the eldest son inherits rights over the land from the father and the eldest daughter inherits from the mother. Through marriage it is possible for the husband to acquire use rights of the wife's land, but he does not become the owner; in case of divorce (which frequently occurs two or more times in the wife's life), she retains her rights, which might be expected from the fact that the property belongs to the house.

The Kaggaba have multiple dwellings, each with different field crops; the dwellings are distributed vertically as well as horizontally. Depending on the available resources but not so much on seasonality (plantain and root crop harvesting is aseasonal), they move from one field crop to the next all year round. This rotation creates a pattern of high mobility in a relatively small territory. Those who do not have land may work fields in a territory of a house or work as a *vasallo* (*Gúa-vasallo*) in exchange for food. The use of the terms vasallo (vasal) and *casta* (caste), which are deeply imbedded in the Kogi language, may have been incorporated from Old Spanish as being homologous to the system of social relations of servant to master or of belonging to the house of a Máma or Makú.

It is important to understand that, even if there is a control of land, this control is integrated into a system of ideological appropriation of the space or landscape (land, resources, territories, temples, villages, and others). We cannot confuse the sources of power, objectives, and inequality that are ideological with other forms of power and objective found in other societies based on subsistence or even land tenure. In the case of the Kagaba, we have to consider that the high ranking priests live in the least productive highland environments of the Sierra Nevada de Santa Marta.

Current Settlement Pattern

The settlement pattern of field temples, religious hamlets, and villages expresses a clear altitudinal hierarchy related to how closely situated the temples of the houses are to the mountain peaks. This altitudinal hierarchy is manifested in differential control of knowledge, which is the basis of inequality between the priest and his peers and at the same time between the commoners (Gúa-vasallo) and the priest. As has been stated, access to the uplands is restricted as part of the religious effort to preserve the upland as a sacred place or to sanctify it as such. The upland is, after all, the place where the centers of learning and transmission of the Mother Laws are found. Furthermore, the ancestors and the masters live in the uplands near the snow and sacred lakes. In addition, the uplands are where the most prestigious Mámas of the high ranking houses have a residence and where the competitions for knowledge take place in hamlets such as Takina and Makotáma on the San Miguel River or Noaváka on the Palomino River.

Countryside temples

Countryside temples or field temples (called *Nuñhua*) always have separate female and male temples. The Máma lives nearby, sometimes with an apprentice. Sometimes, the priests have retired to these temples from the social and religious activities of sacred hamlets. The temples are occasionally visited by neighbors who are members of the priest's house and who go there for consultation or divination in the stone seats near the male temple (Reichel-Dolmatoff 1975b:202; 1976b:275). Access to field temples is difficult because the temples are located on mountain ridges that have splendid views of the landscape (figure 4.3). This location is also chosen in relation to the measure of the Kaggaba year (Mayr 1987). The temples can be a *bohío,* a hut with an apex and walls made of *caña brava* (cane), or they can have a beehive form.

Religious hamlets

Religious hamlets are settlements that have a mythical Kaggaba

Figure 4.3 Male and female temples of Máma Stewa Awiguí and his wife at the headwaters of the Maritza stream, tributary of the Palomino river

origin and more or less correspond to one male and one female house founded by one of the sons and daughters of the Universal Mother. Religious hamlets are usually composed of a small number of huts that differ in architectural features and function.

Each religious hamlet developed its ritual activities in honor of specific lord(s) associated with the founding fathers of the house. The ritual activities necessitate specific paraphernalia passed from one generation of priests to the next one in charge of the house. The ritual calendar of the pilgrimage to these hamlets has not been studied, however, nor is it clear which lords or masters are celebrated. (David Kelley is conducting a very interesting study of the unknown aspects of the ritual calendar that would have enormous importance in archaeology.) Such uncertainty in the ethnographic information is due to the sacred nature of these activities, which makes outsider participation almost impossible.

Religious hamlets are the intellectual centers of the main houses of the Kaggaba world. With the exception of two hamlets, Hukumeiji and Seyua, all are situated in the upper lands (above 1900 msl). Hukumeiji has been recently abandoned, and Seyua remains an important religious and political center (the last house for the design of the Nebbi [Jaguar] cotton bags). Both sites have certain aspects in common: all huts have

a circular base, and almost 50% of the constructions use caña brava in the walls (Hukumeiji: 47%; Seyua: 48%); the other constructions are huts with *bahareque* (mud walls; figure 4.4). Sticks project from the apices of temple roofs, some like sun rays, some in different patterns (figures 4.5, 4.6). Outside the religious hamlets, only one temple has a radial apex—a male temple located in San Miguel at the exit to Takina and Makotáma. Female temples in religious hamlets have similar radial projections. The buildings in the hamlets of the upper lands take the beehive form, and a long horizontal stick with randomly placed potsherds is located on the tip of the apex. The name of the apex is *kagula*, which means deep mountain precipice. The doors of the male temple, *Nuñhuakala* (mountain temple; Hugh-Jones 1995:235), are oriented in an east-west or north-south direction. For example, the doors of the male priest temples in Takina face east-west, and the novices' temple (training for the priesthood), north-south (Preuss 1967:75–76).

The Kaggaba store such ceremonial items as masks, trumpets, flutes, and ornaments for the dances in trunks or chests within the temple; female and male drums are stored in their respective temples. The distribution of trunks, benches, and hearths is the same as in the middle-elevation temples. There is no information about female temples in the upper lands.

There is always a space, sometimes with rock slabs, outside the temples where the ceremonial dances are performed. Slab seats, a distinctive feature of the religious hamlets, for divination and ceremonial meetings are located in front of these spaces (figures 4.7, 4.8). Near the dancing space is a place for the burials of the Mámas, marked by an accumulation of stones (figure 4.9).

The rest of the huts that comprise the hamlets of the upper lands are the homes of the other priests and their families who are linked to the original house by alliances. In Takina, there are only nine dwellings, including the temples. Almost all the other hamlets consist of a few congregated huts surrounded by crops. Seyua and Hukumeiji (middle elevations) have sugar cane crops and *trapiches* (mills) nearby; the settlements in the cold lands, like Takina and Makotáma, have corn crops, potatoes, and other products for the priest's special diet. A mythical father founded all of these hamlets which for generations have been on the property of specific houses headed by specific families under a priest: the Vakunas in Takina; Diñgula in Makotáma and Chindukua; Auigí in Noaváka and Sekaino; Noivita in Hukumeiji; Salavatas in Surivaka, Taminaka (Palomino), Salangaka and Seyua; Moskote in Guamaka; Kontsakala in Sankona; and Daza in Chirúa (Preuss 1967:54; Salavata 1983).

Ceremonial villages

Kaggaba ceremonial villages are uninhabited except during ceremonial meetings or when a Kaggaba family is in need of

Figure 4.4 Mud-wall (*bahareque*) dwellings at Seyua. Note the apex of the male temple in the back

Figure 4.5 Male temple at Hukumeiji

confession or consultation with the local Máma. When the family visits the village, a man sleeps and pursues many of his interests inside the men's temple of the house to which he belongs. In contrast, the woman busies herself with domestic activities, and on occasion the women meet at the female temple (there is no ethnographic information at all on the activities of females in their temples). As with the religious hamlets, there are areas of common activities. This intermediate space is well defined and does not overlap with the separate gender spaces.

It is necessary to differentiate between villages founded by the Catholic church and the traditional Kaggaba because there is a direct relationship between the founding entity and the sizes, types, and functions of buildings. As is explained in the following sections, the settlements founded by the church were part of the political plan of "Indian reduction," where some houses made alliances with the external Catholic and government institutions. This type of settlement corresponds to a village in terms of its size and distinctive features. Villages have a rectangular Catholic church constructed of bahareque with

Figure 4.6 Apex of female temple at Hukumeiji

Figure 4.7 Stone seats of the field temple of Máma Stewa Awiguí, Maritza stream

Figure 4.8 Field temples at the Karaka stream, tributary to the San Miguel river: Field temples of Máma María Pinto *(left);* female house of his wife *(right)*. Kogi pots are in the apex of female house and ceremonial seats are at the center between the structures.

stone bases. Another typical village construction, *la casa de gobierno* (government house), is very similar to the church settlements; this building houses foreign visitors. Another rectangular type of construction is a small bahareque dwelling used as a prison, inside of which is a *cepo,* a medieval European method of punishment. In the last decade, some villages like Don Diego have built schools with bahareque, or different types of buildings made of cement, like the Capuchin Mission in San Antonio.

The three classical A-frame village buildings (church, government house, and prison) are located near one another (figure 4.10). Nearby is the slaughtering area, an open site with three or more poles measuring 3 to 5 m long and having a V-shaped end. On the village's saint's day (for example San Antonio, San Francisco, or San Miguel), the villagers pass a rope through the pole and hoist an animal, strangling it. The Kaggaba kill animals by strangulation or hitting them with a club, but they do not use a knife, according to their beliefs. The slaughter place is used only during the festivities when they kill bulls or oxen.

Hut construction can be divided into secular and sacred. Secular dwellings are made with bahareque or, when the village is surrounded by forest, slats of palm. The same is true of roofing materials. The typical secular construction is a circular hut or rectangular house (figure 4.11), if it is near a non-Kaggaba settlement. Both types of buildings are used by women and children, who sleep and eat inside the dwelling and in the field houses. The husband sleeps at the temple, which functions as a men's club of the house. Thus, the separation of spaces is reproduced in the ceremonial village when the family goes there for the festival or to consult with the Máma. The Máma and his wife have huts with a circular floor plan. The only difference between their huts and those of the common people is the use of caña brava in the walls. In San Miguel, the Makú or Comizario has the same kind of building as the priest, only smaller.

The sacred places in a ceremonial village are the temples and the site of ceremonial divination. In villages, different temples exist for each gender. The male temple is a complex structure that, because of size, needs extra poles to support the heavy roof. In general, the male temple has two doors, in opposite directions, on an east-west axis. To each side of the door is a support pole; more poles are along the walls. These poles have horizontal crosspieces that help to support the roof. In the center of the temple are two vertical poles; lianas (vines) grow onto one of these poles to the center of the roof. Details concerning the symbolic interpretation of the poles and other components of the male temple are found in Reichel-Dolmatoff's article (1975b).

Inside the male temples are two to four long trunk benches oriented on the same axis as the doors. If the temple is really large, other benches may be situated in front of these. At the

Figure 4.9 Divination area at the south of Taminaka, with vertical slab in the back

meetings, the men may string hammocks between the peripheral poles of the temple; the Máma hangs his hammock between the two center poles. A hearth is located in each quarter of the circular floor. It is prohibited to cook meat or any kind of food in the temples; the only ceramics allowed inside are for toasting coca leaves and *ambíl* (a concentrated juice made from tobacco).

Female temples are small, with no center posts and only one hearth in the center. A few small stools are the only material culture inside. They have only one door, whereas the male's temple has an elaborate gate at both doors, like a small passageway to the inside, made of caña brava (figure 4.5).

Another place with sacred connotations is the area for divination. This area, a male space near the temples but outside the village, is formed by a group of natural rocks, some with small depressions. The Kaggaba priest goes to this place with the other men when they need to make a decision about the future. They sit among these rocks and use a *totuma,* a water-filled container made from a tree gourd, resting it upon three round stones. Then they put an ancient stone bead in the water, count the bubbles, and in that way divine a decision. This place is sometimes used for meditation or astronomical observation (figure 4.9).

Figure 4.10 Catholic church at the town of Don Diego. Poles *(right)* are used for hanging bulls during Catholic festivals.

Figure 4.11 General view of settlement of Taminaka

The village cemetery is located outside the settlement but relatively near the Catholic church and government house. Burials are sometimes marked with a stone slab laid flat on the ground. The underground of this area is called *Heisey Huvey*, which means "house of death" (Reichel-Dolmatoff 1974). Either near the cemetery or within it is a provisional hut for married couples, which is used only for the first two nights of marriage. Preuss (1967:192-193) mentions this small hut and that the Kaggaba call it *Gaulhuve, Agakuka Huve* (hut of cohabitation). This hut does not exist in San Miguel; in-

stead, there is a similar hut called *Heisey Huvey*, Heisey being one of the most important lords in Kaggaba mythology and cosmology.

Various agricultural products are cultivated near the village for the Máma, his family, and assistants. These foods are shared communally in the meetings. Each village has a stone wall with gates on both ends, running from the mountains to the river. Its function or symbolic meaning is not clear; it is assumed that its purpose is to keep out large livestock.

Variations between villages of different valleys at similar

elevations are similar to those in field dwellings. Variation exists in the materials used and the apex, as has been described. Another kind of variation is in the proportion of houses with a circular or rectangular base. This proportion depends on how close the settlement is to the contact areas of *Yalyis* (Colombians), an aspect that has a direct relationship with altitude and prestige. It is important to remember that ceremonial villages are found in the middle and lowlands; none of these settlements have a permanent population and they are used only for a short time. The only people who may live in the village or very close to it are the Máma, his family, and a watchman assigned by the Máma; sometimes, the watchman lives there with his family.

Eighteenth- and Nineteenth-Century Ceremonial Spaces

The origin of the ceremonial villages is rooted in the settlements founded by the Catholic church at the end of the last century under government order. One of these is San Jose (1874), located in the middle lands of Guatapurì valley. The objective of these foundations was the integration of the Indians who lived in the upper lands of the Curiva valley or Guatapurì (Simons 1879:692). For example, Santa Rosa (1875) was built to make the Indians more accessible:

> "Palomino....was so isolated that the Prefect of the Sierra Nevada, not being able to visit it, induced the Indians to found Santa Rosa in 1875. They keep all their corn and animals up in the old place, however. A similar case occurred on the Guatapurì when the Indians of Curiva built San Jose near Atanques." (Simons 1881:718).

It is very probable that towns like San Andrés on the Frío River (this town does not exist any more) and Don Diego (Uluejí) in the Don Diego valley were founded under the same policy. In these cases, a few low ranking houses took advantage of making alliances with the government. This policy continued to the beginning of this century when other foundations took place, such as San Francisco and San Javier.

From an ethnohistorical perspective, the gender division of field temples, as well as dwellings, has existed at least since the early eighteenth century, very likely following a pre-Hispanic pattern. Nicolás de la Rosa (1975) gave the first information about how the Indians of the uplands used space, and he makes reference to the sexual separation of dwellings and temples. He indicates that an individual never goes inside a dwelling belonging to a member of the opposite sex; food is served in a place between the dwellings, where a rock may be used as a table. De la Rosa gives an interesting explanation of this sexual division of dwellings. He states that the Indians believe if they have sexual relations inside a dwelling, the children will be born blind (a belief that persists today; see Ma-

son 1926:35). Following de la Rosa, almost every traveler who visited the Sierra mentions the gender division of houses (see Sievers [1886] 1986:6-7; Nicholas 1901:638-639; Brettes 1903; Mason 1926:35). It is interesting, however, that this pattern also existed until a few years ago among the Ijka, neighbors of the Kaggaba (see Bolinder [1925] 1966; Knowlton 1944:264-265). This fact could mean that the pattern was common to many of the Sierra Indian groups.

De la Rosa (1975) gave other important descriptions. He mentions the existence of temples, called *canzamaria,* in the upper lands of the Sierra and explains that these places are for meetings held on the first day of a full moon each month. Furthermore, he says that each rich man has one canzamaria, and that there is one that is greater and more remote to which they go every 2 years for the same feast in the new moon of January. It is not clear if any religious hamlets were associated with these temples, but it is clear that the Palomino valley, from which many of these descriptions come, was out of reach of the Spanish incursions into the Sierra.

The Mysterious Seventeenth Century

Little is known of the seventeenth century in this era. The Spanish port of Santa Marta was at that time a poor city isolated from the main trade routes (Restrepo 1975:291). The Indian population was enslaved and labored in the small Spanish farms around Santa Marta and La Ramada (Dibulla; Douglas 1974:40-44, 57-77). Only a small population composed of members of various houses that were part of different chiefdoms found refuge in the isolated uplands of the Sierra Nevada; they probably became members of the least affected houses on the Palomino River. Seventeenth century chronicles note their historical existence, while mythical origins suggest that the religious hamlets are the result of a migration from the Palomino River to isolated areas of the uplands. The Catholic church, under the direction of Father Romero (1955) at the end of the seventeenth century, began a program of conversion and founded a number of villages. Some traditional Indian temples were destroyed (Bischof 1972). It is possible that the towns of San Pedro del Yucal and San Antonio de la Ramada were formed at this time (Romero 1955; Garcia 1953:195; Bischof 1972). The parish church of San Pedro was abandoned and reestablished with the name of San Miguel; this town is first mentioned in 1848, but it is probably older (Garcia 1953:348).

The Catholic-founded villages have had fluctuating roles since their creation because the Catholic presence in the area has not been historically constant. As Romero (1955) and de la Rosa (1975) mentioned, isolated canzamarias were located in the uplands.

In contrast to the Catholic-founded villages of reduction, the Kaggaba religious hamlets have names in Kogi. The oral and mythological traditions are informative as to the origins of the houses. The Kaggaba consider that the first mythological father, Seizankua, who had three sons, each of whom became a father as well, built the first temples, and he and his sons were the first priests (Mámas). In other words, they gave birth to the first houses:

Father		Ceremonial temple
Seizankua	--------->	Hukuneiji
Sintana	--------->	Mukangalakue
Kultsavitabauya	--------->	Noaváka, Nuameizi
Seokukui	--------->	Takina

The first three temples are located in Palomino; Takina is in the upper valley of San Miguel. The oral tradition of the Kaggaba keeps track of all the genealogy—who were the priests of which house temples—back to the mythological founding fathers. Furthermore, the Kaggaba priest knows the derivations of the temples made for the grandsons of the first father: the house of Makotáma was built by Seizankuae for *Akinmakú* or *Guakinmakú* (note the words terminate in *makú*), and he also built the temple of Kasikiále (Seyua) for *Alukuñña* (Preuss 1967:53). According to Preuss, it is very probable that the founding of temples was a result of a migration from Palomino; Reichel-Dolmatoff (1953) agrees with this interpretation. Based on the mythology and genealogy collected by Preuss (1967), the sequence of temple construction is as follows, with #1 indicating the first temple:

	House temple	Associated river
1.	Hukumeiji	Palomino
2.	Nuameji (Noaváka)	Palomino
3.	Kasikiále (Seyua)	San Miguel
4.	Takina	San Miguel
5.	Chivilongui (Nabuguizi)	Stream of San Miguel
6.	Sekaino	?
7.	Karakas	Stream of San Miguel
8.	Makotáma	San Miguel
9.	Guamaka	Ancho
10.	Sankuna (Avalaji)	Ancho
11.	Surivaka (Sulivaka)	Rancheria
12.	Chirúa (Seilua)	Guatapurì
13.	Chundukua (Sendakua)	Guatapurì
14.	Mamarongui	Rancheria

All the temples existing today are landmarks of the houses. Some are religious hamlets or isolated field temples (see Preuss 1967:53-55). Some sites have begun to grow to form a religious hamlet, the best known of which is Seyua. In 1938, Seyua was a settlement with only three constructions; today, it has eleven. The commonality among religious hamlets and the villages founded by the Catholic missions is that they are uninhabited and used only for meetings or confession; in both instances,

the Máma is present.

Why is it likely that the founding of some of these temples goes back to pre-Hispanic times? The main reason is the clear genealogy that exists for every temple of a house. The list of priests, for example for Hukumeiji, goes back in time to more than 50 priests. Preuss (1967) collected the first list, and it is consistent with lists compiled by Reichel-Dolmatoff's informants, as well as with the information I collected in the field.

Ceremonial Use of Space during the Sixteenth Century

The organization of labor and the political structure of the chiefdoms of the Sierra Nevada during the sixteenth century have been interpreted as being more secular than religious (Bischof 1971). This may be more true in some chiefdoms than in others. At the time of the Spanish conquest, three principal settlements were described: Taironaca, Posigueica, and Bonda. Each of these cities had districts or suburbs with a subchief who depended on the principal cacique.

One chronicle, written in 1625 based on secondary sources (Simon 1882:201), gives interesting information about a village that was different from all the others. This village, called "Pueblo del Mohan" or "Nueva Roma" (Sorcerer's Village or New Rome), was a religious center located in a cold highland valley. It was regularly visited by the Indians from each polity, or more appropriately termed from each house, with each house having its own temple there:

> ...en su mayor parte de buhíos ó canyes del diablo, que tenian hechos cada pueblo de los de la provincia, donde iban en romerias, a pedir cada cual en su buhío remedio de sus nececidades. (Simon [1625] 1882 :201).

> ...in most of the dwellings or huts of the demon, that were made in every town of the province, they used to go for pilgrimages, each to his own hut, to ask for a solution to their needs.

The political organization that the Spanish found reflects strong autonomy of small polities, most of them restricted to the town (this aspect led Bischof [1971] to talk at one point of city-states). Each of these independent towns or clusters of settlements was characterized by autonomous decision-making processes. Sometimes, they made temporary alliances with neighboring chiefdoms. I suspect that more than being alliances of chiefdoms, they were alliances with other houses. The information given by the chroniclers regarding social structure is sparse. They mention merchants, craftsmen, and a large working population dedicated to agriculture. Concerning the positions of upper rank, they mention captains, secondary chiefs, and principal chiefs, and in some zones, they refer to a superior authority called *Naoma* who clearly was a priest (see

Reichel-Dolmatoff 1951a:88-89; Bischof 1971:501-504).

Three independent early accounts from witnesses who participated in expeditions to the area reveal the existence of the priest as the most powerful individual. The first account is the "Relación de Tayrona" (1571) in which it is mentioned that the major center of the Tairona valley was called Yamatague (Tovar N.D.:197–200). This center had two caciques, one with the name Mamanauma, who was the main chief, and the other with the name of Enginay. In this instance, the combination of the name Máma and Naoma, whose meanings were discussed previously, is particularly revealing. The importance of the priest as the major cacique is repeated in other provinces that are relatively close to the Tairona valley (Río Don Diego). This fact is reflected in the following two accounts.

The second account, dated to 1580, refers to a description of the region around the settlement of Tenerife. The description is for the Malibú province which was located on the west margin of the Magdalena River and which has not been considered traditionally part of the Tairona culture. The account clearly states that "...each town has a head (cacique) and some two and three, and the principal head, Macalamama, was the biggest cacique over all, the other heads exist in each town; we, the Spanish, called them caciques, and in their language they are called Malebú" (Tovar N.D.:329). The use of the term *máma* at the end of the title of the main chief is no coincidence. Here, we are dealing with a chief who is a priest. In other parts of the account, the word *mohán* is also mentioned, and it is said that the Indians used the word when they referred to the Catholic priest and medical doctors. The document also indicates an existence of female and male mohárs and a specialization in their duties (Tovar N.D.:332–33).

In 1561, an account tells of an incursion to the Nueva Salamanca de la Ramada, an area where the town of Dibulla is located today (Restrepo Tirado 1943:860). During this trip, the process of the accession of a priest was described: "They obeyed an Indian called mohán who cured them of sickness. At his death he would be succeeded by his son who had been kept enclosed without seeing the sun for ten years." This description greatly resembles the process of training for priesthood noted by Reichel-Dolmatoff (1976b) for the Kaggaba. These three accounts, as well as the description of Nueva Roma, give an idea of priest's importance.

Spanish domination caused the partial destruction of Indian organization at the political, economic, and demographic levels. The ethnohistorical study made by Henning Bischof (1971) demonstrates, however, that the process of domination was never complete. Spanish control was limited to the lowlands, especially near the port of Santa Marta and La Nueva Salamanca de la Ramada. By controlling the coast and lowlands, the conquistadors interrupted the vertical circulation of products like salt, fish, and cotton. Furthermore, the state of war and new diseases reduced the population of the area. Most of the cultural systems collapsed. In less than a hundred years, cities, villages, and hamlets lost their economic and political unity.

Conclusion

The origin of house tied to the religious hamlet is probably pre-Hispanic, as indicated by the case of the sorcerer's village (Nueva Roma) and Romero's visit, as well as by the accounts of the Spanish incursions. Until now, no archaeological evidence of settlements of that kind in the uplands of the Sierra has been found. The process of forming these religious hamlets may have been based on the increasing need for the ritual sanctification of certain persons and mainly of the house as an institution (Rappaport 1971:38-39; Drennan 1976).

Based on evidence available up to the present, there is a pattern that seems to be valid for historical times. Since the seventeenth century, gradual religious expansion led to the consolidation we observe today, with the Kaggaba as a theocratic chiefdom composed of several houses linked to defined territories. The sequence seems to proceed from the rise of a house (Hukumeiji) to the integration of two descent systems, probably as a result of the alliances between two groups, one of which had a patrilineal system and the other a matrilineal system. Then, a process of fission created the formation of new houses and the foundation of new temples in other valleys, such as Takina and Makotáma over the northern area of the Sierra. This process was tied to the expansion of a lignage of priests, as well. Very likely, this process was tied to the house temples of Hukumeiji. Some of these descendant houses then developed into prestigious religious hamlets (Noaváka, Seyua, Takina, Makotáma), creating a religious unification of the area around the figure of the priest and the hierarchy of house in relation to the original founding lignage. At times, the creation of new religious spaces was associated with the control of land by a house and probably was linked to prior prestige through the continual use of the same kind of paraphernalia found archaeologically, such as masks, batons, broad-winged ornaments, and monolithic axes.

The transformation of the temples and spatial structure shows evolutionary flexibility due to a non-material ideology, which in this case is religion. The ideology has permitted the survival of a population and its theocratic power through almost five hundred years of foreign pressure. This theocratic organization of houses is undergoing constant restructuring in relation to the state.

Archaeological research has found evidence of a high density of settlements in different valleys of the northern slope of the Sierra Nevada de Santa Marta. Two examples of urban sites are Pueblito on the coast and Ciudad Perdida in the highlands. In general, the urban sites are surrounded by towns and small villages that were connected to the urban center of a valley by stone roads (Oyuela 1986a, 1987a, 1987b, 1990). The urban center functioned as an economic focus for the distribution and redistribution of different products, as well as for ceremonial activities. After all, the center of each of these settlements is where the ceremonies were conducted and where the ritual paraphernalia has been found.

The villages show clusters of terraces where, at one time, one or more dwellings formed a compound. Normally, each circle had been interpreted as a single one-family household. This interpretation, in fact, contrasts with both the ethnographic and ethnohistorical evidence that suggests that one family may have occupied at least two such circles, as male and female dwelling spaces (see Reichel-Dolmatoff 1951a, 1954b; Serje 1984).

Based on the ethnography, especially the mythology and historiography, we may be dealing with houses represented by a chief. In other words, each settlement may have corresponded to two houses, and where larger settlements existed, such as Ciudad Perdida and Pueblito, there may have been several houses located in separate *barrios* or sectors that characterize such places. Ciudad Perdida, for example, has five well defined sectors that may have corresponded to houses. As should be expected in such settlements, hierarchy was established according to membership in a house and its spatial position in the settlement. In some cases, clusters of settlements having several houses would have been under the umbrella of the domain of the chief or priest of a highly prestigious house, with a genealogical history of its foundation and prestige, and with symbols and emblems of its own. Such a situation would be very similar in form to the Kaggaba today. This situation would also have created a very polymorphic set of relationships among chiefdoms, where the basic unit is not the household or the community but the house. Ranking is not so much related to the individual as to the hierarchy of the houses in which an individual was a member.

The archaeological record of the three regions of Gaira, Parque Tairona, and Buritaca gives no evidence of centraliza-tion (Oyuela N.D.), providing support for Bischof's hypothesis (1971) of small political units (very likely houses) dominating the area, most of which had little control over other towns outside of close neighbors. In this context, the road system and settlement pattern (see Oyuela 1987a) indicate a highly decentralized economic circulation of necessary goods but with the mobilization of labor for the construction of the road system in medium and short distances, possibly thanks to the social organization of alliances between houses.

The only evidence of some higher sphere of integration above the political units of houses seems to be the iconography of gold and stone artifacts. These artifacts have been classified as ceremonialist, suggesting that religion was possibly an integrative factor above the political factions of the houses that operated in the Sierra. At the same time, religion probably gave the houses their hierarchical structure.

Acknowledgments. Thanks to my friends of the Sierra Nevada de Santa Marta who helped me in many aspects since my first fieldwork in the Upper Buritaca and Kaggaba territory (1982–1984), the Tairona Park (1984–1985), and the lower Gaira valley (1986– June 1987). Special thanks are also due to Guillermo E. Rodriguez, who introduced me to the Tairona world and to archaeology, Francisco Rey, Esau Mosquera, Margarita Serje, Maria Cristina Hoyos, Ana Maria Boada, Fernado Salazar, Silvia Botero, Lorain Volmer, Maria Jose Duran, Luisa Fernanda Herrera, Alvaro Soto Holguin, Carlos Castaño, Carmen Lucia Davila, Juan Mayr, Katherina Bernhard, Manuela Fischer, Mathias Wach, Carlos Uribe Tobon, and the late Gerardo Reichel-Dolmatoff and Alicia Dussán, all of whom helped me at one point or another, and collaborated and shared the results and experiences of their own fieldwork in the Sierra, fieldwork that changed us in a way impossible to describe. Renée M. Bonzani, J. Scott Raymond, and Andrew Stein made comments on the chapter.

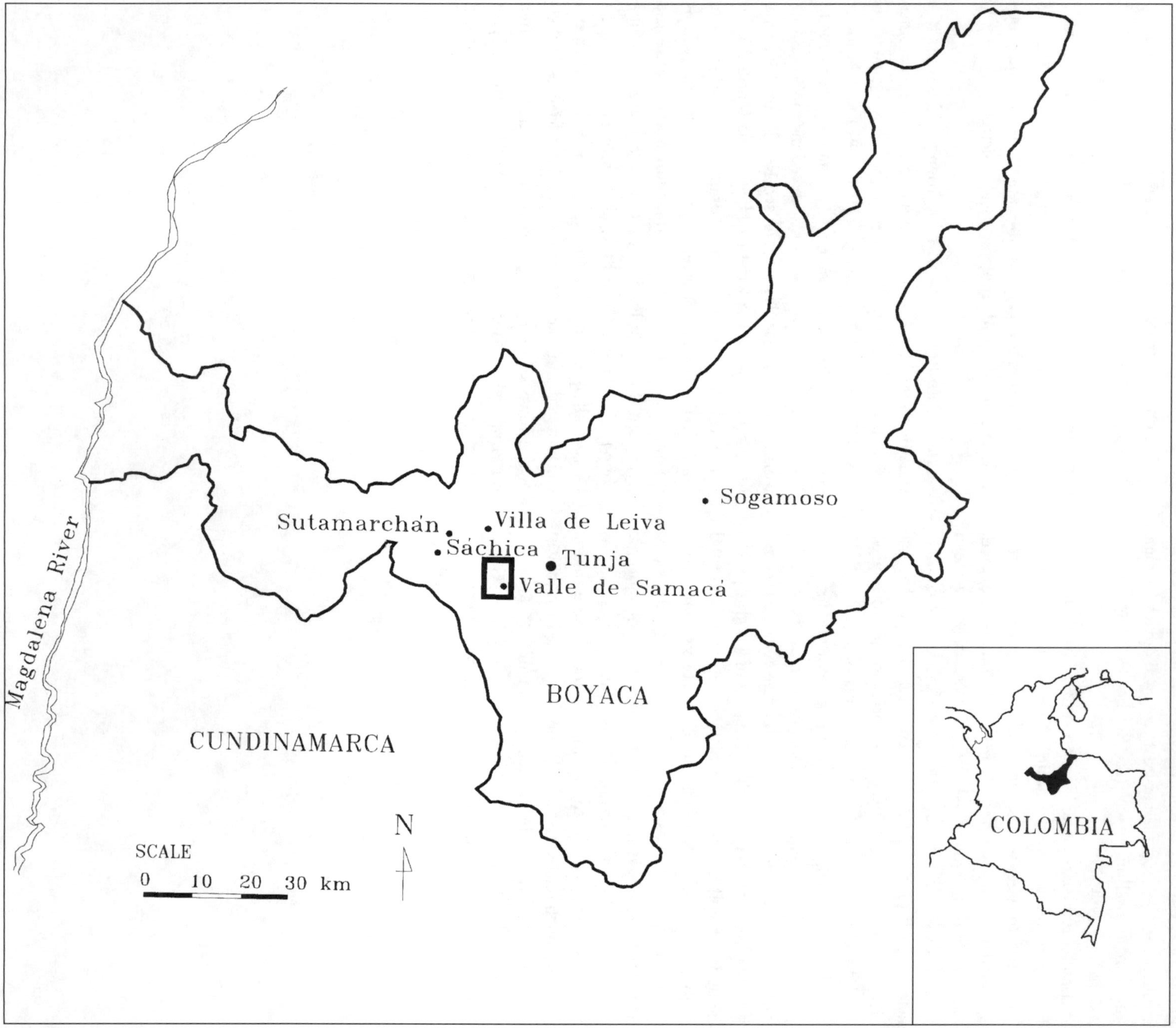

Figure 5.1 Location of the
Valle de Samacá

5

Mortuary Tradition and Leadership
A Muisca Case from the Valle de Samacá, Colombia

Ana Maria Boada Rivas

IN THE SIXTEENTH CENTURY, Muisca groups occupied the northeast Andean region of Colombia known as the Altiplano Cundiboyacense. Most of the information about the Muiscas, particularly that pertaining to sociopolitical organization, is available in chronicles and archival documents. These sources describe Muisca societies as hierarchical, with the political ascendancy of the elite based mainly on wealth accumulation (Aguado 1956, 1:289). However, some scholars have pointed to the lack of evidence of wealth in the archaeological record for the entire Altiplano region (Londoño 1985; Reichel-Dolmatoff 1986).

Regarding the period prior to European contact, however, very little is known about the sociopolitical organization and the basis through which elite obtained and maintained their political preeminence. This chapter addresses the question of the institutionalization of leadership in Muisca society through the analysis of mortuary practices as represented in the archaeological record and supplemented with information from ethnohistorical sources. I suggest that social differentiation reflecting differences in rank is evident in the archaeological record by the fourteenth century and that the elite of one Muisca group, whose archaeological record is discussed below, sustained their positions through prestige acquired via a system of gift-giving.

Current Archaeological Research

At the time of Hispanic contact, four large and several small Muisca chiefdoms inhabited the Altiplano Cundiboyacense. Chroniclers of the sixteenth century described severe political instability among the chiefdoms. Rivalry among the groups was common, with the region characterized by constant confrontations which frequently resulted in territorial gains and losses. The Valle de Samacá, located in the central part of the Departamento de Boyacá (figure 5.1), was no different, and

shortly before European contact the valley was incorporated into the Tunja chiefdom (Londoño 1983).

Preliminary archaeological surveys within the Valle de Samacá (figure 5.2) have indicated a settlement hierarchy which, at least on the basis of size, appears to be three-tier (Boada 1987a, 1991; Boada et al. 1988). The prime settlement, El Venado, is about 12 ha in size and has the longest sequence of occupation and most diverse archaeological assemblage of all the sites in the part of the valley surveyed so far. Unfortunately, little is known about the burials at El Venado, although the four known cases are very similar to the burials excavated at other sites in the valley. Typically, at these sites, little variation is observed in the number and types of burial offerings, body treatment, and tomb shape. However, the settlement of Marín, the focus of this study, exhibits also other traits that have only been reported at the prime center of Tunja, which is located outside the Valle de Samacá.

Marín, a nucleated site approximately 3 ha in size, seems to have been a second order settlement during the fourteenth century AD (Boada 1987b). It is situated at 2600 meters above sea level on the north slope of a small hill facing a small dry lake bed (figure 5.3). The climate is dry, with annual precipitation ranging between 500 and 1000 mm (IGAC 1977:120–127). The soil at the site is of low acidity (pH 7.5 – 8.4 Ingeominas analysis), which has permitted good preservation of archaeological remains, especially bone. The entire area is subject to severe erosion, and the site, in particular, has been heavily disturbed by agriculture since 1988. About thirty-two artificial terraces were placed throughout the settlement at a mean distance of 15.6 m (one standard error=1.5 m) from each other (see figure 5.3). A nearest neighbor analysis was performed on these thirty-two terraces, with corrections for boundary effect as recommended by Pinder, Shimada, and Gregory (1979). This analysis indicated no significance to the depar-

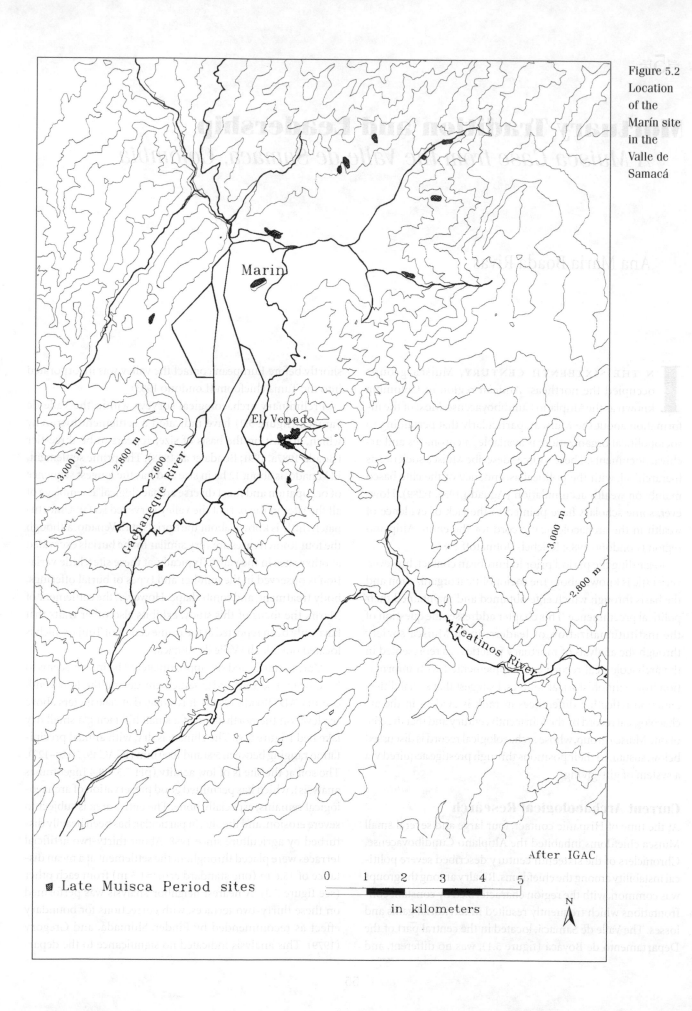

Figure 5.2
Location
of the
Marín site
in the
Valle de
Samacá

Marín

El Venado

3.000 m

2.800 m

2.600 m

Gachaneque River

3.000 m

2.800 m

Teatinos River

After IGAC

■ Late Muisca Period sites

0   1   2   3   4   5

in kilometers

N

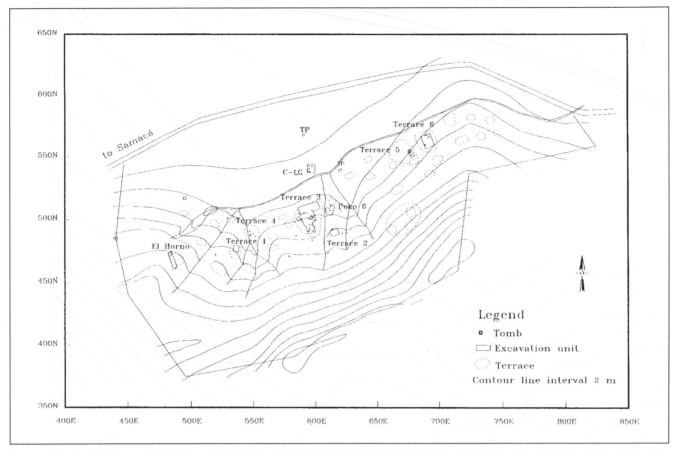

Figure 5.3 The archaeological site of Marín

ture from randomness in the distribution of these terraces within the settlement of Marín (R = 1.059 p>0.5).

From 1986 to 1991 excavation units totaling about 650 m² were placed throughout the site so as to collect samples representing different areas of the settlement (Boada 1987b; González-Pacheco 1991). Excavations on small artificial terraces uncovered postmolds and the earthen floors of circular houses. Although the excavations yielded many interesting features and artifacts, I will focus here on only the burial evidence.

Groups of tombs were found within residential units or in house middens and drainage canals formed by the drip line of the roof (figures 5.4, 5.5). Given their association with the remains of houses, burials are assumed here to represent the remains of household members (Boada 1987b; González-Pacheco 1991).

Most of the tombs contained single burials, except for three cases in which later interments had disturbed the original burials. Three different grave shapes were identified: two types of pits with a circular horizontal cross section (with and without a small chamber) and pits with an oval horizontal cross section. Some graves contained additional "furniture" such as rocks placed at the entrance of the burial or at the entrance of the chamber. The depth of the tombs varied from 10 to 170 cm. The position of the corpse was related to the shape of the

grave. Oval pits had bodies placed in a lateral fetal position, while circular pits without chambers contained skeletons in a vertical fetal position (figure 5.6), except for one case in which the skeleton was in a dorsal fetal position. Circular pits with chambers contained bodies in either a vertical fetal or horizontal fetal position.

The treatment of the corpse also varied. Although all skeletons were placed in a fetal position, some were wrapped in cotton textiles and tied with cords, as shown by imprints on clay layers sometimes present between the textile and the corpse before it was wrapped with textiles. Other interments exhibited a more complex treatment (figures 5.7, 5.8): the bodies were in a seated position on a thin clay layer covering a piece of cotton textile and then wrapped with the textile and plastered with a wet mixture of clay and organic ash. Finally, the bundle was wrapped with additional textiles and tied with cords. Some corpses were wrapped in a net and others in a blanket. In a variation of this treatment the corpse was plastered up to the hip, leaving the torso, upper limbs, and head uncovered, the entire body then wrapped in textiles. Others seem simply to have been wrapped in textiles without clay or ash plastering. Several females, males, and infants had been sprinkled with red ocher at the time of burial. There seems to have been no preferred body orientation, with bodies oriented toward all cardinal points including the zenith (Boada 1987a,

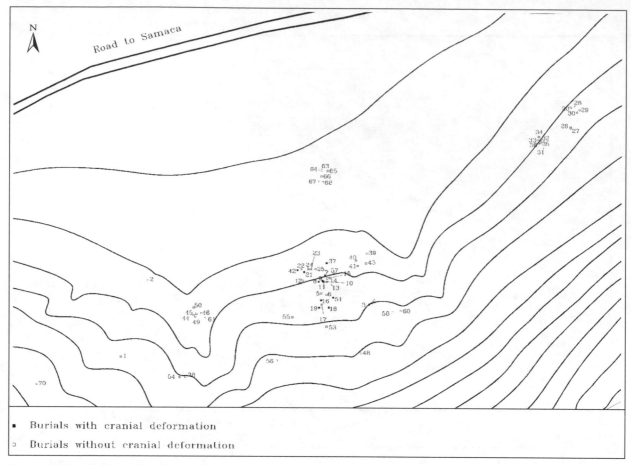

Figure 5.4 Distribution of burials at Marín

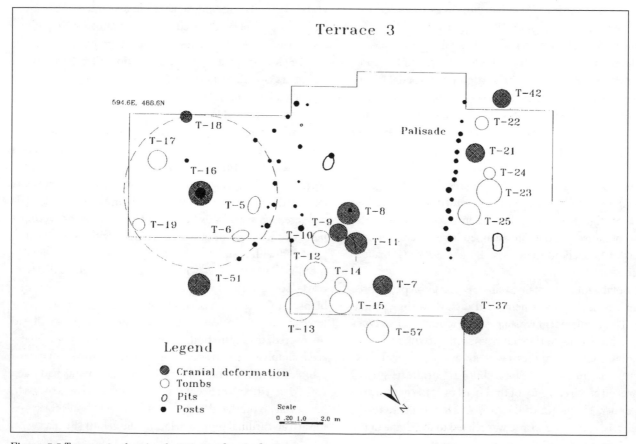

Figure 5.5 Terrace 3, showing locations of main features

Figure 5.6 Shaft tomb with the skeleton in vertical fetal position

Figure 5.7 Bundle burial with plaster of clay and ash

Figure 5.8 Textile impressions in the clay-ash plaster of the bundle burial

1987b). Ethnohistorical accounts describe provision of food and corn beer by the kin of the dead to accompany body preparation prior to the funeral (Simón 1981, 3:406–407).

It is possible that some of the corpses were subjected to smoke drying for slow desiccation. Chroniclers described this custom as a stage of the mummification process performed on high-ranking persons. Bodies were placed in the fetal position on a platform (*barbacoas*) and smoke-dried while some resins (*moca*) were burnt as incense during the process (Simón 1981, 3:406–407). Some bodies were eviscerated, although this practice was not common (Cárdenas 1990). The body was then wrapped in fine decorated textiles and tied with cords. The bundles were taken to a special hut where the mummies were kept (Simón 1981, 3:261, 407). The practice of mummification within the group inhabiting the area can be traced back to at least the ninth century AD; a mummy dated to that time was found in the Valle de Leiva just 20 km away from Valle de Samacá (Holden 1989:7). Mummification was also practiced well after European contact, as shown by the finding of an eighteenth-century mummy (Cárdenas 1989:123).

Although the nature of the human remains at Marín does not allow us to say whether mummification was in fact practiced there, the burn marks left on the elbow of one of the skeletons recovered indicate that at least the desiccation procedure was carried out. Although this possibility had been considered before and almost discarded because of a lack of evidence, these burn marks make us reconsider the possibility of slow desiccation as part of the funerary ritual.

Three excavation units yielded information relevant to understanding the burial data within the social space of the settlement (table 5.1). The excavation of terrace 3, the largest of the settlement, yielded postmolds of a large house 7.40 m in diameter (Boada 1987b;figure 5.5). House posts ranging in diameter from 0.12 m to 0.26 m were located at one meter intervals, some reinforced by thinner posts placed in a double line outside and inside the house. The postmolds from the uphill section of the house were not preserved due to severe erosion. A line of larger postmolds (ranging between 0.20 and 0.30 m in diameter) was also found down the slope in front of the house. Although only part of the alignment was excavated, the postmolds seem to have been part of a palisade surrounding the house. Tombs were found inside and outside the palisade. Significantly, some well preserved skeletons found on this terrace display artificial cranial deformation (tabular oblique;figure 5.9), a characteristic not found in any other part of this or other settlements in the Valle de Samacá (Boada N.D.).

Excavations at unit C-LG, located at the foot of the hill, uncovered postmolds and the sealed dirt floor of a circular house 5 m in diameter (González-Pacheco 1991). Four anthropomorphic figurines and an atlatl made of *tumbaga* (an alloy of gold and copper) were found near the postmolds. The objects may have been used in a household-level ritual since they appear to have been left hanging from wall posts or the roof at the time the house was abandoned (González-Pacheco and Boada 1991). Elsewhere, these kinds of objects do not appear in burials but rather in caves, or springs or in the countryside as offerings (Falchetti 1989). In contrast, ceramic fragments, stone tools, and bones were found in abundance outside the house. Two hearths were also found, one outside the house and the other between two wall postmolds. Broken deer bones were found in and around the fire pit outside the house; none were found around the other hearth, suggesting functional differences in the use of the fire pits. Six burials were uncovered inside and outside the house (González-Pacheco 1991).

The last unit of excavation, El Horno, on the western side of the hill, also yielded interesting information. The soil, a thick layer about 50 cm deep, had a high ash content and an unusual texture similar to the plaster applied to corpses as part of the funerary treatment. The high content of burned vegetal material at that location is possibly associated with the preparation of corpses for the mortuary ceremony. The inference of a ceremony performed at this location is reinforced

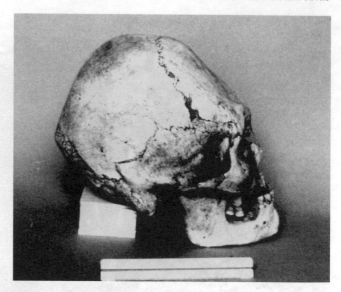

Figure 5.9 Skull with cranial deformation

Table 5.1 Excavation units and features*

UNIT	AREA (M²)	HOUSE DIAM.	BURIALS*	PITS	HEARTHS
Terrace 1	22.5	2.5			
Terrace 2	33.5		2	3	
Terrace 3	231.0	7.4	24	2	
Terrace 4	80.0		6		
Terrace 5	94.0		6		
Terrace 6	40.0		5	1	
Pozo 6	42.0		4		
C-LG	65.0	5.0	6		2
El Horno	40.5	3.0	2	1	

*Ten additional burials were exposed in bulldozer cuts.

by the discovery of a unique ceramic cup decorated with a serpent motif. Nearby, seven postmolds outlined the circular plan of a small (3.0 m diameter) structure which may have had a funerary function, although this conclusion remains tentative until the analysis of associated assemblages has been completed. Two burials were also found in the El Horno unit. In addition to the thirty-one burials found on terrace 3, El Horno, and C-LG, a total of thirty-four of burials were excavated in dispersed areas of the settlement.

Analysis of Marín Tombs and Contents

There are 65 tombs with recorded information, although not all variables could be recorded for each tomb (appendix 5a). The human skeletal sample that could be sexed was composed of 71% (30) females and 29% (12) males. There were twenty-three sexually indeterminate individuals (2 adults and 21 subadults). It is extremely unlikely that the sample of burials from Marín was randomly drawn from a population with an even 1:1 sex ratio (t=2.97, df=41, p>0.01). Several factors might explain this including polygyny and the differential disposal of

DEPTH OF TOMBS		
Subadults		Adults
Leaf	Stem	Leaf
10s cm	100s cm	10s cm
11	0	
22233333	M0	22333333
4555	0	444445555
677	0M	666666777
89	0	88888999
1	1	00000
	1	2222
	1	
	1	7
Mean = 46.9 cm		Mean = 70 cm
		M = Median

Figure 5.10 Stem-and-leaf plot of tomb depth, subadults vs. adults

males (for example, as a result of mummification or male infanticide).

Burial data were first analyzed along the age dimension. Then, data were analyzed against the sex dimension and, finally, against two variables: cranial deformation and wealth. For these tests, identifiable females and males, along with indeterminate adults, were grouped under the label of "adults" while age cohorts such as infants and adolescents, none of whom could be sexed, were labeled "subadults." When standard error is given for a category, the error range is calculated at a 95% confidence level. For this analysis, an estimation (Cowgill 1977) or a scalar approach (Drennan 1996:160–163) was used. In this approach differences within a sample being examined are expressed in terms of probabilities that range in a continuum from very high to very low. In this way, what is being examined is not seen in terms of "yes" or "no" (as the null hyothesis approach does) but rather in terms of probabilities.

The analysis of investment of energy measured through the relationship between the depth of the burials and age was first explored using a back-to-back stem and leaf plot. Figure 5.10 shows that adult graves were on average deeper than those of subadults. Among adults, there is one outlier case of a skeleton buried in a very deep tomb. A significance test made on this sample excluding the outlier indicates that the difference in mean depth of tombs between the two age groups is still very significant (t=2.63, df=61, p=0.011). With regard to the possible significance of such a difference, a significant difference was also found between body position and tomb depth, with seated corpses buried in deeper graves (t = -6.27 df = 61 p = 0.001) than bodies laid out horizontally. It may be that size differences between adults and subadults have something to do with differences in tomb depth, but although these find-

ings point to a functional rather than symbolic/ideological determinant of grave preparation (at least certain depths), other factors to be discussed later clearly suggest an association between high-status and deep graves.

Body treatment was also examined against age groups, although one aspect should be discussed first. It is assumed that complete wrapping in a layer of ash requires a greater expenditure of energy than partial wrapping or no use of ash. This assumption is based on the fact that complete wrapping involves a greater number of steps, makes use of more materials, and is more time consuming. Of the sixty-five burials, 57% (n = 37) have evidence of complete ash plastering and wrapping with textiles, 23% (n = 15) have partial ash plaster and textiles, 17% (n = 11) have no evidence of plaster, and 3% (n = 2) were buried within large cooking pots. Within age categorics, 53% (n = 23) of the adults and 63% (n = 16) of the subadults had complete ash plastering and wrapping in textiles. Despite the greater expenditure of energy associated with such treatments, the high frequency does not point to clear status markers for wrapping and plastering.

The relationship between age and wealth, as measured by the number of grave goods, was first examined using a back-to-back stem-and-leaf plot. For the purpose of the analysis, beads were counted as single necklaces, whether they were found in a burial as a single bead or in the thousands. Other objects, such as emeralds and marine snails, were counted individually since they were not present in large numbers. Figure 5.11 illustrates that both subadults and adults display a similar distribution of grave goods. Each includes a large group associated with a median of two grave goods, as well as a small group representing much wealthier individuals. In other words, each age category includes a few individuals that are wealthier than the majority. A t-test following the removal of 6 outliers in the two groups indicates that the difference in the mean number of grave goods between adults and subadults is of extremely little significance (t=-0.51 df=57 p=0.609). A very similar result was obtained with the outliers included in the data set (t=-0.460 df=63 p=0.647), a finding to be expected since both samples display a similar distribution. Peaks are located at about the same value and the two samples share a similar proportion of outliers with similar values. Peebles and Kus's (1977) "subordinate dimension" predicts differences in the number of items between adults and infants, something that was found not to be significant in the Marín sample.

Another way to assess wealth was to focus on the presence versus absence in the graves of a total of eighteen categories of objects. This was done to compensate for the fact that objects found in large numbers, such as necklace beads, could distort the results. For example, in a given tomb containing 3 ceramic vessels, 1 foreign vessel, 6 emeralds, 300 shell beads, and 15 bone beads, the total category count would be five. In this way, greater wealth would be associated with the higher numbers of object types identified in the graves. Again, the difference in the number of object categories between adults (2.0 ± 0.5) and subadults (2.4 ± 0.8) was also of very low significance (t=-0.85 df=63 p=0.397).

A significance test was also performed on the number of foreign objects. Again, beads were also counted as single necklace whether a single bead or a large number were found. The difference in the mean number of foreign objects between adults (0.95 ± 0.6) and subadults (0.9 ± 0.4) was also of extremely low significance (t=0.005 df=63 p=0.996).

Energy expenditure analysis performed on the sex dimension was first explored using a stem and leaf diagram (see figure 5.12). The graph shows that the graves of males are slightly deeper than those of females. However, a statistical test indicates that such differences have low significance (t=-1.12, df=40, p=0.266), suggesting no preferential investment of labor in the tombs on the basis of sex. Significantly, male tomb depth is highly variable, with some shallow and one very deep. This variability indicates that much more energy was invested in the grave of one male (located at terrace 3) than in those of all other males and females in the sample. The 50 cm difference in depth between the tomb of the terrace-3 male and the rest of the buried individuals is more apparent when we note that an additional 1.5 days of excavation were needed to reach the level of the skeleton. Soils at the site are extremely hard so that the additional depth was not quickly reached. Body-treatment analysis indicates that complete ash plastering and textile wrapping was more frequent among men (N = 8, 67%) than women (N = 15, 50%), although a one-sample Chi-square test indicated a very low significance (χ^2=0.961 df=1 p=0.327). Partial ash plastering and wrapping was found in similar proportions in both sexes, although the absence of ash plastering was more common in women (N = 7, 23%) than in men (N = 1, 8%). (The application of a chi-square test in this situation would be somewhat inappropriate given that more than one-fifth of the filled cells are considered sparse, that is, with values of less than 5.)

The possible relationship between wealth and gender was also explored using a stem-and-leaf diagram (see figure 5.13). The graph shows a very similar distribution in the number of grave goods between men and women. The two sex categories share the same median, as well as a similar proportion of outliers. What is important to notice in the diagram is that very few individuals of either sex category are wealthier than the others. A significance test after having removed these outliers indicates that the difference in the mean number of objects between females and males has low significance (t=-1.190 df=36 p=0.242). The results are even less significant if the test is made using the entire sample (t=-3.75 df=40 p=0.709) because of the spread of both distributions. Wealth was also evaluated by considering the total number of categories present in the tombs. Again, the difference in the mean cat-

	NUMBER OF OBJECTS IN TOMBS	
Subadults		Adults
Leaf	Stem	Leaf
Occurrences	Objects	Occurrences
XX	0	XXXXXX
XXXXX	1	XXXXXXXXXXX
XXXXX	M2M	XXXXXXXX
XXX	3	XXXXXXXXXX
XXX	4	XX
	5	XXX
X	6	
	7	X
	8	XX
XX	9	
	10	X
Mean = 2.9 Objects		Mean = 2.6 Objects
		M = Median

Figure 5.11 Stem-and-leaf plot of number of objects in tombs, subadults vs. adults

egories present in female and male tombs has extremely low significance (t=-0.48 df=40 p=0.631). With regard to the number of foreign objects in the graves, the difference between females and males was also of very low significance (t=0.29 df=40 p=0.770). Thus, none of the above analysis points to significant gender based differences in wealth or energy expenditure.

Interestingly, however, there appears to have been some association between object types and gender in the burials. Atlatl and drug paraphernalia, such as ceramic spoons and bone sticks, were associated with a few of the adult males, suggesting their possible distinct roles in society (for example, hunters or warriors, shamans). Spoons are likely to have been associated with the use of hallucinogenic drugs such as *yopo* and tobacco, the consumption of which was documented by the chroniclers (Simón 1981). Bone sticks might have been associated with the consumption of coca leaves. Kogi men in the Sierra Nevada de Santa Marta (Colombia) presently use similar implements to retrieve the calcium from a gourd which is then mixed in the mouth with the coca leaves, a procedure which releases the alkaloid (Reichel-Dolmatoff 1985c). Spindle whorls, associated with female burials, were also scarce, indicating that spinning probably was not a specialized pursuit in this settlement.

The third type of analysis examines the possible relationship between social differences and two variables: cranial deformation and wealth. An examination of the raw data immediately directs the attention to ten individuals (15%) with cranial deformation. The association between cranial deformation and other variables appears to define one of the most conspicuous social groups in the sample. The following analysis is directed at identifying differences in the degree of energy investment and wealth between the group of individuals exhibiting cranial deformation and the group that lacked such a feature. Figure 5.14 is a stem-and-leaf plot of tomb depth for each group. The graph shows both medians located relatively far from each other with the cranial deformation group characterized by deeper tombs. One such burial containing a male with cranial deformation is particularly deep, indicating a greater expenditure of energy. A significance test indicates that the difference in tomb depth between these two groups has an extremely high significance (t=-4.18, df=62 p=0.0005). Those who were buried in fetal seated position consumed more labor in the construction of the tomb, and this is a distinctive feature of the group with cranial deformation. The most common body treatment in both categories is the practice of complete ash plastering and wrapping in textiles, although these are slightly more common in the group with cranial deformation (N = 6, 60%) than in the other group (N = 31, 56%). (The use of a chi-square test would be inappropriate with this small sample.)

Of the sample of individuals with cranial modification, 70% were buried in pits with circular horizontal cross-sections, 80% were buried in a fetal seated position and 70% were oriented toward zenith. In contrast, the group without artificial cranial modification displayed greater variability in tomb shape, while 78% (N = 43) were buried in a fetal horizontal position with no particular body orientation, and 20% (N = 11) were buried in a fetal seated position. The original burial position of one disarticulated skeleton (2%) is unknown.

A back-to-back stem-and-leaf plot shows that the individuals with cranial deformation tended to be buried with fewer objects, with none of them having more than 5 objects (see figure 5.15). A t-test indicates that the difference in wealth between these two groups has very high significance (t=2.198 df=63 p=0.032). Removing a single outlier in the cranial deformation group and the six wealthiest individuals from the group without cranial deformation, the difference in wealth between the two groups is even more significant (t=3.049 df=56 p=0.004). With regard to the number of object categories, the difference between the two groups following the removal of two outliers (one for each group) also has a very high significance (t=3.038 df=61 p=0.003).

The second group to be analyzed is composed of the 6 individuals that have the largest number of grave goods. This wealthy group is clearly visible in figure 5.11 and is composed of four adults (3 females and 1 male) and two subadults (2 infants) who have between seven and ten objects. The individuals of the wealthy group do not present particularly strong association with any type of tomb shape. None of them was buried in seated position but rather 83% (N = 5) were buried in fetal horizontal position and 17% (N = 1) had no identifiable position. Body treatment for the wealthier group does not differ very much from those without wealth. Wealthy in-

DEPTH OF TOMBS		
Females		Males
Leaf	Stem	Leaf
10s cm	100s cm	10s cm
	0	
333322	0	3
5554	0	4445
777666666	M0	
9888	0M	8899
00000	1	
22	1	22
	1	
	1	7
Mean = 68 cm		Mean = 80.8 cm
		M = Median

Figure 5.12 Stem-and-leaf plot of tomb depth, females vs. males

NUMBER OF OBJECTS IN TOMBS		
Females		Males
Leaf	Stem	Leaf
Occurrences	Objects	Occurrences
XXXX	0	X
XXXXXXXX	1	XX
XXXX	M2M	XXXX
XXXXXXX	3	X
X	4	X
X	5	XX
	6	
	7	X
XX	8	
	9	
X	10	
Mean = 2.8 Objects		Mean = 2.5 Objects
		M = Median

Figure 5.13 Stem-and-leaf plot of number of objects in tombs, females vs. males

dividuals were not clustered in any particular area of the settlement but rather they were buried across the settlement.

In sum, the group of ten individuals with cranial deformation, all of whom are interred on terrace 3 at the center of the settlement, is strongly associated with a number of variables, including seated position and zenith orientation of the body, deeper pit tombs with circular horizontal cross-section, and very few grave goods. A contrasting but small group is composed of six wealthy individuals without cranial deformation and whose tombs are dispersed across the site. None of these six ealthy individuals was buried on terrace 3 at the center of the settlement.

Discussion of the mortuary variability

The analysis of burials from Marín shows the complexities of the social organization of this site. There are two high-status groups that stand out from the population. The first one is a small group of individuals representing both sexes and all ages that appear spatially circumscribed in the center of the settlement. Those individuals show special body position and deeper tombs, and cranial deformation, an additional feature that makes them different from the rest of the population. Performed at an early age, this deformation indicates a special rank that is ascribed from birth for females and males. No wealth is present in these burials, however. The second group, composed of 6 burials, also included females, males, and infants which are wealthier than the rest and have larger amounts of long-distance trade goods. Infants with more abundant burial goods have often been interpreted as indicating an ascribed right that comes through birth (Binford 1971; Peebles and Kus 1977). These wealthier burials do not share the characteristics of the former group (spatial circumscription, cranial deformation, body position, and zenith orientation of the body). The fact that these wealthier burials were not clustered suggests they were not from the same immediate kin group, as opposed to the group of individuals with cranial deformation, who appear to be members of the same kin based on their spatial circumscription.

It is interesting that these two sets of burials, although both possibly reflecting ascribed rank, do not use the same status markers. Initially, this behavior was interpreted as marking equivalencies between social groups, symbolizing horizontal social distinctions. However, manifestations of ascribed status are more probably indicative of vertically ranked social differentiation. Although neither prestige goods nor the amount of energy invested in burials is extremely large, it is clear that there is a modest degree of social differentiation.

It is proposed here that the first group noted above and characterized by artificial cranial deformation had the higher social rank at the settlement of Marín. This is based on the fact that the funerary ceremony associated with these individuals suggests larger, although modest, investments of energy in digging deeper tombs. Also, the larger house (described above) located at the center of the settlement, a privileged location, is associated with this group (see figure 5.4).

Other features also make the large house a special structure. It seems to have been surrounded by a rectangular palisade, a feature that was described in the historical documents as a privilege of chiefs and *"hombres principales"* (Anónimo 1988:177; Simón 1981, 3:184). No hearths or storage pits were found either close to the house or within the excavation units, a trait that suggests that such a large house may have been used to store goods temporarily to be given away quickly. The absence of fire pits and large storage pits seems unusual for the house of a chief who is supposed to be engaged in fre-

DEPTH OF TOMBS		
Cranial deformation		No cranial deformation
Leaf	Stem	Leaf
1s cm	10s cm	1s cm
	1	89
	2	00035
	3	00000000035
	4	000004
00	5M	00006
	6	0000005
	7	45577
50	8	0000
	9	0004
750	M10	05
	11	0
00	12	05
	13	
	14	
	15	
	16	
0	17	
Mean depth= 98.7 cm		Mean depth= 56.0 cm
M=Median		M=Median

Figure 5.14 Stem-and-leaf plot of tomb depth, cranial deformation vs. no cranial deformation

NUMBER OF OBJECTS IN TOMBS		
Cranial Deformation		No Cranial Deformation
Leaf	Stem	Leaf
Occurrences	Objects	Occurrences
000	0	00000
00000	M1	00000000000
0	2M	000000000000
	3	0000000000000
	4	00000
0	5	00
	6	0
	7	0
	8	00
	9	00
	10	0
Mean= 1.2 objects		Mean= 2.9 objects
M=Median		M=Median

Figure 5.15 Stem-and-leaf plot of number of objects in tombs, cranial deformation vs. no cranial deformation

quent social affairs. Rather, it is very likely that cooking was not performed in the large house but in neighboring houses of the same compound with the food delivered to the large house. Chroniclers of the sixteenth century describe a sexual division of houses (the male's house and the female's house, see chapter 4), particularly for chiefs who usually were polygynous. Females, among other tasks, cooked for the chiefs, so it is possible that cooking was done in females' houses (Tovar 1980:51–53). The absence of cooking and storage facilities (present in the rest of the houses of the settlement) suggests that the large house was probably used for social affairs such as entertaining visitors and storage of goods necessary for gifts. In sum, terrace 3, where the group of individuals with cranial deformation was buried, probably was a compound of various houses enclosed by a palisade in which the larger house was the residence of the higher ranked male. However, neither the house nor the burials at terrace 3 yielded evidence of wealth.

The immediate question that emerges from this picture is how this high-status lineage, in which status was ascribed but in which there was no accumulated wealth, managed to obtain and maintain its status. One possibility is that this might have been a group of ritual specialists that maintained their high status by performing ceremonies and had control over esoteric knowledge. This possibility could explain why this group is so poor. However, not a single bit of evidence of ritual paraphernalia was found in any burial, the large house, or in its immediate surroundings.

Two other possible strategies by which the group with cranial deformation could have maintained its high status were ancestor worship and gift-giving. Although I do not think they were the only ones used, they are the ones for which I find more support in the archaeological record and ethnohistorical accounts.

As noted before, the evidence indicates that this group had ascribed status acquired through inheritance. But in addition to an inherited right that entitled these individuals to hold a high social and political position, this lineage seems to have practiced ancestor worship to reassert such high position.

The mortuary variability described for Marín reveals multiple stages of the funerary program, likely representing diverse social dimensions associated with status differences. One of the funerary stages that strongly suggest the practice of ancestor worship is the mummification of certain individuals. Although we do not have direct evidence of mummification performed at the site, such practice has been widely documented in the nearby area by ethnohistoric documents and occasional finding of mummies, so there is no reason to believe that mummification did not take place in Marín.

One of the arguments proposed to explain the importance of mummification among Muisca societies is that it represented an opportunity for the elite to show their capacity to mobilize goods and energy in a kind of social competition for prestige (Langebaek 1992). Competition, as proposed here, was part of the mortuary ceremony when economic resources were displayed actively, particularly prior to the burial, but mummies, since they remained within the community, played a much more active role after the mortuary ceremony. Chroniclers mentioned the mummification of principal individuals such as warriors, but they did not specifically include individuals such as chiefs and priests. Not all chiefs seem to have

been mummified since descriptions were devoted to the burials of paramount chiefs, who were interred with lots of grave goods, several wives and servants (Castellanos 1886:65–66). In fact, mummified individuals of high status included females, males, and children, whose remains have been found in different parts of the Muisca area (see Cárdenas 1989). As seen in this chapter, mummification served more direct political agendas that go beyond the display of the elite's capacity to produce more resources than the rest of the community. The Muisca mortuary complex in general reflects a great emphasis on ancestor worship. It is known from ethnohistorical documents (Simón 1981, 3:254, 261; Castellanos 1886, 1: 183) that ancestors were conserved by mummification and stored within the settlement and in caves spread all over the region. The ones remaining in the village were visited and asked for favors and offered goods through the priest's service. On other occasions, mummies were carried in litters to the battlefield and exhibited to frighten the enemy while inspiring their warriors (Castellanos 1886, 1:98). Some scholars point out the importance of mummies in legitimizing the social status of their descendants but they do not explain how and why such mechanisms are used (that is,, Langebaek 1992; Londoño N.D.). I will expand this topic in two dimensions: political status and land use rights.

Ancestor worship has been interpreted as a mechanism by which individuals directly reinforce their descent from a known ancestor to legitimize claims such as leadership inheritance (Salomon 1995) and also to establish land use rights (McAnany 1995). It is very likely that such claims had been made in the Muisca area particularly under the unstable political environment such as the one described at the beginning of the chapter. Within the Valle de Samacá region (and probably throughout the Muisca region) these claims could have been made through both females and males. Based on historical documents (Broadbent 1964; Londoño 1983; Villamarín 1972) the Muisca kinship system has been described as a matrilineal descent system with avunculocal residence. When the couple got married, the woman left her village to reside in her husband's which was the same as her husband's mother's brother (ego's maternal uncle). This residential pattern maintained the group of males together in spite of the matrilineal system. Leadership was usually inherited through the maternal line, passing on from the leader to his sister's son (Broadbent 1964; Simón 1981, 3:389; Londoño 1983, 1985). The maternal uncle performed the task of actually educating his sister's sons when they had grown enough to go to reside with him (Villamarín and Villamarín 1975:175). The maternal uncle's role was particularly crucial when he was the leader and exerted his right to educate his sister's sons, a long and tedious process for those candidates in the line of inheriting leadership (Castellanos 1886, 1:67; Simón 1981:389).

The most critical moment for those candidates in line to

inherit the chiefdom occurred at the moment of the chief's death. At this moment it was crucial to establish the most direct connection to the ancestor through a direct line in order to claim and legitimize leadership by evoking rights inherited from the ancestors. This claim was facilitated by the fact that mummies were being kept in shrines within the settlement and ancestry could be traced by establishing links between the candidates and their ancestors before the ancestors' (mummified) eyes. Mummies were actually present, known by their names and played an active role by legitimizing a candidate's position. Londoño (N.D.) argues that a chief increased his power (derived from the shrine with or without mummies) when he inherited the shrine upon his ascension to chieftain status.

Ancestor worship may also have had a parallel purpose. Ancestral links might have also been used to claim land-use rights. Although little information is available, the data suggest that these rights were also inherited through the maternal line (Villamarín 1972:101–102, Londoño 1983:63). Although women had to leave their village as soon as they got married, lands might have been used by her family, such as by her sons (Londoño N.D.), if grown enough to live with the maternal uncle, brothers, and/or maternal uncle. By this mechanism, both kinsmen and land were kept in the same place. It has been proposed that the *uta* and the *sybyn* were kinship units as well as territorial units (Rozo 1978; Villamarín and Villamarín 1975; Londoño 1983). As land-use rights were acquired through inheritance, tracing links with the ancestors made it possible to have access to land. Female mummies would have been crucial for the establishment of lines of descent and to legitimize claims over land use rights in a very direct manner.

The situation described applies to high rank lineages where mummification was their prerogative, but what happened at the local level or to the commoners for whom mummification was not allowed? Ancestor worship was also important for lower status lineages, and there is some evidence that might be associated to this practice. The practice of burying the dead within or near the house indicates that links with the ancestors probably legitimized more assertively the current social position than any other material base, as seems to have been the case for the Valle de La Plata as described by Drennan (1995). There is additional evidence that suggests ancestor worship was a generalized practice including the commoners. In one of the houses of Marín a set of four goldwork anthropomorphic figurines and one atlatl were found. Females, warriors and weapons were depicted and kept in the house, probably as representations (as sorts of portraits) of ancestors. Londoño has noted a clay figurine described by the natives as the representation of the chief "*capitán*", Don Alonso (Ibarra y Porras Mexía 1594:253 in Londoño N.D.). Anthropomorphic figurines have not been found in mortuary contexts

but rather as offerings in caves and fields (Falchetti 1989; González-Pacheco and Boada 1991).

Ancestor worship also seems to have been expressed in other ways. One way was through the association of individuals with textiles. Textiles displayed a great variety in length, weaving technique, color, design, and use as clothing and were important in exchange and tribute within the Muisca region (Boada 1989; Cardale 1986; Cortés 1990; Langebaek 1987; Londoño 1990). Mummies were wrapped in textiles. In one recorded example found near the Valle de Samacá, a mummy was wrapped in a textile decorated with anthropomorphic figures (Broadbent 1985). Such designs, painted by native priests and their nephews, were strongly forbidden by the Spanish (Restrepo Tirado 1928:65 in Casilimas and López 1987:43) and could not be used for dress because of the symbolic meaning they conveyed (Friede 1976, VI:460). Although the Spanish did not understand their meaning, it is likely that these figures were related to depictions of ancestors and used as identity symbols by which the wearer's status was immediately recognized.

Leadership, particularly in the absence of tools which guarantee obedience such as coercive force or control over basic resources, needs to be reinforced by the recognition and loyalty of followers. Although leadership was inherited and probably reinforced among the Muisca by ancestor worship, such a prerogative by itself, contrary to the generalized expectation, was not sufficient to maintain leaders in their office, or to sustain their prestige. Other ways to legitimize social and political status had to be developed. One such mechanism may have been gift-giving. Leaders at Marín probably were gift-givers. The archaeological evidence supporting such an idea is that the group with cranial deformation is associated with a house which is the largest of the settlement and which does not have any evidence of domestic activities. The function of the house seems to have been directed toward social affairs. In addition, this group of high status has no evident wealth, while some other individuals scattered through the settlement display greater wealth. Such a distribution could result from a leader giving away prestige goods to other members of the society in order to maintain alliances and loyalties, and to repay social obligations.

The evidence presented here strongly supports the idea that ascribed status was present at Marín, and the scenario described reflects a society where the social hierarchy was based on prestige. Marín emergent elite were probably gaining political ascendance by distributing goods to the point that they became impoverished and had fewer goods than the rest of the population. The fact that Marín elite did not retain goods for their own consumption and were not able to appropriate for themselves part of the goods to be buried with the dead during the mortuary ceremony reveals the small economic control they exerted.

What is distinctive in this case is that the social and political status of the elite does not seem to have been strong enough to be supported by virtue of its inherited rank alone. There is also no evidence whatsoever of control over basic resources and wealth. Instead, the elite at Marín seem to have been competing for political ascendancy through the economic mechanism of giving gifts. However, gift-giving systems are also very unstable mechanisms to maintain status (Sahlins 1963:291–293), and both ancestor worship and gift giving (and probably other strategies), probably were used by the elite to maintain their high status and prestige. None of these strategies on their own may have been sufficiently strong to ensure the maintenance of such high status, but several different strategies used in combination enhanced the likelihood of success.

Ethnohistoric documents of the sixteen century describe mummification of high-status individuals and also of chiefs engaged in generous distributions to other chiefs, high-ranked individuals, and commoners (Simón 1981, T.III:405). Although such distributions were likely more complex than what we have seen in Marín, the documentary evidence for mummification and distributions support the interpretation of the archaeological record offered here.

Conclusion

In general terms, the burials of Marín offer a depiction of an elite impoverished as a result of a political system which relied on prestige gained through gift giving. Another factor that diminished the elite's economic capabilities may have been their relationship to a higher ranked political center. Small local communities, as part of larger political systems, are burdened by obligations to higher political centers, which extract resources. Ancestor worship seems to have played a very important role as a mechanism to legitimize ascribed social and political status at Marín. Elite, however, in spite of having an ascribed status that entitled them to hold the higher positions, engaged in other strategies to maintain their political and social positions. Political and social status in Marín's elite depended on active competition for prestige through gift-giving as opposed to control over goods and basic resources.

It is likely that a higher degree of social differentiation is represented in the central village of the valley. However, what has been envisioned through the study of mortuary variability in Marín might be taken as a reflection of a general trend. In the fourteenth century the political system of the valley seems to have been strongly based on prestige competition through giving gifts and leadership legitimation through an ideological base. Although much more complex, the political organization of the sixteenth century described by the chroniclers seems to represent great continuity of the trends found for the fourteenth century. The description of the chroniclers about a very complex society in the sixteenth century leaves a very short time for such complexity to emerge. A future investigation will be directed to analyze if, how and why such social complexity actually developed in the valley. Leadership was strongly founded in ancestor worship, but the economic basis is still little known and is a basic aspect that will be the topic of future research. The development of ancestor worship within the region and the concurrent conditions that favored such expression is another aspect for research.

Acknowledgments. This investigation was partially financed by the Fundación de Investigaciones Arqueológicas Nacionales, Banco de la República. Several individuals assisted with the fieldwork. I wish to thank Sonia Archila, Andrés Bayona, Inés Cavelier, Ana María Cortés, Camilo Días, Eduardo Fernández, Santiago Mora, Rómulo Novoa, Adriana Suárez, Monika Therrien and Hildur Zea. Thanks also go to the Montejo, Rivas and Uribe families who kindly offered local facilities and continuous support. I want to especially thank Marc Bermann who read this manuscript and improved it greatly with his comments. I am also very grateful to Robert D. Drennan for his continuous advice. Thanks also to Robert Kruger, Dave Anderson and Jon VandenBosch who reviewed the English in this chapter and transformed it into a readable piece. I also thank Augusto Oyuela-Caycedo, who began to explore these data with me a long time ago, and enriched this paper with his comments. I am very grateful to Scott Raymond and Francis Allard who have patiently edited this chapter. I also thank the anonymous reviewers' comments. Finally, I want to thank my mother for her infinite patience and loving support. For more than a year, while I analyzed the material, she kindly tolerated skeletons and sherds "exposed" in her house.

Appendix 5a

Marín site: Data base of variables associated with tombs

TN	X	Y	AGE	SEX	DC	SHP	OR	DTH	POS	TRT	RED	FF	TCE	TFC
1	520	472.2	6	F	A	PO	180	20	FD	SEC	0	0	1	0
2	530	501.6	1	ND	A	.	270	.	FD	ECZ	0	0	1	0
3	614	492.4	1	ND	A	PO	240	25	FD	ECZ	0	1	0	0
4	615	493	1	ND	A	PO	50	18	FD	SEC	0	0	0	0
5	596	496.6	10	F	A	PO	236	33	FD	SEC	0	0	0	0
6	598	496.2	2	ND	A	PO	120	20	FD	ECZ	0	0	0	0
7	597.4	503.4	9	F	P	PC	Zth	100	FS	ECZ	0	0	0	0
8	595	501	6	F	P	PC	Zth	120	FS	ECZ	0	0	0	0
9	596.8	501	6	M	P	PN	Zth	120	FS	ECZ	0	0	0	0
10	598	501	11	F	A	PN	115	60	FD	ECZ	0	0	1	0
11	596.4	501.4	7	M	P	PC	Zth	80	FS	ECZ	0	0	0	0
12	589	501.4	1	ND	A	PC	Zth	110	FS	ECZ	0	0	0	0
13	600	500	6	F	A	PN	Zth	120	FS	ECZ	0	1	0	0
14	598.2	502.2	8	F	A	PO	70	30	FD	SEC	0	0	1	0
15	599	502.4	7	F	A	PN	180	80	FD	ECZ	0	0	2	0
16	596	494	9	M	P	PC	Zth	170	FS	ECZ	0	0	0	0
17	596.2	492.3	1	ND	A	PN	235	60	FD	ECZ	0	0	1	0
18	594.2	492.4	1	ND	A	PN	Zth	74	FS	OLL	0	0	1	0
19	599	491.6	1	ND	P	PC	Zth	50	FS	OLL	0	0	1	0
20	690.2	568	4	ND	A	PN	160	40	FD	ECZ	0	0	2	0
21	589.4	504.6	1	ND	P	PN	150	50	FD	SEC	0	1	0	0
22	588.2	505.7	6	F	A	PC	Zth	90	FS	EPC	0	0	0	0
23	592	505.8	7	F	A	PN	165	60	FD	SEC	0	1	0	0
24	591	505.6	8	M	A	PN	122	56	FD	ECZ	0	0	2	0
25	593.8	505.7	A	F	A	PN	138	100	FD	SEC	0	1	0	0
26	690.2	560.5	7	F	A	PN	Zth	80	FS	EPC	0	1	1	0
27	690.2	560	1	ND	A	PN	52	20	FD	ECZ	1	0	2	0
28	691.8	568.4	10	F	A	PN	15	30	FD	EPC	0	0	0	0
29	693.5	567	7	F	A	PN	230	35	FD	EPC	0	0	1	0
30	692.5	566.2	5	F	A	PC	Zth	75	FS	ECZ	0	0	0	0
31	679.5	552.2	10	F	A	PN	92	80	FD	SEC	0	1	0	0
32	678.6	555.2	5	F	A	PN	215	23	FD	EPC	0	0	1	0
33	677.6	555.4	11	M	A	PN	59	40	FD	EPC	0	0	1	0
34	678	556.6	1	ND	A	PO	160	30	FD	EPC	0	1	0	0
35	678.8	554.4	1	ND	A	PO	272	30	FD	EPC	0	0	2	0
36	678	554	4	F	A	PN	64	77	FD	EPC	0	2	0	0
37	598	508	4	F	P	PC	Zth	105	FS	ECZ	0	0	0	0
38	544.6	464.6	3	ND	A	PN	245	90	FD	EPC	0	0	0	0
39	613.2	511.8	A	ND	A	PO	180	30	FD	SEC	0	0	0	0
40	609	509	8	F	A	PN	3	65	FD	ECZ	0	0	1	0
41	609.6	507	6	F	A	PN	Zth	50	FS	ECZ	0	1	2	0
42	586.8	505.4	8	F	P	PN	40	107	FD	EPC	0	0	0	0
43	612.8	508	1	ND	A	PO	81	19	FD	EPC	0	1	0	0
44	547.6	488	6	F	A	PN	120	60	FD	ECZ	0	0	1	0
45	548.6	488.6	5	F	A	PC	Zth	105	FS	ECZ	1	0	2	0
46	550.5	488.8	1	ND	A	PO	18	30	FD	ECZ	1	0	1	0
48	611	474	6	F	A	PC	201	60	FD	ECZ	1	0	1	1
49	548.2	487.4	10	F	A	PO	190	50	FD	ECZ	0	0	0	0
50	547.6	491	4	M	A	PC	Zth	94	FS	ECZ	1	0	1	0
51	600.4	495	8	M	P	PC	Zth	85	FS	EPC	0	0	1	0
53	598	484	6	F	A	PO	153	40	FD	EPC	0	0	2	0
54	542.4	464.5	4	M	A	PN	Zth	125	FS	ECZ	0	0	0	0

continued

Appendix 5a, *continued*

TN	X	Y	AGE	SEX	DC	SHP	OR	DTH	POS	TRT	RED	FF	TCE	TFC
55	585	487.5	7	M	A	PO	46	30	FD	SEC	0	2	0	0
56	579.4	471	8	M	A	PO	180	90	FD	EPC	0	0	2	1
57	600.4	504	2	ND	A	PN	200	77	FD	ECZ	0	1	1	0
58	622.7	489.5	8	M	A	PN	70	40	FD	ECZ	0	1	1	0
60	626	490.1	6	M	A	PN	165	40	FD	ECZ	0	1	1	0
61	552	487	1	ND	A	PC	Zth	44	FS	ECZ	0	0	0	0
63	596	543.3	1	ND	A	PC	19	30	FD	ECZ	1	0	0	0
64	595	543.4	1	ND	A	PC	.	50	NA	ECZ	1	1	1	0
65	598.2	543	3	ND	A	PO	160	80	FD	ECZ	0	0	1	0
66	594.8	539.3	1	ND	A	PC	355	30	FD	ECZ	1	0	0	0
67	594.4	539	8	F	A	PN	335	50	FD	SEC	0	0	0	0
68	596.4	538.6	8	F	A	PC	335	60	FD	ECZ	1	0	0	0
70	487.8	461.7	9	F	A	PN	170	75	FD	ECZ	1	1	0	0

TN	E	ME	WRL	CLT	HUE	CH	OV	SHB	AU	RX	COL	ATL	AWL	PAL	SPO	TTL	CTG
1	0	0	0	0	0	0	0	0	0	0	0	0	0	0	0	1	1
2	0	0	0	0	0	0	1	289	1	0	1	0	0	0	0	4	4
3	0	0	0	0	0	0	1	0	0	0	0	0	0	0	0	2	2
4	0	0	0	0	0	0	0	0	0	0	0	0	0	0	0	0	0
5	0	0	0	0	3	0	0	0	0	0	0	0	0	0	0	3	1
6	0	0	0	0	0	0	0	0	0	0	0	0	0	0	0	0	0
7	0	0	0	0	0	0	0	2	0	0	1	0	0	0	0	1	1
8	0	0	0	0	0	0	0	0	0	0	0	0	0	0	0	0	0
9	0	0	0	0	1	0	0	0	0	0	0	0	0	0	0	1	1
10	0	0	0	0	0	0	0	0	0	0	0	0	0	0	0	1	2
11	0	0	0	0	2	0	0	0	0	0	0	0	0	0	0	2	1
12	0	1	0	0	0	0	0	1	0	0	1	0	0	0	0	2	2
13	0	0	0	0	0	0	0	1	0	0	1	0	0	0	0	2	2
14	0	0	0	0	0	0	0	0	0	0	0	0	0	0	0	1	1
15	0	0	0	0	1	0	0	0	0	0	0	0	0	0	0	3	2
16	0	0	0	0	0	0	0	0	0	0	0	0	0	0	0	0	0
17	0	0	0	0	1	7	0	15	0	0	1	0	0	0	0	3	4
18	0	0	0	0	3	0	0	0	0	0	0	0	0	0	0	4	2
19	0	0	0	0	0	0	0	0	0	0	0	0	0	0	0	1	1
20	0	0	0	0	0	0	1	0	0	0	0	0	0	0	0	3	2
21	0	0	0	0	0	0	0	0	0	0	0	0	0	0	0	1	1
22	0	0	0	0	0	0	0	0	0	0	0	0	0	0	0	0	0
23	0	0	0	0	0	0	0	0	0	0	0	0	0	0	0	1	1
24	0	0	0	0	0	0	0	0	0	0	0	0	0	0	0	2	1
25	0	0	0	0	0	0	0	0	0	0	0	0	0	0	0	1	1
26	0	0	0	0	0	0	0	0	1	0	0	0	0	0	0	3	3
27	0	0	0	0	0	7	1	561	1	0	2	0	0	0	0	6	5
28	0	0	0	0	0	0	1	0	1	0	0	0	0	0	0	2	2
29	0	0	0	0	0	0	1	0	1	0	0	0	0	0	0	3	3
30	0	0	1	0	0	0	1	0	0	0	0	0	0	0	0	2	2
31	5	0	0	6	0	0	1	6	0	0	1	0	0	0	0	8	6
32	0	0	0	0	0	0	1	0	0	0	0	0	0	0	0	2	2
33	0	0	0	0	0	0	0	0	0	0	0	0	0	1	0	2	2
34	0	0	0	0	0	0	0	0	0	0	0	0	0	0	0	1	1
35	0	0	0	0	0	0	0	0	0	0	0	0	0	0	0	2	1
36	0	0	0	1	0	1	0	0	0	0	1	0	0	0	0	3	3
37	0	0	0	0	0	0	0	0	0	0	0	0	0	0	0	0	0
38	0	0	0	0	0	0	1	0	0	0	0	0	0	0	0	1	1

continued

Appendix 5a, *continued*

TN	E	ME	WRL	CLT	HUE	CH	OV	SHB	AU	RX	COL	ATL	AWL	PAL	SPO	TTL	CTG
39	0	0	0	0	0	0	0	0	0	0	0	0	0	0	0	0	0
40	0	0	0	0	0	0	0	0	0	0	0	0	0	0	0	1	1
41	0	0	0	0	0	0	0	0	0	0	0	0	0	0	0	3	2
42	0	0	0	1	0	0	0	0	0	0	1	0	0	0	0	1	1
43	1	0	0	0	0	0	1	0	0	0	0	0	0	0	0	3	3
44	0	0	0	0	0	0	0	0	2	0	0	0	0	0	0	3	2
45	0	0	0	0	1	0	2	0	0	0	0	0	0	0	0	5	3
46	0	0	0	0	0	0	1	0	0	0	0	0	0	0	0	2	2
48	0	0	1	1	1	65	6	1594	0	8	1	0	0	0	0	10	8
49	0	0	0	0	0	0	0	4	0	0	1	0	0	0	0	1	1
50	0	0	0	0	0	0	2	0	0	0	0	1	0	0	1	5	4
51	0	0	0	0	2	3	0	0	0	0	1	0	1	0	0	5	4
53	0	1	0	0	0	0	0	0	1	0	0	0	0	0	0	4	3
54	0	0	0	0	0	0	0	47	0	0	1	0	0	0	0	1	1
55	0	0	0	0	0	0	0	0	0	0	0	0	0	0	0	2	1
56	1	0	0	0	0	0	2	2	0	0	1	1	0	0	0	7	5
57	0	0	0	0	0	6	0	18	1	0	1	0	0	0	0	4	5
58	0	1	0	0	0	0	0	0	0	0	0	0	0	0	0	3	3
60	0	0	0	0	1	0	0	0	1	0	0	0	0	0	0	4	4
61	0	0	0	1	0	0	0	0	0	0	1	0	0	0	0	1	1
63	0	1	0	0	1	0	1	0	0	0	0	0	0	0	0	3	3
64	0	1	0	0	4	0	2	0	0	0	0	0	0	0	0	9	5
65	0	0	0	1	0	0	2	9	5	0	1	0	0	0	0	9	5
66	0	0	0	0	0	0	0	300	1	0	1	0	0	0	0	2	2
67	0	0	0	0	0	0	0	0	0	0	0	0	0	0	0	0	0
68	0	0	0	0	0	0	2	0	0	0	0	0	0	0	0	3	1
70	4	0	0	0	0	0	1	0	1	0	0	0	0	0	0	8	4

Glossary of variables

AGE: Age cohorts: 1=0-4, 2=5-9, 3=10-14, 4=15-19, 5=20-24, 6=25-29, 7=30-34, 8=35-39, 9=40-44, 10=45-49, 11=50-54, 12=+55 A=Adult
ATL: Number of atlatls
AU: Number of artifacts of *tumbaga* (an alloy of gold and cooper)
AWL: Number of awls
CH: Number of bone beads
CLT: Number of lithic beads
COL: Number of necklaces
CTG: Total number of categories of artifacts
DC: Cranial Deformation: A=Absent, P=Present
DTH: Depth of the tomb
E: Number of emeralds.
FF: Number of ceramic vessel halves
HUE: Number of unmodified animal bones
ME: Number of metates
OR: Body orientation: Zth=Zenith. Numbers indicate degrees in which the head is directed to.
OV: Number of sea snails (*Oliva* spp.).

PAL: Number of bone sticks
POS: Body position: FS= Fetal seated position, FD= Fetal lateral position
RED: Red-ocher pigment sprinkled on the body. 0=Absent, 1=Present RX: Number of resin beads
SEX: M=Male, F=Female
SHB: Number of shell beads
SHP: Tomb shape: PO= Oval cross-section, PC= Shaft tomb, PN= Tomb with shaft and chamber
SPO: Number of spoons
TCE: Number of complete ceramic vessels
TFC: Number of foreign ceramic vessels
TN: Tomb number
TRT: Body treatment: ECZ= Complete ash plaster and textile wrapping, EPC= Partial plaster and wrapping, SEC= Absence of plaster but textile wrapping was likely present, and OLL= Buried within a cooking pot.
TTL: Total number of artifacts. Beads were not included in this count.
WRL: Number of spindle whorls
X: Spatial location on X axis
Y: Spatial location on Y axis

❧6❧

Prestige and Wealth in Chiefdom-Level Societies

A Comparison Between Two Satellite Polities
on the Peripheries of San Agustín and Moundville

Jeffrey P. Blick

REICHEL-DOLMATOFF'S 1961 ARTICLE, "The Agricultural Basis of the Sub-Andean Chiefdoms of Colombia," essentially set the stage for research into Colombian chiefdoms. He recognized many of the concepts that have influenced my work and perceptions of the archaeology of San Agustín and nearby regions. Some of these concepts, such as social differentiation, prestige, and wealth, were the theoretical foundations for my doctoral dissertation (Blick 1993). It is clear from his writing that Reichel-Dolmatoff recognized the distinction between prestige and wealth (1961a:84,87) although he did not specifically formulate these differences. My first preconceptions of the research findings were decidedly Marxist in orientation, but I have come to view the issue of prestige versus wealth through more interpretive eyes through the influence of Reichel-Dolmatoff's writings.

In recent years, there has been a great deal of literature on the nature of chiefdom-level polities regarding economics (Welch 1991), prestige goods (Blitz 1993), political change and "cycling" or the emergence and decline of complexity (Anderson 1994), and, on the other hand, the stability and persistence of chiefdoms (Stemper 1993). Some of these studies have stressed the historical particularist approach in which "different societies have different histories" (see for example Welch 1991:201), while others have stressed the necessity of understanding the differences between developments in various areas in order to better generate explanatory laws to help explain the emergence (as well as the decline) of social complexity in different regions (Drennan 1991; Feinman 1991:261). Rather than review the extensive literature on the subject, and to avoid arguments regarding the utility or evolutionary implications of the term "chiefdom" (see for example Drennan and Uribe 1987:x–xii; Upham 1987; Spencer 1987), I thought it would be interesting to compare findings from two geographically isolated areas and try to draw some generalizations that may help understand the nature of chiefdom-level economics, particularly at lower-level polities on the fringes of larger, more powerful entities.

The inspiration for this chapter is the striking similarity of the findings of Blitz (1993) at Lubbub Creek, a polity on the periphery of the influential Moundville chiefdom in west-central Alabama, and my own findings (Blick 1993) on Cerro Guacas, a polity on the fringe of the large chiefdom centered on San Agustín in southwestern Colombia. At first I thought the similarities were due simply to coincidence; now I am more convinced that they spring from the underlying similarities of the economic and social functioning of the two chiefdom satellite polities on the peripheries of larger, more centralized socio-economic, politico-religious systems. In this regard, I hope that a discussion of the similarities between these two cases, Cerro Guacas on the fringe of San Agustín and Lubbub Creek on the periphery of Moundville, will help contribute to the explanation of the emergence of social complexity, the nature of chiefdom-level economics, and especially the chiefdom-level economics of smaller polities on the peripheries of much larger social entities.

To begin, it is necessary to provide some general information about the nature of the San Agustín and Moundville chiefdoms and the position of the two smaller, peripheral polities, Cerro Guacas and Lubbub Creek, within their respective larger settlement systems. Next, the differences between prestige and wealth are defined. Then the functioning of the Cerro Guacas and Lubbub Creek economies is discussed (with reference to Blick 1993 and Blitz 1993) within the larger San Agustín and Moundville systems, respectively. Finally, the similarities between the economics of Cerro Guacas and Lubbub Creek, the effect of the center-periphery relationship on smaller polities on the fringes of larger systems, and the patterns and implications of restricted, and in other ways not-so-restricted, access to material and immaterial benefits are discussed.

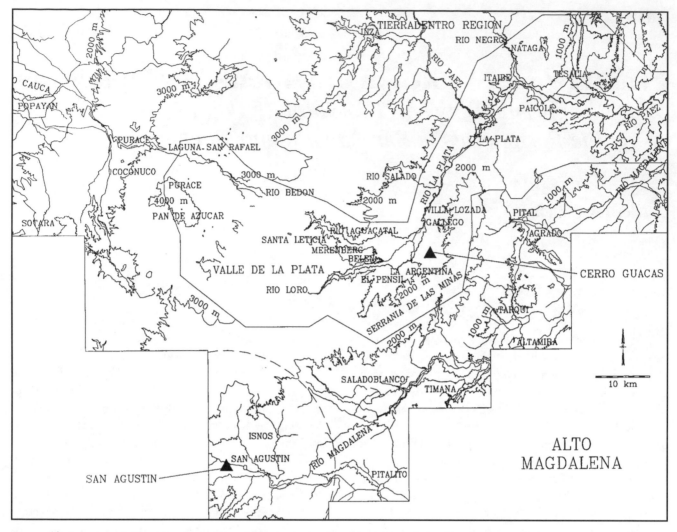

Figure 6.1 Location of San Agustín and Cerro Guacas in the Alto Magdalena, Colombia. The dashed arc is part of a 40 km diameter circle hypothesized to be the limit of effective administrative control of the San Agustín chiefdom, based roughly on one day's walk (20 km) from the chiefdom center. *Map adapted from Drennan et al. 1989:122, Fig. 2, 1991:302, Fig. 5, Blick 1993:23, Fig. 1.2.*

San Agustín and Cerro Guacas

The San Agustín "culture area" is centered around the town of San Agustín in the Departamento de Huila in the southwestern part of Colombia in a region known as the Alto Magdalena, the Upper Magdalena River valley (see figure 6.1). San Agustín was the focus of a mound building and statue carving culture from shortly before the time of Christ to around AD 900 according to the most recent and detailed analysis of radiocarbon dates and ceramics from the region (Drennan 1993:92, 97, 99). While the entire Alto Magdalena has scattered mounds and statues, the heaviest concentration by far is in the immediate environs of San Agustín, thus providing a convenient "geographical center" for this cultural manifestation.

The region is a rugged mountainous terrain which is deeply downcut by steep river valleys. Altitudes range from around 1000 to 4500 m above sea level with average temperatures ranging from around 24 to 0° C; daily temperatures may fluctuate

as much as 10° C (Botero 1985:49). Annual mean precipitation varies between about 1550 and 1600 mm at elevations between 1000 and 1650 m (Botero 1985:60); precipitation reaches as much as 2000 mm per year in the higher elevations, decreasing toward the lower, hotter elevations.

Previous archaeological work in the Alto Magdalena has concentrated mainly on the funerary mounds, statuary, and tombs in the San Agustín and Tierradentro regions (Pérez de Barradas 1937, 1943a; Duque Gómez 1963, 1964, 1966; Duque Gómez and Cubillos 1979, 1983, 1988; Cubillos 1980, 1986; Gamboa Hinestrosa 1982; Llanos Vargas and Durán de Gómez 1983; Sotomayor and Uribe 1987; Llanos Vargas 1988; Cháves Mendoza and Puerta Restrepo 1980, 1984, 1986).

Archaeological investigations in the Alto Magdalena focusing on the sites surrounding San Agustín have, over the years, produced some very good evidence for the existence of chiefdoms (for example, funerary mounds, monolithic sarcophagi, carved statues entombed with certain individuals, and landscaping or terraplaning of natural landforms; Pérez de Barradas 1943a; Duque Gómez 1963, 1964; Cubillos 1980; Llanos Vargas and Durán de Gómez 1983; Cubillos 1986; Reichel-Dolmatoff 1972a, 1986:133–143; Llanos Vargas 1988; Duque Gómez and Cubillos 1988).

While there are some minor differences between the ceramic styles and micro-chronologies of the region, the primary accepted works defining the chronology of the San Agustín region are those of Duque Gómez and Cubillos (1979:224, 1988:101); the work of Drennan (1993), Llanos Vargas (1990), and others working in adjacent areas has successfully applied this chronology to the Alto Magdalena as a whole. The period presently under consideration is the Regional Classic period (AD 1–900) during which status differences became obvious in the archaeological record through the building of funerary mounds and the carving of stone statues.

While systematic settlement pattern data is currently unavailable from the San Agustín region, the work of Drennan and his students (Drennan 1985; Drennan et al. 1989, 1991; Drennan and Quattrin 1995) in the nearby Valle de la Plata has provided some interesting details regarding settlement pattern change and population trends through time in that region. The Valle de la Plata is located centrally within the Alto Magdalena to the northeast of San Agustín and is a naturally defined zone comprised of the drainage basin of the Río La Plata.

According to the findings of Drennan, the Regional Classic period saw strong population growth, the formation of several distinct zones of population concentrations at the regional level, a proliferation of funerary mound building, and monumental statue carving. The common ceramics of the period are poorly fired and erode easily upon handling. However, some of the most ornate ceramics from the Alto Magdalena occur during this period; motifs include anthropomorphic, zoomorphic, and incised and/or punctated geometric designs. As regards source materials for the statues, it seems that the procurement and transportation of stone for carving would not have been comparable, say, to that of the colossal Olmec carved stone heads, because most of the statues derive from the underlying volcanic tobas and andesitic lavas available at practically every location on the hills and small plateaus of the Colombian Massif (Tello Cifuentes 1981:103). The statues found in situ were buried in funerary mounds and tombs (Preuss 1931, Vol. II: Plancha 22, Nos. 3–4, Plancha 57, Nos. 1–3, Plancha 78, Nos. 1 and 3, Plancha 82, No. 2; Duque Gómez and Cubillos 1979:25–219; 1983:9–137; 1988:20–21, 22, Lámina V; Cubillos 1986:25–76; Bermúdez Páez 1992:257–264, 258; and so forth). However, other offerings, such as pottery vessels included with the burials, are few and of moderate quality.

The climate, hotter and drier than present, allowed an increase in agriculturally productive land and a major increase in population (Drennan et al. 1989:15; 1991:309–310). Substantially more population concentration occurred at this time with centers springing up in the San Agustín area and in the Valle de la Plata. During this period, at least three centers of population concentration emerged in the Valle de la Plata.

These population clusters are focused on mortuary complexes of mounds and statues similar to those of San Agustín. Population concentration is relatively dense in the area around these mound and statue groups. The area occupied and the population seem to have approximately doubled from the Formative period (1000–1 BC) to the Regional Classic (Drennan et al. 1991:311) in the area surveyed and analyzed to date. One of these centers of population nucleation, Cerro Guacas, the "Hill of the Tombs" (VP0001), the site of my research focus, lies about 3 km northeast of the modern town of La Argentina and is a typical funerary mound site of this period (see figure 6.1). Approximately six carved statues are known to have originated from this site. Previous stratigraphic test excavations on Cerro Guacas have revealed very low density artifactual remains, raising the distinct possibility that at least part of the site was a ceremonial rather than a habitation zone (Drennan 1993:33–34, 73, Table 2.1). However, Cerro Guacas was the focus of a relatively dense zone of Regional Classic period occupation, indicating that there was some type of socio-political and/or economic attraction to this area. The large-scale population increase, the population clustering, and the boom in mound building and statue carving activities during this period all support the conclusion that social complexity and status differentiation were increasing in the Alto Magdalena and the Valle de la Plata.

Some tantalizing details emerge from several of the excavations in the San Agustín area in terms of differences in mortuary practice according to status, structural and functional differences between households, and possible evidence for the presence of activity areas within houses. Exactly this type of evidence led me to perform archaeological testing and excavations at residential sites in and around Cerro Guacas, one of the small population concentrations, or polities, that emerged in the Valle de la Plata during the Regional Classic period.

It is clear that Cerro Guacas was participating in the San Agustín sphere of influence since its four burial mounds and half-dozen or so carved stone statues fall into the San Agustinian pattern and reproduce the San Agustinian style; the pottery also has similarities to that of San Agustín. Cerro Guacas lies approximately 52 km to the northeast of San Agustín, apparently beyond the theoretical edge of "effective administrative control" (Hally 1987:5) of chiefdom-level societies which are suggested to have maximum diameters of approximately 40 km (Hally 1987). The significance of the peripheral nature of Cerro

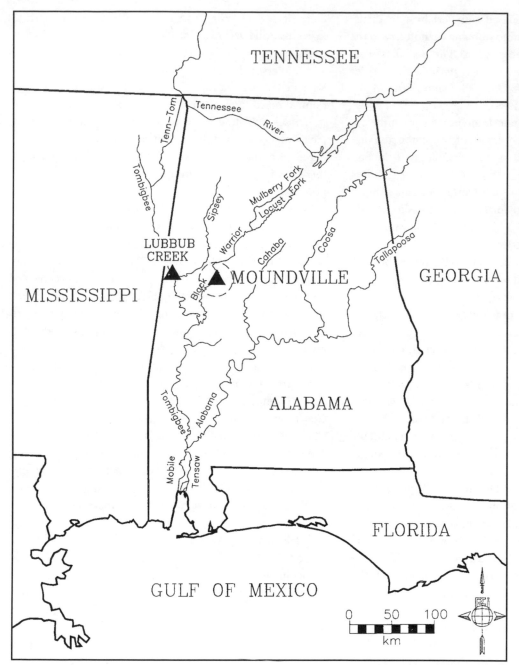

Figure 6.2 Location of Moundville and Lubbub Creek in west central Alabama, United States. The 40 km diameter dashed circle is the hypothetical limit of effective administrative control of the Moundville chiefdom, based on one day's walk (20 km) from the chiefdom center. *After Meyers 1995:4, Fig. 1*

Guacas to San Agustín is discussed further below.

Moundville and Lubbub Creek

The chiefdom-level society of Moundville is centered near the town of the same name near the Tuscaloosa County-Hale County border in central western Alabama in the Black Warrior River valley (see figure 6.2). Like San Agustín, Moundville was the focus of a mound building culture which developed from circa AD 900–1700 and reached its peak during the Mississippian period (AD 1050–1550). While the Black Warrior and nearby Tombigbee River valleys are scattered with single mound sites, the largest concentration of mounds (twenty) is found at Moundville, obviously a major population center for this cultural manifestation. In fact, Moundville has been called the second largest Native American polity in North America, second only to Cahokia.

The region around Moundville is dominated by the floodplain of the Black Warrior River which, below the fall line at Tuscaloosa, "meanders in an alluvial valley 5 to 8 km wide" (Welch 1991:23–25). Moundville sits on the east bank of the Black Warrior in the central portion of an area of floodplain in the Fall Line Hills region almost equidistant between the Cumberland Plateau some 24 km to the north-northeast and the Black Belt some 32 km to the southwest. This geographical position allowed the residents of Moundville to exploit the highly productive floodplain for agriculture and the diverse faunal and floral assemblages of the other nearby physiographic provinces, the river, and oxbow lakes (Welch 1991:23–26, 25). The frost-free growing season is more than 200 days, and monthly precipitation during the growing season averages 800–1200 mm, although it may vary during the summer (Welch 1991:26).

Previous archaeological work at Moundville has been extensive (see for example Peebles 1979, 1981, Peebles et al. 1981; Bozeman 1982; Steponaitis 1983a, 1983b; Powell 1988; Welch 1991); Moundville itself has been subject to archaeological investigations for 155 years (Powell 1988:2) since the very beginnings of archaeology as a scientific endeavor. Much of this work, like that at San Agustín, has concentrated, and in some ways still concentrates, mainly on the mounds at Moundville (for example Knight 1994) and the mounds at other secondary centers, like Lubbub Creek (Blitz 1993:69–97), as well as on the analysis of pottery and certain symbolic objects, focusing heavily on religious, symbolic, and/or iconographic interpretations (for example Knight 1986, 1989; Lacefield 1994).

Despite this mound-oriented archaeology and the art historical interpretation of pottery and symbolic objects, archaeological investigations at Moundville and other nearby sites has, over the years, produced some very good evidence for the existence of a chiefdom-level society at Moundville and surrounding sites in the Black Warrior and Tombigbee river valleys.

While detailed settlement pattern data of the kind available for the Valley de la Plata is not available for the Moundville area, some general trends are apparent. The development of Moundville began at the end of the Terminal Woodland period (AD 900–1050), during which time a small (around 0.5–1.0 ha) West Jefferson phase village was located on the western edge of Moundville (Powell 1988:8–9). At this time, Moundville was one of 30 to 40 small non-mound sites scattered along the Black Warrior River (Welch 1991:32).

Beginning in Moundville I times (AD 1050–1250), the village was replaced by a larger one and the first levels of Mound O were built. During Moundville I, Moundville became one of four single mound sites in the area with "the remainder of the population dispersed in small villages and hamlets" (Powell 1988:9).

During the Moundville II phase (AD 1250–1400) Moundville came to stand out from the other sites in the region. Mound O was completed during this time and "Mounds C, D, H, and F were constructed on the northern and eastern edges of the site;" other mounds may also have been built during this time (Powell 1988:9). According to Powell, the Moundville population was increasing during Moundville II, and the growing size and complexity of the site was based on Moundville's growing importance in the regional settlement system and its ability to "recruit labor for ceremonial construction." During this time, differential mortuary treatment be-

came obvious in the archaeological record, distinguished individuals being interred at Moundville (perhaps brought from surrounding sites) and lesser mortuary distinction being evident at the smaller single mound sites (Powell 1988:9).

The remainder of the mounds were constructed during Moundville III (AD 1400–1550) and a palisade enclosed the site outside the circle of mounds, raising the possibility of concerns for defense; during this time the largest mounds, A and B, took on their final appearance (Powell 1988:10). Six single mound sites, three to the north and three to the south of Moundville, also existed at this time, as well as a number of non-mound sites (Welch 1991:32), thus providing evidence that the Moundville chiefdom had reached a three-tiered settlement pattern by at least this time.

Moundville was probably populated by 3000 inhabitants during this period. From about AD 1450 on, Moundville "witnessed the decentralization of sociopolitical authority and population concentration" (Powell 1988:11). This trend was accompanied by the "dispersal of the occupants of the mound centers into smaller, widely scattered villages," but "no absolute decline in population.... is indicated" (Powell 1988:11). One reason for this apparent decline in complexity is the drop in imported artifacts by more than seventy-five percent, a factor which probably acted to weaken the elite segment of society which had developed at Moundville based on its control of the flow of information and items that served to validate social rank and political connections between communities (Peebles 1983a:10). Other possible contributors to the decline of Moundville that have been discussed include decreasing subsistence surplus caused by increasing population, increasing population pressure on available resources as a result of the climatic fluctuations of the Little Ice Age, the rise of competing chiefdoms that interrupted the flow of exotic items to Moundville, and the collapse of interregional trade networks (Powell 1988:11–12). To support the latter suggestion, the abundance of copper items per dated burial at Moundville (Welch 1991:198) clearly shows a pattern of rise and fall. The abundance of imported shell (as well as non-local stone—see Blitz 1993:173) essentially follows this pattern, while the abundance of imported pottery declines from Moundville I to Moundville II and sees its first rise from Moundville II to Moundville II/III, and then declines.

By 1540 or so, power had shifted to the Alabama River valley to the east, and no mention of any indigenous community that could be associated with Moundville was made in the De Soto chronicles (Powell 1988:12). Moundville IV (AD 1550–1700) or Protohistoric occupation at Moundville appears to have been sparse (Powell 1988:12).

There exists some convincing evidence from the excavations at Moundville and other secondary sites (such as Lubbub Creek—see Blitz 1993:101–104) that there were strong differences in mortuary practice according to social status, and that there were also structural differences between houses, perhaps reflective of status and/or functional differences. However, what I feel is a lack of focus on household archaeology at Moundville limits this site's (otherwise amazing) potential to shed light on such important issues as the nature of economic differences between groups of people and the nature of the rise of economic differences over time.

How does Lubbub Creek fall into the Moundville settlement system, if indeed it does at all? Lubbub Creek is a single mound Mississippian period site in the Tombigbee River valley some 53 km west, and on the periphery, of Moundville (Blitz 1993:2), even further beyond the theoretical limit of "effective administrative control" (Hally 1987:5) than Cerro Guacas was to San Agustín. It dates to the period AD 1000–1600 (Blitz 1993:56) and is thus approximately coeval with developments at Moundville. The presence of Moundville Incised *var. Moundville*, Moundville Engraved, and mold-produced ceramics, copper emblems, as well as certain elements of high status burial ritual (Blitz 1993), all seem to indicate that Lubbub Creek was participating in trade and exchange of information with Moundville. Lubbub Creek appears to have been a smaller single mound center populated by approximately 100 people or less at any one time surrounded by local farmsteads or hamlets (Blitz 1993). In this way, Lubbub Creek occupies a secondary place in the larger Moundville settlement system as does Cerro Guacas in the San Agustín settlement system.

Although Moundville and Lubbub Creek do not occupy the same chronological position as San Agustín and Cerro Guacas (in fact the Mississippian florescence coincides with what is called the Recent period (AD 900–1536) in the Alto Magdalena of Colombia), I feel that the location of Lubbub Creek and Cerro Guacas, peripheral to their respective larger chiefdom centers, makes for some interesting comparisons between the two. In the words of Blitz (1993:2), their "location on [the] periphery raises some very interesting questions about the developmental relationships between small-scale and large-scale polities."

Definitions of Status, Prestige, and Wealth

In the discussions of increasing social differentiation and emerging social complexity, there has been a tendency to conflate the terms "status," "prestige," and "wealth." For example, "high status" has come to be synonymous with "prestigious" or "wealthy." Similarly, some confusion has been created by the alternating use of such terms as "high status goods," "prestige goods" or "prestige goods economy," and "status items," "wealth items," "wealth objects," "primitive wealth," and so forth I prefer to view these terms as separate, although related concepts. For example, status is simply a person's or group's position, rank, or standing in society, whether high, intermediate, or low. Prestige is defined as the power to im-

press or influence and can theoretically operate solely on the basis of intangible or immaterial forces. Wealth, on the other hand, is defined as the possession of a great quantity and/or a high quality of objects. A person can have prestige without having wealth; two prime examples emerge offhand, college professors and priests. Both occupy respected positions in society, while their wealth is moderate to low. Wealth, however, at least in this day and age, seems to engender prestige and high status, although it is possible to imagine a wealthy person, for example a criminal, who, by his or her career or comportment, has little respect in the eyes of society. While it is difficult, if not impossible, to apply western concepts of economics to non-western pre-literate societies (or to compare concepts of status, prestige, and wealth from one indigenous society to another), general distinctions between prestige and wealth, as defined above, can usefully be applied as analytical tools to the societies under consideration.

This research has direct bearing on the distinction between prestige and wealth (see also Drennan 1991; Lange 1992:7; Cooke and Ranere 1992b:244) or "political inequality" and "wealth inequality" (Hastorf 1990:147) in the archaeological record. Prestige, defined above as the power to impress or influence, can theoretically operate solely on the basis of intangible or immaterial forces. Therefore, no wealth items or evidence for unequal access to material goods need be present in the archaeological record to indicate prestige. For example, in the Regional Classic period in the Alto Magdalena generally, and at Cerro Guacas in particular, there is a relatively heavy investment of labor in mortuary architecture (for example, the construction of mounds, the carving of statues), yet there are few or no burial offerings (of ordinary quality) in tombs of otherwise elaborate construction (Blick 1993; Drennan 1995), suggesting the possibility of substantial prestige but little wealth. Furthermore, residences would not be likely to be marked by any significant differences in access to material goods. Wealth, as defined above, is the possession of a great quantity and/or a high quality of objects. Tombs of wealthy individuals are more likely to be marked by many burial offerings of high quality, few very high quality offerings, or many offerings. Wealthy residences would very likely be marked by differential access to higher quality resources, such as imported lithic raw materials like obsidian or greenstone, decorated ceramic vessels, or better quality foodstuffs.

Based on information from the Alto Magdalena, we might hypothesize that forces other than economic (that is, social, ritual, or ideological) were of primary importance in sustaining the system of social differentiation in the Regional Classic period in the Alto Magdalena and at Cerro Guacas. I will argue that a similar pattern is to be found in the Moundville chiefdom and its related settlements such as Lubbub Creek. While certain burials are accompanied by unusual and rare artifacts, these artifacts are characterized not by their nature

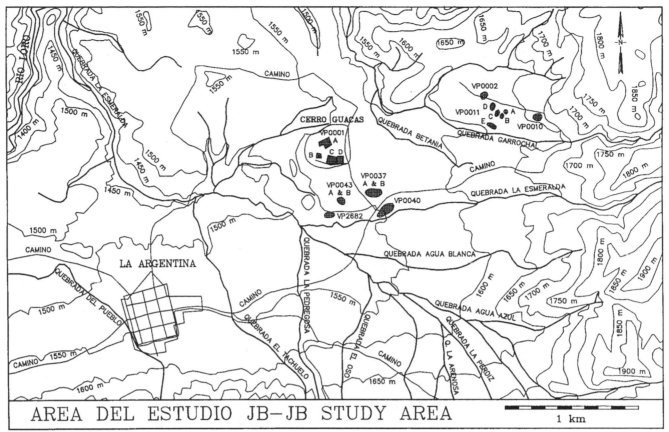

Figure 6.3 Location of Cerro Guacas (VP0001) (north of center) and other sites tested by Blick in 15 km² area near the modern town of La Argentina, Departamento de Huila, Colombia. Contour intervals are every 50 meters; major creeks and roads are also shown.

as objects of wealth, but rather by their nature as objects imbued with ceremonial or sacred meaning (or *sacra* as discussed by Knight 1986). This implies that high status individuals in the Moundville and Lubbub Creek polities really were not actually wealthier than the citizens of these polities but that their higher status was related to their participation in spheres of esoteric knowledge and long distance trading relationships.

Chiefdom-level Economics at Cerro Guacas and Lubbub Creek
Cerro Guacas

As part of my research at Cerro Guacas seventeen archaeological sites were investigated, all except one representing the debris deposited by pre-Columbian households (see figure 6.3). Only artifacts from the Regional Classic period (Guacas Reddish Brown sherds and lithics from pure Regional Classic deposits) from each site were analyzed in the comparison of artifact assemblages from site to site. All the Regional Classic artifacts from the shovel probes, test pits, and/or horizontal excavations from each site were combined and analyzed according to type (ceramic, lithic, and so forth). Distance from the mound center at Cerro Guacas was also recorded for each

site; these distances were used in the statistical analyses to examine the correlation of certain ceramic and lithic variables with distance from the mound center. The results of the data analysis are presented below; for the sake of brevity, only the most significant or theoretically interesting results are discussed (for more details see Blick 1993).

Of the sites with reliable ceramic sample sizes (n>400;see table 6.1), only VP0010 has a percentage of decorated Guacas Reddish Brown sherds that is an outlying value (0.48%). Eleven of the seventeen sites produced no decorated sherds at all, thus indicating the rarity of this sherd type. VP0010 may have had about 2.3 to 9.6 times as many decorated sherds as VP0001-A (0.19%), VP0011-C (0.21%), and VP2682 (0.05%), but the percentages are so minuscule that the differences from site to site appear quite minimal. Only four sites yielded Guacas Reddish Brown tripod feet (diagnostic of tripod ollas), VP0001-A (0.14%), VP0011-C (0.06%), VP0040 (1.10%), and VP2682 (0.02%);however, sample size was so low at VP0040 (n=94) that it casts doubt on the reliability of the percentage from this site. Excluding the percentage from VP0040 (as we have in table 6.1), the percentage from VP0001-A is 2.3 times greater than that from VP0011-C and 7 times greater than that from VP2682. However, considering the very low values, the differences are

Table 6.1 Percentages of ceramic and lithic wealth markers from sites with adequate sample sizes

Ceramic wealth markers (N>400)

	DECORATED SHERDS	TRIPOD FEET	OTHER DIAGNOSTIC SHERDS	TOTAL CERAMIC WEALTH MARKERS
VP0001-A	0.19	0.14	0.04	0.37
VP0010	0.48	0.00	0.00	0.48
VP0011-C	0.21	0.06	0.04	0.31
VP2682	0.05	0.02	0.00	0.07

Lithic wealth markers (N>30)

	OBSIDIAN	QUARTZ	QUARTZITE	CHERT
VP0001-A	33.40	4.50	5.30	2.00
VP0010	0.00	2.90	2.90	2.90
VP0011-C	7.80	1.40	9.80	1.90
VP2682	19.30	1.60	3.70	1.60

not outstanding. Other Guacas Reddish Brown diagnostic sherds such as strap handle fragments, double-spout-and-bridge (*alcarraza*) vessel fragments, and high pedestal cup fragments (described in Blick 1993) were recovered from only three sites, VP0001-A (0.04%), VP0011-C (0.04%), and VP0040 (1.06%), but the low sample size from VP0040 (n=94) makes the percentage from this site unreliable and is therefore excluded from table 6.1. Otherwise the percentages from the other two sites are identical—quite remarkable given the differences in sample sizes—and so low as to be barely distinguishable from zero. Therefore, it appears once again that there were no major differences in access to more elaborate vessels from site to site.

When all of the ceramic wealth markers are combined, the percentages from the four sites with large sample sizes are fairly similar: VP0001-A (0.37%), VP0010 (0.48%), VP0011-C (0.31%), VP2682 (0.07%; see table 6.1). None of these figures are outlying values, although the percentage from VP2682 appears to be a little lower than the rest. These differences are so small, however, I would argue there really is very little difference between sites regarding access to fancier ceramic vessels.

It was originally hypothesized that if residential proximity to the burial mounds at VP0001 (Cerro Guacas), and presumed proximity to the chief's residence, was indicative of higher social status, then perhaps residences closer to the mounds would have greater percentages of higher quality ceramics (it would be interesting to apply this test to Moundville if household data were available). This situation could be expected if fancier vessels were manufactured and/or distributed by some influential entity which could restrict access to vessels that were more labor intensive to create. This hypothesis turned out to be incorrect. Analysis of the ceramic wealth markers with distance from the nearest mound revealed no correlations of any strength or significance. This finding indicates that persons

living closer to the mounds at VP0001 did not have greater access to higher quality ceramics than those living at more distant sites and generally supports Taft's (1991, 1993) conclusion that there was no economic control over ceramic production and distribution.

High quality lithic raw materials, such as rhyolite, obsidian, quartz, quartzite, and chert were thought to be good raw material types to investigate for any potential evidence for differential access to material resources. Rhyolite, as it turned out, was the most ubiquitous raw material type found at 16 of the 17 sites investigated; rhyolite is very abundant in cobbles found in the beds of nearby *quebradas*, or streams, and thus easily accessible as a raw material source. Therefore, there is no evidence of unequal access to rhyolite.

However, when we observe sites with minimally adequate sample sizes (n>30; table 6.1), we find that VP0001-A, one of the four loci tested at Cerro Guacas, appears to have a much greater percentage of obsidian (33.4%) than the other sites, VP0010 (0.0%), VP0011-C (7.8%), and VP2682 (19.3%); in fact, VP0001-A has about 3.7 times as much obsidian as the average of the other three sites. Looking at obsidian weight in grams, VP0001-A has 1.5 to 7.5 times more obsidian weight than the other three sites. In fact, percent obsidian weight is consistently low at sites with adequate sample sizes. Based on this evidence, it appears that the residents of VP0001-A had greater access to obsidian than did the residents of other sites (10 of 17 sites yielded no obsidian at all).

Residents of VP0001-A also had greater access to another high quality lithic raw material, quartz (see table 6.1). The percentage of quartz at VP0001-A (4.5%), an outlying value, is about 1.6 to 3.2 times greater than the percentages of quartz at the other three sites with adequate samples, VP0010 (2.9%), VP0011-C (1.4%), and VP2682 (1.6%). When quartz weight in grams is analyzed, it appears that VP0010 (3.0%) had about 6 to 15 times more quartz weight than the other three sites with large samples, VP0001-A (0.5%), VP0011-C (0.4%), and VP2682 (0.2%). It may be that the apparently high percentage of quartz weight at VP0010 is a result of small sample size (n=35 compared to samples sizes of 2016, 580, and 187 for VP0001-A, VP0011-C, and VP2682, respectively). Thus, it is safer to conclude that the residents of VP0001-A had greater access to quartz than the other sites, with the possibility that VP0010 also had a relatively high percentage of quartz.

VP0011-C yielded an outlying percentage of quartzite (9.8%) when compared with the other sites (see table 6.1); this percentage is 1.85 to 3.4 times greater than the percentages at three sites with adequate sample sizes, VP0001-A (5.3%), VP0010 (2.9%), and VP2682 (3.7%). Perhaps the residents of VP0011-C (and those of other distant sites) relied on alternative lithic raw materials due to the increasing scarcity of obsidian at sites at increasing distances from the mounds at VP0001.

It appears that the residents of VP0010 had about 1.45 to 1.8 times the amount of chert (2.9%) of the other three sites with large sample sizes, VP0001-A (2.0%), VP0011-C (1.9%), and VP2682 (1.6%; see table 6.1). If we examine chert weight in grams, VP0011-C had about 3.9 to 8.5 times more chert weight (5.1%) compared to the consistent and low percentages of chert weight at other sites, VP0001-A (1.3%), VP0010 (0.6%), VP2682 (1.0%), including two other sites with small sample sizes, VP0037-A (1.0%) and VP0040 (1.0%). Thus, it appears that two of the sites more distant from the mounds at VP0001, VP0010 and VP0011-C, had fairly high percentages of chert, perhaps since obsidian was rare at sites at greater distances from VP0001.

It was hypothesized that if the apparent special nature of VP0001 (Cerro Guacas) acted as some type of social attractor, then perhaps certain high quality lithic raw materials (for example, obsidian, quartz, quartzite, chert) would be found in greater amounts at sites closer to the mound center at Cerro Guacas and in lesser amounts further away (once again it would be interesting to apply this model to Moundville if household data were available). Due to small sample size, all sites except VP0001-A, VP0010, VP0011-C, and VP2682 were excluded from the analysis of correlation of the percentages of high quality lithic raw material types and distance from the nearest mound.

Only two of the lithic raw material types correlate strongly with distance from the nearest mound, the percentages of rhyolite and obsidian. The percentage of rhyolite has a strong positive correlation with distance from the nearest mound (Pearson's r=0.877, χ^2=2.204, p=0.123). That is, as the percentage of rhyolite increases, the distance from the nearest mound also increases, although the significance level is fairly low in this case. This relationship and strength of correlation stays virtually the same when all sites, even those with small sample sizes, are included.

Obsidian, due to its desirable qualities for tool making and its sharp cutting edges, was hypothesized to be a potential resource which could have been controlled by high status individuals (see, for example, Winter and Pires-Ferreira 1976:310). Significantly, obsidian consistently had the strongest correlation with distance from the nearest mound. This correlation was found to be strong and negative, meaning that as distance from the nearest mound increases, the percent obsidian decreases (Pearson's r=-0.985, χ^2=5.275, p=0.015). This indicates that sites closer to the mounds (within 900 m) at Cerro Guacas tended to have greater access to obsidian than sites further away (900 to 1900 m). Based on this correlation, the fact that 77.4% of all obsidian flakes and 81.8% of all obsidian weight recovered from Regional Classic contexts come from VP0001-A, and the fact that an analysis of variance of percent obsidian from all sites regardless of sample size divided into site distance classes yields a high F-ratio (8.477) and a very

significant probability (p=0.011), it appears that sites closer to the mounds at Cerro Guacas had greater access to obsidian. These data suggest that the residents of VP0001-A had some type of control over access to obsidian and may have passed more of this lithic material to their neighbors living in sites nearby whereas those living at more distant sites were at a disadvantage in the acquisition of obsidian.

The analysis of all sites regardless of sample size revealed similar patterns for the rhyolite and obsidian data discussed above, but the correlations were not quite as strong although the probabilities were more significant. The correlations of other lithic raw material types (by quantity and/or weight) and distance from the nearest mound were all weak and not very significant.

Evidence for specialized activities at VP0001-A sets off its residents from those of other sites. Such activities included basalt column carving for probable inclusion in tombs and salt and/or ceramic production (for details see Blick 1993). Other sites had no evidence for such specialized activities, although evidence for chipped stone and ground stone tool production was found at most other residential sites, suggesting that these activities were performed in all households.

As the data from Cerro Guacas and surrounding residential sites suggest, wealth distinctions were very weakly developed in this polity during the Regional Classic period. Elsewhere (Blick 1993) it has been suggested that the Regional Classic system of social differentiation at Cerro Guacas, and by extension that of the Alto Magdalena, was based chiefly on access to the esoteric knowledge of the supernatural realm as evidenced by much of the San Agustín and related statuary depicting chiefs as jaguar-men and other chiefly images surmounted by guardian spirit and other bizarre supernatural figures. Apparently, chiefly participation in realms of esoteric knowledge served to create a higher chiefly status based on prestige derived from contact with the spiritual world rather than on material wealth. I would assert that something similar to this system was operating in the Moundville-Lubbub Creek polities, as evidence below will suggest.

Lubbub Creek

The archaeological investigations at Lubbub Creek, as described by Blitz (1993), were conducted by Ned J. Jenkins of the University of Alabama in 1977 and by Christopher S. Peebles of the University of Michigan in 1978–1979 when more than 20,000 m² were excavated (Blitz 1993:53–56).

Blitz (1993:99–101) has suggested that the nucleation of Mississippian communities in the Tombigbee River valley was a result of increasing conflict and the need to store maize harvests in fortified, centralized locations as well as to protect members of the community from attack. He also asserts that this condition could have led to the rise of leaders to "preside over the pooling and disbursement of resources" as well as to preside over military and defense concerns (Blitz 1993:101). Mortuary evidence from Lubbub Creek consisting of two individuals buried with copper emblems with falcon and arrow symbolism, human limb "trophies," and a Moundville Incised vessel indicates that institutionalized leadership roles based on participation in warfare was established by Summerville I (AD 1000–1200) times (Blitz 1993:101–104).

During Summerville times (AD 1000–1500), farmstead subsistence activities at Lubbub Creek and several nearby sites indicate that utilitarian artifact inventories were similar and that there was no site or household specialization regarding basic subsistence activities (Blitz 1993:105–107). Similarly, "the same range of cultivated and wild food-plant remains" were consumed at farmsteads and the local center (Blitz 1993:107–108).

Analysis of Lubbub Creek vessel shape classes (bottles and flaring-rim bowls for serving, standard jars for cooking and storage, and simple bowls for cooking or serving) by mound and general village provenience indicates that the composition of mound and village ceramic assemblages is similar, revealing that the mound was not characterized by a greater proportion of serving vessels (Blitz 1993:92). However, when orifice diameter was examined, there was a significant difference between the median orifice diameters for jars and bowls for the mound and general village samples (Blitz 1993:93–95). Blitz (1993:96) interprets this phenomenon as the result of a "primary emphasis on large-group food consumption and perhaps storage" functions in mound contexts.

Regarding differential access to durable goods such as ceramics and other "prestige goods" (Blitz's 1993:126), Blitz said

> the differential distribution of certain valuables expected from theoretical models of Mississippian chiefly economy has received very limited testing and generally only at the largest regional polities such as Moundville. More investigations are necessary to determine whether patterns of differential distributions and the hierarchical social order they imply operated within smaller Mississippian societies such as Lubbub Creek. Stated another way, does the ranked social order and restricted access to resources so often assumed to be typical of Mississippian chiefdoms crosscut communities of various sizes, or is the degree of social ranking dependent on the size of the polity? (1993:126–127)

This is a very interesting question, equally applicable to the smaller Cerro Guacas polity on the fringe of the larger San Agustín settlement system, and is a matter I will take up later.

Blitz (1993:128) has recognized the problem in distinguishing between status, wealth, and prestige in his attempt to make the distinction between "fineware as a status item (restricted to a specific social status or rank) and fineware as a wealth item (a valued item that confers prestige but is not restricted to a specific social status or rank)."

Distributions of ceramic finewares at Lubbub Creek were examined on an intrasite basis, by comparing mound and village samples, and on the household cluster level. "A high degree of differential distribution" would indicate "restricted or preferential access," while a high degree of similarity in the distributions would indicate unimpeded access to the ceramics (Blitz 1993:129). On the intrasite level, there was no restricted access to Moundville Incised, Moundville Engraved, and Alabama River Applique ceramics which are the diagnostic ceramics of the Summerville I, II-III, and IV phases. In comparing the mound and village samples, the difference in the proportions of decorated sherds was relatively minor (mound=0.04, village=0.06), although higher relative frequencies of the high-cost fineware types were present in the mound sample, perhaps indicative of "greater fineware use in mound contexts" such as feasting (Blitz 1993:135). These differences are, however, considered minor (Blitz 1993:132–136). Finally, at the household level, the evidence indicates that "there was broad access to or use of finewares in household contexts" (Blitz 1993:136–139). In Blitz's words,

> the ubiquitous presence of finewares in all community contexts suggests that fineware ceramics at Lubbub Creek were broadly accessible wealth items and were not restricted to an 'elite.' Possible evidence of greater fineware use in mound contexts, if valid, is consistent with the mound's proposed function as the focus of community rituals and feasts. (1993:145–147)

Another manner of looking at differential access to material goods is to examine the context of their manufacture and use. If elite-supported craft specialization was indeed the norm for Moundville and Lubbub Creek, one would expect to find evidence for restricted manufacture such as workshops or other specialized areas of production including toolkits and hoards or caches of finished products (Blitz 1993:155). Elite supported craft specialization and its products should also be found in restricted contexts since control of production and distribution is implied in this scenario.

Upon examining pottery manufacture and consumption, Blitz (1993:155–158) found that there was no concentration of evidence for ceramic production at any particular location but rather that pottery manufacture of both coarseware and fineware occurred within individual households at Lubbub Creek. No evidence of pottery manufacture was found at smaller farmstead sites near Lubbub Creek (Blitz 1993:155), however, indicating that pottery manufacture was restricted to the local single mound center. On the other hand, Moundville Engraved and other fineware ceramics were found at the farmsteads, indicating a rather broad access to fineware ceramics (Blitz 1993:157).

The evidence for lithic tool production is similar in that low density debris "composed almost completely of local stone" was found in all households (Blitz 1993:158). The most valued lithic raw material, greenstone or green schist, from which celts were manufactured, was found at the local single mound center, Lubbub Creek, and access was open to residents of farmstead sites; evidence for the production of greenstone celts is too scarce to reveal patterns of manufacture (Blitz 1993:158). Discoidal objects or chunky stones were also found at both Lubbub Creek and farmsteads, and production evidence indicates that discoidals were manufactured within individual households (Blitz 1993:158).

Regarding the production of shell beads with microlithic drills, Blitz (1993:160) notes that microdrills were found throughout Lubbub Creek "in the plowzone, in domestic refuse, on structure floors, and in burial contexts." Shell debris is also found in similar contexts. Thus Blitz (1993:160) argues that shell bead production with microlithic drills was apparently carried out on the household level; he also goes on to note that the shell bead industry was based on local freshwater shell. Marine shell was also found at Lubbub Creek and its surrounding farmsteads, usually in burials (Blitz 1993:162). The pattern of consumption of shell beads indicates that shell beads were used almost exclusively as burial offerings at both farmsteads and Lubbub Creek and that "an age-sex pattern for the individual recipients of these beads seems to be evident." At farmsteads only subadults and infants were accompanied by shell beads, "while at Lubbub Creek both sexes and all ages receive beads," but one adult male was accompanied by a larger quantity of beads (Blitz 1993:162). These patterns indicate that shell bead production and consumption was not restricted and that their use in mortuary ritual was characteristic of a society in which status was age and sex related, not ascribed.

An analysis of Moundville, Lubbub Creek, and Lubbub Creek farmstead mortuary ritual indicates that copper items and galena cubes are found only at Moundville and Lubbub Creek, and then only with adult males; other so-called prestige goods such as black bear tooth pendants are found at both farmsteads and Lubbub Creek associated only with subadult burials (Blitz 1993:162–163). Other aspects of mortuary ritual at farmsteads, Lubbub Creek, and Moundville indicate that graves with the most diverse offerings are those of adult males accompanied by skulls, infant bones, or human limb trophy offerings (Blitz 1993:164-166). This pattern indicates that

> High status men at farmsteads, local center, and regional
> center apparently participated in a shared ceremonialism
> that was elaborated in material quantity and diversity at
> each level of site hierarchy....There is some basis to con-
> clude, then, that influential men at the most humble of

settlements had pretensions to symbols wielded by the most exalted at Moundville (Blitz 1993:166).

Thus, according to Blitz's (1993:154) analysis, the Tombigbee sites of Lubbub Creek and its nearby farmsteads produced and consumed wealth items, indicating that there was no craft specialization nor elite control of production and distribution and that individuals at all levels of the three-tiered settlement hierarchy participated in regional exchange networks. Distribution of wealth items was not restricted to Moundville, and high-ranking individuals at local centers, as well as farmsteads, had access to those symbols that marked paramount status at Moundville. "Instead of centralization of production and restriction of access to an elite, the widespread distribution of these wealth items and the materials to make them reveals that the ability of would-be elites to monopolize durable wealth was minimal" (Blitz 1993:178).

Blitz's findings essentially mirror my own findings at Cerro Guacas in the Valle de la Plata and support the contention that, at least in the chiefdom-level societies of San Agustín and Moundville and their peripheral settlements, chiefly control of access to items of wealth was not well developed. While not very surprising in the San Agustín-Cerro Guacas cases (after all, developments in the Intermediate Area have long been thought to have been "stunted" in some way—see Willey 1984:375–378 for example), this finding is perhaps more notable in the Moundville-Lubbub Creek cases since Moundville has long been heralded as one of the more outstanding cultural developments on the North American continent in complexity, scale, and sphere of influence. Blitz's (1993:153–178) overturning of the primary economic models for Moundville (Peebles and Kus 1977; Peebles 1978, 1983b; Welch 1991) suggests that what is apparently a highly complex society may in fact be organized at a much simpler level. This finding has already been suggested for the Cerro Guacas polity; as more systematic data are collected from the San Agustín region, I would not be surprised to find that other chiefdom-level societies of the Alto Magdalena are also organized at a lower, or simpler, level (see Steponaitis 1978:420; Carneiro 1981:47).

Conclusion

The similarities between the economies of Cerro Guacas and Lubbub Creek are quite striking. The investigations around Cerro Guacas yielded no evidence for differential access to decorated ceramics, tripod ollas, or other special vessel types such as strap handled vessels, double-spout-and-bridge vessels or alcarrazas, or high pedestal cups. Taft's (1991, 1993) analysis of the ceramics from the Valle de la Plata indicates that there really was no control over the production and distribution of ceramics and that there was a great deal of competition between potters working at the household level. The Lubbub Creek investigations also indicate that there was no restricted access to production and distribution of fineware ceramics and that production was performed at the household level at the local single mound center, Lubbub Creek, as it was at the regional center, Moundville. Both local centers, Cerro Guacas and Lubbub Creek, were probably involved in ceremonial feasting and/or drinking ceremonies, and perhaps storage, as evidenced by the larger median orifice diameters of bowls and jars from the Lubbub Creek mound and by the higher densities of sherds and fire-cracked rock at Cerro Guacas (VP0001-A); both features indicate greater use and breakage of vessels and greater rate of hearth usage as if more cooking was being performed at this site to feed a larger number of people (Blick 1993). Subsistence at Lubbub Creek and its nearby farmsteads was similar from site to site; subsistence data are lacking from Cerro Guacas, but subsistence data from the earlier Formative period (1000–1 BC) in the Valle de la Plata indicate that sites at varying altitudes had botanical remains of plants typical of their geographical settings and that redistribution of subsistence goods was not being practiced during this period (Quattrin 1995).

Evidence for access to lithic raw materials from residential sites in and around Cerro Guacas indicates that one site in particular (VP0001-A) had greater access to higher quality lithic raw materials, especially obsidian and quartz. The obsidian evidence is extremely interesting in that it indicates that a central figure was procuring obsidian (probably through interregional trade) and then distributing it to his neighbors. In fact, residential proximity to the mounds at Cerro Guacas increased the chances of receiving greater quantities of obsidian; those living further away from the mounds received less as their distance from the mounds increased. People living in sites further from the mounds, and thus on the edge, or outside, this obsidian procurement and distribution network, relied more heavily on alternative raw materials such as quartzite and chert in the absence of obsidian. Lithic raw material evidence was not discussed in detail for Lubbub Creek except to say that lithic debris was low in density but common in domestic contexts; other preferred lithic objects such as greenstone celts and chunky stones were found at the local center and in farmstead residential contexts, indicating no restricted access.

Tombs in San Agustín and Tierradentro (and Cerro Guacas if the rumors of looters are considered reliable) have yielded occasional gold and *tumbaga* (gold-copper-silver alloy) artifacts, although these are quite rare. Simpler items include nose rings and small beads; more ornamental pieces include a flying fish effigy, diadems with jaguar face and anthropomorphic images, a conch shell effigy (from San Agustín), and a jaguar/bird bracelet, a jaguar/caiman breastplate, a jaguar face effigy mask, and a human face ornament (from Tierradentro). While there is some evidence for a gold manufacturing in-

dustry at a couple of sites at San Agustín (Alto de la Piedras, Mesita B), the gold objects in Tierradentro resemble objects more common to other nearby regions of the country such as Calima, Cauca, Quimbaya, and so forth As goldwork motifs, zoomorphic forms such as the jaguar and the caiman predominate ; the mixture of zoomorphic images such as the jaguar/caiman and jaguar/bird seems to indicate the depiction of mythological or supernatural creatures probably utilized by chiefs to associate themselves with ferocious animals and/or supernatural beings in order to validate their position in the social hierarchy (Linares 1977; Helms 1979). Similar motifs can be seen in Mississippian emblems from Moundville and Lubbub Creek such as the falcon copper images, serpent discoidals, and bird-man motif on engraved shell gorgets. Chiefs at Moundville and smaller local centers such as Lubbub Creek probably attempted to associate themselves with these mythological or supernatural creatures as an attempt to validate their position in the social system. Rather than viewing these objects as "wealth items," perhaps they should be viewed literally as "prestige goods" or *sacra*, "representational art, artifacts, and icons that by inference appear to have been charged with conventional supernatural meaning, in the context of ritual activity or display" (Knight 1986:675). These goods would confer prestige (the ability to impress or influence) on their owners rather than giving them actual material wealth. The source of many of these objects, at least the raw materials to produce them if not the objects themselves, seems to be from outside the chiefdom polities, thus imbuing them with an additional aura of mystery and esoterica, and hence prestige (Helms 1979).

What exactly is the result of the center-periphery relationship on the economic expression of emerging social differentiation in secondary, or satellite, polities at the fringe of larger settlement systems? At first thought, one would hypothesize that centralized control of production and distribution (if present) would restrict access to certain specialized products (prestige goods, or wealth items) to residents of regional centers and that such items would be denied, or at least limited, to residents of secondary and lower-level centers. What does the evidence from the San Agustín-Cerro Guacas and Moundville-Lubbub Creek polities have to suggest about this prediction? Although systematically collected, recorded, and published data is not always easy to come by from San Agustín, specialized products such as gold objects and carved statuary seem to be limited to regional and local centers. Thus high status individuals at local centers, such as Cerro Guacas, participated in a shared ceremonialism with the elite of the regional center, San Agustín. Obsidian, on the other hand is found at all three types of settlement from the regional and local centers down to the household farmstead or hamlet. This may have more to do with obsidian's nature as essentially a utilitarian, although highly desirable, material for manufacturing cutting tools. Information is insufficient at this time to discuss patterns of other non-local stone distribution. There appears to have been little control over the production and distribution of ceramics as well as a high degree of competition between household potters; decorated and other special types of ceramics were not unevenly distributed. Examples of what appear to be foreign pottery are found around San Agustín, the regional center, but not at lower level settlements. This is hardly conclusive since museum and other display pieces tend to emphasize the highly ornate and unusual and are often derived from unclear, often looted, contexts.

The evidence from Moundville and Lubbub Creek demonstrates that exotic, imported pottery is found only at the regional center, while copper items and incised stone disks are found at regional and local centers. Other specialized items such as marine shell are found at all three levels of the settlement hierarchy (Blitz 1993:162), and freshwater shell and microdrills to manufacture beads, non-local stone, greenstone celts or axes, and fineware pottery seem not to have been unevenly distributed and were produced and consumed at the ordinary household level and/or in burials.

The evidence presented above seems to suggest two patterns:

- Prestige-enhancing objects such as the San Agustín statues and goldwork (often with representations of mythological or supernatural creatures) and the Moundville-Lubbub Creek copper items (often with the falcon, bird-man, or other symbolism), exotic pottery, and incised stone disks appear to be restricted to the regional and local centers.

- Other "wealth items," (used loosely in Blitz's 1993:128 sense in that they are desirable but are not restricted to a specific status or rank) such as obsidian in the San Agustín-Cerro Guacas cases and marine shell, freshwater shell, fineware pottery, and greenstone celts in the Moundville-Lubbub Creek cases were not of restricted access and thus were available at all levels of the settlement hierarchy and, apparently, to all households.

These patterns suggest that chiefs, or the elite of the regional and local centers, wanted to maintain their monopoly on prestige derived from their ability to communicate with the supernatural world and to mediate and negotiate with, and within, the mundane world, on both the intrapolity and interpolity levels. From their participation in the latter sphere, chiefs maintained their access to the esoteric knowledge of the extrapolity realm, at the same time bringing in foreign items that served to reinforce their connection to the exotic and the mysterious (Helms 1979). Chiefs seemed to have exercised little control over more mundane items such as materials for cutting tools, pottery, and beads (essentially kitchen utensils and bangles). Perhaps this did not matter; the real power was rooted in the control of their subjects' spiritual lives.

Acknowledgments. Fieldwork at Cerro Guacas in the Valle de la Plata, Colombia was supported by National Science Foundation Doctoral Dissertation Improvement Grant No. BNS-9007628. Thanks to Dr. Robert D. Drennan for permission to reproduce figure 6.1.

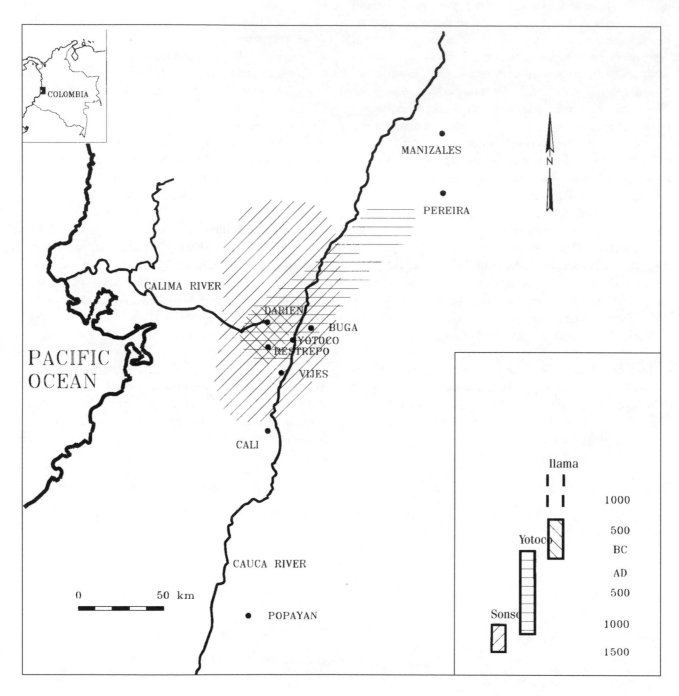

Figure 7.1 General location of the Calima area

7

Pre-Columbian Roads in Calima
A Means of Communication among the Polities of Southwestern Colombia, 500 BC to AD 500

Marianne Cardale Schrimpff

ALTHOUGH GERARDO REICHEL-DOLMATOFF's fieldwork in southwestern Colombia did not match his prodigious output in the northern part of the country he, usually accompanied by his wife Alicia, nevertheless made a number of exceedingly important contributions. These include his excavations in San Agustín during the 1960s and later his interpretative study of the statues found there (Reichel-Dolmatoff 1972a, 1975c), his field work at a La Tolita-Tumaco site on the Mataje River, his monumental survey of the Pacific coast (Reichel-Dolmatoff and Dussan de Reichel 1961, 1962) which enabled him, among other things, to document Tumaco and Tumaco-related sites as far north as the mouth of the San Juan River and, last but not least, his excavations further east in the Guamo area of the Magdalena Valley. At the same time, he carried out pioneering ethnographic fieldwork on the Pacific coast, documenting many aspects of indigenous life that have since disappeared and gaining important insights into the possible significance of certain archaeological materials (Reichel-Dolmatoff 1961a).

To his great regret, a number of the sites he excavated, notably on the Mataje River and those in the Guamo area, were never published in full. The information he obtained from these sites made him realize, more than 30 years ago, that for a period of roughly a thousand years from about 500 BC or earlier, large areas of southwestern Colombia had numerous and highly significant cultural elements in common. It is this period that covers the "golden age" of the Tumaco-La Tolita societies and of the stone carvers and funerary mound builders of San Agustín. It was during this period, too, that the Calima region changed from a society of prosperous and artistic agriculturalists (Ilama) to one whose goldsmiths are deservedly among the most famous in northwest South America (Yotoco).

Initially, in his seminal book *Colombia* published in 1965, he attributed this cultural advancement to successive waves of settlers of Mesoamerican origin who traveled south by boat along the coast and colonized the more favorable areas of the Colombian Pacific lowlands. From there, they gradually moved inland, ascending the rivers that flow down from the Western Cordillera. In his later synthesis of Colombian archaeology (Reichel-Dolmatoff 1986:78-81), he places less emphasis on the Mesoamerican connection and more on links between western Colombia from the north coast to the southern border through the Zambrano-Machalilla tradition.

Although archaeologists do not necessarily agree about either the form or the origins of the elements of unity detectable in the Southwest, few would deny that they exist. As our knowledge of the area increases, so does the list of similarities. Perez de Barradas, as early as 1954, devoted chapter 25 of his book on Calima gold to the many iconographic parallels found on the stone figures of San Agustín, one of the most striking being between the two masked figures represented on statues in San Agustín and the masked figures common on the "pins" or "lime dippers" so characteristic of the Yotoco period in Calima. In the field of metallurgy, Plazas and Falchetti (1985) presented their hypothesis that the Colombian southwest was a single metalworking province that shared several technology and iconography elements and that, at the same time, distinguished the area from the metalworking province of northern Colombia with its ties to Central America.

Communications

The practicalities of these links and communications have, on the whole, received less attention. Reichel-Dolmatoff (1965b:38) pointed out the importance of the coastal route where a light canoe can safely travel through a series of channels in the mangrove swamps from Ecuador as far north as the Bay of Buenaventura without needing to brave the ocean for more than a few brief stretches. It seems likely that there would have also been considerable water traffic on the upper courses of the Magdalena and Cauca Rivers once these entered the broad valleys that characterize much of their course from roughly 2° to 3° north, respectively. All three of these routes follow a north/south axis, and the importance of the Pacific route between 500 BC and AD 500 is amply demonstrated by the distribution of the Tumaco/La Tolita sites registered by Reichel-Dolmatoff (1965b:84) and later by other researchers (Patiño Castaño 1988; Salgado and Stemper 1995).

Of no less significance was the east/west axis, demonstrated, to mention only the tip of the iceberg, by large numbers of Pacific shells, such as *Fasciolaria* conches and *Spondylus* beads, found Calima and the Cauca Valley (Herrera, Cardale de Schrimpff, and Bray 1994:165). Communications across the Central Cordillera are emphasized by the finds of characteristic Yotoco (Calima) gold objects in the valley of the Saldaña River , a tributary of the Magdalena River (Perez de Barradas 1954).

In spite of the inferential evidence for a system of roads or at least of trails, the extent and complexity of this pre-Columbian network comes as something of a surprise, especially when we remember the difficulties the Spaniards encountered once they left the relatively "comfortable" routes of the two main river valleys. To them, Tierradentro was "the land within"—a landlocked region of steep and almost inaccessible mountains. A perusal of contemporary travel diaries reveals that a journey across the Central Cordillera was difficult and hazardous, even at the beginning of the last century. Communications with the Pacific coast also involved considerable hardships, and the route from Cali to the port of Buenaventura was a constant source of complaint from traders and travelers (Eder 1959; Gómez Benitez 1979).

A growing body of information is accumulating on finds that appear to have been trade goods, on roads observed or mapped in the Quindio (Duque Gómez 1965:205–207; Rodríguez 1988:28), and in the La Llanada region of the Western Cordillera (Romoli 1976:30–32; Salgado 1986).[1] Further south along the same mountain range, the roads in the Calima region were first described by Pineda (1945:498), while recently Gähwiler (N.D.) has discovered a well-preserved stretch in the Pavas-La Cumbre region.[2] For the area of San Agustín and La Plata, traces of an important network were published briefly by Moreno (1991 118:120). This network reinforces the observations of Reichel-Dolmatoff (1972a:14) that "another natural advantage the San Agustín region enjoys is the ease of communication by overland trails with many different and more distant geographical districts." It seems more than probable that 2000 or so years ago San Agustín was a sort of cultural bridge linking the populations of the Colombian Massif and steep ranges to the north via the headwaters of the river Caquetá to both the south (Mocoa and Nariño) and southeast with the inhabitants of the tropical forests in the tributaries of the northwest Amazon.[3] At the same time, Tierradentro

may well have enjoyed a central position by no means deserving of the name it currently bears.

Today, these pre-Columbian roads are, in places, as much as 10 m or more wide. Although excavation suggests that this width is partly due to erosion and that the original width was closer to 2 or 3 m, this is considerably more than would be necessary for a casual footpath. Although surprising, the width is not out of line with that of many pre-Columbian road networks reported from other areas of the Americas (Trombold 1991). These roads are particularly prone to erosion becuase, unlike those of the Inka (Hyslop 1984) or of the Tairona in the Sierra Nevada de Santa Marta in northern Colombia (Oyuela-Caycedo 1990), they are not usually stone paved. Much of the southwestern Colombian landscape is covered by a mantle of volcanic ash, and suitable stone is often scarce. Where long stretches of road are still preserved, the observer can hardly fail to be impressed by the straightness of their course, which takes every advantage of the topography. Whenever possible, the roads follow the crest of long natural ridges. Close observation often reveals minor, but equally straight, roads leading off them. Where there is no long ridge leading in the desired direction, the road runs horizontally across a slope. When a descent to cross a stream or a small valley is absolutely unavoidable, the straightness of the route contrasts with the zig-zag routes used by the country people today whose beasts of burden require a smoother gradient. In Calima, at least, it is noteworthy that the pre-Columbian roads reach the streams at points where the banks are high rather than where the valley opens out a little and the stream or river becomes wider and easier to ford. This configuration suggests that the road users crossed the streams on bridges, which would have been less time-consuming than crossing at a ford and, would have enabled travelers to avoid the flash floods that are so common in the Andes. These floods make fords dangerous or impassable for hours and even days.

A Brief History of the Calima Region

Calima is a small area of the Western Cordillera (figure 7.1) centered on the upper course of the river by that name. The area became well known some 50 years ago with the discovery of rich pre-Columbian tombs. At an altitude of about 1500 m (a little under 5000 feet), the relatively gentle rolling landscape, the mild subtropical climate, and the fertile soils make the region ideal for human settlement, and it is hardly surprising to find such settlement documented from the Early Holocene onward. Today, the land is mainly pasture or coffee plantations, complemented by subsistence crops and tropical fruits on the many small holdings. To the east and north in the area where the Calima River rises, the land rises steeply, and forest-clad mountains form an impressive backdrop. Calima has long been considered a natural pass between the Cauca Valley and the Pacific lowlands, and through it today runs the main road from this valley to the Pacific port of Buenaventura.

Archaeological research in the area began 60 years ago with the work of Wassén (1976) and has intensified since the 1970s with the work of the Pro Calima team of archaeologists, persons affiliated with the Instituto Vallecaucano de Investigaciones Científicas (INCIVA), and a number of independent investigators. Although there are still many gaps in the record, a general picture has begun to emerge (see, for instance, Rodríguez 1992; Salgado, Rodriguez, and Bashilov 1993; Herrera et al. 1990; Cardale de Schrimpff et al. 1989; Cardale de Schrimpff et al. 1992). Little is known about subsistence in the preceramic period, although palm fruits appear to have been very important. A characteristic stone tool with nicks for hafting may possibly have been used as a hoe (Salgado 1989; Herrera et al. 1992).

A single date of 2140 ± 90 BC (Beta 16839) for the most recent preceramic occupation at El Pital (Salgado 1989) suggests that pottery came fairly late to the region, but when is not yet clear. Two relatively early dates (Salgado et al. 1993:92) associated with Ilama style pottery remain outliers, but a group of dates from about 700 BC to approximately the start of the Christian Era indicate that, by this period, the Ilama culture was firmly established in the area. These people lived in small settlements on the hillsides, often overlooking a marshy valley where fish and game would have been abundant. Their pottery is characterized by fine-line incision and black-on-red negative painted designs. Both zoomorphic and anthropomorphic vessels are relatively common, and many reflect a complex belief system.

The first century AD was a period of great change in the area when the Ilama society was replaced by that known to archaeologists as "Yotoco." Pottery becomes more varied, and curvilinear polychrome motifs replaced rectilinear designs and fine-line incision. During this period, however, pottery lost much of its importance as a vehicle for representing the society's cosmology—or at least in a form that we can recognize as such. This role was taken over by gold, the Yotoco goldsmiths being among the most skilled in what is now southwestern Colombia. The precise nature of this change is still a matter of debate. There were undoubtedly elements of continuity, but it is interesting to compare the situation in Calima with that at the recently discovered site of Malagana in the Cauca Valley near Cali where the continuity is much more marked.

Still debated is the date and form of the end of the Yotoco period and the beginning of the succeeding Sonso period which survived up to and beyond the time of the Spanish conquest. The changes between the two periods are very marked: the fine polychrome pottery is replaced by simpler forms and clumsier ornamentation; metal items become rare and relatively simple with a high copper content; while perhaps most significant of all, there is no evidence for continuity in belief systems. Some researchers (for example, Bray 1992a:75) believe that the Yotoco culture may have continued, at least in the Calima region, until somewhere about the twelfth century AD. Others (Salgado et al. 1993:104–109; Rodríguez 1992:192) suggest that there was a rather long period of overlap during which Calima was occupied by two separate cultures, Yotoco and Sonso, a situation not, of course, unknown from other parts of the world. The author feels that, if this were the case, there would be clearer evidence for influence and exchange between the two and that many of the later Yotoco radiocarbon dates must have been obtained from charcoal from pre-Columbian agricultural plots or from other contexts where there has been a long history of occupation and where there is a danger that mixing has gone undetected (Cardale de Schrimpff et al. 1989:24–29). With the current information at our disposal and through comparison with similar changes in the San Agustín and Tumaco regions, it seems reasonable to suggest that the Yotoco culture did not last much longer than the fifth or sixth century AD. The situation will undoubtedly become clearer when we have more dates from closed contexts such as tombs or when we have a greater understanding of the internal development of Yotoco and Sonso pottery styles.

Indian roads in the Calima region

It is impossible to visit this area without being impressed by the five majestic roads that plunge down the mountainsides to the once fertile valley of the upper Calima River (now a reservoir), roads which during the past 15 years have been extensively damaged by bulldozers, housing estates, and agricultural activities (figures 7.2, 7.3). The study of the road network in Calima as a whole has become a matter of urgency.

Why so many roads converge on this end of the valley is an unanswered question. It is here that the valley narrows to a gorge down which the river plunges to the Pacific lowlands. The precipitous sides of this gorge would not appear to present an attractive route for the road builders, however, and it has so far proved impossible to locate stretches of road in this area. It seems not impossible that there was once an important site or settlement at this end of the valley, now covered by the waters of the reservoir.

Of these five roads, we have been able to follow one due east, in the direction of the Cauca River, for some 15 km (10 miles) before losing it where it runs down into another, smaller flat valley bottom (Bray et al. 1981). A second road runs southeast, while a third, and possibly a fourth, appear to join a major east-west route that takes advantage of a long natural crest a little further to the south. The fifth leads directly from the western end of the valley due west and at first sight appeared to be the most promising candidate for a direct route to the Pacific. After a little more than a kilometer, it enters a dense

Figure 7.2 Road Madroñal no. 4. One of the five roads that run down to the reservoir now occupying the upper valley of the Calima River. The road crosses a large, artificial platform about halfway up before disappearing into the woods.

coffee plantation, and it has not so far been possible to locate a continuation on the far side. This road is particularly interesting in that, soon after leaving the valley, it climbs to a windy hilltop and passes through the middle of what has been interpreted as a goldsmith's workshop. This workshop was discovered in the 1930s or 1940s, and the deposit was washed to recover the discarded droplets of gold and fragments of wire.[4] It is attractive to think of this workshop as being situated on a route along which the gold was being brought directly from the rich alluvial deposits of the Pacific lowlands.

The search for the route to the Pacific led to a number of difficulties, such as that of the coffee plantation. Sometimes, the trail vanished in dense vegetation or under the plough or bulldozer. Sometimes, a promising route has been so heavily used in recent times that deep ruts make it impossible to tell

whether it was pre-Columbian in origin, while at other times the presence of the guerrilla or other disruptive elements made it unwise to follow further. What did become clear was that, in this area at least, there are not just one or two main roads but an impressive network of interconnecting routes. Aerial reconnaissance reveals two promising natural routes (one on either side of the modern main highway) to the upper Dagua River, which has traditionally been a favored route to the Pacific. Hopefully, some of these possibilities may be explored in the future. It seems probable that these routes eventually linked up with stretches of road from the Pacific slopes, as reported by Salgado and Stemper (1995:36–45), particularly that from the middle course of the Dagua River.

In the opposite direction, we have been able to document at least one of the principal routes that led from the Calima

Figure 7.3 Part of the road that runs from the Cordillera to the Cauca Valley. Here it can be seen near the eastern edge of the uplands, crossing a landscape of pre-Columbian field lines.

uplands to the Cauca Valley some 500 m (1500 feet) below, taking advantages of natural ridges and of a point where an arm of the flat valley bottom runs west into the mountains, providing unusually comfortable walking conditions. This route has so many natural advantages that it was one of the main points of entry for settlers moving down from Antioquia in the north during the early years of this century, and it was necessary to confirm its pre-Columbian origins by excavation.

Dating the roads is not an easy task, but the fact that, on all the stretches excavated (a total of four cuts), there are sherds of the Yotoco period in the primary silt leaves little doubt that the roads were in use during the early centuries of the first millennium AD. In two cases, the roads turn out to run through a landscape of the Ilama period, which suggests that, in some cases at least, they may date from the final half of the last millennium BC. There appears to be no mention of them in early colonial documents, and some of them at least were abandoned in pre-Columbian times, such as the stretch at Rancho Grande which was later cut by field lines. While such lines were in use during the final pre-Columbian period, Sonso, they first appear in the earlier Yotoco period, so they do not in themselves provide a precise date. At one of the points excavated (Hacienda La Mesa), the road was covered over with slope-wash from above that contained abundant sherds of the Sonso period. Because the slope above was covered with grass and probably trees until recently, it seems likely that the slope-wash accumulated during the Sonso period and that by this time

travelers and other trail users made do with a narrow path at the edge of the original road.

When walking the roads, it becomes clear that every possible step was taken to make traveling as swift and easy as possible. This extends beyond the optimal layout—surely the work of "engineers"—the straightness and the bridges. Where the road crosses a slope horizontally, the route was built up to extend the flat area and ensure that the road was sufficiently wide. Where it must cross a small depression where water may build up in the rainy season and boggy conditions result, a causeway was constructed, as was the case where the natural terrain dips, forming a small irregularity which, nevertheless, would have taken precious seconds to negotiate.

To conclude, we must ask ourselves what these roads can tell us about the societies that laid out and used them.

First, we will consider one of these societies that was linked by this road system, in this case Calima. The differences between these pre-Columbian roads and the winding, modern trails that turn aside here for a fallen log and make a considerable detour to avoid a house or skirt a field boundary is so marked that one cannot avoid the conclusion that the layout of the ancient roads was in the hands of engineers. He or she would surely have been either a secular or religious figure in authority, perhaps a shaman with engineering skills, who would have enjoyed sufficient powers of persuasion or of compulsion to allow him to direct the public works necessary for constructing and maintaining bridges, embankments, and so forth. The straightness invites comparison with Roman or

Inka roads, both laid out by invading armies in conquered territory where "social" obstacles, such as houses or field boundaries, could be ignored because their subjugated owners had lost the right to protest.

There is no evidence, however, that these roads were conquest roads. Perhaps we should think rather in terms of a different social or political system in which the property rights of the individual were voluntarily ceded for the public good. Or perhaps, as in many indigenous societies today, the land belonged to the community as a whole, with an individual and his family granted the right to use it during his lifetime or as the necessity arose. A careful study of what remains of the road network should provide a key to the whole social landscape of the area. Logic suggests that the most important roads must have linked the most important settlements, and so with time and determination, it should be possible to reconstruct a map of these centers.

Second, we must consider what these roads can tell us about the southwest as a whole at that time. Because, as we have mentioned above, there is no evidence for imperial expansion but rather for coexisting polities, it seems reasonable to conclude that the roads were constructed to facilitate communications between them. Societies of roughly equal strength (as opposed to empires in expansion) that find themselves at war tend to close roads, not improve them. Furthermore, the construction and layout of these roads are such that these communications would probably have surprised us with their swiftness.

Until recently when the river was less contaminated, it was common for people living in the Calima uplands to walk down the Indian road to the Cauca for a day's fishing, returning the same evening. It seems not unlikely that a journey from Calima to, for instance, San Agustín could have been accomplished in a matter of a few days. Not only would the journeys have been swift, they must surely also have been frequent for it to have been worthwhile to maintain roads of this size.

The roads appear to reflect a very strong desire for close links and communications in the southwest at that time. These links were almost certainly not restricted to trade in the purely commercial sense of the term. They would have probably included visits between, for instance, chiefs and shamans, or perhaps between goldsmiths and other specialists in search of an interchange of both sacred and secular knowledge, somewhat in the way described by Helms (1979) for the chiefdoms of Panama at the time of the Spanish conquest.

Acknowledgments. During the past year, I received a grant from the Colombian Institute of Culture to study pre-Columbian roads in the Calima region as part of the Pro Calima project for research on the pre-Columbian history of this area which Warwick Bray, Leonor Herrera, and I have worked on for the last 15 years. For financial support, I am extremely grateful to COLCULTURA for the grant under their program "Fransisco Paula de Santander" as well as to the Foundation Pro Calima that supplemented these funds and helped finance occasional road research during the last 15 years. Much of the material in this chapter was collected in the company of Pro Calima colleagues Bray and Herrera, and the latter read and commented on a draft of this chapter. The study would have met with little success had it not been for the kindness and enthusiasm of many in the Calima region, especially landowners who cheerfully agreed to their pastures being trampled over or trenches dug across their "tracks." A number of people walked different stretches of roads with me; particular thanks go to Bernardo Rendon whose endurance and enthusiasm was proof against all weather.

Notes

1. Roads and routes in the Colonial period is a fascinating subject, as is the information found in sources such as the early Spanish chroniclers concerning the routes in use at the time of the Conquest. There is no time to cover these aspects in a short article, but useful information can be found in the publications of, for instance, Duque Gomez (1945), Trimborn (1949), Wassén (1955), and Pineda (1991).

2. These roads were not, of course, restricted to the southwestern part of the country. The best preserved and probably the most impressive network is the stone-paved roads of the Sierra Nevada de Santa Marta on the North Coast (Oyuela 1990). In Antioquia, a number of well-preserved stretches are being investigated by Castillo, and by Botero and Velez.

3. A number of writers (Preuss 1931:162; Duque 1967:318; Reichel-Dolmatoff 1972a) emphasize features in the stone sculptures of San Agustín that appear to reflect themes prominent in the cosmology of contemporary indigenous groups in the northwest Amazon region, particularly the Múrui-muinane or Witoto. Unfortunately, their approach has been hampered by the fact that, among these contemporary groups, the themes are now only partly remembered (Yepes 1982), while the prehistory of this vast region is still poorly understood.

4. This information was given to us by Don Bernardo Rendon, whose father and uncles had worked the site.

⫷8⫸

Cupica (Chocó)
A Reassessment of Gerardo Reichel-Dolmatoff's Fieldwork in a Poorly Studied Region of the American Tropics

Richard Cooke

T HE FRONTIER REGION between Panama and Colombia was, at contact, occupied by scattered, but in places quite large, agricultural villages that were closely linked culturally and commercially (Bray 1984:305–308). Described in detail by early sixteenth-century Spanish chroniclers (for example, Cieza de León 1956; Martyr 1912; Oviedo y Veldes 1849-53), some sections of this population, such as the Cueva of early Colonial Darién, are considered by many researchers to be archetypal of Intermediate Area chiefdoms before the Spanish conquest and of drastic deculturation after it (see Helms 1976, 1979, 1981; Romoli 1987; Sauer 1966; Steward and Faron 1959). The territory occupied by the Cueva is indicated in figure 8.1 (after Romoli 1987).

The Spanish quickly abandoned settlements at Santa María la Antigua and Acla in favor of Panama Viejo on the Pacific side. The regenerated forests of the Darién Gap became havens for small groups of Native Americans who survived the violent confrontations, sociopolitical dislocation, and obligatory subsistence reorientation caused by contact with the Spanish (Cooke et al. 1996; Piperno 1994a). Their modern descendants, the Kuna, Waunaan, and Eperã, continued to oppose European and neo-African encroachment and still retain a considerable degree of political and cultural independence (Isacsson 1981; Vargas 1990, 1993).

Current knowledge of the pre-Columbian archaeology of this region does not do justice to its importance in understanding local and regional histories of cultural development (Bray 1984; Isacsson 1975). During the last 15 years or so, several Colombian projects within and bordering the Darién Gap have provided welcome information about site distribution and function, subsistence, environmental history, and material culture (for example, Bouchard 1982; Cardale de Schrimpff et al. 1992; Castillo 1988; Patiño 1988; Rodríguez 1992; Salgado 1986; Salgado et al. 1993; Santos 1989). A flurry of interest in the Bayano valley in Panama in the early 1970s produced con-

textual information (Cooke 1976a). But, in general, Darién Gap archaeology has been exploratory, largely nonstratigraphic, and geographically disjunct—a far cry from the multidisciplinary, multiseason regional projects that are required objectively to evaluate Spanish colonial observations about contact period social organization and cultural geography.

Cupica, on the Pacific coast of the Department of Chocó, Colombia, is one of the few stratified sites that has been reported in detail (figure 8.1). Here, Gerardo and Alicia Reichel-Dolmatoff (henceforth, the Reichels) conducted excavations in 1961 as part of an international research program entitled "Interrelationships of New World Cultures," sponsored by the Inter-Andean Research Foundation and financed by the National Science Foundation (Reichel-Dolmatoff and Dussán de Reichel 1961).

In spite of the paucity of comparative material from adjacent regions, it was clear to the Reichels that Cupica ceramics bore resemblances closer to materials from Panama and the Atrato and Sinú drainages than to culture areas further south, such as Tumaco-Tolita or Calima. Much more recently, Bray proposed that the entire Pacific coast of the Panama Bight from Chame (Panama) to Cupica (figure 8.1) be considered a "significant culture area in its own right and...not...a mere buffer zone between the high chiefdoms of Coclé (Central Panama) and Colombia"(1984:331). He suggested that maritime trade, in which the Pearl Islands on the Pacific and the Gulf of Urabá on the Atlantic played important entrepôt roles, was the motor behind "continuous and vigorous contact" among native polities.[1]

The Cupica Site
Geography
The pre-Columbian site of Cupica is located in the high tidal zone of a small mangrove estuary at the northern edge of

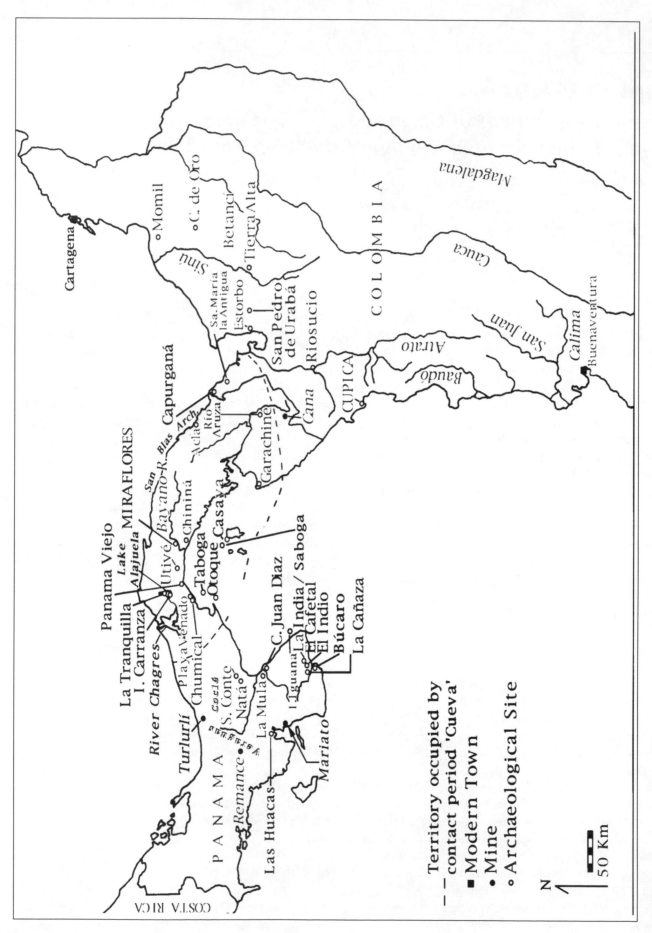

Figure 8.1 Map of Panama and northwest Colombia showing location of Cupica and Miraflores in relation to other archaeological sites and major geographical features

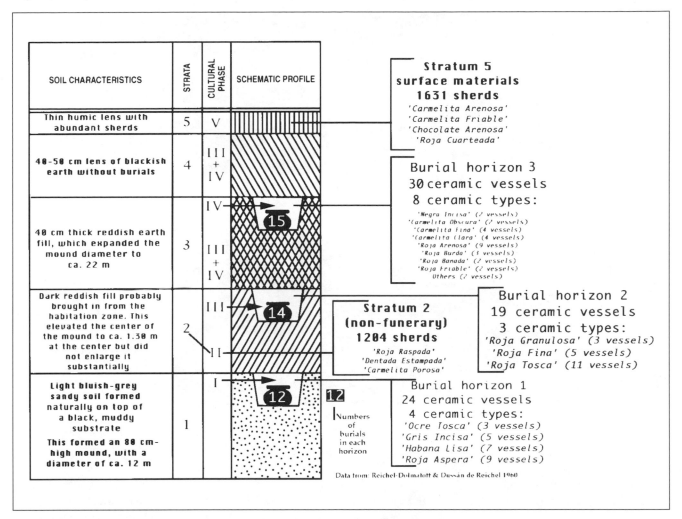

SOIL CHARACTERISTICS	STRATA	CULTURAL PHASE	SCHEMATIC PROFILE
Thin humic lens with abundant sherds	5	V	
40-50 cm lens of blackish earth without burials	4	III + IV	
40 cm thick reddish earth fill, which expanded the mound diameter to ca. 22 m	3	IV, III + IV	
Dark reddish fill probably brought in from the habitation zone. This elevated the center of the mound to ca. 1.30 m at the center but did not enlarge it substantially	2	III, II	
Light bluish-grey sandy soil formed naturally on top of a black, muddy substrate. This formed an 80 cm-high mound, with a diameter of ca. 12 m	1	I	

Stratum 5
surface materials
1631 sherds
'Carmelita Arenosa'
'Carmelita Friable'
'Chocolate Arenosa'
'Roja Cuarteada'

Burial horizon 3
30 ceramic vessels
8 ceramic types:
'Negra Incisa' (2 vessels)
'Carmelita Obscura' (2 vessels)
'Carmelita Fina' (4 vessels)
'Carmelita Clara' (4 vessels)
'Roja Arenosa' (9 vessels)
'Roja Burda' (3 vessels)
'Roja Banada' (2 vessels)
'Roja Friable' (2 vessels)
Others (2 vessels)

Burial horizon 2
19 ceramic vessels
3 ceramic types:
'Roja Granulosa' (3 vessels)
'Roja Fina' (5 vessels)
'Roja Tosca' (11 vessels)

Stratum 2
(non-funerary)
1204 sherds
'Roja Raspada'
'Dentada Estampada'
'Carmelita Porosa'

Burial horizon 1
24 ceramic vessels
4 ceramic types:
'Ocre Tosca' (3 vessels)
'Gris Incisa' (5 vessels)
'Habana Lisa' (7 vessels)
'Roja Aspera' (9 vessels)

Numbers of burials in each horizon

Data from: Reichel-Dolmatoff & Dussán de Reichel 1960

Figure 8.2 Schematic diagram of the stratigraphy of the Cupica burial mound, summarizing the ceramic types found in funerary and non-funerary deposits

Cupica Bay, a 30-km-long indentation on the Pacific coast of the Department of Chocó 75 km from the Panamanian frontier (figure 8.1). It is about 4 km northeast of the township of Cupica, a late eighteenth-century foundation (West 1957:103). The Reichels identified habitation and mortuary zones, the former consisting of a shallow (200 x 100 m) accumulation of sherds and stone tools, and the latter, a low sandy mound that abutted the main estuary channel. They proposed that substantial changes in coastal geomorphology had occurred since the pre-Columbian occupation but were unsure of the causes. (West [1957:16] suggested that the Cupica region shows evidence of recent uplift but does not indicate how recent.)

The Colombian coast at this point is steep, humid, and largely forested, but it is not as inhospitable and marginal as Reichel-Dolmatoff and Dussán de Reichel (1961:242–43) imply. According to West (1957:27, 153), annual rainfall is nearer 4,000 mm than 6,000 to 10,000 mm, while the sandy alkaline soils of the narrow coastal plain provide "optimum edaphic conditions" for modern citrus farms.

Linné's excavations

In 1927, Swedish archaeologist Linné visited Cupica where he conducted excavations at a burial ground he called La Resaca. Cupica had washed into the sea by 1961 but was, according to one of the Reichels' informants, about 500 m southeast of the burial mound.

Linné recorded 27 subrectangular graves, but his photographs (1929:Figure 52) suggest that his field procedures may not have been appropriate for defining features in humid tropical soils (the Reichels [Reichel-Dolmatoff and Dussán de Reichel 1961:307] were skeptical of his grave floor plans). He recovered approximately sixty pottery vessels and two spindle whorls, one of which is similar to figure 8.5m. One of his graves (L [= Linné] 18) contained a cache of six celts, a granulated clay ball, quartz crystals, two polishing stones, and a gold ornament, which subsequent compositional analysis showed to contain platinum. Linné (1929:186) speculated that the person buried there was a chief or a celt worker who had bartered his produce for the gold trinket, perhaps used originally to adorn a ceramic figurine. A short distance inland, Linné visited an 800-m-long ridge with approximately one hundred mostly looted burials (El Cementerio, called Loma de Balboa by the Reichels [Reichel-Dolmatoff and Dussán de Reichel

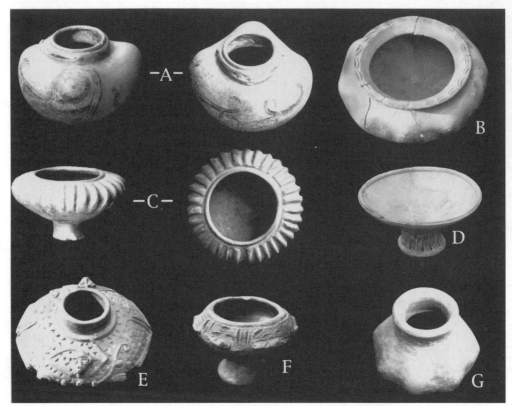

Figure 8.3 Ceramic vessels from Cupica, Department of Chocó, Colombia. phase IV (vessel numbers and typology refer to G. and A. Reichel-Dolmatoff's [1961] catalog): *a*, vessel 71, Roja Bañada (height: 10.4 cm, width: 15.8 cm); *b*, vessel 16, atypical (height: 12.2 cm, width: 21 cm); *c*, vessel 42, Negra Incisa (height: 6.6 cm, width: 13 cm); *d*, vessel 17, Carmelita Fina (height: 17.6 cm, diam. plate: 31.6 cm) *e*, vessel 53, Carmelita Fina (height: 17 cm, width: 25.4 cm); *f*, vessel 47, Negra Incisa (height: 10 cm, diam: 17 cm); *g*, vessel 41, Carmelita Fina (height: 11 cm, width: 15.4 cm). *Photograph by Richard Cooke*

1961:308]). Here, he excavated an intact grave with a 3.5-m vertical shaft and a 2.5-m horizontal side chamber.

The Reichels' excavations

The Reichels excavated only in the burial mound. Hounded by constant rain showers and daily tides that swamped the site, they opted to dig 2 x 6 m trenches with intervening walls, most of which were eliminated as work proceeded. They left three long profiles, however, for stratigraphic control. Because they were unable to expose large areas of the site at any one time, they were concerned that they may not have identified the inception of every grave feature. Nevertheless, they were confident that their five strata, three burial horizons, and five cultural phases formed a coherent sequence (figure 8.2).

The Reichels excavated forty-one graves dug into the underlying strata (figure 8.2). These were cylindrical pits about 1 m in diameter, and most of them less than 0.5 m deep. None contained human bone. Ceramics were the only burial goods found in all but five of the graves, which contained between two and five whole or broken vessels. Non-ceramic artifacts consisted of one gold object, spindle whorls, and a few stone tools and raw materials.[2]

Ceramic Typology and Periodization

The Reichels' ceramic typology highlighted surface treatment and temper qualities. They established five ceramic phases, three defined exclusively from mortuary vessels (phases I, III, and IV) and two from sherd samples (phases II and V; Reichel-

Dolmatoff and Dussán de Reichel 1961:Figure 6; figure 8.2).

A charcoal sample recovered at 0.76 m below the surface in stratum 2 (which coincides with Cupica phase II) returned a radiocarbon date of 735 ± 100 BP (AD 1215; M-1313; Reichel-Dolmatoff 1963). This calibrates at 1 sigma to cal AD 1285 (1326, 1353, 1361, 1367, 1389) 1419 (Stuiver and Becker 1993:35-65). Bray (1984:330) rejected it as too recent and "out of line with the rest of the stratigraphic evidence." It does not agree with my reevaluation of the data either.

Table 1 of the Cupica report (Reichel-Dolmatoff and Dussán de Reichel 1961) shows a mutually exclusive relationship between ceramic types and grave periodization. In spite of this, the Reichels were convinced that they were describing the diachronic transformation of a single local pottery tradition. (They considered only two vessels to be atypical, one of which is illustrated in figure 8.3b). For this reason, they believed that the typological differences between each mortuary horizon (Cupica phases I, III, and IV) were the result of hiatuses between burial episodes.

Cupica Sequence and External Connections
Interpretations by Linné and the Reichels

Linné (1929:184, 195) believed that the pottery from La Resaca and El Cementerio was broadly comparable to materials he had found elsewhere while on his Pacific coast cruise, but he assumed that these two localities represented different time periods. The Reichels proposed that the La Resaca pottery correlated with their own Cupica III and Cupica IV phases,

Figure 8.4 Ceramic vessels from Cupica *(a-h)* and Chinina, Darién, Panamá *(i)*: *a*, vessel 13, Gris Incisa (height: 5.2 cm, diam: 17 cm); phase I. *b*, vessel Carmelita Obscura (height: 13.7 cm, width: 17.7 cm); phase IV. *c*, vessel 15, Gris Incisa (height: 16 cm, diam: 17 cm); phase I. *d*, vessel 5, Gris Incisa (height: 12.8 cm, width: 20 cm); phase I. *e*, vessel 14, Gris Incisa (height: 11.5 cm, diam: 18 cm); phase I. *f*, vessel 49, Roja Fina (height: 18 cm, width: 13.8 cm); phase III. *g*, vessel 60, Roja Tosca. phase III. *h*, vessel 11, Roja Tosca. phase III. *i*, Chinina, Darién, Panamá. *Photograph by Richard Cooke*

drawing particular attention to two decorative modes:

- Circumferential triangular punctated zones enclosed within incised lines on collared jar exteriors (figure 8.4g, h)

- Outflaring pedestals with excised decoration (figure 8.3d)

They considered that the El Cementerio materials were dissimilar to those of Cupica phases III and IV, basing their opinion on differential pottery manufacturing techniques. They observed that coiling was the only technique present in the Cupica burial mound and Linné's La Resaca cemetery, while surface sherds collected by Oppenheim (Recasens and Oppenheim 1945) at El Cementerio were made by modeling, a technique modern Eperã women use.

Having recently completed excavations at Momil and Ciénaga de Oro in the Sinú drainage, it is not surprising that the Reichels should have seen modal similarities between the pottery from those sites and the Cupica phase I and II materials. They also noted a stylistic connection with Tierra Alta (equivalent to Cupica phase III) and Betancí (equivalent to Cupica phase IV). In translation of their own words:

Cupica and Sinú are considered to be culturally interrelated and approximately synchronous. This makes sense because the Sinú river basin is quite close to the Cupica region, especially if we bear in mind that the Atrato river and its tributary, the Napipí, offer an easy avenue of communication between the two." (Reichel-Dolmatoff and Dussán de Reichel 1961:310)

The Reichels were disillusioned that so few data were then available for eastern Panama (the Darién sector of the Interrelationships project [MacGimsey 1964] was never adequately published). Some of their cross-cultural comparisons (that is, with early first millennium BC material from La Mula-Sarigua in Panama's Central Region [Willey and McGimsey 1954]) are no longer viable in the light of current chronologies (Cooke 1995). Still plausible, however, is their attribution of four vessel types, all from the Cupica phase IV, to "Panamanian developments": a polychrome humpback effigy (figure 8.3a), gourd effigies (figure 8.4c, g), a beveled pedestal vessel with incised decoration (figure 8.3f), and plates whose pedestals are decorated with excised triangular zones (figure 8.3d). Although the Reichels included the humpback effigy, along with an eroded vessel, in a "local" type (Cupica Roja Bañada), they state in another section of their paper that

…these two pieces…are not similar to any of the established types. The differences are above all in the color and the composition of the paste, surface treatment and shape.

In a later publication, Gerardo Reichel-Dolmatoff (1986:100) reaffirmed the Cupica-Panama connection, emphasizing the "sophistication" of the Cupica ceramics over the "crudity" of pottery found south of the San Juan river.

Figure 8.5 Incised and modeled sherds, pottery stamp, spindle whorls, and gold artifact from Cupica, Colombia and Miraflores, Panama: *a*, Cupica, vessel 45, Roja Aspera; *b*, Miraflores, fill, tomb 2; *c*, Miraflores, fill, tomb 2; *d*, Miraflores, tomb fill; *e*, Cupica, Roja Fina, phase III; *f*, Miraflores, tomb fill; *g*, Cupica, Roja Fina, phase III; *h*, Miraflores, tomb fill; *i*, pottery stamp, Miraflores, tomb 2; *j*, Miraflores, tomb fill; *k*, Isla Carranza, Lake Alajuela or Madden, Panama. Associated with a ^{14}C date of 2020 ± 155 BP (cal BC 201 [36,34,18,13, cal AD 1] cal AD 132); *l*, incised spindle whorl, Miraflores, confiscated from looters; *m*, incised red-painted spindle whorl, Cupica, surface. See G. and A. Reichel-Dolmatoff 1961: Figure 16, 10; *n*, gold nose-ring, Miraflores, tomb 2, floor. *Photograph by Richard Cooke*

Bray's reinterpretation

In Bray's (1984:330) opinion, Cupica phase I vessels, "although within the usual Darién repertoire," could "be compared in a general way with those of Momil and Ciénaga de Oro." Incised Relief Ware sherds (figure 8.5a, c; Biese 1964) found "in the same deposit" were "identical to those from Panamá Viejo and [Playa Venado], Utivé, the Pearl Islands (for example, Linné 1929:Figure 21), Miraflores (CHO-3), and several other sites in the Pacific lowlands of eastern Panama." Like the Reichels, Bray noted correspondences between Cupica phase III, and Tierra Alta (Alto Sinú) and Estorbo (Gulf of Urabá). He also suggested that Cupica phase IV burials contained "imported Macaracas Polychromes from Coclé, alongside local wares with deeply carved designs allied to those of Betancí,

the most recent phase in the Sinú" (for example, figure 8.3e). Bray concluded:

> In Panamanian terms the Cupica pottery styles come out in their right relative order and also correlate quite correctly with the styles of Urabá and of Caribbean Colombia right across to Cartagena. All along the Pacific coast there was continuous and vigorous contact for some 900 years. The presence of just about every important trade ware in the Pearl Islands, together with Coclé goldwork, suggests that much of this traffic was by sea...Darién was probably the intermediary by which Colombian metallurgy reached central Panama. (1984:331)

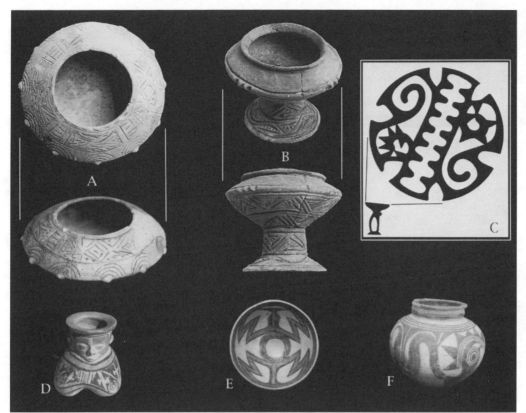

Figure 8.6 Pottery from Miraflores (Bayano River), Venado Beach, and the Azuero Peninsula, Panama: *a*, Miraflores, confiscated from looters (diam: 13.2 cm) *b*, Miraflores, tomb 1, (height: 11 cm, width: 13.5 cm); *c*, Miraflores, tomb 2, interior design of vessel illustrated in figure 8.8b (black on red); *d*, human effigy vessel, Venado Beach, in Museum of the American Indian, Cubitá style; *e*, Black on Red plate, Ciruelo-Black-on-Red type, Cubitá style, Azuero Peninsula; *f*, Black on Buff jar, Cubitá style, Azuero Peninsula

A Reconsideration of Cupica's Chronology and External Connection

Miraflores, River Bayano, Panama

In 1973, I excavated three tombs at Miraflores (CHO-3), a large settlement in the Bayano flood plain 320 km across the Panama Bight (figure 8.1) from Cupica. Published only in Spanish with poor illustrations (Cooke 1976a), this site is understandably little referenced outside Panama. Two tombs, dated radiometrically, contained pottery categories that also occur at Cupica. Hence, they are useful for cross-dating the Reichels' Cupica sequence, and they provide data appropriate for reassessing the nature and scope of this site's external connections. The Miraflores tombs were cut through bedrock to a depth of about 2m (figure 8.7). They are quite complex, with interior niches, steps, and (in tomb 1) postholes in the floor (for suspending the dead in a hammock?). One hundred pottery vessels were recovered from the tombs. Two wood charcoal samples, trowelled off the floors of tombs 1 and 2 and sent immediately to Teledyne, returned dates of 1185 BP ± 80 [cal AD 734 (785, 786, 877) 981] for tomb 2, and 2) 1135 BP ± 80 [cal AD 781 (898-976) 997] for tomb 1 calibration (see Stuiver and Becker 1993).

Most Miraflores vessels are well-finished red-painted and plain wares with moderate to good firing control. Their physical properties recall those of the Reichels' Cupica red and plain ware types (for example, Roja Fina, Roja Arenosa, Carmelita Clara, and Carmelita Fina). Stylistically, however, I believe that the Miraflores and Cupica samples are sufficiently dissimilar

to suggest manufacture by local artisans in obeisance to local tastes. The rectangular stamp with a perforated handle (figure 8.5i), and a few vessel shapes found at Miraflores have not been reported elsewhere in Panama, nor, as far as I know, at Colombian sites (for example, subrectangular trays, some with rocker feet [figure 8.8e, f] and a striking human face effigy [figure 8.8c]).

Unpublished sherd collections in the Anthropology Museum in Panama City and Linné's report (1929) show that other Miraflores pottery modes occur at rudimentarily studied sites on the Pacific littoral of Panama province, in the Darién, and on the Pearl Islands. They include:

- Double vessels (one of which is zoomorphic) conjoined with a straight and a looped bridge (figure 8.8d),

- Plates with elongated pedestals modeled like realistic animals (figure 8.8b),

- Round-bodied jars with almost vertical handles joined to the collar rim (figure 8.8g),

- Flat-bottomed bottles with sharply angled shoulders and sometimes slanting mouths (figure 8.8h),

- Globular bottles with necks shaped like house roofs (figure 8.8i),

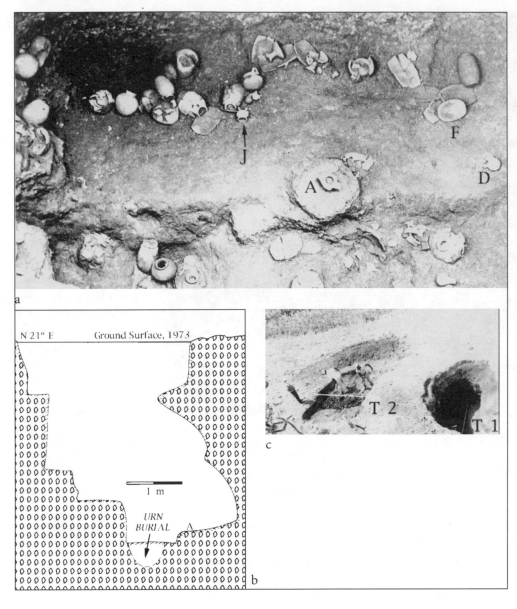

Figure 8.7 Burial features at Miraflores, Bayano River, Panama: *a*, Miraflores, floor of tomb 2, March 1973; Letters refer to vessels illustrated in figure 8.8.); *b*, Miraflores, profile of tomb 2 (A: position of vessel illustrated in figure 8.8a); *c*, Miraflores, excavation of tombs 1 and 2, March 1973. *Photographs and drawing by Jacinto Almendra*

- Small collared jars with tripod feet (figure 8.8j),

- Globular bottles with a strongly grooved neck (for suspending with a string?; figure 8.8k; see also Linné 1929: figure 31e,k),

- Globular jars with short necks and flattened bases (figure 8.8l),

- Globular vessels with necks shaped like parrots (figure 8.8a),

- Effigies of psittacid birds (figure 8.8m).

There are also several painted and incised pottery modes, including spindle whorls, which Miraflores and Cupica shared. For example:

- Strongly beveled pedestal vessels with elaborate, deeply incised decorations, probably always filled with calcium carbonate (see figure 8.3f, Cupica, with figure 8.5a, b, Miraflores)

- Triangular punctated zones enclosed within incised lines (figure 8.4g, h, Cupica, with figure 8.5j, Miraflores)[3]

- Jars (some double spouted [for example, figure 8.4f]) and decorated on the exterior with a rectilinear design consisting of combinations of fine linear incisions and punctations (figure 8.5e g, Cupica [Cupica Roja Fina]), with figure 8.5d, h, Miraflores)

- Incised Relief Ware (figure 8.5a, Cupica, with figure 8.5c, Miraflores)[4]

- Modeled bird heads at the juncture of a vessel body and

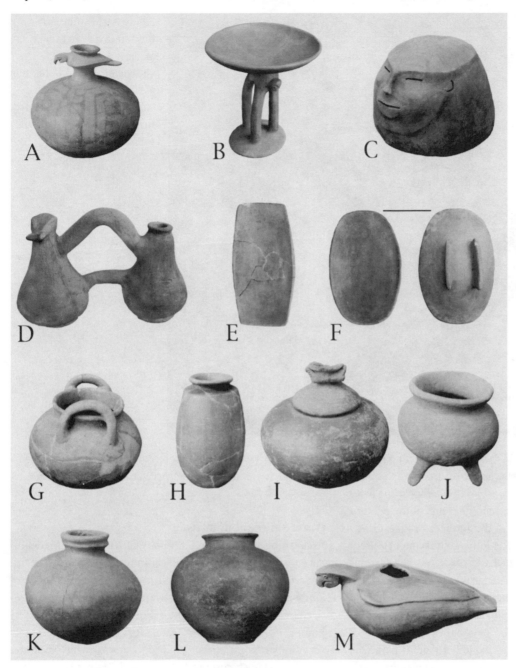

Figure 8.8 Pottery vessels from Miraflores, Bayano River, Panama. *a*, tomb 2, floor (see figure 8.7), (height: 30.5 cm, width: 30.3 cm); *b*, surface find, (height: 44 cm, diam: 39 cm); *c*, tomb 1, (height: 19 cm, max width: 28 cm); *d*, tomb 2 (see figure 8.7), (height: 19 cm); *e*, tomb 2, length: 21.6 cm; *f*, tomb 2 (see figure 8.7), length: 24.4 cm; *g*, tomb 2, (height: 11.9 cm, width: 11.8 cm); *h*, tomb 2, (height: 18 cm, width: 11.2 cm); *i*, private collection; *j*, tomb 2, floor (see figure 8.7), (height: 8.1 cm, width: 7.5 cm); *k*, surface find, width: 12.1 cm; *l*, tomb 2, (height: 14 cm, width: 15 cm); *m*, confiscated from looters. *Photograph by Richard Cooke*

neck (figure 8.5b, Miraflores, with a vessel from grave L7 at La Resaca [Linné 1929:Figures 50e, 52d; see also Recasens and Oppenheim 1945: Plates 1, 2])

- Polychrome pottery that incorporates purple paint (figure 8.3a, Cupica, with figure 8.9, Miraflores)

- Spindle whorls with radiating incised decoration at the waist (figure 8.5m, Cupica, with figure 8.5l, Miraflores [see also Linné 1929:Figure 51h; Recasens and Oppenheim 1945: Plates 2, 4])[5]

There are sound stylistic reasons for believing that the Cupica polychrome humpback (illustrated also in Reichel-

Dolmatoff 1986:Figure 56; Herrera 1989:137) is contemporaneous with the Macaracas painted pottery style of Panama's Central Region (for example, Lothrop 1942:Figure 601). Although Bray (1984:330) believed that this vessel was brought to the site from Coclé (figure 8.1), I believe that its paste and surface finish are more similar to those of other humpback effigies recorded from the eastern half of Panama Bay (see Biese 1964: Plate 15b) than to examples found in Coclé and the Azuero Peninsula sites.[6]

On the other hand, the Macaracas style polychrome sherds found in the tomb fills at Miraflores—and, hence, either contemporary with or earlier than the graves—exhibit surface finish, color balance, and pastes that are indistinguishable from those of Parita Bay material (figure 8.9a is a fragment of a ham-

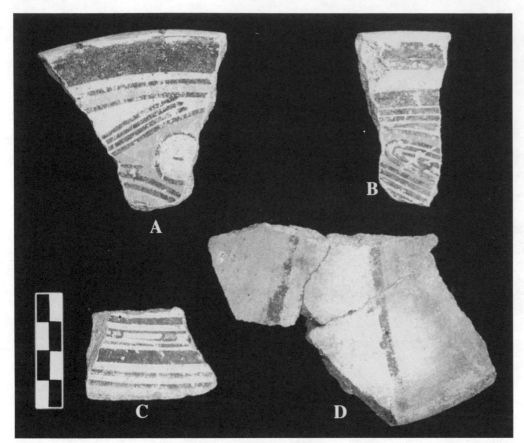

Figure 8.9 Miraflores,
Bayano River, Panama.
Macaracas style poly-
chrome sherds from the fills
of tombs 1 and 2. Scale in
cm. *Photograph by Richard
Cooke*

merhead shark motif; see Labbé 1995: Frontispiece). They are likely to be genuine imports, and are, in fact, the only Macaracas style material that has associated radiocarbon dates from anywhere in Panama (the 1 sigma range of the relevant samples is cal AD 735–1000, and the intercept range, cal AD 785–975). In Panama's Central Region, the subsequent pottery style, called Parita (Cooke 1995; Ladd 1964), has been associated with dates whose intercept range is cal AD 1030–1275. On the basis of these and other data currently under analysis, I estimate a timespan of cal AD 750-1000 for the Macaracas pottery style.

As Bray (1984) points out, Incised Relief Ware (figure 8.5a, c; Biese 1964) is widespread in Panama in the area occupied by the contact period Cueva, both on the Atlantic and Pacific watersheds (Drolet 1980). It is decorated with bas relief animal designs and embellished with incisions and marine bivalve edge-stamping (generally *Anadara* spp). Vessels usually have red surfaces (in Panama, the red slip is fugitive, which is probably why it is usually described as "brown ware"). Although Incised Relief Ware has not been found in radiocarbon dated contexts,[7] several whole vessels at Playa Venado and Panama Viejo were associated with painted pottery, which clearly belongs to the recently described Cubitá style from central Panama (Sánchez Herrera 1995; see also Biese 1964: Frontispiece; Labbé 1995:Figure 16). At Cerro Juan Díaz, Cubitá vessels and sherds have been associated with ten radiocarbon dates whose 1 sigma range is cal AD 415–860 and intercept

range is AD 435–755.[8] Therefore, I believe that Incised Relief Ware was manufactured no earlier than cal AD 400 and no later than cal AD 750.

Other Colombian sites

Archaeologists from the University of Antioquia (Medellín) have worked hard to establish ceramic sequences and define settlement patterns on the northwestern Atlantic coast of Colombia from the Sinú river westward to the Panamanian frontier. Surface-collected materials from surveys conducted by Linné (1929), Higgins (1986), and Horton (1979) suggest that very similar ceramics were made during late prehistoric times (AD 900–Spanish conquest) along the Panamanian San Blas coast to the vicinity of Acla (contact period Careta, a Cuevan chiefdom).

At Capurganá at the western edge of the Gulf of Urabá, Bedoya and Naranjo (1985) identified two ceramic phases, the earlier of which (Capurganá phase I) contained plastically decorated sherds mixed in with others painted with black, white, and red. Santos Vecino (1989:45) and Groot de Mahecha (1989:27) relate this material to Momil; it has not been dated radiometrically. In my opinion, some of the incised modes are significantly similar to those present in sherd samples from the three Panamanian sites of Isla Carranza (Lake Alajuela), Búcaro (Azuero Peninsula), and La Mula-Sarigua (Parita Bay; Cooke and Ranere 1992b:Figure 8; Ichon 1980:Figure 11; see also Stirling and Stirling 1964 [Taboguilla-1]). These sherds

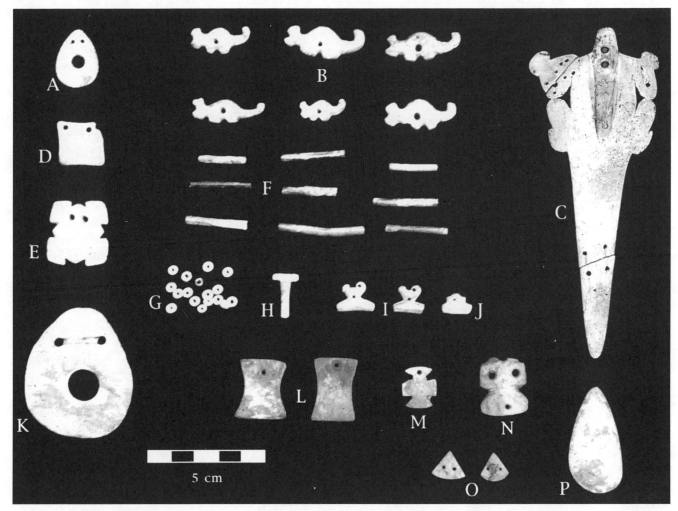

Figure 8.10 Shell jewelry, Cerro Juan Díaz, Los Santos, Panamá: *a,b,d-k*, feature 16, multiple secondary burial. *a, b, d, e, h, i* & *j* definitely and possibly *f* and *g* are made of *Spondylus*; *c*, feature 94, primary flexed burial (probably Strombus). Ciruelo Black-on-Red type plate of the Cubitá style, illustrated in figure 8.6e, was found in the same feature); *l-p*, feature 41, primary semiflexed burial, all Pinctada mazatlanica. *Photograph by Richard Cooke*

are associated with five dates whose intercept range is cal 35 BC–AD 140 (Cooke 1995). An Isla Carranza sherd from a thin-walled collared vessel, decorated with V-shaped slashes, is illustrated in figure 8.5k. Handling the Colombian sherds themselves (rather than comparing often poor-quality illustrations) might alter my opinion. I believe that Capurganá I represents the same time period. Sherds illustrated by Linné (1929:Figure 10, labeled Triganá, but not described in his text) may be coeval.

There is no material comparable to Capurganá phase I at Cupica. There are close stylistic similarities, however, between a group of plastically decorated collared vessels from Cupica and the Colombian ceramic tradition Incisa con Borde Doblado. The Incisa con Borde Doblado tradition has not been identified around the Gulf of Urabá, but, rather, in the lower Atrato river, Río Sucio drainage, and the eastern slopes of Eastern Cordilleran Cauca valley (Castillo 1988). The corresponding Cupica material comprises subglobular vessels, often quite strongly waisted. They have lightly outflaring collars decorated

on the exterior rim with incised, impressed, and appliqué strips. Bodies are sometimes adorned with undulating appliqué fillets crossed by incisions or punctations (figure 8.4b,c). Fifteen of the twenty-four vessels from the first burial horizon (Cupica phase I) present these kinds of decorative modes (Habana Lisa, Gris Incisa, and Ocre Tosca). This typological integrity confirms the Reichels' opinion that the three Cupica burial episodes occurred at different times.[9] If a cal AD 735–1000 time frame for Cupica phase IV can be inferred by cross-dating with the Miraflores tombs, then Cupica's phase I should be older than these dates, but not by much. One phase I vessel from the first burial horizon is Incised Relief Ware, which I suggested earlier was manufactured between cal AD 400 and 750.[10]

Cupica, Miraflores, and Regional Cultural Geography

The cultural geography of pre-Columbian cultures in the Intermediate Area is grosso modo regional-diachronic. Archaeologists arrange blocks of national territory into discrete culture areas for which the diachronic development of lifeways is, generally speaking, better known than the synchronic relationships among regions. In Colombia, recent syntheses apply an overtly physical geographical approach. Cupica, for example, is placed in the sub-Region Pacífico Norte. In Panama, modern researchers rejected a close relationship between physical geography and pre-Columbian culture areas, preferring to divide the isthmus vertically into three regions—Western, Central, and Eastern—each of which comprises contrasting life zones. They argue that ecological heterogeneity was a stimulus for, rather than a barrier to, sociopolitical integration (Cooke 1984; Linares and Ranere 1980).

Bray (1984:308) believed that the distribution of pottery complexes in Lower Central America and Colombia demonstrated that culture areas were stable over very long periods of time and shared more traits with their neighbors than with regions further away. On the other hand, metalwork gave him a contrary impression of considerable conceptual homogeneity from southern Nicaragua to northwest Colombia. To accommodate this dialectic between local conservatism and stability, and regional commercial and intellectual interaction, Bray (1984:308) proposed a chain model in which "each link, or culture province, has its own identity, but at the same time interlocks with its neighbors to form a continuous and unbroken whole."

Recent studies of the genetic and linguistic relationships among modern Native American inhabitants of lower Central America and northern Colombia are broadly harmonious with Bray's model. With a few notable exceptions (that is, the Teribe), surviving cultural groups, which clearly represent the *in situ* fissioning of an ancient human lineage, are most closely related to their nearest neighbors (Barrantes et al. 1990; Constenla 1991, Torroni et al. 1993). Although the data are of better quality for speakers of Paya-Chibchan languages (Constenla 1991), than for Chocoan speakers, there is growing evidence for the Kuna (Paya-Chibcha) and Eperä (Chocoan) having been in closer reproductive and cultural contact than sometimes supposed (see Herlihy 1986). In the next paragraphs, I reconsider Cupica's relationship to Bray's chain model in the light of new data concerning ceramic distributions and commerce in the Panama Bight.

Metalwork, Exotic Marine Shells, and pre-Columbian Commerce

The earliest metal items found on the isthmus of Panama (Bray 1992b:Figure 3.2) have clear iconographic and technological counterparts in northern Colombia. Remarkably striking are similarities among pieces found at five sites in Panama's Central Region (Las Huacas, El Indio, La India, El Cafetal, and Cerro Juan Díaz) and at San Pedro de Urabá in northwest Colombia (Uribe 1988). Whether or not it was the commodities,

ideas, or specialists (that is, Oviedo's tequinas) that moved, it is clear that these sites participated in the same socioeconomic network, which appears to have extended into Tairona lands at this time (Falchetti 1987). Radiocarbon dates and grave associations at El Cafetal and Cerro Juan Díaz suggest that the earliest (Initial and Openwork Group) gold artifacts from Panama (Bray 1992) accompany the Tonosí and Cubitá ceramic styles (Ichon 1980; Sánchez 1995), which I now believe were manufactured between cal AD 300 and 750 (Bray 1992; Cooke and Bray 1985). [11]

At the time metallurgy was being established in Panama, small ornaments made from inter- and sub-tidal marine molluscs were used for personal embellishment (figure 8.10). The majority were made from thorny oysters (*Spondylus princeps* and *Spondylus calcifer*) and the pearl oyster (*Pinctada mazatlanica*). This industry has been identified at three sites: Cerro Juan Díaz (Cooke et al. 1994), Playa Venado (Lothrop 1957), and La Cañaza (Ichon 1980:277–82). Cerro Juan Díaz and La Cañaza are located in Cooke's (1984) Central Region, while Playa Venado is in the Eastern Region (that is, in the territory occupied at Spanish contact by the Cueva [Cooke and Ranere 1992:Figure 1]). These three sites share the Cubitá ceramic style (figure 8.6d-f) and many aspects of mortuary behavior (Cooke et al. 1994; Ichon 1980:292-98; Lothrop 1954).

Thorny and pearl oysters are still common around coral-fringed islands in Panama Bay. The two Panamic *Spondylus* species are sub-tidal. They encrust into the substrate and must be prised off—no mean feat for divers without tanks. I do not know whether they can be collected on rockier sectors of the mainland coast (that is, near Playa Venado). Even if they can, I doubt that large specimens are as easy to obtain there as on the Pearl Islands, Taboga, and Otoque (figure 8.1). They are certainly not found in or near turbid estuaries. This fact, in addition to finds of worked and unworked *Spondylus* debris at Cerro Juan Díaz, suggests that beads and pendants were made at this site from raw materials acquired outside Parita Bay. *P. mazatlanica* seeks clear water, but can be found in both inter- and sub-tidal zones. I recently found it common at low tide on a rocky promontory at Isla Iguana, at the southeastern tip of the Azuero Peninsula, 57 km southeast of Cerro Juan Díaz (figure 8.1). Unless the prograding Parita Bay estuarine sediments have buried suitable habitats, I doubt whether it was available much nearer to this site in pre-Columbian times. [12]

At Cerro Juan Díaz, *Spondylus* and *Pinctada* shell ornaments and perforated pearls are found in graves together with Cubitá-style ceramics (for example, figure 8.6e, from feature 94). They occur in large numbers with only a few individuals, including subadults (Cooke et al. 1994). The extensive Playa Venado excavations have never been published in detail. On a recent visit to US museums, however, Sánchez noted that the abundant marine shellwork ornaments found here are mostly coeval with Cubitá-style painted pottery (figure 8.6d; Bull 1958,

1961; Lothrop 1954, 1956, 1957, 1964:Figure 18b; Sánchez 1995). At La Cañaza, *Spondylus* and *Pinctada* ornaments appear to occur with both Cubitá and later Macaracas style vessels (Ichon [1980:295] found a child's skeleton with more than 600 pearls); but, since Ichon's excavations were salvage (Ichon 1980:292), I am cautious about the stratigraphic integrity of shell-pottery associations here. [13]

It seems clear, then, that during the period cal AD 300-750 commercial activity around Panama Bay centered on the manufacture and exchange of goods made of colorful shells, pottery painted in the Tonosí and Cubitá styles, and hammered and cast gold pieces. [14] Shell ornaments found in graves outnumber both pottery and metalwork.

If we turn the clock forward to the time of the Miraflores burials and Cupica phase IV (cal AD 735-1000), we find a different situation. At Miraflores, only one vessel is polychrome (a beveled jar with an eroded design). The interior of one pedestal plate (figure 8.8b) is decorated with a black-painted YC design reminiscent of Conte style designs from the Central Region (figure 8.6c). The remaining 98 vessels do not show affinities with samples from contemporary sites in the Central Region (Coclé, the Azuero Peninsula, and southern Veraguas). On the other hand, many of the pottery types found at Miraflores were reported from the Pearl Islands by Linné, and also appear at surface-collected sites situated between Chame Point and the Gulf of San Miguel.

According to current ceramic chronology, the well-known Sitio Conte burials in Coclé province, Panama (Lothrop 1937, 1942; Hearne and Sharer 1992) date between cal AD 700 and 1000. They do not contain marine shell artifacts (Ichon 1980:289). Sitio Conte is situated only 40 km as the crow flies from Cerro Juan Díaz. During its major occupation, it would have been less than 10 km from the coast, up a navigable river. Hence, had shell trinkets been available to adorn important personages, this village would have been well placed to receive them.

No Cubitá style pottery has been found at Sitio Conte. A few metal objects from the earliest graves are typologically and technologically similar to the Initial and Openwork Group goldwork from Playa Venado (Bray 1992; Lothrop 1956), but most of the metal artifacts belong to the later International and Conte groups (Bray 1992; Cooke and Bray 1985). Moreover, much larger numbers of gold objects were found at Sitio Conte than in graves associated with Tonosí and Cubitá pottery at other sites. Some individuals were buried with scores of objects of diverse function, technology, and semiotic content (Lothrop 1937).

Contrary to ideas advanced by Sauer (1966) and developed by Helms (1979), Panama is well endowed with sources of alluvial gold, a fact that induced the Spanish to open mines very soon after contact (Castillero Calvo 1967). Finds of gold-working kits and exploded molds archaeologically document evidence for the manufacture of cast gold pieces (Cooke and Bray 1985). Cori, chief of a town in the environs of Panama Viejo, was an expert metallurgist, according to Pedrarias (Jopling 1994:21): "the present chief of Panamá is called Cori. He and all his ancestors were great melters of gold and masters at working it, and they make very fine pieces there." Deposits of alluvial gold are found in far eastern Darién (Cana), along the San Blas coast, in Caribbean Veraguas (Turlurlí), on the Gulf of Montijo (Mariato), in the southern Veraguas foothills (El Remance), and in the western cordillera (Tisingal; the names of Spanish mines are all in parentheses).

If gold objects were manufactured at major population centers, as Pedrarias implies, one can assume that well-established exchange routes connected them with the auriferous areas of the isthmus. These routes would have taken very different directions from the exclusively coastal and maritime routes that developed around the acquisition and manufacture of *Spondylus* and *Pinctada* ornaments. Fernández de Oviedo (1853) recalled a similar situation while he was living at Natá, head town of a populous territory, in 1527, only 12 years after the Spanish invasion. He would send his slaves to Concepción, the port for the Turlurlí mines, to exchange cotton mantles for gold items.

In conclusion, I propose that, during the period cal AD 750-1000, goldwork displaced *Spondylus* and *Pinctada* shells as the primary semiotic correlate of social status, engendering a spatial reorganization of commercial and social relationships and (in a strictly material sense) culture area distributions. Oviedo (1853:140), for one, was convinced that trade was a major stimulus to social contact in our study area: "When the Cueva are not at war they spend all their time dealing and trading all their worldly goods with each other…their loads are carried on the backs of slaves: some carry salt, and others maize, blankets, hammocks, raw and spun cotton, salt fish, and gold (which the Cueva call *yrabra*)."

Summary

The data recovered by the Reichels at Cupica indicate that this important site belonged to a social network that looked north and east towards the Atrato and Sinú rivers and Panama Bay rather than south towards Tumaco-Tolita and Calima. If the Reichels' typology and in-site distributional analysis are sound (and their report offers few reasons for questioning them), the focus of Cupica's social relations shifted somewhat through time, just as they did around Panama Bay. During the first occupation (Cupica phase I), which seems to have occurred between cal AD 400 and 750, pottery styles suggest interactions with the Atrato, Sinú, and Middle Cauca rivers. This axis accords well with current knowledge about regional geography and the postcontact distribution of native groups. Although the linguistic affiliations of the peoples who lived in the Cupica area after conquest are not clear (the people of Birú, the

Gorgonas, the Idibáez), they were certainly in constant contact with Chocoan speakers whose settlements were widely distributed in the San Juan, middle and upper Atrato, and upper San Juan drainages (Isacsson 1975, 1981; Romoli 1976; Rowe 1950; Vargas 1987). The Eperã still inhabit this zone, traveling among their widely scattered settlements mostly by river (Isacsson [1975] says it is possible to portage canoes from the headwaters of the Atrato to the San Juan).

By the time of the Reichels' phase IV (ca. cal AD 735–1000), Cupica's external connections acquired a more northwesterly and coastal orientation. Pottery used for daily chores was probably still manufactured at or near the village. Decorated wares may also have been locally made, but the cognitive information they contained appealed to a wider audience, including people who lived 300 km away on the Pearl Islands and up the Bayano river in Panama.

When metallurgy was introduced into Panama from northwestern Colombia, probably after circa cal AD 300, it was a scarce commodity with an exotic iconography. It soon acquired a regional symbolism, however, sharing icons with the burgeoning painted pottery tradition. After circa cal AD 700, important people had access to very large numbers of gold adornments. Although some shell jewelry continued to be manufactured until contact times (Cooke 1976b), *Spondylus* and *Pinctada*, which are most abundant on offshore islands, were used far less for making ornaments than during the period cal AD 300–700.

I propose that this readjustment in regional commercial relationships would have enhanced the importance of Cupica's access to major gold-producing centers in the middle Atrato and Sinú drainages, stimulating an increasing involvement with Panama Bay populations. However premature this model might appear, it seems more prudent to attribute subtle changes in the distribution of ceramic styles to the reorganization of social relations than to catalytic events, such as the establishment of "Panamanian colonies" on the Gulf of Cupica (Herrera 1989:138).

Peroration

Gerardo Reichel-Dolmatoff was a very international person: of Belorussian ancestry, born and educated in Hapsburg Austria-Hungary, the protégé of a Frenchman, and resident of a rather conservative Latin American country with an enviable intellectual tradition. The chapter I have presented for this memorial volume was constructed around a piece of work that, I imagine, was not high on the list of Gerardo's favorite jobs. Neither was the description of pottery types; but, unfortunately, he did not find much else at perennially humid Cupica.

The data I have presented are imperfect, and my interpretations are not necessarily more robust than those of former researchers whose opinions I have questioned. My main point has been to cast doubts upon an earlier premise, which I have

shared with my thesis advisor (Bray), namely, that the geographic stability of culture areas in Lower Central America and Colombia goes hand-in-hand with stylistic conservatism in pottery. In the light of my ongoing research at Cerro Juan Díaz, this position is less defensible than it was 10 years ago.

Geographers, historians, and anthropologists have gotten a lot of mileage out of the famous Cueva—somewhat ironically because sixteenth-century documents present a contradictory account of the true nature of this society (for example, Loewen 1963). Good regional, multidisciplinary field archaeology, with the appropriate doses of chemistry and physics, is required objectively to evaluate what Oviedo, Andagoya, and Martyr wanted us to believe about these and other people, who lived in the oft-maligned, infrequently visited, and rudimentarily studied Darién Gap and who probably spawned the successful Kuna, Waunaan, and Eperã societies.

It would be much easier to integrate the ideas that wove through the above text into a robust model if there had been more frequent and prolonged contact among researchers from Panama and Colombia. The frontier between the two countries was the result of a nascent foreign power's desire to make its mark in the world. In pre-Columbian times, the inhospitable and marginal Department of the Chocó was not a frontier.

Acknowledgments. The photographs of the Reichels' Cupica materials were taken in the Instituto Colombiano de Arqueología and the Museo Nacional in Santa Fé de Bogotá at the end of 1995. I am extremely grateful to Leonor Herrera and the staffs of these two institutions for helping me with this assignment. I also thank Rolf Schrimpff and Marianne Cardale de Schrimpff, Ana María Falchetti, Gonzalo Correal, Germán Peña, Clemencia Plazas, and Channah Nieuwenhuis for their kind hospitality and assistance in Colombia. Alejandro Caballero helped me scan slides and prepare the plates. I have much appreciated Scott Raymond's and Augusto's impatience and encouragement. I found reviewers' comments most useful and hope that the final manuscript is an improvement on the turgid earlier versions. Lastly, a special word of gratitude to Alicia Dussán *viuda* de Reichel, who kindly let me see color photographs of the Cupica pottery.

Notes

1. While he was Visiting Professor at UCLA, Gerardo Reichel-Dolmatoff frequently stopped at the Smithsonian Tropical Research Institute in Panama to use the library and to consult with tropical forest biologists. On one memorable occasion, he and Junius Bird dined at my house. It is a shame that I did not tape their conversation, which was tantamount to a "song contest" between the two venerable archaeologists: tropical forest versus Patagonian and Eskimo anecdotes; histrionic demonstrations of the effects of hallucinogens versus protracted eulogies of cor-

morant and sea-gull stew; Bird and Reichel versions of the follies and foibles of famous colleagues. Cupica was the nearest Gerardo Reichel-Dolmatoff came to doing fieldwork in Panama, the country where I have spent all my working life. There are personal, as well as professional reasons, then, for constructing this short contribution to his memory around this site.

2. Grave R (designation used in Reichel-Dolmatoff and Dussán de Reichel 1961) 4: a circular cast gold object, perhaps a nose ring, grave R5: a polished stone ax, grave R18: a possible pumice polisher and a stone bar, grave R19: four quartz scrapers or knives, and grave R26: two spindle whorls, twenty-nine black mineral balls, an irregular piece of pumice-like material, and four quartz scrapers.

3. This decorative mode is frequent at Cupica where it occurs in the Reichels' burial mound and in Linné's La Resaca cemetery. On Miraflores' examples, which are common in the tomb fills, the apex of the triangular punctated zones points towards the waist of the vessel rather than towards the rim (figure 8.4g, h, Cupica, with figure 8.5j, Miraflores). A vessel very similar to figure 8.4g was reported by Torres de Araúz (1975:68) from the River Aruza, Darién. Sherds decorated with the downward-pointing triangles are widespread in eastern Panama Bay, for example, Chame (materials in the Panama City Anthropology Museum), Taboga (Stirling and Stirling 1964: Plates 46h, j and 48c, e), Chininá (Darién; figure 8.4i), Casaya and Saboga (Pearl Islands), and Garachiné (Darién; Linné 1929:Figures 21h, 31g, 44g, i).

4. The Reichels assigned Cupica Incised Relief Ware sherds to their phase I and III types, Cupica Roja Áspera and Cupica Roja Granulosa, respectively. Although they did not illustrate whole vessels, they refer to a large sherd from the first burial horizon (Cupica phase I) as "vessel 45" (figure 8.5a). At Miraflores, Incised Relief Ware sherds occurred only in the tomb fills.

5. These have not been reported west of Chame Point. They are frequent at Panama Viejo, however (Biese 1960), and also occur on the Pearl Islands (Linné 1929:Figure 18h).

6. My implication that these humpbacks were manufactured in the eastern part of Panama Bay appears to contradict my hypothesis that the zone of production of polychrome pottery shifted westward after circa cal AD 700 in response to sociopolitical reorganization. Cubitá-style pottery from Panama Viejo and Playa Venado is, however, stylistically very similar to materials from Coclé and the Azuero Peninsula, whereas the group of polychrome humpbacks to which I refer here is notably different from those recorded in Coclé and the Azuero Peninsula. To preempt accusations of subjective sophistry, I admit that a viable alternative model to the one I am proposing here attributes the distribution of polychrome and nonpolychrome pottery to differential trading opportunities among inland and coastal populations. In other words, sites like Miraflores, which is 15 km inland, would have had fewer opportunities to obtain exotic polychromes from western Panama Bay than villages located on the coast.

7. The two dates published for Playa Venado (Lothrop 1959, 1960) are worthless because pottery associations have not been satisfactorily described.

8. The Central Region polychrome "styles"—or, more correctly, "painted decoration modes"—represent arbitrarily defined apogees in a longevous iconographic tradition (Cooke 1985). Each style grades almost imperceptibly into its sequel, and probably lasted only two or three potters' generations, that is, considerably less than the 1 sigma 160-220 year span of most available radiocarbon dates. The Cubitá style, which lacks purple paint, is intermediate between the earlier Tonosí and later Conte (or Early Coclé) styles (Ichon 1980; Labbé 1995; Lothrop 1942). At Cerro Juan Díaz where stratigraphy is very precise, Tonosí-style sherds predominate in a recently excavated stratum dated by four charcoal samples with a 1 sigma range of cal 410-660 and an intercept range of cal AD 540–645 (Sánchez 1995). Conte materials have not yet been radiometrically dated (Cooke et al. 1994).

9. To judge from the Reichels' illustrations, the Carmelita Obscura vessel (from grave R 36; figure 8.4b) belongs to this stylistic group. The Reichels assigned it, however, to Cupica phase IV. Whether this assignment represents a mistake in their analysis or points toward a long-lived decorative tradition rather than a short-lived phase, as I am arguing, will only be clarified by future research.

10. A second and later Urabá complex (Tradición Modelada-Incisa; Complejo Estorbo) has been associated with two ^{14}C dates: AD 1055 ± 40 BP [cal AD 905 (996) 1021] and 925 ± 45 BP [cal AD 1029 (1069, 1083, 1124, 1137, 1153) 1207] (Santos 1989:44). The only similarity that I detect between this material and the Cupica sample is Santos' F5B rim (a tall collar with indentations on the edge of the lip).

11. Metalwork has been found at Cerro Juan Díaz in three tombs, which are stratified beneath a circular arrangement of stone-lined pits. Charcoal from the fills of these pits has returned seven radiocarbon dates whose intercept range is cal AD 540–755. Whole metal artifacts in the tombs include three hammered plaques with divergent raised spirals, two openwork modeled animals, and a large ring with a high percentage of copper. The plaques with spirals are very similar to an example from El Cafetal (Ichon 1980:Figure 56h). One plaque was found in a cylindrical tomb containing multiple secondary interments, among which is a human bone AMS date of cal AD 410 (430) 510 (Cooke et al. 1994). Feature 94, which contained the Cubitá style plate illustrated in figure 8.6e, has been dated by two charcoal samples: 1570 ± 80 BP (cal AD 416 [435,446,536] 600) and

1380 ± 80 BP (cal AD 606 [656] 761).

12. Linné (1929:132-3) speculated that the absence of pearl and thorny oysters at the Pearl Island middens he investigated was due to the islanders having exported these materials to other communities.

13. At Cerro Juan Díaz, burials associated with Macaracas polychromes were found introduced within earlier features. In a salvage situation like that of La Cañaza, I can envisage serious difficulties with regard to the sequential definition of features.

14. In the absence of compositional analyses of ceramics and goldwork, and isotopic evaluations of shell populations, arguments concerning the direction and mechanisms of this exchange will remain circular. The paste, surface finish, and design details of Cubitá style sherds and vessels found at Eastern Region sites, such as Playa Venado, Chumical, Panamá Viejo, Taboga, Casaya, and Saboga (Pearl Islands), suggest local manufacture rather than trade from the Azuero Peninsula (see also Linné 1929:138). It is hoped that compositional analyses of pottery undertaken by the Université de Montréal (Québec) will resolve some of these problems.

PART III
Shamanism and Iconography

⚜9⚜

Shamanistic Elements in a Terminal Valdivia Burial, Northern Manabí, Ecuador
Implications for Mortuary Symbolism and Social Ranking

James A. Zeidler, Peter Stahl, and Marie J. Sutlif

THE VALDIVIA CULTURE, which flourished throughout the lowlands of western Ecuador between 3500 and 1500 BC, is the foremost expression of Early Formative life thus far documented for pre-Columbian South America. Valdivia is often described as precocious, a particularly apt description for an archaeological culture whose vibrant material record appears with such great antiquity. This unusually rich legacy has afforded archaeologists an extraordinary opportunity to contemplate inferences about space-time systematics, settlement and subsistence patterns, and the ideological and spiritual realms of an Early Formative society.

Over the past 40 years of research into the Early Ecuadorian Formative period, few themes have occupied the attention of archaeologists more than the nature of ancient ceremonialism. In this chapter, we present further evidence for ritual activity and religious symbolism in the terminal stages of the Early Ecuadorian Formative. Our presentation continues in the legacy inspired by Colombian anthropologist Gerardo Reichel-Dolmatoff, whose seminal research served as a strong inspiration for students of the Ecuadorian Formative. We begin with a brief overview of Early Formative ritual in Ecuador, with particular emphasis on the role of Reichel's work and his key insights into native South American shamanism and religious symbolism. We then describe a Terminal Valdivia (Piquigua phase) burial from the site of Capa Perro (M3D2-065) in the Middle Jama Valley of northern Manabí province in western Ecuador (figure 9.1). Here, several different lines of evidence coalesce into one archaeological context to argue convincingly for an analog to contemporary shamanism from a prehistoric culture over 3000 years ago. Moreover, the placement of these shamanistic elements in a Terminal Valdivia burial raises intriguing questions regarding mortuary symbolism and social ranking in Valdivia society.

Early Formative Ceremonialism in Ecuador

We have at our disposal a large body of literature that productively explores various material expressions of Valdivia ceremonial life in the surviving material record. Survey and lateral excavation have enabled us to consider the appearance and subsequent evolution of Early Formative ceremonial blueprints for community patterning. Archaeological evidence suggests that the Valdivia phase I and II village consisted of small houses dispersed around a central open space in a circular or U-shaped pattern. By analogy to contemporary indigenous villages, such as the Gê-Bororo groups of central Brazil, archaeologists argue that such patterns reveal early ideological expressions demarcating sacred and profane space. Excavations at Real Alto reveal the beginning of a ceremonial plaza and dual mound-building as early as Valdivia phase II. By phase III, a clear segregation occurs in funerary ritual with the construction of a charnel house on one of the ceremonial mounds. A subsequent increase in ceremonialism is suggested by the appearance of rebuilt public structures, delineated plazas, and axial alignments. Real Alto appears to have evolved into a ceremonial center with a reduced on-site population supported by outlying hamlets. It disappears as a ceremonial center by Middle Formative Machalilla (for example, Damp 1979; 1984; Lathrap et al. 1977; Marcos 1978; 1988a; Marcos et al. 1976; Marcos and Norton 1981; Raymond 1993; Stahl 1984; 1985a; Zeidler 1984; 1986). Substantial evidence for ceremonial mound-building is also accruing from recent excavations in areas to the north and south of coastal Guayas Province (Staller 1994:319; Zeidler 1994a).

Ceramics are the cornerstone of Valdivia archaeology, and our normal preoccupation with pots is intensified by an unusually fertile iconography that informs on various issues of prehistoric ritual life. From its earliest appearance, the ceramic inventory includes a relatively restricted range of vessel categories, including tall-necked jars, squat-rimmed pots, and

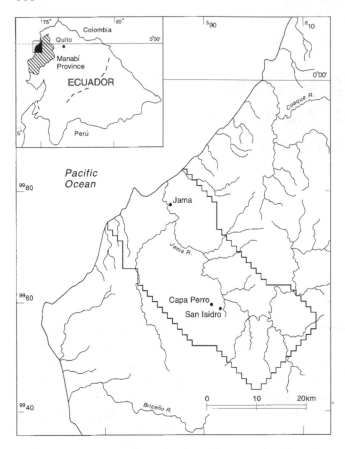

Figure 9.1 The Jama Valley study area, northern Manabí Province, Ecuador, showing the location of the Capa Perro site in the middle reaches of the valley

hemispherical bowls (Lathrap et al. 1975:27). Ritual activities inferred from contextual associations of surviving pottery involve the use of dedicatory caches and episodes of ceremonial drinking. In particular, the red-slipped and iconographically bold bowl forms have been implicated by analogy to shamanistic themes and a corpus of hallucinatory motifs (Damp 1979, 1982, 1984; Lathrap et al. 1975, 1977; Marcos 1978, 1988a; Marcos et al. 1976; Raymond 1993; Stahl 1984, 1985a, 1985b).

The surviving material record also includes a remarkable array of ritual paraphernalia, unprecedented for assemblages of this great antiquity. Ecuadorianist archaeologists have convincingly explored the analogous linkage between contemporary ritual practices of indigenous South America and the prehistoric material record. Some of the earliest and finest exemplars find their expression in Early Formative Valdivia context. These include feline effigy mortars from Terminal Valdivia contexts in the Jama River drainage of northern Manabí province (Zeidler 1988). Snuffing paraphernalia have been described from Valdivia contexts in present-day Guayas provinces (Lathrap et al. 1975:47; Marcos 1988a II:331; Marcos and Manrique 1988:43) and Manabí (Holm 1987:9), as have lime pot *coqueros* (Lathrap et al. 1975:47; Stahl 1984:226; Zeidler 1984:394) and iconographic depictions of coca usage (Holm 1987:12; Lathrap et al. 1975:48; Marcos 1988a II:330; Marcos and

Manrique 1988:42). To this list we can also add miniature, often zoomorphic, ceramic stools found in archaeological context. Most archaeologists accept their interpretation as analogous representations of shaman's stools (Damp 1979:107; Holm 1987:12; Lathrap et al. 1975:47; Marcos 1988a I:99; II:317, 322; 1988b: 175; Marcos and Manrique 1988:37; Stahl 1984:174; Zeidler 1988:254). Various authors have discussed the possible early role of hallucinogens and stimulants, especially within the context of shamanic religion (for example, Holm 1987:12; Klepinger et al. 1977; Lathrap et al. 1975:45; Stahl 1984:56; 1985b:116; Zeidler 1988:244). Finally, we must also consider the important ritual role of shell (particularly *Spondylus* spp.) acquisition, consumption, and exchange throughout the pre-Columbian Andes, which finds its early expression in Valdivia contexts (Marcos 1977/78:107; Marcos and Norton 1981; Paulsen 1974; Zeidler 1977/78:28–29; 1991:254).

Perhaps no other material category has received as much attention as the famed Valdivia figurines whose exact functions continue to be debated but which are unanimously implicated in ancient ceremonial activities. These figurines have long captivated worldwide attention for their antiquity, beauty, and abundance in a pre-Columbian context seemingly preoccupied with their manufacture. The repetition of an overtly feminine form typically prompted early speculations about a fertility cult similar to cults suggested for other ancient world areas (Estrada 1956:8; 1958:26; Zevallos and Holm 1960b:10). Interest in fertility, particularly connected to agriculture, has persisted (Zevallos 1971:23; Holm 1987:11); however, some archaeologists began to speculate on the depiction of both sexes in early figurine art (Holm 1987:10; Lathrap et al. 1975:39; Marcos 1988b:175; Marcos and Manrique 1988:37). This point is disputed by Di Capua (1994; see also 1973:110) who suggests that figurine variability can be explained by reference to physical stages of feminine development. She suggests their use in rituals pertaining to puberty, a point repeated by others (Damp 1979:75; Holm 1987:11). Alternative functional interpretations, such as effigies (Damp 1979:74), good luck amulets (Lubensky 1991:31), and votives in rain ceremonies (Porras 1973:145), have been offered; however, much of the literature has stressed a role in curing rituals, (Evans and Meggers 1958:181; Evans et al. 1959:10; Meggers 1966:41; Meggers et al. 1965:108; Porras 1973:145), particularly within the context of ecstatic shamanism (Stahl 1984:176; 1986).

A final aspect of Valdivia ceremonialism that deserves mention is mortuary behavior. Little of this information has been systematically assembled. Here, we wish to provide only a general spatial and temporal context for the Terminal Valdivia burial that is the subject of this study. On the basis of earlier archaeological studies of Valdivia society at Buena Vista (Meggers et al. 1965) and San Pablo (Zevallos and Holm 1960a; 1960b) in coastal Guayas Province, Meggers characterized Valdivia mortuary practices in the following terms: "The poor condition of the remains makes posture difficult to discern, but most skeletons lie on their right side with legs tightly flexed and arms extended along the hips. It is probable that the body was wrapped for burial in a mat or cloth.... Tools and ornaments were seldom placed in the grave, but a polished stone axe, a shell scoop or a pottery vessel sometimes occurs. Infants were buried in jars" (Meggers 1966:42).

Burial orientation, where it could be discerned, was usually toward the west, with the few exceptions being oriented toward the north (Meggers et al. 1965:19, 21; see also Zevallos and Holm 1960b:Lámina 6, superior). At San Pablo, Zevallos and Holm (1960b:11) reported finding fractured human bones throughout the upper layers of cultural midden, suggesting that they may have been discarded in the garbage with no special treatment. Mortuary evidence of social ranking or special status (see, for example, Brown 1981; Wason 1994:67–102) is lacking at both sites.

While these descriptions provide crucial information pertaining to Valdivia funerary customs, they offer a relatively homogeneous picture, perhaps because they are based on relatively small sample sizes. At Buena Vista, thirteen individuals were found, while at San Pablo, nine individuals were recovered, all of which pertain to Late Valdivia times (phases VI-VII in the Hill [1972-1974] chronology and phase C in the Meggers et al. [1965] chronology). A single human burial reported from excavations in Early Valdivia (phase II) deposits at the Loma Alta site (Stahl 1984:226–229; see the description below) conforms to this general picture, as does a series of four Terminal Valdivia (phase VIII) burials at the site of La Emerenciana in southern El Oro province excavated by Staller (1994:304). The latter tend to be upright, flexed interments, with red ochre, shells, and faunal remains in lined pits. Disarticulated secondary burials are also reported from these two sites (Stahl 1984; Staller 1994).

A more heterogeneous picture of Valdivia mortuary practices emerges when burials are documented from different kinds of archaeological contexts across a site and sample size is dramatically increased. For example, intensive excavations at the Real Alto site (Marcos et al. 1976, Lathrap et al. 1977; Marcos 1978; 1988a; Klepinger 1979; Zeidler 1984) yielded a sample of more than 100 individuals spanning phases I through VII, seventy-two of which pertain to phase III. Even the contemporaneous phase III burials from Real Alto demonstrate a remarkable degree of mortuary variability indicative of a complex "burial program" (as defined by Brown 1981:31). The latter are defined as "treatment sequences of the corpse (and skeleton if secondary burial is involved) particular to specific status categories" (Brown 1981:31).

First and foremost is a clear segregation between ceremonial (sacred) and domestic (profane) burial within the village limits. Interment in the phase III charnel house of the central ceremonial precinct appears to have been the prerogative of a distinct high-status social group (Lathrap et al. 1977; Marcos 1978, 1988a). Here, the remains of some 20 individuals were

recovered, eleven on the interior floor area and wall trench on the northern half of the structure and nine in a tomb complex underneath the threshold (Marcos 1988a:163). At least three of the eleven individuals found inside the structure proper were juveniles, one of whom had associated grave goods, including a ceramic figurine and fourteen *Spondylus* beads, and another had a polished stone axe (Marcos 1988a:169–170) . Of special importance was the placement of an adult female within the threshold tomb complex in a special crypt lined with fragmented manos and metates (Lathrap et al. 1977:9–10; Marcos 1988a:165). The threshold tomb complex also contained the remains of a spatially isolated, partially disarticulated male and secondary interments of seven additional males (one adult and six subadults). Although these male burials were earlier interpreted as sequential sacrificial offerings to the female burial (Lathrap et al. 1977:10), Klepinger (1979:308) convincingly argues that the close association of an adult female, two adult males, and six subadults of various ages is suggestive of a high-status family group . Likewise, the inclusion of juvenile burials in the charnel house suggests that status differences "must have been at least in part hereditary, since young children would have had little opportunity to achieve honor" (Klepinger 1979: 308; see also Zeidler [1984:637–640] for further elaboration of this point).

The sparseness of grave goods in these charnel house interments, goods that do not differ appreciably from those found in domestic burials, should not be interpreted as evidence for the lack of status distinctions during the phase III occupation at Real Alto. We would agree with Brown that "contrary to some statements in the literature, wealth distinctions are not as indicative of specific social variables as are rights to *symbolically special burial locations*" (1981:29; emphasis is the authors') such as a charnel house located in the central ceremonial precinct of a large village.

The domestic burials at Real Alto, located in the ring of residential midden around the central plaza, also demonstrate considerable variability during phase III. The most common type of adult and subadult interment is flexed burial in a shallow grave immediately adjacent to the wall trenches of individual dwellings (Zeidler 1984:277–279; Marcos 1988a:161–162). Fully extended burials in deep pits, secondary bone bundles in communal graves, and disarticulated and mixed human bone in communal ossuaries are also found. Prenatal infants are commonly interred in overturned cooking ollas and placed in dwelling wall trenches (for example, Marcos 1988a:68, 69), while infants were placed either in wall trenches without a ceramic container or unceremoniously incorporated into midden deposits. Grave inclusions are usually restricted to adult burials and are minimal in quantity, but can include ceramic figurines, stone axes, shell ornaments, and miscellaneous food items.

The wide variability represented by these phase III mortuary practices at Real Alto suggests equally varied energy expenditure in tomb preparation, funerary ritual, and treatment and disposal of the corpse. It no doubt obeyed a set of philosophical-religious beliefs that provided the ideological underpinning for a simple, yet clearly hierarchical, social order. Interestingly, this variability does not extend to grave goods in an appreciable way. It is against this background that Valdivia mortuary practices documented at other sites and in other temporal phases of the Valdivia sequence must be examined.

Shamanism and Valdivia

In most works, shamanism appears as the focal motif for interpreting Valdivia ceremonialism from the surviving record. Many recent analyses or reviews of Early Valdivia ceremonialism either directly mention or treat shamanism as a dominant interpretive motif (Damp 1979, 1982; Holm 1987; Klepinger et al. 1977:507; Lathrap et al. 1975; Lubensky 1991; Marcos 1988a,1988b; Marcos and Manrique 1988; Marcos and Norton 1981:149; Raymond 1993; Stahl 1984, 1985a, 1985b, 1986; Zeidler 1988). In Ecuadorian archaeology, this interpretive paradigm appears with the pioneering work of Saville (1910:206) who described seated pottery figurines from excavations at Cerro Jaboncillo near present-day Portoviejo. One ornamented specimen with a bag hanging from its left wrist particularly drew his attention, as the left hand grasped a tube resting upon a bird's back and extending to below the figurine's mouth. He argues that "the whole figurine unquestionably represents sorcery, exorcism, or some shamanistic ceremony, and [that] probably all of these seated figures may be interpreted in like manner" (Saville 1910:206). Despite this earlier reference, the intellectual trajectory of shamanic interpretations into Early Formative studies can be traced directly to the inspiration of Gerardo Reichel-Dolmatoff.

We refer, of course, to the ideas expressed in his influential paper "Anthropomorphic Figurines from Colombia, Their Magic and Art." Although this article was published in 1961, its contents influenced Ecuadorian archaeology at an earlier date. In 1958, Evans and Meggers published a popular piece in the journal *Archaeology* which included a lengthy 1957 personal communication from Gerardo and Alicia Reichel-Dolmatoff concerning the use and discard of figurines among various groups within the Chocó and Cuna. A similar quotation also appears in Evans and Meggers (1958:181–182) and is repeated again in Evans, Meggers, and Estrada (1959:10). Reference to Reichel-Dolmatoff by way of their 1959 work is repeated in Meggers, Evans, and Estrada (1965:108), whereas later, Meggers (1966:41) reiterates these ideas, but with no reference to Reichel-Dolmatoff.

In this article, Reichel (1961b; see also 1965b:76–77) published his observations of various Chocó and Cuna curing practices, with specific emphasis on the use and eventual discard of figurines. A connection between figurines and curing rituals had been known for some time; however, it took the

broad perspective of a renaissance anthropologist to recognize its significance for prehistory. He emphasized the sheer quantities of figurines needed by the shaman as a factor of both the number of figurines used and the frequency of curing rituals. He stressed that the figurine repositories of shamanic spirit helpers were often no longer needed and subsequently discarded upon termination of the ceremony; however, he also mentions different situations in which they were curated. Reichel (1961b: footnotes 4,7) refers to Nordenskiöld's much earlier work on the Chocó and Cuna which clearly describes the role of figurines in curing (1929:145, 151; see, for example, Stout 1945:266), as well as their loss of value upon termination of the ritual amongst the Chocó (1929:145). He also agrees with Lehmann's (1953, 1967; originally presented in 1949) observation that New World figurines depicting prone and restrained individuals on beds were representations of curing rites (Reichel-Dolmatoff 1961b:238). He was, however, the first to tie these ethnographic observations to archaeological expectations, noting that figurines throughout nuclear America were both highly abundant and appeared in garbage contexts.

Few scholars have been as effective in communicating the essence of native South American ritual and religion as Reichel-Dolmatoff. This was demonstrated early in his career in his monumental ethnography of the Kogi or Kaggaba Indian of the Sierra Nevada de Santa Marta in northern Colombia (Reichel-Dolmatoff 1950, 1951a; 1974). In wider circles, he is perhaps best known for his celebrated works on tropical lowland shamanism, particularly among the Desana of eastern Colombia. These works, found in numerous scholarly journals and written over an extraordinarily productive career, are probably best explicated in his classic books *Amazonian Cosmos* (1971), *The Shaman and the Jaguar* (1975a), and *Beyond the Milky Way: Hallucinatory Imagery of the Tukano Indians* (1978a).

The shaman is, of course, a highly trained expert capable of ecstatic flight through cosmological time and space. As a focal mediator with metaphysical realms, the shaman spiritually alters his corporeal state by transforming himself into a dominant animal avatar, often with the aid of ritual paraphernalia and powerful stimulants. In particular, Reichel explored the epistemological basis of contemporary cosmology and detailed the intimate relationship among the shaman, powerful felines, and the important role of hallucinogens. Moreover, his study of Kogi funerary customs and religious symbolism demonstrated in rich ethnographic detail how native South American burial rites can be viewed as "act[s] of cosmification" (Reichel-Dolmatoff 1974:298) in which the deceased is entombed in a microcosmic universe that mimics the dynamic macrocosmic structure of Kogi religious beliefs. Together, these studies provide us with a rich corpus of information for developing archaeological inferences regarding shamanistic

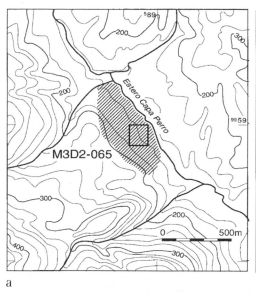

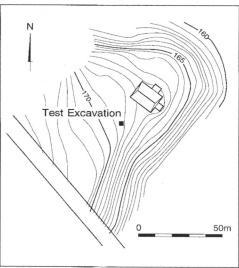

Figure 9.2 The Capa Perro site: *a*, general location within Estero Capa Perro drainage; *b*, inset showing location of test excavation in central area of site

a   b

ritual and mortuary symbolism in Terminal Valdivia society.

Burial 1 at the Capa Perro Site

The archaeological context we examine in this chapter comes from the large multicomponent Capa Perro site (M3D2-065; figure 9.2) that first appeared in the extensive alluvial bottomland of the Jama Valley during Terminal Valdivia times. Capa Perro was one of several satellite communities near San Isidro (M3D2-001), the valley's major civic-ceremonial center throughout most of its 3500-year prehistoric sequence (Zeidler 1994a, 1994b; Zeidler et al. 1996). It was discovered during a probabilistic regional archaeological survey of the valley landscape carried out between 1989 and 1991 (Zeidler 1995; see also Zeidler and Pearsall 1994). It is situated on a right bank terrace of the Estero Capa Perro approximately 160 msl, just 1.5 km west and upstream from San Isidro. The long linear site northwest/southeast axis of this parallels the adjacent watercourse. Up to 6.5 m of culture-bearing fill and fluvial deposits all along its northeastern side have been exposed by progressive down-cutting (Donahue and Harbert 1994). Fine sands and silts characterize the upper layers, although intermittent layers of gravel-to-pebble-size sediments indicate periods of high-energy stream flow (Donahue and Harbert 1994:Figure 3.3, Table 3.1). From these thick cut-bank exposures, the archaeological deposits thin out rapidly as the terrace approaches the base of a slope and colluvial deposition begins to affect the cultural stratigraphy.

A Terminal Valdivia burial context (feature 2) was encountered in a site testing operation carried out in the southern half of the site approximately midway up the terrace. Various factors influenced the decision to conduct site testing at Capa Perro. One important reason included the presence of three clearly defined tephra deposits visible in the Capa Perro cut-bank. Another was the long cultural sequence represented by the cut-bank deposits. Surface collections along the length of the site and the adjacent cut-bank recovered ceramic mate-

rial dating to Terminal Valdivia (Piquigua phase), Chorrera (Tabuchila phase) and to both the Jama-Coaque I (Muchique phase 1) and Jama-Coaque II (Muchique phases 2 through 4) occupations, indicating that Capa Perro was a deep multicomponent site spanning the entire pre-Hispanic cultural sequence in the Jama Valley. Site testing at Capa Perro also afforded the opportunity to enhance our understanding of the chronological sequence in the middle valley of the Jama drainage because its stratigraphic sequence could be correlated with the "master sequence" previously defined at the nearby site of San Isidro (Zeidler 1994a).

Testing was initiated in 1989 as a single deep 1 x 1 m pit for examining the cultural stratigraphy away from the cut-bank. This unit was excavated in arbitrary 20-cm levels to a depth of 160 cm below the surface. At this level, the partial exposure of human remains at the end of the field season necessitated back-filling the site so that the entire burial context could be excavated again during the 1990 field season. The excavation site was located in the levelled patio area 12 m southwest of the landowner's residence (figure 9.2). It consisted of a 2 x 2 m area (including the original 1 x 1 m test pit) that was excavated through nine distinct stratigraphic deposits to a depth of 210 cm (figure 9.3).

Five phases of cultural occupation were identified from diagnostic potsherds associated with these stratigraphic units. The top four layers (deposits 1 through 4) probably represent colluvial deposition with a compressed mixture of Tabuchila and Muchique 1-3 components. The top portions of deposits 1 and 3 may represent more stable surfaces, judging from paleosol formation and the presence of cultural features. A fragmented clay floor feature in the upper 10 cm of deposit 1 yielded a radiocarbon determination of 1195 ± 85 BP (cal AD 689 [821, 838, 855] 953), placing it at the early end of Muchique phase 3. Subsequent cultural occupation may have been eliminated when the current residents removed up to 50 cm of soil while leveling the patio area. Deposits 5 through 9

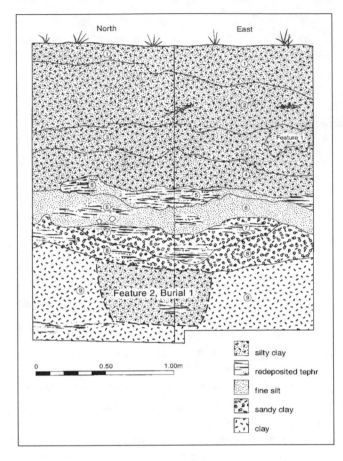

Figure 9.3 North and east profiles of unit 1 showing strati-graphic position of feature 2 burial pit

pertain to the Terminal Valdivia Piquigua phase, while deposits 5 through 8 represent reworked tephra probably accumulated in rapid succession as colluvial slopewash and/or sheetwash. These redeposited tephra layers contain admixtures of silts and clays along with cultural materials. They represent the Tephra I airfall documented elsewhere in the Jama Valley (Zeidler 1994a, 1994b; Isaacson 1994) which dates to approximately 2000 cal BC (Zeidler et al. 1996).

Underlying these strata is a compact deposit of olive-colored clay (deposit 9) mottled with inclusions of light green clay. The abrupt change in soil from the overlying silts and ash indicates an entirely different landscape and living surface, as the clay is very hard and compact. The outline of the feature 2 burial pit was identified just below the top of this clay deposit in the 1989 test pit (unit 1) at approximately 160 cm below the surface. The tomb first appeared as an elongated trench oriented in a northeast/southwest direction extending across the entire 1 x 1 m unit, with a maximum width of 60 cm. The fill of the trench was distinguished from its surrounding matrix (D 9) by its notably darker brown color and the fine-grained mottling of charcoal flecks, small fragments of burnt clay, and small inclusions of tephra. According to local *huaqueros*, pre-Hispanic human burials are commonly marked by *queso rallado* or 'grated cheese' in the tomb fill. This

refers to the speckled appearance of the white tephra intermixed with the tomb fill. The northeast corner of the trench, clearly extending well into the north and east sidewalls, revealed the severely fractured cranium and shoulders of a single individual (burial 1).

Three additional 1 x 1 m units were opened up to the north, northeast, and east in the 1990 field season to expose the remaining portion of the burial. Stratigraphic excavation of the overlying deposits permitted full exposure of the feature 2 burial pit (figure 9.4). The fully exposed tomb (feature 2) had a minimum length of 225 cm and a maximum width of 70 cm. The interment was situated just 25 cm below the top of the burial pit, indicating that the tomb was dug as a long shallow trough with slightly sloping walls. Orientation of the burial is northeast/southwest, with an azimuth of approximately 250°.

The skeleton, that of a young adult female with no observable skeletal pathologies, was found lying in a fully extended supine position with the cranium turned toward the right shoulder (figure 9.4). Both arms are extended along the thoracic region and crossed at the wrist above the pelvic area. The incomplete fragmentary bones of the left hand may have resulted from postinterment disturbance. The lower extremities are extended and slightly twisted toward the right side. The original condition of the feet cannot be determined because the bones were removed during looting intruded into the northern end of the tomb just prior to our 1990 field season. It is also likely that postinterment compaction affected the position of the skeleton (particularly that of the cranium and legs) and contributed to fracturing the cranium. Age at death is estimated at 15 to 20 years based on the absence of fully erupted third molars (D. Ubelaker, personal communication, 1995). The significance of the gender and age characteristics is discussed more fully below.

Shamanistic Elements in Burial 1 at Capa Perro

The assorted grave goods associated with the interment of burial 1 are of considerable interest because they shed light on shamanistic ritual. These items include a miniature ceramic vessel (*coquero*), a polished greenstone pendant, a concentration of unmodified claystone, a ceramic figurine within a fragmented feline snout, and the osseous remains of a bat (figures 9.5, 9.6). Continuities with some of these themes can be traced to earlier phases of the Valdivia cultural continuum, arguing for the progressive development of shamanistic ritual in Early Formative Ecuador.

The small ceramic vessel or *coquero*, situated above the right elbow, has a restricted bowl form whose body is decorated with fine-line incising and modeling; the rim and base are slipped in red. Incision consists of a narrow band of cross-hatching below the rim and a broad band of concentric triangles with modeled nubbins at the vertices. The incision and modeled nubbin motif, similar to that found on a Valdivia phase VI olla form illustrated by Lathrap et al. (1975: Speci-

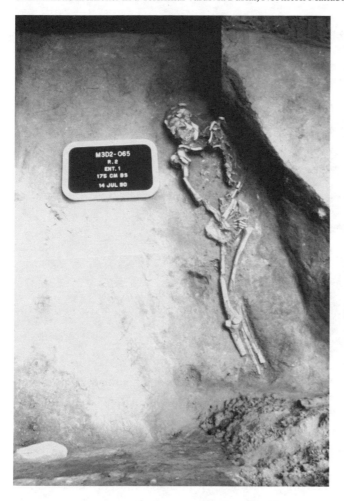

Figure 9.4 Overview of burial 1 during excavation. Note cluster of claystone fragments exposed at bottom of thoracic cavity

men 33), may represent an archaism whereby an earlier ceramic design motif was copied in this phase VIII context. Alternatively, the vessel may represent an actual phase VI *coquero* that was curated and passed down though several generations. Such items are commonly thought to have greater supernatual power because of their antiquity and ancestral associations. DeBoer (chapter 10) has observed this practice among the modern Chachi of Esmeraldas Province, where archaeological figurines and stone axes are carefully curated by Chachi shamans and considered to have greater curing power than their modern counterparts.

Ceramic *coqueros* are relatively rare components of Valdivia pottery assemblages. Nevertheless, four such items have been documented in house floor middens dating to the Valdivia phase III occupation at Real Alto (Zeidler 1984:394, Maps 82, 95, 96), suggesting a fairly widespread domestic use. Their ritual use in ceremonial contexts, such as grave inclusions, appears to be more restricted. One undecorated specimen has been described from a Valdivia phase II burial context at Loma Alta (Stahl 1984:226, Figure 56). Here, a small, round *coquero* was found near the left hand of a flexed burial lying on its left

side in a well-defined pit on the east-central portion of the sterile site center. The approximate placement of the fragmented cranial bones with respect to the postcranial skeleton suggests a northerly burial orientation (see Stahl 1984:Figure 57). The remains appear to be those of an adult male around 30 years of age. Interestingly, the grave also contained a few highly fragmented remains of a second male between the ages of 20 and 25 years (J.S. Raymond, personal communication letter March 10, 1995). Other grave inclusions consisted of marine shells, polished pebbles, and worked fish bones (Stahl 1984:229).

An oval 3.8 x 3.3 cm polished greenstone pendant was found over the abdominal region (figures 9.5; 9.6). It was probably suspended from the neck via a biconically drilled perforation through the longer axis, measuring approximately 0.8 cm at each end. This burial item forms part of a well-developed lapidary industry identified in other Terminal Valdivia contexts in the Jama Valley (Zeidler 1988), and may represent a distinctive sumptuary category. Another interesting element of this burial context is a dense concentration of more than 250 unworked light green clay stone fragments placed directly underneath the thoracic area of the deceased (figures 9.4, 9.6). Although the exact purpose of this cache is unknown, it is clear that it formed an integral part of the funerary ritual.

By far the most intriguing and diagnostic find associated with this Terminal Valdivia burial was a fragmented ceramic figurine found nestled within the disarticulated remains of a feline snout. These remains, in turn, were capped by a large fragment of ground stone. Ground stones, especially in the form of manos and metates, appear as ceremonial items and burial inclusions throughout the archaeological record of Valdivia (Marcos 1988a:165; Marcos et al. 1976:5; Staller 1994:330). The figurine (figure 9.7), standing only 6 cm tall, has a torso with unusually bulbous proportions and short stubby arms and legs. As is common in the Valdivia figurine tradition, the torso exhibits a surface finish of polished red slip. The facial features, with their protruding beaked nose and slanted arched lines to mark the eyes, show clear affinities with the Late Valdivia Chacras style of central Manabí (see especially Lathrap et al. 1975: specimen 114).

Unlike most Valdivia figurines, this piece lacks distinctive gender characteristics. It is also stylistically different from the other Terminal Valdivia figurines found throughout the middle Jama valley which are characterized by their large size, seated posture, and circular flattened head (for example, Schávelzon 1981). Its stylistic affinities with the Late Valdivia Chacras figurines of central Manabí may represent another case of archaism alluded to above with reference to the ceramic *coquero*. Interestingly, Di Capua (1994:Figure 45) depicts a looted figurine, purportedly from the San Isidro area, that shows marked similarities to the Capa Perro figurine in the configuration of the torso, arms, and legs, and presence of an aquiline nose. The "hooded" head and pregnant appearance

Figure 9.5 Oblique view of burial 1 and associated grave offerings

of this specimen are not present on the Capa Perro specimen, however.

The figurine was found nestled within the disarticulated maxillary and mandibular remains of a medium-size feline identified as an ocelot (*Felis pardalis*). This spotted cat is a solitary, secretive, and often nocturnal hunter that tolerates a variety of terrestrial habitats, usually near cover, and adapts readily to anthropogenic conditions (Eisenberg 1989:281; Emmons and Feer 1990:149). Ocelot remains are found in a variety of archaeological contexts throughout the long pre-historic habitation of the Jama Valley; however, the actual number of skeletal fragments tends to be low (Stahl 1994, 1995). Similar observations have been made for other neotropical areas (for example, Cooke 1993).

The feline remains included both maxillary and mandibu-lar elements which, prior to overburden compaction, likely represented the whole snout. It is interesting to speculate on the nature of these remains at the time of interment. The more fragile bones of the sinus area are missing, and the basal bor-ders of the mandible show fracturing typically associated with fresh bone. Although speculative, we suggest that these ros-tral elements were originally included within the facial por-tion of a feline skin that was utilized as a cape or poncho. When the ocelot was skinned up to and over the cranium, we sug-gest that the lower jaw was loosened and snapped downward, with an opposite, upward force applied to the upper jaw. The young woman might have been buried with the skin poncho placed over her body, the ocelot head resting in her abdomi-nal area with the fragmented figurine placed in its jaw. This interpretation is discussed at greater length below.

Finally, a mandible and teeth from a large neotropical fruit-eating bat (*Artibeus*) were found in the abdominal region. Flo-tation fraction from the general abdominal region also re-vealed a deer (*Odocoileus*) phalangeal fragment, one isolated tooth each from a cotton rat (*Sigmodon*) and a rice rat (*Oryzomys*), a fragment from a small reptile, and isolated up-per and lower dental elements from the same bat. On the ba-sis of these latter dental remains, we suggest that the entire bat head might have been included in the original interment.

Discussion

In recent years, archaeologists concerned with the interpreta-tion of mortuary practices have increasingly attempted to go beyond the sociological inferences of 'mainstream' North American mortuary analysis by systematically addressing the realm of mortuary symbolism and its underlying philiosophical-religious beliefs (see, for example, Parker Pearson 1982; Shanks and Tilley 1982; Hodder 1984; David 1992; Wason 1994; Carr 1995). This shift has stemmed largely from the growing recognition that the social factors usually re-garded as strong determinants of mortuary behavior (see, for example, Saxe 1970; Binford 1971; Chapman and Randsborg 1981; Bartel 1982) are themselves dramatically affected by philosophical-religious beliefs and that reasonable archaeo-logical inferences regarding these belief systems are possible through detailed analysis of mortuary symbolism and the nonarbitrary iconic properties of material culture items placed in grave contexts (Wason 1994; Carr 1995; see also Hodder 1986). Thus, any approach to the study of prehistoric mortu-ary practices must provide a more balanced, holistic anthro-pological perspective than that of the Northern American "mortuary sociology" school of the 1960s and 1970s, one in which "social organization, beliefs, and *their interaction* are considered together for their effects on mortuary practices

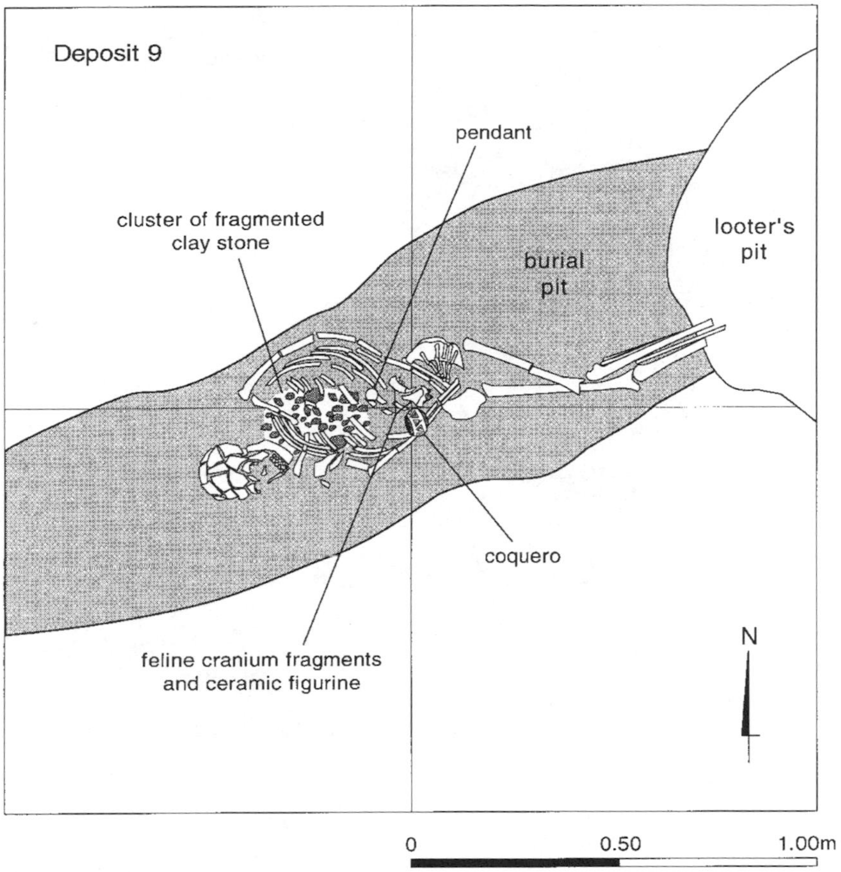

Figure 9.6 Plan map of burial 1

Deposit 9

pendant

cluster of fragmented
clay stone

burial
pit

looter's
pit

coquero

feline cranium fragments
and ceramic figurine

N

0   0.50   1.00m

(Carr 1995:121; original emphasis)

This recent shift in archaeological mortuary studies has resulted in a rekindling of scholarly interest in the work of French sociologist Robert Hertz, whose seminal study of death ritual and mortuary symbolism (1907, 1960) provides a unique holistic framework for the anthropological study of death (Huntington and Metcalf 1979; David 1992; Carr 1995). Hertz argued that the structure and content of mortuary practices are determined by a triadic relationship between (1) the living and the mourners, (2) the corpse and the burial, and (3) the soul and the dead (Hertz 1907, 1960; Huntington and Metcalf 1979; David 1992; Carr 1995).

The relationship between (1) and (2) defines the scale of the funerary rites and expresses the social personae of the deceased. It is social-organizational in nature, entailing the obligations of the living to the dead (Carr 1995:176). As such, it has been the traditional focus of the 'mortuary sociology' school in North American archaeology. The relationship between (1) and (3) involves the procession of funerary rites and the gradual transformation or extinction of the social personae of the deceased. It is social-psychological in nature, involving diverse issues of inheritance and culturally appropriate expressions of grief (Carr 1995:177). Finally, the relationship between (2) and (3) is essentially philosophical-religious as it involves eschatology, the metaphorical relationship of the body and soul, the symbolic content of the funerary rites. As Huntington and Metcalf (1979:67) point out, this relationship

has "unique power...[for] it enables us to penetrate the meaning of mortuary rituals by paying attention to the details of the treatment of the corpse." Following Hertz (1960:45), the symmetry or parallelism between the condition of the body and the condition of the soul has a symbolic character that "makes it possible to derive eschatology from the metaphorical relationship of body and soul" (Huntington and Metcalf 1979:67).

The pertinence of this premise for ethnographic analysis or mortuary ritual is obvious, as preoccupation with eschatological issues appears to dominate mortuary beliefs and practices in many areas of the world. Indeed, in Carr's survey of thirty-one non-state societies listed in the Human Relations Area File (HRAF), "the philosophical-religious factors that were found most often to determine mortuary practices and remains include [in order of relative importance] beliefs about the soul and the afterlife, the nature of the soul's journey to the afterlife, universal orders and their symbols, the cause of illness and death of the deceased, and responsibilities to and punishments of the deceased's soul" (1995:190). Hertz's premise, however, is no less relevant for the archaeological analysis of mortuary contexts. As Carr (1995:119; original emphasis) notes, the structured variation of mortuary remains (including corpse disposal and related grave goods) can be examined as "contrasting and associated *sets* of symbols" within their synchronic and historical context. We adopt the approach below by examining, both temporally and spatially,

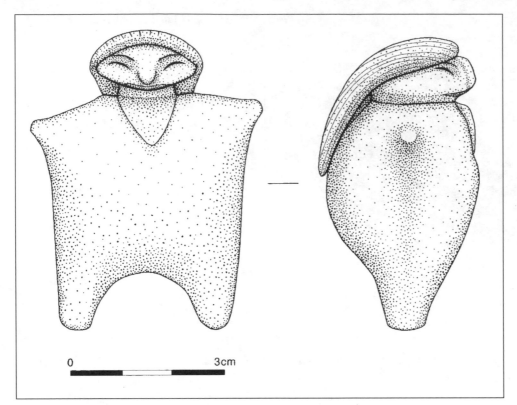

Figure 9.7 Reconstructed rendering of ceramic figurine from burial 1

the structure and content of burial 1 at Capa Perro with reference to the forms of symbolic expression documented elsewhere in the Valdivia cultural continuum. Here ethnographic analogies with lowland South American societies can be productively explored for interpretive purposes, particularly those provided by the work of Reichel-Dolmatoff.

We consider the coalescence of various associations within this contemporaneously deposited Terminal Valdivia burial as convincing evidence that mortuary ritual practiced in the Jama Valley over 3000 years ago was analogous to shamanism, eschatology, and beliefs in the afterlife common to many indigenous groups in the tropical lowlands of South America. We can take as an arbitrary starting point the feline remains associated with the burial. The intimate relationship between shamans and felines is, of course, well known. Furst (1968:163) earlier argued that, under spiritual alteration, a transformation between shamans and jaguars does not necessarily take place; rather, the shaman realizes the jaguar that exists within. As a key feature in ecstatic human/animal metamorphosis, the feline thus assumes an important role as mediator or messenger for otherworldly realms (for example, Lathrap 1973:97). It is therefore not surprising that an anthropomorphic figurine is found inside the feline mouth. An essential feature of the shaman is his interpretive power gained from ecstatic flight to hidden worlds where understanding is achieved with the aid of intermediary spirit helpers. If, as earlier suggested, Valdivia figurines functioned "as repositories for spirits contacted by the shaman during ecstatic visits to hidden domains" (Stahl 1986:141), then this contextual relationship is understandable.

Certainly, the role of stimulants in the afterlife is also implicated by the association of a *coquero* with the other grave goods. Coca leaves may have been an additional grave good for which no archaeological traces have been found. Alternatively, coca may have been an essential ingredient in the mortuary ritual itself, as in the case of the Kogi where crushed coca leaves are used by the Kogi priest (*Máma*, for more detailed information on the priest, see chapter 5) for delimiting and preparing the tomb (Reichel-Dolmatoff 1974:292–293). As noted previously, the processing of hallucinogenic plant remains (probably *Virola* snuff) in feline effigy mortars of polished stone is also a hallmark of the Terminal Valdivia Piquigua phase in the Jama Valley (Zeidler 1988). The use of these substances would have likely been essential for ecstatic shamanistic ritual involving feline transformation.

The purposive inclusion of the bat cranium within this burial context is certainly interesting as it may be suggestive of some prehistoric notion of ritual flight. Bats, of course, appear throughout Ecuadorian antiquity as a recurring iconographic motif and are especially prevalent on pottery seals and spindle whorls from Manabí Province (see, for example, Parducci [1966] and Wilbert [1974:55–68]). In much of Mesoamerican and South American myth and iconography, the bat is characteristically a multivocalic symbol that is often associated with felines and the notion of fertility (Wilbert 1974). As Furst (1972:66) noted: "The bat is an animal of night and of caves, it is the only animal that nurtures its young from two breasts like a human, it has fangs like a jaguar, it has the characteristics of a bird, so it incorporates many concepts...." Its association with night and darkness may explain why it would be appropriate in a funerary context.

The close association of the perforated greenstone pendant is suggestive of "cosmological luminescence," which is central to the shaman's power and often embodied in stones or crystals that are focal elements of shamanic equipment (see the references in Stahl 1984:92). Here, we might also tentatively add the dense concentration of over 250 unworked light green clay stone fragments. Reichel (1975a:79) mentions the "thunder-stones" of the Tukano payé, used both in curing and in assaulting enemies. In a later publication (Reichel-Dolmatoff 1979), he expanded on the role of translucent rock crystals in Desana cosmology. These crystals contain condensed solar energy and, as the principal power objects of shamans, are "among their most treasured possessions" (Reichel-Dolmatoff 1979:117). We are also reminded of Palmatary's (1960:75–84) lengthy discussion of Amazonian *pedras-verdes*, especially those suspended by cords, which were highly valued as talismans possessing great power over evil.

The precise motive for this particular burial will, of course, remain elusive. We can, however, offer a number of scenarios, all or any of which may be interrelated. First, the burial may represent a young (apprentice?) female shaman, which the ethnographic literature suggests is not at all uncommon (see references in Stahl 1984:52). The associated grave goods might be her important ritual paraphernalia from the mundane world, but the iconic nature of their specific configuration with respect to the corpse may relate to concepts of the soul and its journey to the afterlife. In this sense, it is worthwhile to reprint a lengthy quote that Reichel-Dolmatoff (1975a:47) found to be of great importance. Whiffen (1915:139–140; emphasis ours) observed that among the Witoto (Huitoto):

When a medicine-man dies he returns as a tiger, and even during his lifetime he can make excursions in tiger-form, and be so absolutely tiger that he can slay and eat the beasts of the wild. Every medicine-man possesses a jaguar skin that he is said to use when he turns tiger. By possession of a skin he has the power of resuscitating the tiger. He can thus work his will, afterwards returning to human form. An ordinary tiger might be killed, but a medicine-man in tiger form could not be. On one occasion a medicine-man I met had a bag made of tiger-skin hung around his neck, in which he carried all his paraphernalia. But the medicine-men never wear these skins as wraps or coverings. Each hides his tiger skin away, when not in actual use for magic purposes. The power to return after death in the shape of the dreaded jaguar is a further defensive measure, a precaution against hostile peoples, as in this shape *both before and after death* the medicine-man can attack the tribal enemies, and carry obnoxious individuals away into the bush whenever opportunity offers.

Interestingly, Reichel-Dolmatoff, himself (1944), observed the use of such jaguar skins in shamanistic rituals among the Guahibo Indians of eastern Colombia in which "the shaman wears a crown of jaguar claws and a cover of jaguar skin" when he ingests narcotic snuff (Reichel-Dolmatoff 1972b:62).

Closer to home in the western lowlands of Ecuador, Di Capua (1986) notes that modern Tsachila (Colorado) oral history makes reference to shamanic jaguar skin ponchos in a myth known as "Quela" in the Tsachila language or "Los Tigres" (Mix 1982:58–61). As transcribed by Mix, the following passage leaves no doubt as to the transformative power of the feline skin or pelt nor to its use as a poncho:

Los tigres se convierten en hombres para ir a espiar a la casa de la gente. Asi acostumbraban ir a espiarlo todo. Tenian unas pieles. Cuando se las ponian se convertian en tigre. Eran como ponchos. Al ponersela se convertian en tigre. Asi hacian bastantes veces.

The jaguars transform themselves into humans in order to spy on people's houses. They became accustomed to spying on everything. They had some pelts and when they put them on, they transformed themselves into jaguars. They were like ponchos. When they wore them, they became jaguars. They did this repeatedly. (Mix 1982:59; authors' translation)

Di Capua (1986:165–166) also convincingly demonstrates the prehistoric use of the jaguar skin poncho in the iconographic designs engraved on the body of a ceramic male figurine (shaman?) of clear Guangala stylistic affinity dating to the Regional-Developmental Period (ca. 100 BC to AD 800). Here the head of the figurine protrudes through the back of the jaguar skin, and the cranial portion of the skin is clearly draped over the abdominal region of the figurine's body (Di Capua 1986: Figura 3.1) in an anatomical location identical to that of the jaguar cranial fragments in burial 1 at Capa Perro. Below the tail area of the engraved jaguar skin is another smaller feline depiction rendered in a slightly different iconographic style. Di Capua (1986:166) interprets this figurine and its attendant iconography as a shaman whose jaguar skin is dominating (with the help of magic darts) a feline/shaman of a different ethnic group. The jaguar poncho, then, is clearly a major item of shamanic ritual paraphernalia in the western Ecuadorian lowlands from prehistoric to modern times.

In many lowland South American societies, the afterlife of shamans is conceptually distinct from that of other members of society (see, for example, Wilbert 1975:170–174), especially in their ability to "return after death." The preceding quotation from Whiffen (1915) adequately illustrates the unique status that shamans hold within their society. It also demonstrates why the interment of a deceased shaman might include items of his or her ritual paraphernalia, in this case a jaguar skin, because their use continues after death. Such a distinction might also explain the uniqueness of the burial 1 grave inclusions when compared to the corpus of other Valdivia burials documented to date.

As an alternative scenario, the burial may represent some form of ritual offering with shamanistic overtones that resulted from a failed curing ceremony. Here, the relationship between felines and fecundity, which Reichel-Dolmatoff stressed throughout his works (for example, 1971:71), may be of particular importance, as we see an association of these traits in the abdominal area of the burial. Circumstantial factors surrounding the death (for example, the kind of illness, the place and timing of death, and so forth) may also be important in determining the uniqueness of the grave associations.

Finally, in any or all of these cases, the burial and its associated remains may be suggestive of gender hierarchy in the Terminal Valdivia occupation of northern Manabí and of the persistence of ascribed social status accorded certain female members of Valdivia society. It is important to emphasize that these particular grave features were associated with the remains of a subadult female whose relatively young age would seem to preclude the attainment of sufficient status to merit such unique grave offerings. Special mortuary treatment of females, subadults, and juveniles is a pattern with clear precedents in phase III of the Valdivia cultural continuum and provides the strongest evidence for ascribed hereditary ranking. We refer, of course, to the high-status adult female buried with subadult retainers under the threshold of Real Alto's ceremonial charnel house, as well as the presence of juvenile interments inside the structure (Lathrap et al. 1977; Klepinger 1979; Marcos 1988a). The mortuary ritual documented at Capa Perro may be further evidence for such ranking in a Terminal Valdivia (phase VIII) context. It is interesting to note that the southwesterly orientation of burial 1 coincides with the axial location of the charnel house mound in the southwestern quadrant of Real Alto's rigid spatial configuration (Zeidler 1984, 1992). This intercardinal direction may have had eschatological significance for the deceased who were placed in the charnel house.

If our interpretation of this burial context as that of a young female (apprentice?) shaman is correct, it raises intriguing questions regarding political leadership in Valdivia society. As Santos Granero (1986:658) has observed, in many lowland South American societies, the shaman wields considerable social and economic power and often plays a political leadership role because he or she is intimately involved in the "mystical means of reproduction—[that is,] the mystical knowl-edge and ritual operations which are thought, symbolically and literally, to ensure the well-being and reproduction of both the social group and the natural environment." Was the apical social rank in Valdivia society expressed in the dual role of shaman-leader? Did this role consistently fall to female members of an apical corporate group through hereditary succession? The archaeological evidence amassed thus far seems to point in this direction, but it is based on a relatively small sample of the kinds of archaeological contexts needed to address these issues. Future analyses of Valdivia mortuary contexts would shed valuable light on the questions posed above, but only if they are carried out in the holistic anthropological perspective advocated herein.

In closing, it is fitting that this unique archaeological context be presented in a volume honoring the late Gerardo Reichel-Dolmatoff, who contributed so significantly to our knowledge of native South American religion. His ethnographic observations were particularly accessible to us for he, himself, was a great archaeologist, and his work on the Colombian Formative motivated decades of fruitful research in Ecuador. His love of native South America, both present and past, is reflected in his classic works that remain monumental inspirations representing anthropology at its very best.

Acknowledgements. Funding for this research was made possible through grants from the National Science Foundation (BNS-8709649, BNS-8908703, BNS-9108548) awarded to James A. Zeidler and Deborah M. Pearsall. Permission to undertake this work was provided by the Instituto Nacional del Patrimonio Cultural (Guayaquil Office). We are indebted to the extended family of the late Joel Solorzano of San Isidro for permission to excavate on their property and for their generous hospitality during and after our field work. Identification of the faunal material was facilitated through access to comparative materials in the Department of Mammology, American Museum of Natural History, whose kind staff we thank. Thanks also to Bill Isbell (Department of Anthropology, Binghamton University, NY) and Dennis Mortenson (Nanticoke Taxidermy Studio, Whitney Point, NY) for their thought-provoking observation on the possibility of a feline cape and to Constanza Di Capua (Quito, Ecuador) for her stimulating comments on Valdivia figurines and for pointing out iconographic and ethnographic references to jaguar skins used as shamanic ponchos in Ecuador. Finally, we thank Douglas Ubelaker (Department of Anthropology, Smithsonian Institution, Washington, DC) for his timely examination of the human skeletal remains.

☙10❧

Figuring Figurines
The Case of the Chachi, Ecuador

Warren DeBoer

FIGURINES are common artifacts in the archaeological record of northwestern South America. As iconic artifacts, figurines lend themselves to interpretive speculation and continue to spawn a large literature (for example, Drolet 1974, Lubensky 1991, Di Capua 1994). Despite this attention, figurines remain a kind of archaeological Rorschach test and are seen variously as toys, fertility symbols, markers of rites of passage, or shamanic paraphernalia. In this chapter, I turn to figurines made by the contemporary Chachi, native Americans of coastal Ecuador, in an attempt to cast new light on figurine function and form in northwestern South America.

With respect to function or to address the question "what are figurines for?," Gerardo Reichel-Dolmatoff (1961b) offered an influential interpretation in his paper "Anthropomorphic Figurines from Colombia, Their Magic and Art." In this landmark study, he noted that any satisfactory account of archaeological figurines would have to explain two observations. First, figurines tend to be abundant. Second, they tend to be found in everyday domestic middens; rarely do they occur in burials or other specialized contexts. In accounting for these two observations, Reichel-Dolmatoff cited the case of modern Chocó shamans who use figurines in curing sessions. Every Chocó community is likely to have at least one, if not several, shaman who recurrently conducts such cures. After their use in a particular session, figurines are believed to be spent and are discarded unceremoniously, producing over time figurine-rich middens that, if Chocó figurines were only made of durable clay rather than perishable wood, effectively mimic the archaeological situation.

Figurines also have form, specifically representational. Only alluded to by Reichel-Dolmatoff, the question "what do figurines represent?" has been raised recently by Michael Taussig (1993). Following puzzlement expressed earlier in this century by the ethnographer Erland Nordenskiold (in Wassén 1938:345, 423-426) and his pupil Henry Wassén (1940), Taussig is intrigued by the fact that the wooden figurines used by Cuna and Chocó shamans do not resemble Indians at all, but rather Europeans, or at least non-Indians (see the sample reproduced in figure 10.1). Why, Taussig asks, do these figurines mimic non-Indian "others," and why do they do so in the specific context of shamanic curing? Taussig does not directly answer this query, but he prods the issue in delightful and provocative ways. Perhaps a straightforward sympathetic magic is at work

Figure 10.1 Cuna figurines. *After Wassén 1938: Figs. 25–26*

121

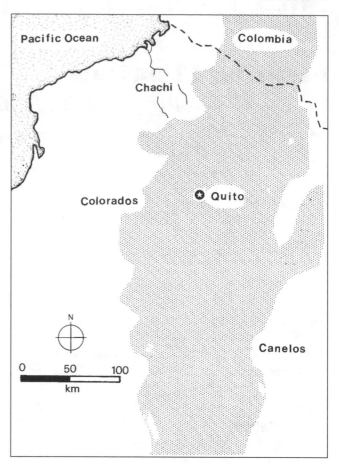

Figure 10.5 Northern Ecuador showing the location of the Chachi, Colorado, and Canelo. Stippling indicates the Andes

TOP: Figure 10.2 First view of anthropologist and native: the other. MIDDLE: Figure 10.3 Second view of anthropologist and native: the self. BOTTOM: Figure 10. 4 Third view of anthropologist and native: the self becomes the other. *Illustrations by Ainsley DeBoer*

in which "one can protect oneself from evil spirits by portraying them" (Taussig 1993:12). But Taussig, whose book bears the threatening title *Mimesis and Alterity*, is unlikely to end in such simple musing. Building on the works of Walter Benjamin and others, he goes on to sketch a general critique of the anthropological encounter in which the confronted "other" (figure 10.2) is requisite to constructing "self" (figure 10.3). Then, in a twist, this constructional process culminates in a transference[1] in which "self" becomes the "other" (figure 10.4). In this post-modern house of mirrors, what image of figurines could be the correct one?

It may seem that Reichel-Dolmatoff's shamanic analogy for figurine function and Taussig's reflections on figurine form are worlds apart. The Chachi evidence, however, suggests that the two approaches, although analytically separable, have an unanticipated engagement.

A Chachi Curing Session (1986)

Like their Cuna and Chocó counterparts, Chachi shamans use wooden figurines in curing. The Chachi (formerly known in the ethnographic literature as the Cayapas) number some three thousand individuals, most of whom inhabit the inland reaches of the Cayapas basin of Esmeraldas Province, Ecua-

Figure 10.6 Layout of Perdomo's curing session, Guadual on the Río Cayapas, 1986 Only a portion of the house floor is shown. *a,* two wooden statues; *b,* bottle of aguardiente; *c,* two stone axes on a white cloth; *d,* bench; *e,* palm whisk; *f,* back of the house to where the patient walked at the end of the curing ceremony. See text for discussion.

dor (figure 10.5). They are a river people, equally at home in a dugout canoe as on land; fish and plantains are dietary staples; and the preferred settlement pattern continues to be one of single houses dispersed along the Cayapas and its major tributaries. Although most Chachi have access to Western medicines, shamans who cure continue to be important and are consulted regularly. Ailments particularly amenable to shamanic treatment involve soul loss or, alternatively, invasion by a malevolent spirit, often objectified in the form of a small dart or stone. Through a combination of songs, power-laden objects (including figurines) that the Chachi collectively call *arte,* and the ingestion of tobacco smoke, aguardiente, and *pildé* (the local term for the hallucinogen ayahuasca), the shaman is able to see the invasive material causing sickness or to find the vagrant soul and attract it back to the patient.

Before turning to the figurines themselves, a sketch of their context of use may be helpful. The following account of a curing session and the accompanying diagram (figure 10.6), which gives the physical layout of the proceedings, are based on 1986 field notes. It was dusk and the anthropologists were invited to watch a curing ceremony in which Perdomo, our neighbor-shaman, was to attend to several visiting patients. Perdomo sat cross-legged in the middle of the floor of his particularly large house. To his right was a wooden bench (D in figure 10.6) upon which he rested his right arm. Immediately in front of Perdomo stood a bottle of aguardiente (B) and an assortment of *arte,* including two wooden figurines (A) and two stone axes (C) laid upon a white cloth. The patient sat upon a mat to Perdomo's left facing the riverfront outside. One of Perdomo's daughters, who acted as his assistant during the session, sat immediately across from her father, a palm leaf

whisk (E) at her side. The atmosphere was hardly solemn. Waiting patients talked to themselves at one end of the house, children played, and household residents engaged in such casual activities as sweeping, cooking, or swinging in a hammock.

Perdomo was singing in Chapalachi, but his songs were studded with words in Spanish and Quichua. Periodically, he took a mouthful of aguardiente and sprayed the liquor over the wooden statues and stone axes. Later, he explained that the songs activated the *genios* (spirits) in the figurines and axes that then, in turn, entered the patient and expelled the foreign illness-causing objects. The spraying of the *arte* with aguardiente warded off bad spirits intent on preventing the cure. After about 10 minutes of this singing and spraying, the patient arose and walked to the back of the house (F). There, the assistant gently swept the patient's back and arms with the palm whisk. Finally, the assistant took a mouthful of water from a calabash and sprayed the patient's back, much as Perdomo had formerly done to the *arte.* This final act ended the treatment. Following much the same procedure, Perdomo treated a dozen patients during the night and into the morning. Almost every aspect of this account can be matched by shamanic practices recorded for other groups of the Andes and Amazon.[2]

Genealogy of Figurines and Shamans

Perdomo's figurines and stone axes were on loan from his half-sister Milena, also a shaman. Both Perdomo and Milena are children of a famous Chachi shaman Jesusito, who had died the year before our arrival on the Cayapas. Throughout Chachi-land, Jesusito continues to hold a legendary status as

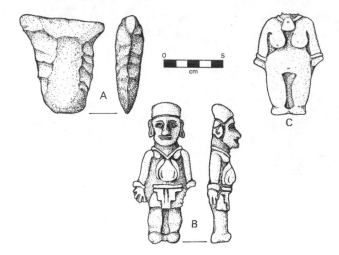

Figure 10.7 Archaeological objects included in Jesusito's *arte*: *a,* stone axe; *b-c,* ceramic figurines

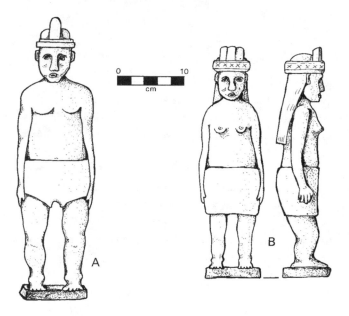

Figure 10.8 Wooden figurines in Jesusito's *arte*

a great shaman. His power stemmed from several sources: first, his *arte* was unsurpassed in efficacy; second, as a youth, he had apprenticed himself to a prominent shaman of the nearby Colorados; and third, he had visited Canelo shamans in the Ecuadorian Amazon from whom he learned curing songs and obtained particularly potent strains of pildé.

Both Perdomo and Milena received their shamanic training from Jesusito. Sons of shamans, if so disposed, are often instructed by their fathers. Female shamans, however, are rare among the Chachi, and Milena came to this role through what might be considered a natural predisposition. As an adolescent, Milena is said to have been "media loca," often going into trances that lasted several days. She actively sought out shamanic instruction from her father. Of his two shamanic offspring, Jesusito evidently preferred Milena and bequeathed his *arte* to her.

Although Milena was reluctant to have her inherited *arte* photographed, she allowed us to draw many of the objects. Among these were two ground stone axes (one is shown in figure 10.7) and several ceramic figurines (two are shown in figure 10.7). The axes and figurines were acquired from local archaeological deposits and are of types characteristic of the Cayapas region during the La Tolita period, ca 200 BC to AD 350 (DeBoer 1996). In the Chachi view of ethnic history, the earliest occupants of the Cayapas were the people who built the large mound site of La Tolita. These ancient folk were followed by the Indios Bravos, an uncivilized, cannibalistic, and otherwise nasty bunch. Finally, the Chachi came to the Cayapas from their former home in the Andes (Barrett 1925; DeBoer 1995). In Chachi archaeology, La Tolita was a time of extraordinary shamans, and La Tolitan axes and figurines are valued accordingly as *arte*.

In addition to these archaeological artifacts, recycled for shamanic purposes, Jesusito's *arte* included six wooden figurines. These can be considered in terms of three pairs. The first consists of a male and female, nude except for three-pronged headdresses and shorts in the case of the male, and a skirt in the case of the female (figure 10.8). Both figurines are considered to represent Chachi, although nothing like the three-pronged headdress is worn today, nor was such attire mentioned by Barrett in his 1925 ethnography.

The second pair also consists of a male and female. The male, dubbed Cipriano, is nude except for a brimmed hat (figure 10.9a). Although the brimmed hat suggests a European model, similar headgear is, in fact, found on prehistoric figurines from the Cayapas (figure 10.9b). Cipriano bears two other features of note. First, his exposed penis appears to be tied to his abdomen, a decidedly non-Chachi practice. Wassén (1935:64-65) recorded a similar penial treatment in toy figurines among the Nonamá of the southern Chocó. A connection is possible as the Chachi believe the shamans of coastal Colombia to be particularly powerful and deserving of emulation (Barrett 1925:352), and Chocó shamans are said to have visited the Chachi (Stout 1948:271). A second noteworthy feature is that, at some time, Cipriano lost his right arm. Perhaps this missing limb is merely an accident. Amputations and deformities are, however, common shamanic attributes (Reichel-Dolmatoff 1961b:236; Ginzburg 1991; Taussig 1993:17-18). Cipriano's female partner, named "Mama Grande" or "Mama Negra," is also nude except for a pillbox hat otherwise unrecorded in Chachi material culture (figure 10.10). As one of her appellations suggests and as the Chachi aver, the Mama Negra represents a black. Although little love is lost between the Chachi and their black neighbors, neither are reluctant to visit the other's curers.

The third pair is of a different order entirely. These two carvings clearly represent European figures of authority, a clergyman ("El Obispo," figure 10.11a) and a soldier ("El Capitán," figure 10.11b). Figure 10.11c shows a second example of an El

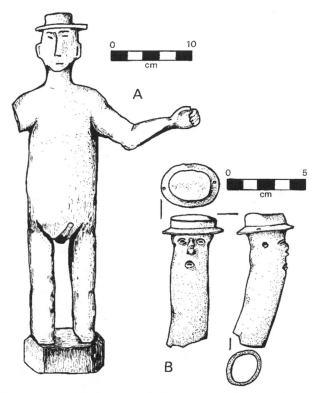

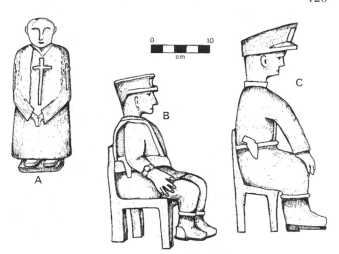

Figure 10.11 More of Jesusito's *arte*: *a*, "El Obispo"; *b*, "El Capitán"; *c*, another version of the "capitán" theme produced for sale in Quito. *a and b are after drawings by Milton Herrera; c is after a drawing by Leon Doyon*

Figure 10.9 *a*, Cipriano; *b*, a hollow ceramic figurine with brimmed hat from the prehistoric site of Herradura (C55), Río Cayapas. *a is after a drawing by Milton Herrera*

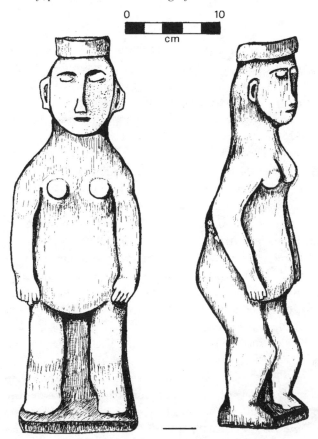

Figure 10.10 The "Mama Grande" or "Mama Negra." *After a drawing by Milton Herrera*

Capitán statue that was purchased in a tourist shop in Quito. I include this specimen to point out that carvings of the kind used in *arte* are increasingly popular in the folk art market (Einzmann 1985). As they have not been activated through shamanic songs and drugs, however, these carvings for sale are inert and do not qualify as *arte*.

The six figurines discussed above have a complex history that can be appreciated by placing them in genealogical context (figure 10.12). The first pair was commissioned by Vicente (no. 2 in figure 10.12), Jesusito's father and a very powerful shaman in his own right. The carver of these statues was Vicente's wife's grandfather (no. 1) who was not a shaman himself. After acquiring the first pair of statues, Vicente commissioned another carver to make Cipriano and the Mama Grande (shamans themselves rarely produce their own *arte*). Upon Vicente's death, Jesusito (no. 3) inherited these four statues. To supplement this power-laden inheritance, Jesusito commissioned the Obispo and the Capitán from another non-shaman carver. When Jesusito died, Milena (no. 7) became heir to what now amounted to three generations of arte.

This accumulated *arte* is not of equal power. The first pair of statues is believed to be the most powerful, followed by the odd couple of Cipriano and Mama Grande, with the Obispo and Capitán of least potency. This ranking is based evidently on genealogical time depth: the older the carving, the more power it possesses. This power becomes accessible, however, only through the knowledge of songs and drugs. Without this knowledge, the *arte* is ineffectual. Yet this crucial knowledge is never passed on with perfect fidelity—neither Milena nor Perdomo would claim to rival the shamanic accomplishments of Jesusito. There is a seeming conundrum at work in which the passage of time creates power while simultaneously dissipating access to that very same power.

But receding time is only part of the story. Distant space

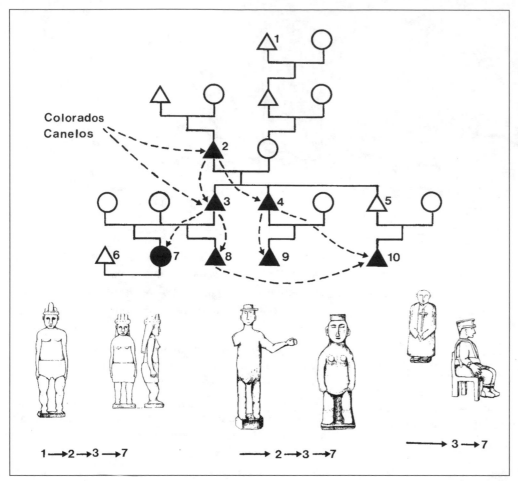

Figure 10.12 A partial genealogy of Chachi shamans and their *arte*. Solid symbols represent shamans. Dashed lines indicate shamanic learning routes. *1*, the carver of the statues shown in figure 10.8; *2*, Vicente; *3*, Jesusito; *4*, Vallejo; *5*, one of Jesusito's brothers who did not become a shaman; *6*, Vicente, the husband of Milena; *7*, Milena; *8*, Perdomo; *9*, Zamoro; *10*, Manuel. See text for discussion.

also plays a role. The privileged shamanic status of Jesusito and Vicente depended, in large part, on the fact that both traveled to obtain instruction from Colorado shamans and, later in their lives, from even more distant Canelos. Jesusito, in particular, received a double dose of such wisdom, visiting the groups for himself as well as receiving the exotic knowledge acquired by his father. In contrast, Vallejo (no. 4 in figure 10.12) never visited these foreign sources of shamanic power and, as a consequence, never achieved the renown of either Vicente or Jesusito. The same untraveled stigma befell the shamanic careers of Vallejo's son (no. 9) and nephew (no. 10). There is something almost Lacanian in this diagnosis in which the ontogenetic present is always withering away only to be resurrected (namely re-erected) by seeking the phylogenetic sources of power lodged long ago or far away. This quest, embodied in the nervous business of shamanism, prefigures what latter-day invaders would call anthropology.

Archaeology of Mimesis and Alterity

Does the Chachi case conform to Reichel-Dolmatoff's model for figurine use? Yes and no. Yes, in that Chachi shamans regularly use wooden, as well as ancient ceramic, figurines in their curing rites. No, in that these figurines are curated assiduously. As a result, figurines would leave

scant trace in the archaeological record. This is indeed the case. In more than thirty Chachi archaeological sites sampled to date, figurines and other shamanic paraphernalia are completely absent (DeBoer 1996).

Of more interest, however, is the apparent reason that the Chachi curate their *arte*. This *arte* accrues value over time, just as foreign knowledge exceeds local knowledge in its potency. As Taussig (1987:179) points out, the field of shamanic play is a fundamentally decentered one in which players are always on the periphery, the core always elsewhere, receding into the past or over the horizon.[3] This diagnosis also recalls arguments made by Mary Helms (1979, 1991, 1992) in which distant time, as congealed in Chachi *arte*, and distant space, as evinced in Jesusito's travels to the Colorado and Canelo, are accessed to create and maintain shamanic power. These observations lead to Taussig's opening query: Why do figurines represent non-Indians?

With respect to this question, the Chachi evidence is instructive. Three generations of shamanic figurines show major changes in representational form. The oldest cohort apparently displays Chachi, but extraordinary Chachi as marked by unusual three-lobed headdresses. It is as if these statues portray the strange in the familiar. The next pair shifts theme, and a foreign Indian who, from the Chachi point of view, has his genitalia shamelessly exposed is matched with a black female. Finally, the twin agents of state power—church and police—are represented by the Obispo and Capitán, respectively. These six figurines can be viewed as a kind of successional alterity in which the distant reaches of time and space are joined by the added dimension of social distance in which the strange "other" is made familiar.

If this diagnosis carries any merit, then a further puzzle is raised. If the other is so salient in the shamanic art of the Cuna, Chocó, and Chachi, then why are archaeologists so disposed to interpret prehistoric figurines as if they were windows into the local, the intra-societal, and the commonplace rather than, as ethnography suggests, mirrors reflecting and refracting the foreign and the exotic? How odd to remind anthropologists, as strategic shamans in their own right, that their gaze upon the other is returned.

Notes

1. I use this word in an everyday sense, but it is of interest to compare psychoanalytic usage:

> Transference - a process of actualization of unconscious wishes. Transference uses specific objects and operates in the framework of a specific relationship established with these objects. In the transference, infantile prototypes re-emerge and are experienced with a strong sense of immediacy. (Laplanche and Pontalis 1973:455)

2. For the Chachi proper, consult Carrasco (1983:168-169), Altschuler (1964:100), and Haro (1971:14-15), as well as Barrett's pioneer account (1925:344-352). Among other groups, the use of palm whisks to sweep away malevolent spirits is reported for the Colorado (Barriga 1986) and Canelo (Whitten 1976:146). Citing Zerries, Oberem (1980:278) argues that the palm whisk, as used in shamanic healing, may be a regional surrogate for the gourd rattle, otherwise widespread in South American shamanism. For a comparative account of spraying, see Parsons (1945:71). The ground stone axes, so prominently placed on Perdomo's "mesa" (Sharon 1976), also figure in a larger arena. These axes, invariably retrieved from archaeological sites, loom largely in the shamanic ideology of the Canelo (Whitten 1976:148-149), Colorado, and Cuna (Wassén 1949:37).

3. The lament over the passing of great shamans is widespread. In the early years of this century, Barrett noted that Chachi shamans seemed to be losing their influence, although great ones could still be found among the Cholo in neighboring Colombia (Barrett 1925:351-352). Langdon (1990) reports a similar case among the Siona of the upper Putumayo who, like the Chachi, perceive an erosion of their own shamanic power while believing that powerful shamans still exist among the Secoya, Sibundoy, and Cofán. The Coto (Mai huna) of the lower Napo give the same diagnosis (Bellier 1994:112), as do the Quijos of the upper Napo (Oberem 1980:278-279). As Nordenskiold's Cuna informant Ruben Pérez Kantule summarized: "The neles of the old days possessed much greater powers than those of the present time." (Wassén 1938:85)

The Spectacled Bear in Iconic Imagery of Ancient Panama and Colombia

Mary W. Helms

IN MANY REGIONS OF THE WORLD, one of the animals most celebrated and symbolized in myth, ritual, and ceremony is the bear. Bear sacrifices, ritualistic bear hunts, and recognition of the bear in shamanic contexts have been widespread and very likely have great antiquity in areas inhabited by bears (Campbell 1959:334–347; Hallowell 1926; Ohnuki-Tierney 1984:70–71, 74, 90–96, 99; see also references in Shepard and Sanders 1985). In the northern hemisphere of Europe, Asia, and North America, the bear has been accorded a wide range of exceptional and supernatural qualities. It has been associated with wildness and fearlessness; rebirth, curing, and success in the hunt; and mediation with the spirit world, particularly as a liminal being that, as cave dweller, moves between the earth's surface and the underworld or conjoins water, land, and sky with its skills as fisher and swimmer, terrestrial walker, and arboreal climber.

The bear is also noted for its very human-like appearance and behavior, including its frequent use of upright stance; its large head with broad skull, heavy forehead, strong cheekbones, and eyes nearly in a frontal plane; its close attendance on its playful and expressive cubs, including nursing in a sitting position and occasional cuffs and spankings; its plantigrade five-toed footprint and agile use of forepaws for digging, handling, and climbing; its tendancy, when walking, to create and utilize narrow trails that look like human footpaths; and its very human-like anatomy when skinned (Shepard and Sanders 1985:Chapter 1). In light of such anatomical and behavioral characteristics, the bear is frequently anthropomorphized as a furry human. Beliefs that the bear is kin to humans, in shamanic bear-human transformation, and in the bear as human ancestor were and are widespread, as are beliefs in the bear as animal king or Master of Animals associated with treasure and properly hunted only by chiefs (Shepard and Sanders 1985:Chapter 3; Goldman 1975:147–148, 234; Locher 1932:18–19; Ingold 1987:257).

In this chapter, I review evidence suggesting that the spectacled bear (*Tremarctos ornatus*), the single remaining member of the genus *Ursus* native to South America and the only bear still found in the southern hemisphere (where several species of bears once roamed), may have been accorded comparable qualities by indigenous peoples of the Andes and portions of adjacent lower Central America. I also suggest that the spectacled bear may have served as the zoological prototype for certain design motifs found on various expressions of pre-Columbian art from Panama and Colombia. My position rests initially on the logical argument that an animal accorded so much ideological attention elsewhere in the world might be expected to receive comparable attention here. More specifically, I argue that certain physiological characteristics of the spectacled bear may be identified in the iconography associated with San Agustín, Colombia, and Coclé, Panama. Further support for the spectacled bear as a symbolically significant animal may be found in the scattered ethnographic comments and fragments of tales and myths that I have encountered in the ethnographic literature.

Range and Characteristics of *Tremarctos ornatus*

The ecological range of the spectacled bear, or Andean bear as it is sometimes called, extends from western Venezuela and Colombia (and possibly portions of adjacent Panama) south through the Andes to Bolivia and Chile. Its territory in general has included the eastern and western Andean slopes and coastal foothills of Chile and Bolivia, Peru, Ecuador, Colombia, and western Venezuela. Unconfirmed sightings have also been reported from southern Panama. In the Pleistocene, its range was much wider; fossil remains have been found as far north as Mexico and Florida (Davis 1955:25). Within these regions, spectacled bears can thrive in very diverse habitats from 600 to 13,800 feet (180 to 4,200 m) altitude, but are most com-

Figure 11.1 A spectacled bear (*Tremarctos ornatus*). Facial markings are highly individualistic. This cub shows partial spectacles around the eyes. *Photograph by Jessie Cohen. By permission of Jessie Cohen and the National Zoological Park, Smithsonian Institution, Washington, DC*

mon in cloud forest and *páramo* (6,000 to 8,800 feet; Weinhardt 1993:134). More specifically, "most of its year is spent in deep, wet forests, from which it moves with the seasons to alpine forest and páramo, or even into the high elfin forest, steppe, or thorn forest and desert" (Shepard and Sanders 1985:49; Peyton 1980; van Gelder 1990:733; Lumpkin 1986:4; Walker 1975:1171). With its territory increasingly reduced by human encroachment, the spectacled bear, formerly abundant throughout its range, is reported now to inhabit only the more inaccessable (to humans) portions of its potential range (Peyton 1980:652).

Tremarctos ornatus typically grows to about 5 to 6 feet in head and body length. It has a short, stubby (2 to 3 inches) tail and stands about 30 inches high at the shoulder. It may weigh as much as 300 pounds. The spectacled bear can be striking in appearance because its blackish-brown coat is often marked with "a whitish or yellowish coloration on the muzzle that extends upward to encircle each eye, like comic spectacles, and downward over the throat to the chest, where it forms an irregularly defined ring" (van Gelder 1990:733; Walker 1975:1171; see figure 11.1). These markings are highly variable among individuals, however, and do not appear uniformly on all individuals. This plant-eating bear is also distinguished by an unusually wide and massive skull, porportionate to its size, due to the development of heavy jaw muscles needed to crush

branches, stalks, palm nuts, bromeliad hearts, and other plant materials (Shepard and Sanders 1985:50, 53; Peyton 1980:642–647; Allen 1942:398–399; Lumpkin 1986:6; Davis 1955).

As with bears in general, the incisors are not specialized, but the canines are elongate, and the molars are broad and flat with tubercular crowns (figure 11.19; Walker 1975:1169; Davis 1955:Figure 2). Also as with bears in general, the paw print made by the spectacled bear appears very human-like, displaying five digits (actually nonretractile claws) and with the entire sole touching the ground (van Rosen 1990:301). *Tremarctos ornatus* is an agile climber on cliffs and in trees, where it constructs platforms of broken branches by pulling thin fruit-bearing branches toward itself until they break and then repositioning itself on top of the resulting "platform" to reach more distant branches. Such platforms are said also to be used for day bedding (Peyton 1980:644).

Hunting and Lore

Spectacled bears, being humid forest residents much of the time (Lumpkin 1986:4; Weinhardt 1993:134; Peyton 1980), generally have remained apart from humans. Yet, since pre-Columbian times, bears have been hunted or killed as nuisances if caught raiding cultivated fields (Shepard and Sanders 1985:51; Rowe 1946:217; Gilmore 1950:454; Allen 1942:399–400; Steward and Métraux 1948:569; Bennett 1946:103; Hernandez de Alba 1948:394; Peyton 1980:648–650). The bear, frequently anthropomorphized (Peyton 1980:647), also has figured in tales, myths, and legends, and can be accorded a degree of ceremonial significance. Body parts, too, are considered to have some curing value as charms or medicine (Weinhardt 1993:136).

Data on these topics (which are of particular interest as evidence of ideological and symbolic contexts that might underlie artistic representation of the bear) are few but suggestive. Gilmore states that the bear of the high eastern Andean slopes "seems to be an important animal in legends in the southern part of its range, and many fantastic qualities and even shapes are attributed to it" (1950:376). Speaking of the fifteenth century Cañari of southern Ecuador, Murra says that bears were "mentioned among deities" (1946:801). According to a late sixteenth or early seventeenth century Augustinian friar, "the Indians of the Andes, who live in the lands behind snow-capped mountains, where it always rains and where it is very hot (like in Panama and Cartegena), and the Indians who live in the mountains, worship Tigers, Lions, *Bears* and Serpents, because there is an abundance of these species in their countries. Those [people] of Guanuco [worship] a rampant Lion, ... those of Tomebamba [the present-day city of Cuenca in Ecuador] a *Bear*..." (quoted in Zuidema 1985:234, parentheticals by Zuidema, my italics).

Urton reports, with reference to the twentieth century southern Peruvian Andes, that, while few villagers have actually seen a real spectacled bear, or *ukuku*, they are nonetheless "among the most common animals represented by dancers in Andean villages," the dancers always being unmarried (that is, unsocialized) adolescent men (see note 2; Urton 1985:270, 271–272).[1] In this region, there are also numerous myths about bears (many of which are similar to Spanish tales), including the allegation that *ukukus* will run away from men but not from women, and tales about women being raped by, or having sexual intercourse with, bears and subsequently giving birth to bear-human children (Urton 1985:271). Because of their combination of human and non-human (wild, natural) traits, bears (like adolescent males) are regarded overall as representing the boundary between true humans and true animals (Urton 1985:272, 274).[2]

Further north, contact-era accounts by Europeans note that, among the indigenous chiefdoms of northern Venezuela, "some of the most distinguished warriors were clad in puma or bear skins, with the animal's mouth placed over the head" (Kirchhoff 1948:489). Among the Muisca of highland Colombia, the bear is said to have been the patron of drunkards, weavers, and cloth dyers (Labbé 1986:155), while in postcontact Panamanian (Kuna) tales, the bear is briefly mentioned as a "brother" (along with a number of other animal brothers) of the culture-hero Iberorkun (Nordenskiöld 1979:281, 283). Twentieth century native herbalists and healers of southwest Colombia (the widely traveled Inganos) include among their wide assortment of medicines and charms "dessicated paws of the jaguar and the bear" (Taussig 1980:237). In mountain towns, bear fat may be sold to treat rheumatism (Taussig 1987:272).

Also speaking of the Ingano and Kamsá peoples of southwestern Colombia (ancient residents of the Sibundoy Valley), McDowell says, "There are no longer any bears in the Sibundoy Valley, but the elders still remember seeing them there, and what is more, the bear has left behind quite a presence in the lore of the native communities of the valley. In mythic narrative among the Kamsá and Ingano people, the bear figures as a somewhat oafish character, often the blundering victim of tricksters like the rabbit and the squirrel. In another guise, known generally as the 'Juan Orso' tale, the bear as a animal-person shows an unwarranted interest in human females" (McDowell 1989:51).

McDowell also mentions a favorite story episode concerning the bear and the trickster squirrel in which the physically strong, but apparently not very intelligent, bear (also portrayed as the *gobernador*, political leader of the community) is tricked and outwitted by his wily opponent (1989:55). In another Sibundoy tale, an origins myth in which the bear is portrayed in a more flattering light, an ancestral hunter acquires the necessary spirit power to become a Master of Animals, "one which is able to *transform himself into the jaguar or the bear*" (McDowell 1989:119; my emphasis). The U'wa (Tunebo) of

the Sierra Nevada de Cocuy also recognize shamanic transformation into jaguar, bird, or bear as a result of hallucinogenically induced visionary power (Osborn 1990:151).

Finally, there is the elusive boráro or kurupíra, a fearsome creature of the forest known among many Amazonia tribes and described by Reichel-Dolmatoff for the Desana. The boráro is suggestive of the bear in many respects, although descriptions also seem to combine bear and jaguar motifs such that Reichel-Dolmatoff queries whether a single basic concept may ultimately be involved. Basically, however, the essential creature seems very bear-like. As a supernatural being, the Desana described the boráro as "a tall naked man with a hairy chest, short hair cut horizontally, and a huge penis. His eyes are red and glowing, and he has large, curved fangs like those of a jaguar" (Reichel-Dolmatoff 1971:86). A more generalized description, focusing on the basic characteristics of the boráro common to many tribal accounts, describes him as "a monstrous man-like being, covered with shaggy black hair, with huge pointed fangs protruding from his mouth" (Reichel-Dolmatoff 1975a:182–190). The boráro's name comes from its roar, likened to that of an enraged jaguar. Its ears are large, erect, and pointed forward, and it has various physiological anomalies, such as feet that are twisted backward and no knee joints.

The boráro lives in the cliffs and hills and spends much time in the forest or on headwaters of streams where it gathers crabs, its favorite food. Sometimes, the boráro is seen sunning himself in a jungle clearing. This creature kills unwary hunters, either by urinating on them or by embracing the person and holding him tightly to its chest until the body is crushed and pulverized. It is generally viewed in a very negative context, being foul smelling and destructive. The boráro is called a "chief of the animals" by the Desana, although it does not interact with hunters in this capacity. Reichel-Dolmatoff suggests, however, that in the past the boráro was the Master of Animals and that it was accorded its negative image relatively recently, at least among the Desana (Reichel-Dolmatoff 1971:86–88; 1975a:182–190).

Although Reichel-Dolmatoff does not suggest a zoological prototype for this creature, seeing it instead as totally imaginary (1975a:190), the description appears largely compatible with the bear, that is, a large, hairy, man-like being that lives in the forest or on headwater regions, is seldom seen by humans, and can kill with a deadly hug.[3] The description contains jaguar-related features, too, such as the large fangs, which are discussed further below. In fact, Reichel-Dolmatoff notes that "the boraro and the jaguar have many characteristics in common that makes one suspect that only one basic concept is involved" (1971:86, note 13). This comment is interesting in light of the ethnographic data mentioned above where dessicated paws of both bear and jaguar are peddled by traveling curers and

where the ancestral hunter as Master of Animals or the shaman can transform into either a bear or a jaguar. It also is in
accord with observations by Lévi-Strauss (1978:427) concerning the interchangeability of the bear with felines (as well as
with large deer and horned snakes) in North American mythology.

The Bear in Ancient Panamanian Art

Although there are no confirmed sightings of spectacled bears
from twentieth century Panama, it seems reasonable to suggest that a thousand years ago the range of *Tremarctos ornatus*
may well have included cordilleras of the Isthmus. At the very
least, ancient Panamanians would have known of the bear
from their extensive Colombian and western Venezuelan con-
tacts. Assuming that the spectacled bear was known to Panamanians, and given the symbolic and cosmological significance accorded the bear in other regions of North and South
America, it also seems reasonable to assume that the bear
would have been considered a very special animal relative to
humans in Panamanian ideology, especially to hunters and to
others, such as chiefs and shamans, associated with cosmo-
logically "outside" (including forest) phenomena.

Special supernatural qualities very likely were attributed
to the bear, and it is quite conceivable that indigenous Panamanian belief systems recognized shaman-bear transformation (among other forms) or identified the bear as a type of
Master or Mistress of Animals. In fact, given the virtually universal attribution of special qualities to bears wherever they
have been known, it would be strange indeed if such were not
the case not only in pre-Columbian Panama but also in the
adjacent northern Andes. Evidence for such attributions may
exist in the pre-Columbian indigenous art of the Isthmus, for
there are several motifs that suggest that the spectacled bear
may have served as the zoological prototype for creatures depicted in both ceramic and metallurgical art associated with
prehistoric Panama. The materials I consider are known primarily from excavations in central Panama, at the Sitio Conte,
involving caches and burials of high-status individuals dating from approximately AD 500 to 1100 (Lothrop 1942; Cooke
1985; Hearne and Sharer 1992). Let us begin with metallurgical art, focusing on depictions embossed on several gold sheet
plaques probably worn on the chest.

The designs on these plaques depict a four-limbed, planti-
grade-footed anthropomorphic figure with small ears, large
head, and (sometimes) distinctive circular or triangular chest
marking standing upright and facing forward with out-
stretched arms. Two long-tailed creatures usually hang from
its waist (Hearne and Sharer 1992:70–77, Plates 1–7; Plates 1
and 2 are shown in figures 11.2 and 11.3). In a previous publication (Helms 1977), I argued for an identification of the waist-
suspended animals as iguanas, and described in passing the
being carrying them as a sacred-secular authority figure, such
as a Master of Animals, a shamanic priest or chief, or a culture

Figure 11.2 Design on embossed gold plaque from Sitio
Conte. *The University Museum, University of Pennsylvania,
no. 40-13-26. Drawing by Mary Helms*

Figure 11.3 Design on embossed gold plaque from Sitio
Conte. *The University Museum, University of Pennsylvania,
no. 40-13-3. Drawing by Mary Helms*

Figure 11.4 Coclé polychrome ceramic plate depicting front-facing, bipedal figure with large head and chest markings. *From Lothrop (1976:42 left). By permission of Dover Publications*

hero-cum-hunter who is carrying game attached (belted) to his waist in the manner of hunters. (This imagery was suggested largely by Kuna and Talamancan Indian myths and by Desana, Sherente, and Boróro myths with themes appropriate for the Panamanian materials; see Helms 1977).[4]

I wish to argue for the spectacled bear as zoological prototype for these culture-heroes, Masters of Animals, or shamanic or chiefly personages. Representations of the central figure in question depict several characteristics relative to the proposed identification. The figure is upright in stance and shows flat rows of rectangular teeth with no extended canines, both anthropomorphic signifiers. The hands and feet, or paws, however, are clawed but often with palms and soles embossed in such a way as to suggest a plantigrade (full-footed, with sole and heel touching ground) print. The head, trapezoidal in outline, is large relative to the body and appears to be enhanced by a headdress. (It is noteworthy that the boráro wears a feather headdress; Reichel- Dolmatoff 1975a:187). The prominent eyes appear ringed, the nose is broad with nostrils clearly portrayed, and, as mentioned above, the chest, in several examples, has a distinctive marking, sometimes either triangular (Hearne and Sharer 1992:71, 72, 74–77) or circular (Easby and Scott 1970:Figure 237).

The upright stance, with four limbs ending in plantigrade hands and feet, and the uniform rectangular teeth can readily be construed as human signifiers. That the extremities are also clawed suggests an animal combining both claws and plantigrade stance, which, zoologically, could reference the bear. In addition, the broad head, which can easily be described as

"massive" relative to the rest of the body, is particularly suggestive of *Tremarctos ornatus*, whose head shape is unusually wide for a bear (actually more panda-like) due to its heavy jaw and musculature. The broad nose with frontal flaring nostrils could be interpreted as animal as readily as human. The seemingly ringed eyes can be related to the distinct coloration that produces "spectacles" in the bear's appearance, and the triangular or circular chest markings that appear on some depictions may also reference the bear's distinctive coloration. Combining all these features, with particular reference to the large, broad headshape, plantigrade but clawed extremities, possibly ringed eyes, and distinctive chest markings, I am persuaded that the spectacled bear could easily be the zoological prototype of the form depicted here. It is also apparent, however, that the depiction (specifically, the upright posture; the flat, rectangular teeth; and perhaps the nose style) also speaks of an anthropomorphic identification for the bear and/or of a human-animal duality or transformation theme.

The postulated imagery of the anthropomorphic bear as mythical hunter or Master of Animals carrying iguanas as its game is particularly interesting in light of a Sibundoy tale, briefly mentioned above, involving the bear and the trickster squirrel in which the wily, intelligent squirrel outwits the physically strong, but dull-witted, bear. More specifically, the squirrel tricks the bear into crushing his own testicles with a rock (McDowell 1989:55). This incident is identical to an incident in a tale of the Kuna Indians of Panama in which the protagonist is also a physically very strong but not very bright personage known as Iguana-chief who competes with an intelligent, solar-related hero, Tad Ibe.[5] These two also compete in various power struggles and competitions including a pain endurance contest in which they are to beat their testicles with stones. The intelligent Tad Ibe wins this contest by using his wits (he pushes his testes back into his abdomen so that the rock strikes only empty skin) while Iguana-chief goes through with the contest as planned. Although Iguana-chief easily endures the physical challenge of this trial, he eventually is defeated and killed by his wily challenger, who strips him of his supernatural power and turns him into an edible iguana, condemning him henceforth to serve as food for people (Helms 1977:74–77).

The bear and Iguana-chief hold identical structural positions in these two episodes, both seeming to represent Nature in contrast with Culture. As such, the bear would also appear suitable as tangible embodiment of the primordial (and presumably forest-dwelling, that is, natural) Master of Animals as suggested by the Sibundoy origins myth mentioned above (McDowell 1989:119). Considered overall, and recognizing that the details of myths and stories may change over the centuries, there seems nonetheless to be suggestive evidence of an indigenous symbolism supporting an anthropomorphic, spectacled bear-cum-Master of Animals or hero-hunter carrying

Figure 11.5 Coclé polychrome design depicting four-limbed, bipedal, front-facing, large-headed figure with small ears, chest triangle and headdress. *From Lothrop (1976:25 center left). By permission of Dover Publications*

Figure 11.6 Two quadrants of this polychrome plate depict a four-limbed, bipedal, front-facing large-headed creature with distinctive circle on abdomen. *From Lothrop (1976:15 lower left). By permission of Dover Publications*

Figure 11.7 Front-facing four-limbed bipedal creatures with rounded heads and distinctive chest or abdominal markings. *From Lothrop (1976:14 lower right). By permission of Dover Publications*

Figure 11.8 Front-facing four-limbed bipedal creatures with rounded heads, small ears, and distinctive abdominal markings. *From Lothrop (1976:14 top right). By permission of Dover Publications*

Figure 11.9 More abstract rendering of broad-headed front-facing creature with small ears and circled eyes and, perhaps, headdress. *From Lothrop (1976:15 right). By permission of Dover Publications*

Figure 11.10 Abstract rendering of broad-headed, front-facing creature with small ears and circled eyes and delineated nose or snout. *From Lothrop (1976:15 top left). By permission of Dover Publications*

Figure 11.11 Coclé polychrome plate depicting plantigrade footprints. *From Lothrop (1976:29 lower left). By permission of Dover Publications*

Figure 11.12 Coclé polychrome plate possibly depicting plantigrade footprints. *From Lothrop (1976:49 lower left). By permission of Dover Publications*

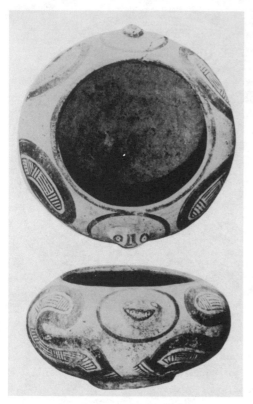

Figure 11.13 Coclé effigy bowl depicting the round-headed creature with ringed eyes and delineated nose or snout. Note stubby tail. *From Lothrop (1976:37 top left and center left). By permission of Dover Publications*

Figure 11.14 Coclé effigy ceramic depicting round-headed creature with small ears. *From Lothrop (1976:38 top left). By permission of Dover Publications*

iguanas from his waist as the central figure on the Sitio Conte gold plaques.

Turning from Panamanian goldwork to ceramics, elaborately patterned polychrome wares, also associated with the Sitio Conte, show several design motifs that also suggest the spectacled bear as zoological prototype. These also involve a large-headed, four-limbed, bipedally stanced, forward-facing personage sometimes with definitive chest markings.[6] Figures 11.4 and 11.5 (see also Lothrop 1976:25 top right and left, 91 top; Labbé 1995:Figures 12, 38, 106, 107–109), for example, look quite similar to the figures on the gold plaques discussed above in terms of general body form and overall depiction. Other ceramic designs may also reference the spectacled bear, though in a somewhat different manner. Two of the quadrants of figure 11.6,[7] for example, again reveal a four-limbed but upright stanced, forward-facing, broad-headed creature with rounded ears and round midsection that contains a central circle. Sometimes the head, with its round eyes, long nose, and occasionally small ears, is more rounded (figures 11.7, 11.8; see also Lothrop 1976:14 top left, 13 right).[8] Because some descriptions of the boráro-type creature say that the animal has a very tough skin *except* around the navel (see note 3), it is interesting that many Coclé ceramic depictions of this crea-

Figure 11.15 Front-facing, small-eared creature of female gender with ringed eyes and abdominal marking. *From Lothrop (1976:16 lower right). By permission of Dover Publications*

Figure 11.16 Stone sculpture from mesita A, west barrow, San Agustín depicting stocky four-limbed figure in bipedal stance. Note very large rectangular head, outlined eyes, and tooth patterning contrasting overlapping and pointed canines with even rectangular incisors and molars. *From Reichel-Dolmatoff (1972a:17, Figure 3). Copyright Praeger Publishers*

Figure 11.17 Stone head from mesita B, northwest barrow, San Agustín. Note encircled eyes and tooth patterning contrasting overlapping and pointed canines with even, rectangular tooth rows. *From Reichel-Dolmatoff (1972a:35, Figure 11). Copyright Praeger Publishers*

ture also show a distinct abdominal circle that could be a navel as readily (or more so) as a stylized chest marking (figures 11.6–11.8; see also Helms 1995:55–56).

Sometimes, the round-eared, broad-faced figure with circled eyes appears in more abstract form (figures 11.9, 11.10; see also Lothrop 1976:16 top right). Several representations (figures 11.11, 11.12) appear to depict plantigrade paws or footprints with narrower heels and broader fronts made by an animal that stands on the entire sole of the foot with the heel touching the ground and suggestive of bear prints (although several other possibilities could be considered, too, including human prints or coati prints; see the discussion in Helms 1995:66).[9] Still other ceramic pieces in effigy form (for example, figures 11.13, 11.14; see also Labbé 1995:Figure 134) depict a round-eared and round- (or encircled) eyed snouted creature with a stubby tail whose facial portrayals appear similar to some of the facial portrayals shown before and which may also reference the spectacled bear.[10]

Some of the ceramic "bear" designs obviously are of female gender (figures 11.15, 11.5; see also Lothrop 1976:25, 6 lower left; Labbé 1995:Figure 107), which raises the question of whether they may depict a Panamanian variant on the very widespread myth of the Bear Mother in which a human girl becomes wife to, or is raped by, a bear and produces bear-sons who are capable of human-animal transformation and become great hunters (Shepard and Sanders 1985:58–61; Urton 1985:271; see also the ancestral hunter who transforms into a bear in the Sibundoy tale mentioned above). McDowell (1989:111–112) notes an association between a probable bear and a young man transformed into a woman, in a Sibundoy valley tale. There are also references in Colombian tribes to herbivores associated with female principles or female identification as opposed to male attributes associated with carnivorous predator animals (Labbé 1986:124; Reichel-Dolmatoff 1972b:57). The supernatural Great Mother of the Kuna (Muu) and of the Kogi also come to mind, especially beliefs among the latter that all animal spirits (as well as the doubles of all men) dwell at Great Mother's sacred temple mountain (that is, Great Mother as Mistress of Animals) and that the remote mountain highlands—the bleak and silent *páramos*—are the sacred abode of the Mother Goddess, creator of the universe and humankind and provider of good harvest, good health, and protection against evil (Reichel-Dolmatoff 1978c:13–25; Reichel-Dolmatoff 1974:297; Nordenskiold 1979:372–374, 385–386, 437–438). Although no explicit association is made between Great Mother and a mammalian prototype today, the bear as seasonal denizen of the *páramo* and more permanent occupant of the mountain forests, that is, as resident of isolated, sacred places frequented by religious specialists, conceivably could have been associated with Great Mother in more ancient times.

Considered overall, evidence appears suggestive of iconography referencing the spectacled bear on Coclé polychrome

Figure 11.18 Stone figure from Alto de Lavaderos depicting upright stanced, four-limbed creature with very large head. Note circled eyes and dental pattern contrasting overlapping and pointed canines with even, rectangular incisors and molars. *From Reichel-Dolmatoff (1972a:80, Figure 49). Copyright Praeger Publishers*

wares, though the identification must remain tentative. It is well to remember that other animals may have some of the same characteristics associated with bear imagery. For example, other animals have plantigrade paws—the coati, for one, which also sports small rounded ears, white-ringed eyes, and whitish muzzle, chin, throat, and chest (as well as a long ringed tail), and is definitely portrayed in Coclé art (Lothrop 1976:65 lower right; 60 center left; 57 lower left; 43 lower right; 66 top left and right). The squirrel monkey also presents a definitely spectacled appearance with its mask-like white face and white-ringed eyes (Boinski 1992; Helms 1995:71).

If the facial expression of the round-headed, front-facing, open-mouthed or "smiling" creatures is considered alone, the sloth might be a possibility, too. This parallel is enhanced in depictions where the paws are shown as being strongly clawed. Because sloth ears are very inconspicuous, however, this possibility seems to weaken if ears are distinctly depicted (Lévi-Strauss 1969:355, Figure 25).[11] Conceivably, too, all these diverse animals were considered variations on a basic theme in which the spectacled bear stood as the primary zoological prototype for an important "personage" in Coclé symbolism, cosmology, and art.

The Bear at San Agustín

The extensive archaeological area known as San Agustín, situated near the headwaters of the Magdalena River in the mountainous country (the Colombian Massif) where Andean highlands and tropical lowlands meet, is famous for its freestanding stone sculptures, relief carvings on stone slabs, and other remains of a pre-Columbian society. Among the sculptures are a number of tall (6 to 8 feet) or medium height (2 to 4 feet) columnar statues depicting standing beings portrayed as "top-heavy figures with oversize heads, squat bodies, contracted arms, and dwarfed legs" (Reichel-Dolmatoff 1972a:66; and illustrations). More specifically, the representations of body form portray

> an almost straight-sided trunk, with high square shoulders, ... surmounted by an enormous head; the thin flat arms hang down or are bent stiffly at the elbows, ... The lower part of the body, the legs and feet, are barely outlined, the whole figure, because of the hunched shoulders, appearing to lean slightly forward.... It is the face, the grim mouth, and the huge eyes, in which all expressive force is concentrated.(Reichel-Dolmatoff 1972b:51)

Reichel-Dolmatoff goes on to note the "human" quality of the body, indicating, for example, that its arms end in fingers, not claws, and stressing the human-like facial depictions (1972b:52).[12]

Supporting his iconographic data with an impressive body of relevent ethnographic information, Reichel-Dolmatoff focuses his interpretation of these sculptures on the feline qualities they also seem to depict. In this context, the pieces were said to show a "jaguar-monster," once again emphasizing

> a heavily compressed human body with an enormous head whose composite features—bared fangs, glaring eyes, and flaring nostrils—represent a snarling feline. (Reichel-Dolmatoff 1972a:69)

and whose primary feline feature was the fanged mouth (Reichel-Dolmatoff 1972b:52; see figures 11.16 through 11.18

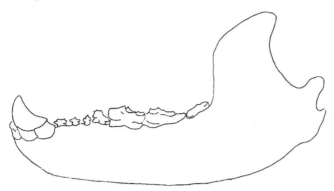

Figure 11.19 Tooth pattern of *Tremarctos ornatus*. Adapted from Davis (1955:Figure 2). *Drawing by Mary Helms*

and additional illustrations in Reichel-Dolmatoff 1972a).

Without denying the strong possibility that feline referencing is included in these sculptures, I should like to argue the additional possibility that the zoological prototype for these carvings also references the spectacled bear and that the underlying themes include a bear-human or bear-jaguar-human transformation motif that may also reference the bear as Master (or Mistress) of Animals. The basis for this argument rests primarily on general sculptural form: the solid, stocky body with high, square, "hunched" shoulders and disproportionately large (wide) head with large outlined eyes that appears to lean slightly forward and the overall anthropomorphic quality—a description that would seem to fit the spectacled bear very well (the general block carving style for San Agustín statues notwithstanding).

The major objection to this identification would appear to lie in the depictions of large overlapping canines—the "fangs" of the "jaguar." Although there is no reason why the features depicted could not reference both bear and feline attributes, I think it advisable, nonetheless, to consider further the nature of tooth depiction overall. The dentition portrayed on these statues consistently reveals flat, rectangular incisors (or row of front teeth) and flat, rectangular molars in addition to the overlapping pointed canines. This tooth pattern can be considered as representative of a zoologically known animal or, alternatively, the dental representation can be considered as thematic or symbolic rather than literal. If the latter position is pursued, it can be argued that the intent may be to *contrast* two very distinctive tooth forms—the elongated and pointed canines with the flat, rectangular "other" teeth—and to do so by stylistically overemphasizing *both* the evenness and regularity of the rectangular tooth rows and the elongation and pointedness of the canines. Such a contrast presumably would encode either a transformation theme (from one type of animal to another) or a multiple persona theme (a being combining the attributes of both animals). The most general transformation or multiple persona thematic reading that can be given this style of dental depiction identifies the rectangular

teeth as connoting humanness and the pointed canines as connoting a non-human being.

In a paper also discussing the monumental sculpture of the northern Andes and lower Central America, Bruhns suggests that a particular zoological identification associating fangs with a definite species of animal is irrelevant in a given depiction. She believes that fangs are, instead, a stylistic device signifying in general terms the presence of the supernatural, that is, identifying the figure so adorned as being in some manner or degree supernatural (1992:337). Applied to the San Agustín sculpture, Bruhns' persuasive point would seem to fit very well with a general human-nonhuman transformation theme. It is intriguing, nonetheless, to consider what, if any, categories of fanged creatures might have served as tangible prototypes or archetypes of such supernaturalism for pre-Columbian societies. Even if (following Bruhns) in sculpture, such as that at San Agustín, pointed and overlapping canines are taken to signal non-human in general, it is still reasonable to consider various animal identifications as possible zoologically known prototypes or tangible manifestations of supernatural non-humans. From this perspective, any animal with reasonably distinctive canines could be a candidate for the animal portion of the San Agustín sculptures under consideration, including the bear, whose canines are somewhat elongate. In addition, the spectacled bear is also characterized by generalized incisors and broad flat molars (figure 11.19), which could be easily rendered stylistically as rectangular teeth, as on the San Agustín sculptures, suggesting that the anthropomorphic nature of the sculptures could reference the bear as readily as it could humans.

Alternatively, it is possible that the large canines represent the jaguar while the large head and stocky body represent the bear. Indeed, as we have seen ethnographically, the bear and the jaguar could easily have filled comparable ideological roles or statuses as tangible zoological prototypes for mythological or supernatural beings and/or as iconic themes and design motifs in northern Andean belief systems in general. Thus, there would be good reason why they could be jointly represented on the San Agustín sculptures. In addition, Campbell has pointed out that when the significance of the Eurasian circumpolar bear as Master Animal is extended into Africa, the role played by the bear in the north is taken by the great felines—lion, leopard, panther, and so forth (Campbell 1959:347, 340 Figure).

In the corresponding southern portion of the Western hemisphere, of course, the great feline version of the Master Animal is the jaguar. Given that San Agustín is uniquely situated where highlands meet lowlands and given the extensive range of both the bear and the jaguar, it seems entirely plausible that the widespread and pervasive jaguar symbolism of the tropics should meet an equally potent and fundamental Andean bear symbolism at such a place, and that the supernatural role (such as Masters of Animals or as transformational forms of living shamans and/or primordial bearhunters) accorded these animals in their respective domains should merge.

Depiction of a stocky, large-headed, bear-like being with jaguar fangs contrasted with human-like teeth, as well as other human or cultural appurtenances also depicted on the various sculptures (for example, headdresses, ornaments, loincloth, hands rather than front paws), would perfectly express all these conjunctions. One wonders, too, if the same basic associations continue to be expressed in the boráro, for the boráro as a monstrous man-like being with huge pointed fangs protruding from its mouth seems to fit the San Agustín sculptures extremely well. The boráro also can wear a headdress and may carry a stick-rattle or a long-handled hoe (Reichel-Dolmatoff 1975a:187–188) just as the San Agustín sculptures wear headdresses and, in some cases, carry staffs. The San Agustín statues and the boráro thus may be conceptualizations of the same mythological-cum-zoological personage(s). Both may combine zoological prototypes of the spectacled bear and the jaguar with ancient concepts regarding the Master of the Animals and human-animal transformation.

Conclusion

In addressing issues of indigenous iconography, it is always well to remember, as Bruhns does, that the most important point intended by the artists is not what zoological specimens are portrayed but what such portrayals mean, what concepts they convey relative to the general cosmological principles that indigenous art makes tangible. However, to Western viewers, who often are not very well grounded in the principles and nuances of those cosmologies, identification of zoological species often appears to be the more manageable, more concrete analytical objective, especially when dealing with ancient art. Indeed, zoological identification may provide one of the best ways for Western viewers initially to approach the conceptual worlds of these societies, provided guidelines and comparisons are also sought in relevant ethnographic materials pertaining to more directly known cultures where the intricacies of the interwoven symbolic and cosmological associations accorded the diversity of flora and fauna, colors and odors, sounds and surfaces may be rendered more explicit and where the scholar may begin to learn to think in terms more appropriate to the social, symbolic, and cosmological settings in which the art was originally made, appreciated, and used. I first learned this vital guiding principle by reading the works of Reichel-Dolmatoff. It is a good and lasting legacy, in appreciation of which this essay is offered as a small token of thanks.

Notes

1. Urton reports that "the costumes of these ukuku dancers are virtually identical from one village to the next in the southern highlands of Peru. They consist of a tubular-shaped garment with arms, which is pulled on over the head; the garment is covered with overlapping layers of black, multicolored or, in some cases, white fringe. A small doll ..., which is itself dressed like an ukuku dancer, hangs on the front of the costume, usually on the left side of the chest; a bell or whistle hangs on the right side. The dancer wears a knitted "ski" mask that covers his head and face and has white circles around the eyes (like the spectacled bear) and a mirror over his forehead. Each dancer carries a whip of braided leather affixed to a wooden handle that is carved in spiral grooves" (1985:270).

2. Urton points out that, just as adolescents are young people on their way to becoming responsible community adults but are not yet full human beings in that respect, so bears are regarded as animals on their way to becoming human but are not truly human. That is, bears have a two-legged gait, alleged human-like mating practices, and the ability to eat wild and domestic animals and garden produce, but they are also unruly, destructive, and sexually aggressive and do not have language. In other words, bears are like adolescents (Urton 1985:272).

3. The boráro is known by many names and frequently occurs in Brazilian Indian legend. It has been described by other authors as a human-sized, reddish-haired creature that sits or stands upright, has long claws, is sometimes fanged, makes a loud shouting sound, has feet turned backward, and has an extremely bad smell. It also is said to eat palm hearts and fruits, and to have a very tough skin except around the navel. Although much of this description could fit the spectacled bear, there is speculation in some quarters that the beast may be a giant ground sloth generally thought to be long extinct (a skeleton of which was recovered some forty years ago from central Panama; see Conover 1994:20–23).

4. In earlier decades, these figures were frequently identified as "crocodile gods" or "alligator gods" (Lothrop 1937:119, 134–136; 1964:142,143; Easby and Scott 1970:Figures 236–238).

5. The bear is identified, as we have seen, with the town gobernador or political leader. Similarly, Iguana-chief is identified as a man of power.

6. Sometimes, chest markings appear to represent inner organs of the chest cavity (for example, the figures referenced in Labbé 1995) rather than external body markings. The two, of course, may easily be related.

7. The "bears" are paired with curassows in this figure (see Helms 1995:39–43, Figure 22).

8. This style of eye and nose depictions is also found on other animal forms depicted on Coclé ceramics, especially the serpent. Consideration of possible relationships between the themes of the serpent and bear are not pursued here.

9. The "footprints" in figure 11.12 are depicted in pairs, and allow an alternative identification as bivalve shells because the "digits" in each pair are asymmetrical in number, five and four, respectively, and would interdigitate well. In light of the implication discussed below that the bear may be associated with the Great Mother in Intermediate Area symbolism, it is intriguing to read that the Kogi of Colombia offer shells, including bivalves, to the Great Mother to increase fertility (Reichel-Dolmatoff 1974:298–299).

10. The depictions of the paws on these effigy pieces appear similar to a widely used "animal limb with paw" kenning frequently found on Coclé ceramic plates and effigy forms that may be another referent, in kenning form, to the bear in Panamanian ceramic art. See the discussion in Helms (1995:65, 66–67).

11. Some of the animals with "sloth" countenances also show definite tails, but in the world of myth the primordial sloth was originally well-tailed, as was the presumably extinct Pleistocene ground sloth (Conover 1994). In mythology, the sloth lost its tail due to greediness and unwillingness to share food (Pressmann 1991:84). A mythical tailed sloth may be depicted in Coclé art. See also note 3 regarding sloths and the boráro. It is quite conceivable that conceptual parallels existed in ancient isthmian lore linking the bear and the sloth (tree and/or ground) as primordial animals, and that such ideas still contribute to boráro themes.

12. One of the "beings" frequently portrayed on Panamanian ceramics sometimes also has flat digits on the upper limbs but claws on the lower, or vice versa (figure 11.15). Sometimes these depictions show a large-headed, stocky-bodied creature facing front; sometimes a side view of a long-faced creature with a stocky body is shown. See, for example, Lothrop (1976:45 bottom) and Labbé (1995:Figures 38, 109, 110). Sometimes, the contrast of the anthropomorphic versus the animal (digits versus claws) appears to be expressed by depicting limb ligatures, those representing anthropomorphic limbs, I suggest, being contained within the limb outlines while those representing animal limbs being extended beyond the limb outlines. See, for example, Lothrop (1976:25 top left).

Afterword

A Personal View of Gerardo Reichel-Dolmatoff and Venezuelan Archaeology

Erika Wagner

MY FIRST PERSONAL CONTACT with Don Gerardo was in March 1965 in New Haven, while I was writing my Ph.D. dissertation on the Carache area of the Venezuelan Andes. I was looking for information on the so-called bat-wing pendants that I had excavated—for the first time in a controlled archaeological context—in Miqumú, with an associated ^{14}C date of 650 AD. In those days there were few sources for comparison outside Venezuela, and specialists were even scarcer. Ben Rouse, my adviser, suggested that I write to Gerardo Reichel-Dolmatoff, then head of the Anthropology Department of the Universidad de Los Andes in Bogotá. I hesitated writing at first because I didn't think that such an internationally known and eminent scholar would be interested in an obscure graduate student from Yale. I was pleasantly surprised when he answered my letter promptly and politely. He not only gave me some useful references but he also aroused my curiosity in the Kogi or Kaggaba Indians of the Sierra Nevada de Santa Marta, a remarkable group, who he came to know over the years as well as his own family. Regarding the Kogi, he mentioned in the letter that "these *placas* are worn hanging from the elbows in pairs, while the Kogi priests dance." He believed the pendants—whether Colombian or Venezuelan—were Central American in origin and diffused southward with some kind of painted pottery.

Once my thesis was published by the Yale University Publications in Anthropology series (Wagner 1967), he wrote me again and expressed some disagreement with my comparisons of my Andean and Sub-Andean Patterns (comparable in those days to a co-tradition) with his Colombian Sub-Andean Chiefdoms (conceived as a developmental stage). These comparisons included agriculture, pottery, trade, shaft graves and other aspects of culture and were based on his stimulating article "The Agricultural Basis of the Sub-Andean Chiefdoms of Colombia" (Reichel-Dolmatoff 1961a), published in 1961

and later reprinted in 1973 in Daniel Gross's influential reader *Peoples and Cultures of Native South America* (Gross 1973). These patterns and stages, now considered old-fashioned, need to be revised once the new models proposed for northern South America have a more solid data base. Nevertheless, in retrospect, the concepts have been useful to some younger colleagues who have extended Murra's concepts of *vertical archipelago and ecological complementarity* (Murra 1972, 1975) to the northern Andes (especially Ecuador and Colombia), where a model of micro-verticality has been proposed (Oberem 1976, Salomon 1986, Langebaek 1986, Wagner 1993).

I met the Reichel-Dolmatoffs in person only once. It was in 1975, in Panama, at the memorable and exciting symposium "Tropical Agro-Ecosystems: An Experimental Design" organized by Olga Linares of the Smithsonian Tropical Research Institute (STRI). An informal gathering for discussion of ideas and experiences, it benefited from the experience of the Reichel-Dolmatoffs, the late Earl "Doc" Smith, Alan Covich, Tony Ranere, Richard Cooke, Alberta Zucchi, myself and several Panamanian and STRI colleagues. We visited Barro Colorado Island, Tony Ranere's preceramic rock shelters in Aguadulce and Richard Cooke's Sitio Sierra, among other sites, and saw the human side of the people involved. "Doc" Smith, with infectious humor, made us aware of the importance of looking at Tropical American plants from a non-European, non-temperate climate viewpoint. Nervous and seemingly troubled before reading his paper, Don Gerardo gave nonetheless an excellent account of the state of the anthropological research in Colombia, touching on Puerto Hormiga, Canapote, Monsú, Momíl, agricultural systems, environmental awareness, the Tukano and the Kogi. Once his presentation was over, he was pleasant and charming .

Impact on Archaeology

Regarding the early stages of research in northern South

America, there is no doubt that the continuing efforts of the Reichel-Dolmatoffs have provided a wealth of information, especially in regard to the ceramic history. The ceramic record provides archaeologists with their primary source for understanding culture history in the tropical lowlands of South America. As early as 1950, the Reichel-Dolmatoffs divided polychrome pottery of northern Colombia into two great horizons, which they labeled the First Painted Horizon and Second Painted Horizon (G. and A. Reichel-Dolmatoff 1951). These are still valid and have been a source, together with later contributions by Don Gerardo, for comparisons for all of us who have worked east of the Sierra Nevada de Santa Marta, that is, in the Lake Maracaibo Basin and its interaction sphere. Even Reichel-Dolmatoff's chronological "guesses"—in a time when radiocardbon dating was unknown—still largely hold true. In this context, I would like to quote his original statement on this issue: "When my wife and I excavated at the Ranchería river valley in 1950, the dating technique of radiocarbon was not known. Thirty years later, Gerardo Ardila (1991) developed a rescue excavation program to obtain absolute dates. The dates confirmed the original chronology" (Reichel-Dolmatoff 1986:230; editor's translation).

The impact of Reichel-Dolmatoff's work in Venezula is best illustrated by considering the findings of recent researchers in the area: Gallagher (1976), Sanoja and Vargas (1974), Wagner (1978b, 1992), Tarble (1982), Nuñez-Regueiro et al. (1985), Arvelo (1987) and Oliver (1989).

Gallagher—Guajira Peninsula and Maracaibo Basin

Patrick Gallagher (1976) conducted excavations in 1959 at La Pitía, an early ceramic coastal shell mound located on the eastern coast of the Guajira Peninsula (figure 1.1). He established a sequence of three successive phases revealed by stratigraphy and seriation—Kusu, Hokomo, and Siruma—that range from period I to IV of Rouse and Cruxent's regional chronology (1963). The Kusu phase represents a period I, Meso-Indian occupation which Gallagher related, albeit remotely, to Puerto Hormiga and Malambo in Colombia. The second phase, Hokomo, represents the major occupation of the site and comprises periods II and III in Rouse and Cruxent chronology (1000 BC–AD 1000). Gallagher established eleven types of pottery, which share many traits with the Tocuyanoid series of western Venezuela and with Reichel-Dolmatoff's First Painted Horizon and probably gave rise to the Betijoque phase, now belonging to Arvelo's Hokomo tradition. Gallagher's Siruma phase, corresponding to period IV (AD 1000–1500), is associated with a shift toward hunting land mammals and a marked decline in the number and variety of pottery modes.

Gallagher also established a modified sequence for the Maracaibo Basin, but his main contribution was to test two hypotheses regarding the culture history of northwestern South America. First, he examined Willey's (1958) hypothesis of the existence of a non-agricultural ceramic horizon, extending from Panama through Colombia and into Venezuela during Period I (before 1000 BC), from which arose the earliest pottery styles of northeastern South America, those of the Barrancoid series. Second, he evaluated Rouse and Cruxent's (1963) hypothesis about the origin of a western Venezuelan center of pottery style. The center, they argued, was the result of cultural influences from the Ranchería area of Colombia during the latter part of Period II, producing the classical dichotomy of culture in Venezuela. Gallagher concluded that his investigations tended to confirm Willey's hypothesis and suggested that the western center seems to be a local development and not the result of influences from northeastern Colombia (Wagner 1978a).

Sanoja and Vargas—Lake Maracaibo

Sanoja and Vargas worked in several regions in western Venezuela and along southern Lake Maracaibo (figures 1.1, 1.2), for which they established the El Guamo, Onia, Zancudo, Caño Grande, and El Danto phases (Vargas, 1985). Detailed information is available from the Zancudo phase, which Sanoja (1970) estimates lasted from AD 760 to 1377. Zancudo was divided into two periods, I and II. Period I is characterized by pottery with fabric impression and modeled or applique fillets. Subsistence was based on agriculture, fishing, and hunting, and burials were primary-direct or in urns. During Period II, pottery tended to be simpler and more monotonous, settlements were located on elongated mounds, and subsistence was based on manioc and maize cultivation. Sanoja concluded that the Zancudo phase showed cultural relationships with other phases from the Maracaibo Basin, such as Rancho Peludo and Dabajuro, with the Venezuelan Andes (Miquimú, Chiguará and Mucuchíes), northern Colombia (Ciénaga de Oro, Tierra Alta, Momíl, Crespo), and perhaps with some of the Antilles, such as Haiti (Sanoja, 1970).

Wagner—Maracaibo Basin

My own research in the Maracaibo Basin started in 1972 and has centered in two regions: the eastern Lake Maracaibo shore where Lagunillas and Bachaquero were excavated (Wagner and Tarble de Ruíz 1975) and along the Perijá piedmont zone where Las Tortolitas, San Martín, El Diluvio, Berlín, Caño Pescado, Las Minas, Puerto Nuevo, Sirapta, and Toromo have been studied (figures 1.1, 1.2; Arvelo 1987; Arvelo and Wagner 1984, 1986). Briefly, the Lagunillas study enabled us to establish a new phase characterized by subsistence based on maize, by pile-dwellings (the oldest so far reported for northern South America with dates ranging between 480 and 210 BC), and by pottery with plastic decoration. Lagunillas' closest similarities can be found in Venezuela with Santa Ana (Tarble 1982), Caño del Oso, and Tocuyano. Lagunillas was also related to northern Colombia, particularly the 'First Painted Horizon'

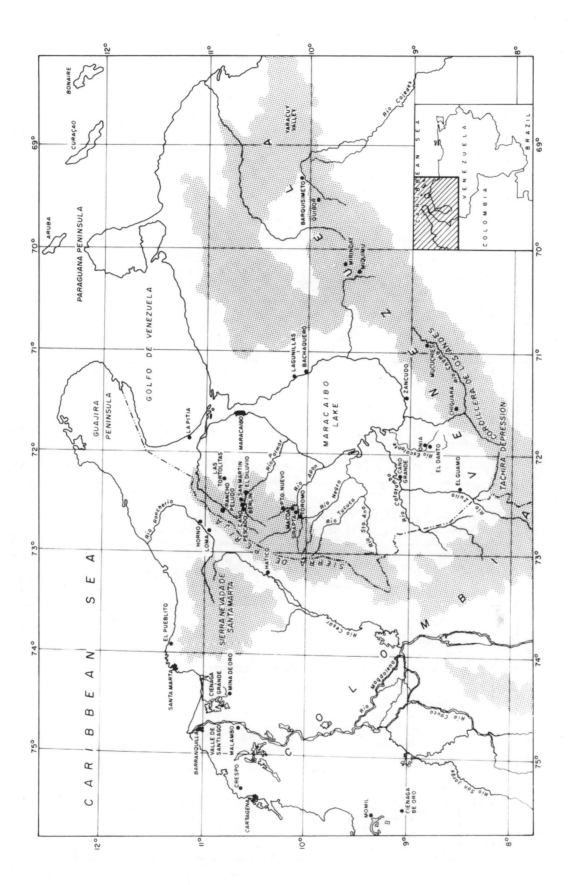

Figure A.1 Map of northern Colombia and Venezuela, showing locations of archaeological sites

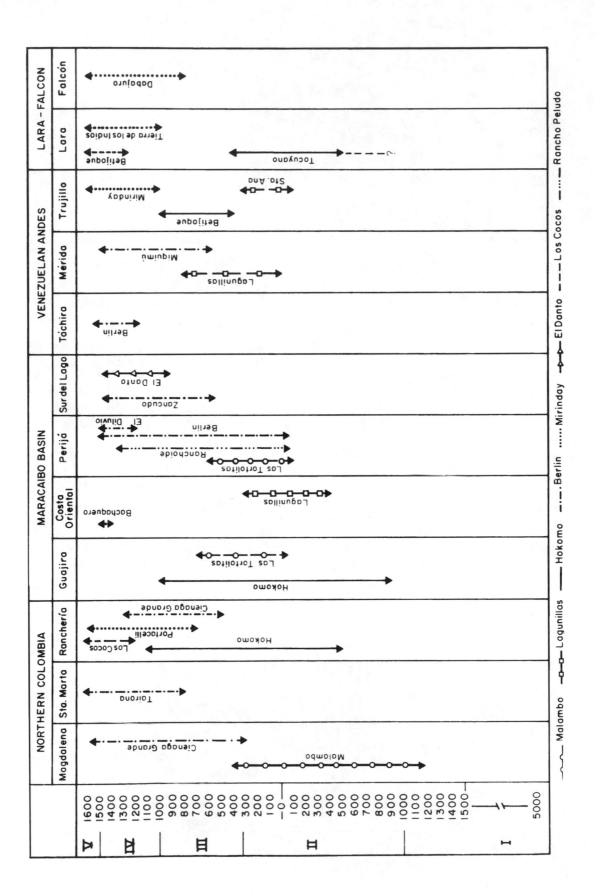

Figure A.2 General chronology of northwestern South America

Malambo, the Tairona area, and the Crespoid series. In its broadest sense, Lagunillas pottery shows some sort of relationship with pottery of the 'modeled-incised horizon,' extending perhaps from Ecuador to the Colombian coast and to Venezuela over 2000 years ago, and also shows indirect Amazonian influences.

For the Perijá piedmont zone we established a new Berlinoid series related to the Lagunillas, Ranchoid, and Pitioid series of the Maracaibo Basin and to northern Colombia, especially the Ciénaga Grande de Santa Marta, el Valle de Santiago, the Sierra Nevada de Santa Marta, and the Ranchería areas. These relationships suggest a more direct and intense process of interaction than simple cultural diffusion. The northern South American piedmont area of Colombia and Venezuela is an exciting but so far neglected region, which combines highland Andean and lowland Amazonian characteristics. It should be studied in more detail, once the current problems of personal safety, drug dealings, and border conflicts have been settled.

Nuñez-Regueiro, Tartusi, and CORPOZULIA—Western Venezuela

In 1979 Víctor Nuñez-Regueiro, Marta Tartusi, and their CORPOZULIA team started a Salvage Archaeology Program in the Guasare-Socuy and Guajira regions of Venezuela. In addition to systematically re-excavating Rancho Peludo and offering a solid chronology for that controversial site, they located a series of new sites and postulated three traditions for the area: Ranchoid, Hornoid and Malamboid, which characterize several localities in northwestern Venezuela and northeastern Colombia. For Rancho Peludo they obtained 50 radiocarbon dates and 25 thermoluminescent dates ranging between AD 300 to 400 and 1300 (Nuñez-Regueiro et al. 1985). They also advanced a theory about the existence of a funerary horizon of anthropomorphic burial urns frequently associated with a *duho* (carved wooden stools), based on a religious system that spread all the way from northwestern Venezuela to northeastern Argentina, perhaps similar to the Wari-Tiwanaco expansion in the Central Andes (Tartusi et al. 1984).

Arvelo and Oliver—Models for the peopling of western Venezuela

In recent years two models based on migrations have been proposed for the peopling of western Venezuela, one by Arvelo (1987) and the second by Oliver (1989). Research has shifted from the excavation of single sites and refining chronology and cultural relationships to a more regional perspective with the objective of integrating archaeological, linguistic, and ethnohistorical data.

In her 1987 MA thesis, *Un Modelo de Poblamiento Prehispánico para la Cuenca de Maracaibo*, Arvelo undertook an analysis of the information produced during the last 40 years on the past and present aboriginal populations of the Maracaibo Basin. This study shows that this region has been the setting for complex cultural developments. Arvelo has proposed a synthesis for the pre-Hispanic occupation of the region based on a compilation of the results of archaeological investigations, complemented by ethnohistorical and linguistic data. Her study spans a period of 3000 years, from 1500 BC to AD 1500, which she divided into three periods: 1500 BC to AD 1; 1 to AD 600; and AD 600 to 1500. She proposed that population movements to and from the basin area were a principal cause of the cultural heterogeneity evident both in the archaeological and historical records. In this model she traces migratory waves from northern Colombia, the Colombo-Venezuelan piedmont, and the Orinoco River Basin as well as emigrations from the study area (Arvelo 1987, Wagner 1992). The construction of the model required a careful comparative analysis and reclassification of the different series, traditions, styles, and phases proposed for the study area, based on a thorough review of the literature and examination of archaeological collections available for western Venezuela and northern Colombia. In order to unify the data, she used the concepts of stylistic tradition and ceramic style, both of which refer explicitly to the ceramics made by potters sharing similar norms for the elaboration of their wares. For the comparison with Colombia, the Reichel-Dolmatoffs were a key element since she consulted sixteen references by them, starting as early as 1942 with the article *La Cueva Funeraria de la Paz* (Reichel-Dolmatoff 1942).

Arvelo proposed that during the last 3000 years the Maracaibo Basin was an area of cultural confluence where two great migratory waves met. The first, represented by the Hokomo and Mirinday traditions, emphasized polychrome pottery and was distributed in the arid northeastern zone; the second, marked by plastic decorative techniques, was represented by such traditions as Malambo and Berlin and was located in the more fertile and humid southwest region of the Maracaibo Basin. In Arvelo's view, the Maracaibo Basin has been a natural corridor, an area of culture encounters, and a region that has generated local developments.

José Oliver's dissertation "The Archaeological, Linguistic and Ethnohistorical Evidence for the Expansion of Arawakan into northwestern Venezuelan and northeastern Colombia," a provocative thesis à la Lathrap, provides a model of the prehistoric to protohistoric expansions of Arawakan-speaking groups into northwestern Venezuela and northeastern Colombia. It is based on research conducted in coastal Falcón State between 1981 and 1983. Three independent data sets are analyzed: archaeology, linguistics, and ethnohistory. The resulting model of Arawakan expansion stands in contrast to previous models that have predominated in the interpretation of the culture history of Venezuela and Colombia, namely Osgood's Theory of the H (Gassón and Wagner 1994:132,134), the dichotomy of Venezuela by Cruxent and Rouse, and Willey's Pre-Agricultural/Early Pottery Horizon.

An early Proto-Maipuran/Arawakan expansion is hypothesized to have originated out of the Central Amazon into the Orinoco-Apure River confluence, reaching the area by 3600 BC and carrying an ancient Amazonian polychrome tradition. This expansion continued westward along the Apure and into the Llanos, splitting northward into the Barquisimeto Plateau via the Cojedes and into the Maracaibo Basin, via the Táchira Depression, in Venezuela. The archaeological evidence correlated with this early movement is defined as the Macro-Tocuyanoid pottery tradition. According to Oliver, by about 1200 to 900 BC, the Macro-Tocuyanoid tradition had already colonized the Lower Magdalena and the Ranchería valleys in northeastern Colombia. The latest ceramic complex of the Pitían Sub-tradition (Macro-Tocuyanoid) survived until shortly after conquest in the Lower Guajira. Ethnohistorical documents of the fifteenth century show that the Arawakan-speaking Onoto, Paraujano, and Guajiro inhabited the area at the time La Pitía was in its terminal stage.

An intermediate stage of Proto-Maipuran divergence and subsequent expansion is hypothesized to have taken place possibly as early as 1500 BC, and certainly by 500 BC. It involved the eventual emergence of Taino, Island Carib (Antilles), Lokono (Guayanas), and Caquetío (western Venezuela). The ancestors of the latter expanded westward along the Apure and north into the Cojedes river (Upper Llanos). At some point on this journey, the Pre-Caquetío Arawakans developed a ceramic style of the Macro-Dabajuroid tradition. By at least AD 700 to 800, two related but distinct archaeological traditions emerged, the Dabajuroid tradition and the Tierroid tradition. The latter, by AD 900, had already expanded into the Barquisimeto Plateau, the valley of Quibor, and the Yaracuy valley. The distribution of the Tierran styles correlates with the Barquisimeto-Yaracuy Caquetío polities.

The Dabajuroid tradition had also expanded via the Yaracuy Valley, where it split into several component sub-tra-

ditions and spread in opposite directions along the coast of Venezuela. The Dabajuran sub-tradition expanded into the west coast of Venezuela, rapidly spreading through Aruba, Curaçao, and Bonaire by AD 900. At about AD 1300 and up to post-Conquest times, the Bachaqueroan sub-tradition diverged from the Dabajuran sub-tradition, spreading westward into the Maracaibo Basin. This process of expansion was interrupted by the Spanish conquistadores.

Impact on Ethnoecology

In the later years of his career, after joining Johannes Wilbert at the Latin American Center at UCLA, Reichel-Dolmatoff turned more to ethnology and ecology, particularly to symbolic theory and cognitive anthropology. This is not surprising since he always believed that one should not separate archaeology and the ethnology of tribal societies. An excellent ethnographer, he was always attuned to the native point of view; in his writings he mentions that there existed and still exist intellectuals in the forest and philosophers among the mountains (Reichel-Dolmatoff 1976a).

Thus beyond his impact on archaeology, he has also been a source of inspiration for researchers working in the ethnoecology of Venezuela's lowland tribes. Kay Tarble's team (1993), doing research in the Barraguan area of the Middle Orinoco River, among other aspects, focused, for example, on trying to understand the symbolic conception of land use by such tribes as the Piaroa (Wothuha) and Mapoyo (Wa'nai). As Reichel-Dolmatoff has emphasized, many tropical forest tribes conceive the relationship between man and nature as a delicate balance where compensations are called for, especially if something is taken from nature, particularly during hunting and fishing (Reichel-Dolmatoff 1975a).

For the Indians, according to Reichel-Dolmatoff (1982a), environmental conservation has profound ethical significance. This message is repeated in many of his writings and should be his lasting lesson to all of us, especially at this time of accelerated negative change.

Bibliography

Acuña, Victor

1975 Florencia-1, un sitio precerámico en la vertiente Atlántica de Costa Rica. *Vínculos* 9:1–14.

Aguado, Pedro Fray de

1956 *Recopilación historial. Biblioteca de la Presidencia*. 4 vols. Bogotá: Empresa.

Allen, Glover M.

1942 *Extinct, and vanishing mammals of the Western Hemisphere with the marine species of all the oceans.* Special Publication no. 11. Ms. on file, American Committee for International Wild Life Protection, Washington DC.

Altschuler, Milton

1964 The Cayapa: a study in legal behavior. Ph.D. dissertation in Anthropology, University of Minnesota.

Anderson, David G.

1994 *The Savannah River chiefdoms: Political change in the late historic Southeast.* Tuscaloosa: University of Alabama Press.

Anónimo

1988 Epítome de la conquista del Reino de Granada. In *No hay caciques ni señores*, edited by Hermes Tovar Pinzón, Barcelona: Ediciones Sendai.

Aprile-Gniset, Jacques

1991 *La Ciudad Colombiana*. Bogotá: Banco Popula.

Ardila, Gerardo

1990 Acercamiento a la historia prehispanica de la guajira. In *La guajira*, edited by G. Ardila, 59–80. Bogotá: Universidad Nacional de Colombia.

1991 The peopling of northern South America. In *Clovis: Origins, and adaptations*, edited by R. Bonnichsen, and K. Fladmark, 261–282. Orono, Maine: Center for the Study of the First Americans.

Ardila, Gerardo, and Gustavo Politis

1989 Nuevos datos para un viejo problema. *Boletín Museo del Oro* 23:3–47. Bogotá.

Arvelo, L.

1987 Un modelo de Poblamiento prehispánico para la cuenca del Lago de Maracaibo. Master's thesis Scientiarum en Biología, Mención Antropología, Instituto Venezolano de Investigaciónes Científicas.

Arvelo, L., and E. Wagner

1984 Relaciones estilísticas cerámicas del noroeste de Suramérica con Las Antillas. In *Relaciones prehispánicas de Venezuela*, edited by E. Wagner, 51–66. Caracas: Fondo Editorial Acta Científica Venezolana.

1986 La Serie Berlinoide de la Cuenca de Maracaibo y sus nexos culturales. *Acta Científica Venezolana* 37(3):302–310.

Bailey R., G. Head, M. Jenike, B. Owen, R. Rechtman, and E. Zechenter

1989 Hunting, and gathering in tropical rain forest: Is it possible? *American Anthropologist* 91:59–82.

Bailey R., M. Jenike, and R. Rechtman

1991 Reply to Colinvaux, and Bush. *American Anthropologist* 93:160–162.

Barrantes, Ramiro, P. E. Smouse, H. W. Mohrenweiser, H. Gershowitz, J. Azofeifa, T. D. Arias, and J. V. Neel

1990 Microevolution in lower Central America: Genetic characterization of the Chibcha-speaking groups of Costa Rica, and Panama, and a taxonomy based on genetics, linguistics, and geography. *American Journal of Human Genetics* 46:63–84.

Barrett, Samuel A.

1925 *Cayapa Indians of Ecuador.* Indian Notes, and Monographs no. 10, 2 vols. New York: Museum of the American Indian, Heye Foundation.

Barriga Lopez, Franklin

1986 *Etnología Ecuatoriano I: Colorados.* Quito: Instituto Ecuatoriano de Crédito Educativo y Becas.

Barse, William

1990 Preceramic occupation in the Orinoco River Valley. *Science* 250:1388–1390.

Bartel, Brad

1982 A historical review of ethnological, and archaeological analyses of mortuary practice. *Journal of Anthropological Archaeology* 1(1):32–58.

Bartholomäus, Agnes, Alberto De la Rosa Cortés, Jaime Orlando Santos Gutiérrez, Luis Enrique Acero Duarte, and Werner Moosbrugger

1990   *El manto de la tierra: Flora de los Andes. Corporación*
       Autónoma Regional de las Cuencas de los Ríos Bogotá,
       Ubaté y Suárez. Bogotá: Ediciones Lerner Ltda.

Bedoya, Maria del C., and Maria E. Naranjo

1985   Reconocimiento arqueológico en el litoral Atlántico:
       Capurganá. Bachelor's thesis, Universidad de
       Antioquia.

Bellier, Irene

1994   Los Mai huna. In *Guía etnográfica de la alta*
       Amazonía, edited by Fernando Santos y Frederica
       Barclay, vol. 1:1–179. Quito: FLACSO-SEDE.

Bennett, Wendell

1946   The archaeology of the central Andes. In *Handbook of*
       South American Indians, edited by Julian H. Steward,
       Bureau of American Ethnology, Bulletin 143, vol. 2:
       61–147. Washington, DC: Smithsonian Institution
       Press.

Bermann, Marc

1994   *Lukurmata: Household archaeology in prehispanic*
       Bolivia. Princeton: Princeton University Press.

Bermúdez Páez, Alvaro

1992   Reconstrucción de un conjunto funerario en el alto de
       las Piedras—Isnos. *Revista Colombiana de*
       Antropología 29:257–264.

Biese, L.

1960   Spindle whorls from Panama Viejo. *Panama Archae-*
       ologist 3(1):35–45.

1964   The prehistory of Panama Viejo. *Bureau of American*
       Ethnology Bulletin 191:1–51. Washington DC.

Binford, Lewis R.

1971   Mortuary practices: Their study, and potential. In
       Approaches to the social dimensions of mortuary
       practices, edited by James A. Brown. *Memoirs of the*
       Society for American Archaeology 25:2–29.

1972   Mortuary practices: their study, and their potential.
       In *An archaeological perspective,* 208–342. New York:
       Academic Press.

1980   Willow smoke, and dog's tails: Hunter-gatherer
       settlement systems, and archaeological site forma-
       tion. *American Antiquity* 45(1):4–20.

1983   *Working at archaeology.* New York: Academic Press.

Bird, Junius R., and Richard G. Cooke

1977   Los artefactos mas antiguos de Panama. *Revista*
       Nacional de Cultura 6:7–31.

1978   The occurrence in Panama of two types of
       Paleo-indian projectile points. In *Early Man in the*
       New World from a circum-Pacific perspective, edited
       by A.L. Bryan, 263–272. Occasional Papers no. 1.
       Edmonton: Dept. of Anthropology, Univ. of Alberta.

Bischof, Henning

1971   Die Spanish-Indianische Auseinandersetzung in der
       nordlichen Sierra Nevada de Santa Marta (1501–1600).
       Bonner Amerikanitische Studien 1. Bonn.

1972   Una colección etnográfica de la Sierra Nevada de
       Santa Marta, Siglo XVII. *Atti del XL Congresso*
       Internazionale Degli Americanisti 2:390–398. Roma-
       Genova.

Blanton, Richard E.

1994   *Houses, and households: A comparative study.* New
       York: Plenum Press.

Blick, Jeffrey P.

1993   Social differentiation in the regional classic period
       (A.D. 1–900) in the Valle de la Plata, Colombia. Ph.D.
       dissertation, University of Pittsburgh. Ann Arbor:
       University Microfilms International.

1995   Prestige versus wealth in the Cerro Guacas polity
       during the regional classic period (A.D. 1–900) in the
       Valle de la Plata, Colombia. Paper presented at the
       60th Annual Meeting of the Society for American
       Archaeology, Minneapolis.

Blitz, John H.

1993   *Ancient chiefdoms of the Tombigbee.* Tuscaloosa:
       University of Alabama Press.

Boada Rivas, Ana María

1987a *Asentamientos indígenas en el Valle de la Laguna.*
       Bogotá: Banco de la República.

1987b Excavación de un asentamiento indígena en el Valle
       de Samacá. Informe final. Ms. on file, Fundación de
       Investigaciones Arqueológicas Nacionales, Banco de
       la República. Bogotá.

1989   Elementos de uso cotidiano, elementos de uso
       funerario. *Boletín Museo del Oro* 25:71–91. Bogotá.

1991   Patrón de asentamiento a lo largo de ríos y afluentes
       del valle de Sutamachan. Ms. on file, Fundación de
       Investigaciones Arqueológicas Nacionales, Banco de
       la República, Bogotá.

N.D.   La deformación craneana como marcador de
       diferenciación social. *Boletin Museo del Oro.* In press.

Boada, Ana María, Santiago Mora, and Monika Therrien

1988   La arqueología: Cultivo de fragmentos cerámicos,
       debate sobre la clasificación cerámica del Altiplano
       Cundiboyacense. *Revista de Antropología* 4(2):163–
       197.

Boinski, Sue

1992   Monkeys with inflated sex appeal. *Natural History*
       101(July):42-49.

Bolinder, Gustaf

1966   *Del Troiska Snöfjällests Indianer.* Translated by Frieda
       Schutze. Originally published 1925. Human Relations
       Area Files, New Haven: Yale University.

Bombin, Miguel, and Gustavo Huertas

1981   Los mastodontes de Colombia (Nota Preliminar).
       Revista CIAF 6(1–3):19–42.

Bonzani, Renee M.

1995   Plant diversity in the archaeological record: a means toward defining hunter-gatherer mobility strategies. *Journal of Archaeological Science* 24:1129–1139.

1995   Seasonality, predictability, and plant use strategies at San Jacinto 1, Colombia. Ph.D. dissertation, Department of Anthropology, University of Pittsburgh.

Bordieu, Pierre

1977   *Outline of a theory of practice.* New York: Cambridge University Press.

Botero, Pedro José

1985   Soilscapes. In *Regional archaeology in the Valle de la Plata, Colombia*, edited by R.D. Drennan, Technical Report no. 16, 41–79. Ann Arbor: University of Michigan Museum of Anthropology.

Bouchard, J.F.

1982   Excavaciones arqueológicas en la región de Tumaco, Nariño, Colombia. *Revista Colombiana de Antropología* 24:125–334.

Bozeman, Tandy K.

1982   Moundville phase communities in the Black Warrior River Valley, Alabama. Ph.D. dissertation, University of California, Santa Barbara.

Bray, Warwick M.

1984   Across the Darién Gap: A Colombian view of Isthmian archaeology. In *The archaeology of lower Central America*, edited by F. Lange, and D.Z. Stone, 305–338. Albuquerque: University of New Mexico Press.

1990   Cruzando el Tapón del Darién: Una visión de la arqueología del Itsmo desde la perspectiva colombiana. *Boletín Museo del Oro* 23:3–52. Bogotá.

1992a   La cultura Yotoco. In *Calima: Diez mil años de historia en el suroccidente de Colombia*, edited by Cardale de Schrimpff, M., W. Bray, T. Gwiler-Walder, and Leonor Herrera, 73–124. Santa Fe de Bogotá: Fundación ProCalima.

1992b   Sitio Conte metalwork in its Pan-American context. In *River of gold: Precolumbian treasures from Sito Conte*, edited by P. Hearne, and R. J. Shearer, 333–46. Philadelphia: University of Pennsylvania.

Bray, Warwick, Leonor Herrera, and Marianne Cardale de Schrimpff

1981   Precolombian roads in the Calima area. *Pro Calima* 2:7–10.

Brettes, Joseph de

1898   Chez les Indiens du nord de la Colombie. *Le tour du monde* 4.

1903   Les Indians Arhouaques-Kagabas. *Bulletins et Memoire de la Societe D'Anthropollogie de Paris* 4:318–357.

Broadbent, Sylvia M.

1964   *Los Chibchas, organización socio-política.* Serie Latinoamericana 5, Facultad de Sociología, Universidad Nacional de Colombia, Bogotá.

1985   Chibcha textiles in the British Museum. *Antiquity* 59:202–205.

1990   More Chibcha textiles. *Antiquity* 64:841–843.

Brown, James A.

1981   The search for rank in prehistoric burials. In *The archaeology of death*, edited by Robert Chapman, Ian Kinnes, and Klavs Randsborg, 25–37. Cambridge: Cambridge University Press.

Brücher, Heinz

1989   *Useful plants of neotropical origin, and their wild relatives.* Berlin: Springer-Verlag.

Bruhns, Karen O.

1992   Monumental sculpture as evidence for hierarchical societies. In *Wealth, and hierarchy in the Intermediate Area*, edited by Frederick W. Lange, 331–356. Washington, DC: Dumbarton Oaks Research Library, and Collections.

Bryan, Alan L., J. M. Cruxent, R. Gruhn, and C. Ochsenius.

1978   An El Jobo mastodont kill at Taima-Taima, Venezuela. *Science* 200:1275–1277.

Bull, T.

1958   Excavations at Venado Beach, Canal Zone. *Panama Archaeologist* 1(1).

1961   An urn burial – Venado Beach, Canal Zone. *Panama Archaeologist* 4(1):42–47.

Campbell, Joseph

1959   *The masks of God: Primitive mythology.* New York: Viking Press.

Cane, Scott

1989   Australian aboriginal seed grinding, and its archaeological record: A case study from the western desert. In *Foraging, and farming: The evolution of plant exploitation*, edited by D. R. Harris, and G. C. Hillman, 99–119. Boston: Unwin Hyman.

Cardale de Schrimpff, Marianne

1986   Painted textiles from caves in the eastern Cordillera, Colombia. In *The Junius Bird conference on Andean textiles*, edited by Ann Rowe, 205–18. Washington, DC: Dumbarton Oaks.

Cardale de Schrimpff, M., W. Bray, T. Gwiler-Walder, and Leonor Herrera

1992   *Calima: Diez mil años de historia en el suroccidente de Colombia.* Santa Fe de Bogotá: Fundación ProCalima.

Cardale de Schrimpff, Marianne, Warwick Bray, and Leonor Herrera

1989   Reconstruyendo el pasado en Calima: resultados recientes. *Boletín del Museo del Oro* 24:2–33. Bogotá.

Cardale de Schrimpff, Marianne, and Leonor Herrera

1995   Caminos y comerciantes en el suroccidente de Colombia entre 2500 and 1500 AP. In *Perspectivas regionales en la arqueología del suroccidente de Colombia y northe del Ecuador*, edited by Cristobal Gnecco, 195–222. Popayan, Colombia: Editorial Universidad del Cauca.

Cardenas, Felipe
1989   La momificación indígena en Colombia. *Boletín Museo del Oro*, 25:121–123. Bogotá.
1990   La Momia de Pisba, Boyacá. *Boletín Museo del Oro* 27:3–13. Bogotá.

Carneiro, Robert L.
1970   A theory of the origin of the state. *Science* 196:733–738.
1981   The chiefdom: Precursor of the state. In *The transition to statehood in the New World,* edited by Grant D. Jones, and Robert R. Kautz, 37-79. Cambridge: Cambridge University Press.

Carr, Christopher
1995   Mortuary practices: Their social, philosophical-religious, circumstantial, and physical determinants. *Journal of Archaeological Method, and Theory* 2(2):105–200.

Carrasco, Eulalia
1983   *El Pueblo Chachi.* Quito: Ediciones Abya-yala.

Carsten, Janet, and Stephen Hugh-Jones
1995   Introduction. In *About the house: Lévi-Strauss, and beyond*, edited by Janet Carsten, and Stephen Hugh-Jones, 1–46. Cambridge: Cambridge University Press.

Cashdan, Elizabeth
1990   *Risk, and uncertainty in tribal, and peasant economies.* Boulder, CO: Westview Press.
1992   Spatial organization, and habitat use. In *eEvolutionary ecology, and human behavior,* edited by Eric Alden Smith, and Bruce Winterhalder, 237–266. New York: Aldine de Gruyter.

Casilimas, C. Inéa, and López, María I.
1987   El templo Muisca. *Maguaré* 5:127–150.

Castañeda, Rafael Romero
1965   *Flora del centro de Bolivar.* Bogotá: Banco de la Republica.

Castaño, Carlos
1985   Secuencias y correlaciones cronológicas en el Río de La Miel. Ms. on file, Fundación de Investigaciones Arqueológicas Nacionales, Bogotá.

Castellanos, Juan de
1886   *Historia del Nuevo Reino de Granada.* Madrid: Imprenta de A. Pérez Dubrull.

Castillero-Calvo, A.
1967   *Estructuras sociales y económicas de Veragua desde sus orígenes historicos, Siglos XVI y XVII.* Panamá.

Castillo, N.
1988   Complejos arqueológicos y grupos étnicos del siglo XVI en el occidente de Antioquia. *Boletín Museo de Oro* 20:16–34. Bogotá.

Castro, Jaime E.
1994   La actividad de molienda en San Jacinto 1, los liticos de moler. Tesis de grado. Ms. on file, Departamento de Antropología, Universidad de Los Andes, Bogotá.

Celedon, Rafael
1886   Gramática de la lengua Koggaba. *Biblioteca Linguistique Americane* 10. Paris.

Chapman, Robert, and Klavs Randsborg
1981   Approaches to the archaeology of death. In *The archaeology of death*, edited by Robert Chapman, Ian Kinnes, and Klavs Randsborg, 1–24. Cambridge: Cambridge University Press.

Chauchat, C.
1977   Problemática y metodología de los sitios líticos de superficie: El Paijanense de Cupisniques. *Revisita del Museo Nacional* 43:13–26.

Cháves Mendoza, Alvaro, and Mauricio Puerta Restrepo
1980   *Entierros primarios de Tierradentro.* Bogotá: Banco de la República.
1984   *Tierradentro.* Bogotá: El Ancora.
1986   *Monumentos arqueológicos de Tierradentro.* Bogotá: Biblioteca Banco Popular.

Cieza de León, Pedro de
1956   *Crónica del Perú.* Madrid: Espasa-Calpe.

Colinvaux P., and M. Bush
1991   The rain-forest ecosystem as a resource for hunting, and gathering. *American Anthropologist* 93:153–159.

Conover, Adele
1994   The object at hand. *Smithsonian* 25(7):20–23.

Constenla-Umaña, A.
1991   *Las lenguas del area intermedia: Introdución a su estudio areal.* San José: Editorial de la Universidad de Costa Rica.

Cooke, Richard G.
1976a   Informe sobre las excavaciones en el sitio CHO-3 (Miraflores), río Bayano, febrero de 1973. *Actas del IV Simposium Nacional de Antropología, Arqueología y Etnohistoria de Panamá*, 369–426.
1976b   Rescate arqueológico en El Caño (NA-20), Coclé. *Actas del IV Simposium Nacional de Arqueología, Antropología y Etnohistoria de Panamá*, 447–482. Panamá: I.N.A.C.
1984   Archaeological research in central, and eastern Panama: a review of some problems. In *The archaeology of lower Central America*, edited by F. W. Lange, and D.Z. Stone, 263–302. Albuquerque: University of New Mexico Press, and School for American Research.
1985   Ancient painted pottery from central Panama. *Archaeology* 38:33–39.
1993   Animal icons, and pre-Columbian society: The Felidae, with special reference to Panama. In *Reinter-*

preting prehistory of Central America, edited by Mark Miller Graham, 169–208. Niwot: University Press of Colorado.

1995   Monagrillo, Panama's first pottery (3800–1200 CAL BC): summary of research (1948–1993), with new interpretations of chronology, subsistence, and cultural geography. In *The emergence of pottery*, edited by W.K. Barnett, and J. Hoopes, 169–184. Washington, DC : Smithsonian Institution Press.

Cooke, R., and W. M. Bray

1985   The goldwork of Panama: an iconographic, and chronological perspective. In *The art of precolumbian gold: The Jan Mitchell Collection*, edited by J. Jones, 35–49. London: Weidenfeld, and Nicholson.

Cooke, R.G., L. Norr, and D.R. Piperno

1996   Native Americans, and the Panamanian landscape. In *Case studies in environmental archaeology* 15, edited by E.J. Reitz, L. Newsom, and S. Scudder, 103–125. New York: Plenum Press.

Cooke, R.G., and A. J. Ranere

1984   The Proyecto Santa María, a multidisciplinary analysis of prehistoric adaptations to a tropical watershed. In *Recent developments in Isthmian archaeology: Advances in the prehistory of lower Central America*, edited by F. Lange, 3–30. BAR International Series 212. Oxford: British Archaeological Reports.

1992a   Prehistoric human adaptations to the seasonally dry forests of Panama. *World Archaeology* 24(1):114–133.

1992b   The origin of wealth, and the hierarchy in the central region of Panama (12,000-2,000 BP), with observations on its relevance to the history, and phylogeny of Chibchan-speaking polities in Panama, and elsewhere. In *Wealth, and hierarchy in the Intermediate Area*, edited by F.W. Lange, 243–316. Washington DC: Dumbarton Oaks Research Library, and Collection.

Cooke, R., L.A. Sánchez, A. Pérez, I. Isaza, O. Solís, and A. Badilla

1994   Archaeological investigations at the Cerro Juan Diaz site in central Panama. Progress report on work undertaken between January, 1992, and July, 1994, by the Smithsonian Tropical Institute, and the 'National Hertitage' department of the Panamanian National Institute of Culture.

Correal, Gonzalo

1973   Artefactos líticos en la hacienda Boulder, Municipio de Palermo, Departamento del Huila. *Separata de la Revista Colombiana de Antropología*, vol. 6. Bogotá.

1977   Exploración arqueológica en la costa Atlántica y en el Valle del Magdalena: Sitios precerámicos y tipologías líticas. *Caldasia* 11:35–111.

1981   *Evidencias culturales y megafauna Pleistocénica en*

Colombia. Bogotá: Banco de la República.

1983   Evidencia de cazadores especializados en el sitio de la Gloria, Golfo de Urabá. *Revista de la Academia Colombiana de Ciencias Exactas, Físicas y Naturales* 15:77–82.

1988   Apuntes sobre el medio ambiente pleistocénico y el hombre prehistórico en Colombia. In *New evidence for the Pleistocene peopling of the Americas.* edited by Alan Bryan. 115–131. Orono: Center for Study of Early Man, University of Maine.

1990   *Aguazuque: Evidencias de cazadores, recolectores y plantadores en la altipalnicie de la Cordillera Oriental.* Bogotá: Banco de la República.

Correal, G., F. Piñeros, and T. van der Hammen

1990   Guayabero I: Un sitio precerámico de la localidad de Angosturas II, San José del Guaviare. *Caldasia* 16–17:245–254.

Correal, G., T.,. an der Hammen, and K. C. Lerman

1969   Artefactos líticos de abrigos rocosos en El Abra, Colombia. *Revista Colombiana de Antropología* 14:9–46.

Correal, Gonzalo, and T. van der Hammen

1977   *Investigaciones arqueológicas en los abrigos rocosos del Tequendama*. Bogotá: Banco Popular.

Cortés Moreno, Emilia

1990   Mantas Muiscas. *Boletín Museo del Oro* 27:61–75. Bogotá.

Cowgill, George L.

1977   The trouble with significance tests, and what we can do about it. *American Antiquity* 42:350–368

Cruxent, J. M.

1970   Projectile points with Pleistocene mammals in Venezuela. *Antiquity* 44:223–225.

Cubillos, Julio César

1980   *Arqueología de San Agustín: El Estrecho, El Parador, y Mesita C.* Bogotá: Banco de la República.

1986   *Arqueología de San Agustín: Alto de El Purutal.* Bogotá: Banco de la República.

Damp, Jonathan E.

1979   Better homes, and gardens: The life, and death of the early Valdivia community. Ph.D. dissertation, Department of Archaeology, University of Calgary, Calgary.

1982   Ceramic art, and symbolism in the early Valdivia community. *Journal of Latin American Lore* 8:155–178.

1984   Architecture of the early Valdivia village. *American Antiquity* 49:573–585.

David, Nicholas

1992   The archaeology of ideology: Mortuary practices in the central Mandara highlands, Northern Cameroon. In *An African commitment: Papers in honour of Peter Lewis Shinnie*. Bogotá: Biblioteca Banco Popular.

DeBoer, Warren
1995 Returning to Pueblo Viejo: History, and archaeology of the Chachi (Ecuador). In *Archaeology in the lowland American tropics*, edited by Peter Stahl, 243–262. Cambridge: Cambridge University Press.
1996 *Traces behind the Esmeraldas shore: Prehistory of the Santiago-Cayapas region, Ecuador*. Tuscaloosa: University of Alabama Press.

DeBouck, D.
1992 Verbal communication to Bonzani, July.

de la Rosa, Nicolás
1975 *Floresta de la Santa Iglesia Catedral de la Ciudad y Provincia de Santa Marta*. Originally published in 1756. Bogota: Biblioteca Banco Popular.

Di Capua, Costanza
1973 Analisis morfológico y estético de algunos fragmentos de la cultura Valdivia. *Boletín de la Academia Nacional de Historia* 121:102–114.
1986 Shamán y jaguar: Iconografía de la cerámica prehistórica de la costa Ecuatoriana. *Miscelánea Antropológica Ecuatoriana* 6:157–169.
1994 Valdivia figurines, and puberty rituals: A hypothesis. *Andean Past* 4:229–279.

Dillehay, T., G. Ardila, G. Politis, and M. Beltrao
1992 Earliest hunters, and gatherers of South America. *Journal of World Prehistory* 6(2):145–204.

Doebley, John
1990 Molecular evidence, and the evolution of maize. In *New perspectives on the origin, and evolution of New World domesticated plants*, edited by Peter K. Bretting, 6–28. Economic Botany 44 (Supplement).

Donahue, J., and W. Harbert
1994 Fluvial history of the Jama River drainage. In *Regional archaeology in Northern Ecuador. Volume 1: Environment, cultural chronology, and prehistoric subsistence in the Jama River Valley*, edited by James A. Zeidler, and Deborah M. Pearsall, 43–58. Memoirs in Latin American Archaeology 8, University of Pittsburgh.

Douglas, Clarke W.
1974 Patterns of Indian warfare in the Province of Santa Marta. Ph.D dissertation, Department of History, University of Wisconsin, Madison.

Drennan, Robert D.
1976 Religion, and social evolution in Formative Mesoamerica. In *The early Mesoamerican village*, edited by Kent V. Flannery, 345–368. Orlando: Academic Press.
1984 Long-distance movement of goods in the Mesoamerican Formative, and Classic. *American Antiquity* 49(1):27–43.
1985 *Regional archaeology in the Valle de La Plata,*

Colombia: A preliminary report on the 1984 season of the proyecto Arqueológico Valle de La Plata. Museum of Anthropology, University of Michigan, Technical Reports no. 16.
1991 Pre-Hispanic chiefdom trajectories in Mesoamerica, Central America, and northern South America. In *Chiefdoms: Power, economy, and ideology*, edited by T. Earle, 263–287. Cambridge: Cambridge University Press.
1993 Part one: Ceramic classification, stratigraphy, and chronology. In *Prehispanic chiefdoms in the Valle de la Plata, Volume 2: Ceramics—chronology, and craft production*, edited by R. D. Drennan, M.M. Taft, and C.A. Uribe, 3–102. University of Pittsburgh Memoirs in Latin American Archaeology 5. University of Pittsburgh, Pittsburgh, and Universidad de los Andes, Bogotá.
1995 Mortuary practices in the Alto Magdalena: the social contex of the San Agustín culture. In *Tombs for the living: Andean mortuary practices*, edited by Tom Dillehay, 79–110. Washington, DC: Dumbarton Oaks Research Library, and Collection.
1996 *Statistics for Archaeologists: A common sense approach*. New York: Plenum Publishing Company.

Drennan, Robert D., and Dale W. Quattrin
1995 Social inequality, and agricultural resources in the Valle de la Plata, Colombia. In *Foundations of social inequality*, edited by T.D. Price, and G.M. Feinman, 207–233. New York: Plenum

Drennan, Robert D., L.G. Jaramillo, E. Ramos, C.A. Sánchez, M.A. Ramírez, and C.A. Uribe
1989 Reconocimiento Arqueológico en las Alturas Medias del Valle de la Plata. In *Memorias del Simpósio de Arqueología y Antropología Física, V Congreso Nacional de Antropología*, edited by S. Mora Camargo, F. Cárdenas Arroyo, and M. Angel Roldán, 119–157. Bogotá: Instituto Colombiano de Antropología, and ICFES.
1991 Regional dynamics of chiefdoms in the Valle de La Plata, Colombia. *Journal of Field Archaeology* 18:297–317.

Drennan, Robert D., and Carlos A. Uribe
1987 Introduction. In *Chiefdoms in the Americas*, edited by R.D. Drennan, and C.A. Uribe, vii–xii. Lanham: University Press of America.

Drolet, Robert
1974 Coqueros, and shamanism: An analysis of the Capulí phase ceramic modeled figurines from the Ecuadorian northern highlands, South America. *Journal of the Steward Anthropological Society* 5(2):99–132.
1980 *Cultural settlement along the moist Caribbean slopes of eastern Panama*. Ph.D. dissertation, University of

Illinois. Ann Arbor: University Microfilms.

Duque Gómez, Luis

1945   Apuntes sobre el Comercio entre los indios Pre-
colombinos. *Boletín de Arqueología* 1(1):31–35.

1963   *Reseña arqueológica de San Agustín.* Bogotá:
Editoriales de Librería Voluntad.

1964   *Exploraciones arqueológicas en San Agustín.* Revista
Colombiana de Antropología, Suplemento no. 1.
Bogotá: Imprenta Nacional.

1965   Etnohistoria y arqueología. *Historia extensa de
Colombia*, vol. I: Prehistoria, tomo 1. Bogotá:
Academia Colombiana de Historia.

1966   *Exploraciones arqueológicas en San Agustín.* Bogotá:
Instituto Colombiano de Antropología.

1967   Tribus indígenas y sitios arqueológicos. *Historia
extensa de Colombia*, vol. I: Prehistoria, tomo 2.
Bogotá: Academia Colombiana de Historia.

Duque Gómez , Luis, and Cesar Cubillos

1979   *Arqueología de San Agustín: Alto de los idolos,
montículos y tumbas.* Bogotá: Banco de la República.

1981   *Arqueología de San Agustín: La Estación.* Bogotá:
Banco de la República.

1983   *Arqueología de San Agustín: Exploraciones y trabajos
de reconstrucción en las Mesitas A y B.* Bogotá: Banco
de la República.

1988   *Arqueología de San Agustín: Alto de Lavapatas.*
Bogotá: Banco de la República.

Earle, Timothy

1991   The evolution of chiefdoms. In *Chiefdoms: power,
economy, and ideology,* edited by T. Earle, 1–15.
Cambridge: Cambridge University Press.

Easby, Elizabeth, and John F. Scott

1970   *Before Cortes: Sculpture of Middle America.* New York:
The Metropolitan Museum of Art.

Eder, Phanor James

1959   *El Fundador Santiago M. Eder.* Bogotá: Antares Ltda.

Einzmann, Harald

1985   Artesanía indígena del Ecuador: Los Chachis
(Cayapas). In *Artesanías de América* 19:13–78.

Eisenberg, John F.

1989   *Mammals of the neotropics.* Volume 1, The northern
neotropics. Chicago: University of Chicago Press.

Emmons, Louise H., and Françoise Feer

1990   *Neotropical rainforest mammal: A field guide.* Chicago:
University of Chicago Press.

Estrada, Emilio

1956   *Valdivia. Un sitio arqueológico en la costa de la
Provincia del Guayas, Ecuador.* Publicación del Museo
Víctor Emilio Estrada, No. 1, Guayaquil.

1958   *Las culturas Pre-Clásicas, formativas o arcaicas del
Ecuador.* Publicación del Museo Víctor Emilio Estrada
no. 5, Guayaquil.

Evans, Clifford, and Betty Meggers

1958   Valdivia—An Early Formative culture of Ecuador.
Archaeology 11:175–182.

Evans, Clifford, Betty Meggers, and Emilio Estrada

1959   *Cultura Valdivia.* Guayaquil: Museo Víctor Emilio
Estrada.

Falchetti, Ana María

1987   Desarrollo de la orfebrería Tairona en la provincia
metalúrgica del norte colombiano. *Boletín Museo del
Oro* 19:3–23. Bogotá.

1989   Orfebrería prehispánica en el altiplano central
colombiano. *Boletín Museo del Oro* 25:3–42. Bogotá.

FAO

1986   *Food, and fruit-bearing forest species. 3: Examples
from Latin America.* Rome: FAO.

Feinman, Gary

1991   Demography, surplus, and inequality: Early political
formations in highland Mesoamerica. In *Chiefdoms:
Power, economy, and ideology,* edited by Timothy
Earle, 229–262. Cambridge: Cambridge University
Press.

Fischer, Manuela

1989   *Mitos Kogi.* Quito: Ediciones Abya-Yala.

Friede, Juan

1976   *Fuentes documentales para la historia del Nuevo Reino
de Granada. Desde la instalación de la Real Audiencia
de Santafé 1581–1590.* Bogotá: Biblioteca Banco
Popular.

Fritz, G. J.

1994   Are the first American farmers getting younger?
Current Anthropology 35(3):305–309.

Furst, Peter T.

1968   The Olmec were-jaguar motif in light of ethnographic
reality. In *Dumbarton Oaks Conference on the Olmec,*
edited by Elizabeth P. Benson, 143–174. Washington,
DC:Dumbarton Oaks Research Library, and Collections.

1972   Commentary on Gerardo Reichel-Dolmatoff's The
feline motif in prehistoric San Agustín sculpture. In
*The cult of the feline: A conference in Pre-Columbian
iconography,* edited by Elizabeth P. Benson, 66.
Washington, DC: Dumbarton Oaks Research Library,
and Collections.

Gähwiler-Walder, Theres

N.D.   Präkolumbische Kulturen im Pavas-Gebiet,
Kolumbien. Archäologische Befunde und
ethnohistorische Daten. Zürich.

Gallagher, P.F.

1976   *La Pitía: An archaeological series in northwestern
Venezuela.* Yale University Publications in Anthropology no. 76. New Haven: Yale University.

Gamboa Hinestrosa, Pablo
1982   *La Escultura en la Sociedad Agustiniana*. Bogotá:
        Ediciones CIEC.
García Barriga, Hernando
1992   *Flora medicinal de Colombia*. Tomo I, II, III. Second
        edition. Bogotá: Tercer Mundo Editores.
Garcia Benitez, Luiz.
1953   *Reseña histórica de los obispos que han regentado la
        diócesis de Santa Marta*. Bogotá: Editorial Pax.
Gasson, Rafael, and Erika Wagner
1994   Venezuela: Doctors, dictators, and dependency (1932
        to 1948). *In History of Latin American archaeology*,
        edited by Augusto Oyuela-Caycedo, 124–136. Hamp-
        shire: Avebury.
Gawthome, Linda.
1985   Cogui kinship. In *South American kinship: Eight
        kinship systems from Brazil, and Colombia*, edited by
        W. R. Merrifield, 35–42. Dallas: International Museum
        of Cultures.
Gentry, Alwyn H.
1993   *A field guide to the families, and genera of woody
        plants of northwest South America (Colombia,
        Ecuador, Peru)*. Washington, DC: Conservation
        International.
Gilmore, Raymond M.
1950   Fauna, and ethnozoology of South America. In
        Handbook of South American Indians. edited by Julian
        H. Steward. Bureau of American Ethnoolgy, Bulletin
        143, vol. 6:345–464. Washington, DC.
Ginzburg, Carlo
1991   *Ecstasies: Deciphering the witches' sabbath*. New York:
        Pantheon Books.
Gnecco, Cristóbal
1989   Adaptaciones precerámicas en el suroccidente de
        Colombia. *Boletín Museo del Oro* 24:34–53. Bogotá.
1990   El paradigma paleoindio en Suramérica. *Revista de
        Antropología y Arqueología* 6(1):35–78.
Goldman, Irving
1975   *The mouth of heaven*. New York: John Wiley & Sons.
Gomez Benitez, Piedad
1979   El camino de Buenaventura. Bachelor's thesis,
        Departamento de Historia, Universidad del Valle, Cali.
Gonzalez-Pacheco, Laura
1991   Una vivienda en el cercado indígena del Santuario.
        Bachelor's thesis, Departamento de Antropología,
        Universidad de los Andes.
Gonzalez-Pacheco, Laura, and Ana María Boada
1991   Tunjos y accesorios: Elementos de dos contextos
        diferentes. *Boletín Museo del Oro* 27:55–60. Bogotá.
Groot de Mahecha, A. Maria
1989   La Costa Atlántica. In *Colombia prehispánica:
        Regiones arqueológicas*, edited by L. Herrera, A.M
        Groot, S. Mora, and M. C. Ramírez de Jara, 19–52.

Bogotá: Instituto Colombiano de Antropología.
Gross, Dave
1973   *Peoples, and cultures of Native South America*. New
        York: Doubleday, and Natural History Press.
Grove, David, and Susan D. Gillespie
1992   Ideology, and evolution at the pre-state level:
        Formative period Mesoamerica. In *Ideology, and
        precolumbian civilization*, edited by A. Demarest, and
        G. W. Conrad, 15–36. Santa Fe: School of American
        Research.
Hallowell, A. I.
1926   Bear ceremonialism in the Northern Hemisphere.
        American Anthropologist 28:1–175.
Hally, David
1987   Platform mounds, and the nature of Mississippian
        chiefdoms. Paper presented at the 44th Annual
        Meeting of the Southeastern Archaeological Confer-
        ence. Charleston, South Carolina.
Hancock, James F.
1992   *Plant evolution, and the origins of crop species*.
        Englewood Cliffs, NJ: Prentice Hall.
Harlan, Jack R.
1989   Wild-grass seed harvesting in the Sahara, and Sub-
        Sahara of Africa. In *Foraging, and farming: The
        evolution of plant exploitation*, edited by D. R. Harris,
        and G. C. Hillman, 75–95. Boston: Unwin Hyman.
Haro Alvear, Silvio Luis
1971   Shaminismo y farmacopea en el Reino de Quito.
        *Instituto Ecuatoriano de Ciencias Naturales,
        Contribución* 75:1–28.
Harris, David R.
1980   Commentary: Human occupation, and exploitation of
        savanna environments. In *Human ecology in savanna
        environments*, edited by David R. Harris, 31–39. New
        York: Academic Press.
Hastorf, Christine A.
1990   One path to the heights: Negotiating political
        inequality in the Sausa of Peru. In *The evolution of
        political systems: Sociopolitics in small-scale sedentary
        societies*, edited by S. Upham, 146–176. Cambridge:
        Cambridge University Press.
Hastorf, C. A., and V. S. Popper , eds.
1988   *Current paleoethnobotany: Analytical methods, and
        cultural interpretations of archaeological plant
        remains*. Chicago: University of Chicago Press.
Hearne, Pamela, and Robert J. Sharer, eds.
1992   *Rivers of gold: Precolumbian treasures from Sitio
        Conte*. Philadelphia: The University Museum,
        University of Pennsylvania.
Helms, Mary W.
1976   Competition, power, and succession to office in pre-
        Columbian Panama. In *Frontier adaptations in lower
        Central America*, edited by M. W. Helms, and F. L.

Loveland, 25–35. Philadelphia: Institute for the Study of Human Issues.

1977   Iguanas, and crocodilians in tropical American mythology, and iconography with special reference to Panama. *Journal of Latin American Lore* 3:51–132.

1979   *Ancient Panama: Chiefs in search of power.* Austin: University of Texas Press.

1981   Succession to high office in Pre-Columbian Circum-Caribbean Chiefdoms. *Man* 15:718–31.

1987   Art styles, and interaction spheres in Central America, and the Caribbean: Polished black wood in the Greater Antilles. In *Chiefdoms in the Americas*, edited by R. D. Drennan, and C. A. Uribe, 67–83. Lanham, MD: University Press of America.

1991   Esoteric knowledge, geographical distance, and the elaboration of leadership status. In *Profiles in cultural evolution*, edited by A. Terry Rambo, and Kathleen Gillogly, 333–350. Anthropological Papers 85, Museum of Anthropology, University of Michigan.

1992   Thoughts on public symbols, and distant domains relevant to the chiefdoms of lower Central America. In *Wealth, and hierarchy in the Intermediate Area*, edited by Frederick W. Lange, 317–330. Washington, DC: Dumbarton Oaks.

1995   *Creations of the rainbow serpent: Polychrome ceramic designs from ancient Panama.* Albuquerque: University of New Mexico Press.

Henley, P.

1982   *The Panare: Tradition, and change on the Amazonian Frontier.* New Haven: Yale University Press.

Herlihy, P.

1986   A cultural geography of the Emberã, and Wounaan (Chocó) Indians of Darién, Panama, with emphasis on recent village formation, and economic diversification. Ph.D. dissertation, Louisiana State University, Departments of Anthropology, and Geography, Baton Rouge.

Hernandez de Alba, Gregorio

1948   The Betoi, and their neighbors. In *Handbook of South American Indians*. edited by Julian H. Steward, Bureau of American Ethnology, Bulletin 143, vol. 4:393–398. Washington, DC.

Herrera, L.

1989   Costa del Océano Pacífico y Vertiente Oeste de la Cordillera Occidental. In *Colombia prehispánica: Regiones arqueológicas*, edited by L. Herrera, A.M. Groot, S. Mora, M. C. Ramírez de Jara, 135–157. Bogotá: Instituto Colombiano de Antropología.

Herrera, Leonor, Marianne Cardale de Schrimpff, and Warwick Bray

1990   La arqueología y el paisaje en la región Calima. In *Ingenierias prehispánicas,* edited by Santiago Mora Camargo, 111–150. Bogotá: Fondo FEN Colombia, Instituto Colombiano de Antropología.

1994   Los sucesos de Malagana vistos desde Calima. Atando cabos en la arqueología del suroccidente colombiano. *Revista Colombiana de Antropología* 21:145–174.

Herrera, Leonor, Warwick Bray, Marianne Cardale de Schrimpff, and Pedro Botero

1992   Nuevas fechas de radiocarbono para el Precerámico en la Cordillera Occidental de Colombia. In *Archaeology, and environment in Latin America*, edited by Omar R. Ortiz-Troncoso, and Thomas van der Hammen, 145–163. Proceedings of a Symposium held at the 46th International Congress of Americanists, July 4–8, 1988. Instituut voor pre-en Protohistorische Archeologie Albert Egges van Giffen (IPP). Universiteit van Amsterdam.

Hertz, Robert

1907   Contribution a une étude sur la representation collective de la mort. *Année Sociologique* 10:48–137.

1960   A contribution to the study of the collective representation of death. In *Death, and the right hand*, translated by Rodney Needham, 25–86. Glencoe, IL: The Free Press.

Higgins, D.A.

1986   Aglatomate Bay 1985. Archaeological survey, and excavation of Indian, and early Colonial sites in the San Blas Province of Panama. Report describing archaeological work carried out by Operation Raleigh. Manuscript, 47 Dirección Nacional de Patrimonio Histórico, Panamá.

Hill, Betsy D.

1972–74   A new chronology for the Valdivia ceramic complex from Guayas Province, Ecuador. *Ñawpa Pacha* 10–12:1–32.

Hodder, Ian

1984   Burials, houses, women, and men in the European Neolithic. In *Ideology, power, and prehistory*, edited by Daniel Miller, and Christopher Tilley, 51–68. Cambridge: Cambridge University Press.

1986   *Reading the past: Current approaches to interpretation in archaeology.* Cambridge: Cambridge University Press.

Holden, Timothy

1989   Preliminary work on South American mummies held at the British Museum. *Paleopathological Newsletter* 65:5–9.

Holldobler, Bert, and Edward O. Wilson

1990   *The Ants.* Cambridge, MA: Harvard University Press.

Holm, Olaf

1987   *Valdivia: Una cultura Formativa del Ecuador, 3500–1500 a.c.* Quito: Museos del Banco Central del Ecuador.

Horton, M.

1979   Caledonia Bay, Panama. Operation Drake, London.
       Ms. on file at the National Institute of Culture,
       Panama.

Hugh-Jones, Stephen

1995   Inside-out, and back-to-front: The, androgynous
       house in Northwest Amazonia. In *About the house:
       Lévi-Strauss, and beyond*, edited by Janet Carsten, and
       Stephen Hugh-Jones, 226–252. Cambridge: Cambridge
       University Press.

Huntington, Richard, and Peter Metcalf

1979   *Celebrations of death: The anthropology of mortuary
       ritual.* Cambridge: Cambridge University Press.

Hurt, W.R., T. van der Hammen, and G. Correal

1972   Preceramic sequences in the El Abra Rock-Shelters,
       Colombia. *Science* 175:1106–1108.

Hyslop, John

1984   *The Inka road system.* New York: Studies in Archaeol-
       ogy, Academic Press.

Ichon, A.

1980   L' Archéologie du Sud de la Péninsule d' Azuero,
       Panama. *Études Mésoamericaines-Serie II.* Mission
       Archéologique et Ethnologique Francaise au Méxique,
       Mexico DF.

IGAC (Instituto Geográfico Agustín Codazzi)

1973   *Magdalena.* Color Osprey Impresores Limitada,
       Bogotá.

1975   *Estudio general de suelos de los municipios de Carmen
       de Bolivar, San Jacinto, San Juan Nepomuceno,
       Zambrano, El Guamo y Cordoba.* Volumen XI no. 3.
       Bogotá: Instituto Geográfico Agustín Codazzi.

1977   *Zonas de vida o formaciones vegetales de Colombia.*
       Vol. XIII(11). Bogotá: Subdirección Agrológica,
       Instituto Geográfico Agustín Codazzi.

1980   *Estudio general de suelos de los municipios de
       Barrancabermeja, Puerto Wilches, Sabana de Torres y
       San Vicente de Chucurí. Departamento de Santander.*
       Bogotá: Instituto Geográfico Agustín Codazzi.

1982   *Los suelos del Departamento de Antioquia y su aptitud
       de uso.* Bogotá: Instituto Geográfico Agustín Codazzi.

Ingold, Tim

1987   *The Appropriation of nature.* Iowa City: University of
       Iowa Press.

Instituto Colombiano de Antropología

1991   Un viaje por el tiempo a lo largo del Oleoducto—
       Cazadores recolectores, agroálfareros y orfebres.
       Informe Final. Ms. on file, Bogotá.

1994   Arqueología de rescate oleoducto Vasconia-Coveñas:
       Un viaje por el tiempo a lo largo del oleoducto—
       Cazadores recolectores, agroalfareros y orfebres.
       Bogotá: Instituto Colombiano de Antropología-
       Oleoducto de Colombia S.A.

Issacs, Jorge

1951 [1884]. *Estudio sobre las tribus indígenas del Magdalena.*
       Bogotá: Biblioteca Popular Colombiana.

Isaacson, J.

1994   Volcanic sediments in archaeological contexts from
       western Ecuador. In *Regional archaeology in northern
       Ecuador, Volume 1: Environment, cultural chronology,
       and prehistoric Subsistence in the Jama River Valley*,
       edited by James A. Zeidler, and Deborah M. Pearsall,
       131–140. University of Pittsburgh, Memoirs in Latin
       American Archaeology no. 8, Pittsburgh.

Isacsson, Sven-Erik

1975   Biografía atrateña. *Indiana* 3:93–109. Berlin.

1981   *Gentilicios y desplazamientos de la población aborigen
       en el suroeste colombiano (1500–1700). Indiana* 6:209–
       225. Berlin.

Johannessen, Sissel, and Christine A. Hastorf eds.

1994   *Corn, and culture in the prehistoric New World.* San
       Fransisco: Westview Press.

Jones, Rhys, and Betty Meehan

1989   Plant foods of the Gidjingali: Ethnographic, and
       archaeological perspectives from northern Australia
       on tuber, and seed exploitation. In *Foraging, and
       farming: The evolution of plant exploitation*, edited by
       D. R. Harris, and G. C. Hillman, 120–135. Boston:
       Unwin Hyman.

Jopling, Carol F. (compiler)

1994   *Indios y negros in Panamá en los siglos XVI y XVII:
       Selección de documentos del Archivo General de
       Indias.* (Memoria que da Pedrarias sobre la provisión
       a Vasco Núñez de Balboa de la gobernación y
       adelantamiento [1510]). Centro de Investigaciones
       Regionales de Mesoamérica, Serie Monográfica 7.
       Vermont: S. Woodstock.

Kirchhoff, Paul

1948   The tribes north of the Orinoco River. *Handbook of
       South American Indians,* edited by Julian H. Steward,
       Bureau of American Ethnology, Bulletin 143, vol.
       4:481–493. Washington, DC.

Klepinger, Linda L.

1979   Paleodemography of the Valdivia III phase at Real
       Alto, Ecuador. *American Antiquity* 44(2):305–309.

Klepinger, Linda L., John K. Kuhn, and Josephus Thomas, Jr.

1977   Prehistoric dental calculus gives evidence for coca in
       Early Coastal Ecuador. *Nature* 269:506–507.

Knight, Vernon James, Jr.

1986   The institutional organization of Mississippian
       religion. *American Antiquity* 51(4):675–687.

1989   Symbolism of Mississippian mounds. In *Powhatan's
       mantle: Indians in the Colonial Southeast*, edited by P.
       H. Wood , G. A. Waselkov, and M. T. Hatley, 279–291.
       Lincoln: University of Nebraska Press.

1994   Evidence for the dating of mounds A, B, P, R, and S, Moundville. Abstracts of the 51st Southeastern Archaeological Conference, and the 39th Midwest Archaeological Conference, November 9-12, 1994, Lexington, Kentucky. Southeastern Archaeological Conference Bulletin 37:44.

Knowlton, E.

1944   The Arhuaco Indians, 20 years after. *American Anthropologist* 46:263–266.

Labbé, Armand J.

1986   *Colombia before Columbus.* New York: Rizzoli International Publications.

1995   *Guardians of the life stream.* Santa Ana: Cultural Arts Press, Bowers Museum of Cultural Arts.

Lacefield, Hyla

1994   Some iconographic comparisons of crested birds from Moundville. Abstracts of the 51st Southeastern Archaeological Conference, and the 39th Midwest Archaeological Conference, November 9–12, 1994, Lexington, Kentucky. *Southeastern Archaeological Conference Bulletin* 37:44.

Ladd, J.

1964   *Archaeological investigations in the Parita, and Santa María zones of Panama.* Smithsonian Institution Bureau of the American Ethnology, Bulletin 193. Washington DC.

Langdon, Jean

1990   La historia de la Conquista de acuerdo a los Indios Siona del Putumayo. *Los meandros de la historia en Amazonía,* edited by Roberto Pineda Camacho, and Beatriz Alzate Angel, 13–42. Quito: Ediciones Abya-yala.

Lange, Frederick W.

1992   The Intermediate Area: An introductory overview of wealth, and hierarchy issues. In *Wealth, and hierarchy in the Intermediate Area,* edited by F.W. Lange, 1–14. Washington, DC: Dumbarton Oaks.

Langebaek, Carl H.

1986   *Mercados, poblamiento e integración entre los Muiscas. Siglo XVI.* Bogotá: Colección Bibliográfica, Banco de la República.

1992   Competencia por prestigio político y momificación en el norte de Sur América y el Istmo de Panamá. *Revista Colombiana de Antropología* 29:7–26.

Laplanche, Jean, and J.B. Pontalis

1973   *The language of psycho-analysis.* New York: Norton.

Lathrap, Donald W.

1970   *The upper Amazon.* London: Thames, and Hudson.

1973   Gifts of the cayman: Some thoughts on the subsistence basis of Chavín. In *Variation in anthropology: Essays in honor of John C. McGregor,* D. W. Lathrap, and Douglas, 91–105. Urbana, Illinois: Illinois Archaeological Survey.

Lathrap, Donald W., Donald Collier, and Helen Chandra

1975   *Ancient Ecuador. Culture, clay, and creativity 3000–300 B.C.* Chicago: Field Museum of Natural History.

Lathrap, Donald W., Jorge G. Marcos, and James A. Zeidler

1977   Real Alto: An ancient ceremonial center. *Archaeology* 30 (1):2–13.

Lehmann, Henri

1953   On Noel Morss' "Cradled Infant Figures." *American Antiquity* 19:78–80.

1967   (orig. 1952) Le personnage couché sur le dos: Sujet commun dans L'archéologie du Mexique et de l'equateur. In *The civilizations of Ancient America, Selected Papers of the XXIXth International Congress of Americanists,* edited by Sol Tax, 291–298. New York: Cooper Square.

Le Roy Gordon, B.

1983   *El Sinú: Geografía humana y ecología.* Bogotá: Carlos Valencia Editores.

Lévi-Strauss, Claude

1969   *The raw, and the cooked.* New York: Harper & Row.

1978   *The origin of table manners.* New York: Harper & Row.

1981   *La vía de las Máscaras.* México: Siglo Veintiuno Editores.

Linares, Olga F.

1977   *Ecology, and the arts in Ancient Panama: On the development of social rank, and symbolism in the Central Provinces.* Studies in Pre-Columbia Art, and Archaeology no. 17. Washington, DC: Dumbarton Oaks.

Linares, O.F., and A. J. Ranere

1980   *Adaptive radiation in Prehistoric Panama.* Peabody Museum Monographs no. 5. Harvard University, Cambridge, Massachusetts.

Linares, O.F., P.D. Sheets, and E.J. Rosenthal

1975   Prehistoric agriculture in tropical high lands. *Science* 187: 137–145.

Linné, S.

1929   *Darién in the past.* Goteborg: Elanders Boktryckeri Aktiebolag.

Lippi, R.D., R. McK. Bird, and D.M. Stemper

1984   Maize recovered at La Ponga, an early Ecuadorian Site. *American Antiquity* 49:118–124.

Llanos Vargas, Hector

1988   *Arqueología de San Agustín: Pautas de asentamiento en el Cañón del Río Granates—Saladoblanco.* Bogotá: Banco de la República.

1990   *Proceso histórico prehispánico de San Agustín en el Valle de Laboyos (Pitalito-Huila).* Bogotá: Banco de la República.

Llanos Vargas, Hector, and Anabella Durán de Gómez

1983   *Asentamientos prehispánicos de Quinchana, San*

Agustín. Banco de la República, Bogotá.

Locher, Gottfried W.

1932   *The Serpent in Kwakiutl Religion* E. J. Brill, Leyden.

Loewen, J.A.

1963.   Choco 1: Introduction, and bibliography. *International Journal of American Linguistics* 29:239–362.

Londoño, Eduardo

1983   La conquista de la Laguna de Cucaita para el Zaque: Un hecho militar prehispánico Muisca conocido por documentos de archivo. Sexto Semestre. Ms. on file, Departamento de Antropología, Universidad de los Andes, Bogotá.

1985   Los cacicazgos Muiscas a la llegada de los conquistadores Españoles. El caso del Zacazgo o Reino de Tunja. Undergraduate Tesis. Departamento de Antropología, Universidad de los Andes. Bogotá.

1990   Mantas Muisca—Una tipología colonial. *Boletín Museo del Oro* 27:121–126.

N.D.   El lugar de la religión en la organización Muisca. *Boletín Museo del Oro*. Bogotá. In press.

López, Carlos E.

1989   Evidencias Paleoindias en el valle medio del Río Magdalena (Municipios de Puerto Berrío, Yondó y Remedios, Antioquia). *Boletín de Arqueología* 4(2):3–23.

1992   Cazadores-Recolectores tempranos en el Magdalena Medio (Puerto Berrío-Antioquia). Ms. on file Banco de la República, Bogotá.

1994   Aproximaciones al medio ambiente, recursos y ocupación temprana del valle medio del Río Magdalena. *Informes Antropológicos* 7:5–15.

López C., and P. Botero

1994   La edad y el ambiente del precerámico en el Magdalena Medio. Resultados de laboratorio del Sitio Peñones de Bogotá. Ms. on file, Banco de la República, Bogotá.

López, Carlos, H. Correcha, and E. Nieto

1994   Estudio de arqueología de Rescate Línea San Carlos-Comuneros. Ms. on file, Interconexión Eléctrica S.A., Medellín.

Lothrop, Samuel K.

1937   *Coclé, an archaeological study of central Panama, Part 1*. Memoirs of the Peabody Museum of Archaeology, and Ethnology 7, Harvard University, Cambridge.

1942   *Coclé, an archaeological study of Central Panama, Part II*. Memoirs, Peabody Museum of Archaeology, and Ethnology, vol. 8, Harvard University, Cambridge.

1954   Suicide, sacrifice, and mutilations in burials at Venado Beach, Panama. *American Antiquity* 19:226–234.

1956   Jewelry from the Panama Canal zone. *Archaeology* 9:34–40.

1957   Text, and critical analysis. In *The Robert Woods Bliss Collection of Precolumbian Art*, edited by S.K. Lothrop, W.F. Foster, and J. Mahler. New York: Phaidon.

1959   A re-appraisal of Isthmian archaeology. *Amerikanistisch Miszellen.* Hamburg: Mitteilungen aus dem Museum für Völkerkunde XXVV: 87–91.

1960   C-14 dates for Venado Beach, Canal Zone. *Panama Archaeologist* 3:96–98.

1964   *Treasures of ancient America*. Skira, Geneva.

1976   *Pre-Columbian designs from Panama: 591 illustrations of Coclé pottery*. New York: Dover Publications.

Lubensky, Earl H.

1991   Valdivia figurines. In *The New World figurine Project*, Vol. 1, edited by Terry Stocker, 21–36. Provo: Research Press.

Lumpkin, Susan

1986   Spectacular spectacled bears. *Zoogoer* 15 (4):4–6.

Lynch, Thomas

1990   Glacial-age man in South America? A critical review. *American Antiquity* 55(1):12–36.

MacArthur, Robert H.

1972   *Geographical ecology*. Princeton, NJ: Princeton University Press.

MacGimsey, C.R., III

1964.   Informe preliminar sobre las temporadas de 1961-62. *Hombre y Cultura* 1:39-55.

Marcos, Jorge G.

1977/78 Cruising to Acapulco, and back with the thorny oyster set: A model for a lineal exchange system. *Journal of the Steward Anthropological Society* 9 (1/2):99–132.

1978   The ceremonial precinct at Real Alto: Organization of time, and space in Valdivia society. Ph.D dissertation, Department of Anthropology, University of Illinois, Urbana.

1988a *Real Alto: La historia de un centro ceremonial Valdivia*. (Primera y Segunda Partes). Quito: Corporación Editora Nacional.

1988b Economía e ideología en Andinoamérica septentrional. In *Nueva historia del Ecuador*, vol. 2, edited by Enrique Ayala Mora, 171–183. Quito: Corporación Editora Nacional.

Marcos, Jorge G., and Mariella García de Manrique

1988   De la dualidad fertilidad-virilidad a lo explicamente femenino o masculino: La relación de las figurinas con los cambios en la organización social Valdivia, Real Alto, Ecuador. In *The role of gender in Pre-Columbian art, and architecture*, edited by Virginia E. Miller, 35–51. Lanham, MD: University Press of America.

Marcos, Jorge G., and Presley Norton

1981   Interpretación sobre la arqueología de la Isla de la

Plata. *Miscelánea Antropológica Ecuatoriana* 1: 136–154.

Marcos, Jorge G., Donald W. Lathrap, and James A. Zeidler
1976   Ancient Ecuador revisited. *Field Museum of Natural History Bulletin* 47(6):3–8.

Markgraf, Vera
1989   Palaeoclimates in Central, and South America since 18,000 BP Based on pollen, and lake-level records. *Quaternary Science Reviews* 8:1–24.

Martyr de Anghlera, P.
1912   *De Orbe Novo. The eight decades of Peter Martyr d'Anghlera.* Translated from the Latin with notes, and introduction by F.A. MacNutt. 2 vols. New York: Putnam's.

Mason, Alden J.
1926   Coast, and crest in Colombia. *Natural History* 26(1):31–43.

Mayer-Oakes, William J.
1963   Early man in the Andes. In *Readings from Scientific American.* 51–59. San Francisco: Freeman, and Company.

Mayr, Juan
1987   Contribución a la astronomía de los Kogi. In *Etnoastronomías Americanas*, edited by Elizabeth Reichel, and Jorge A. de Greiff, 57–68. Bogotá: Ediciones de la Universidad Nacional.

McAnany, Patricia A.
1995   *Living with the ancestors: Kinship, and kingship in ancient Maya.* Austin: University of Texas Press.

McDowell, John H.
1989   *Sayings of the ancestors: The spiritual life of the Sibundoy Indians.* Lexington: University of Kentucky Press.

McGimsey, C.R. III
1956   Cerro Mangote: A preceramic site in Panama. *American Antiquity* 22(2):151–161.

McGimsey, Charles
1964   Investigaciones arqueológicas en Panama: informe preliminar sobre la temporada de 1961–1962. Panama: *Hombre y Cultura* 1(3):39–55.

Meggers, Betty J.
1966   *Ecuador.* New York:Praeger Publishers.

Meggers, Betty J., Clifford Evans, and Emilio Estrada
1965   *Early Formative period of Coastal Ecuador: The Valdivia, and Machalilla phases.* Smithsonian Contributions to Anthropology, vol. 1. Washington DC: Smithsonian Institution.

Meyers, Allen Dale
1995   Charactersitics of Historic Creek household organization: Evidence from plow-disturbed contexts. Master's thesis, Department of Anthropology, University of Alabama, Tuscaloosa.

Mix, Robert
1982   Matu to cuenta: Cuentos tradicionales de los Tsáchila Colorados. *Miscelánea Antropológica Ecuatoriana* 2:56–101.

Mora, S, L. Herrera, I. Cavelier, and C. Rodriguez
1991   *Plantas cultivadas, Suelos antrópicos y estabilidad.* University of Pittsburgh Latin American Archaeology reports no. 2. Pittsburgh.

Moreno, Leonardo
1991   *Pautas de asentamiento Agustinianas en el Noroccidente de Saladoblanco (Huila).* Bogotá: Banco de la República.

Murra, John
1946   The historic tribes of Ecuador. *Handbook of South American Indians,* edited by Julian H. Steward, Bureau of American Ethnology, Bulletin 143, vol. 2:785–821. Washington, D.C.

Murra, J.V.
1972   El control vertical de un máximo de pisos ecológicos en la economía de las sociedades Andinas. In *Visita de la Provincia de León de Huánuco en 1562*, vol. II, edited by J. V. Murra, 427–468. Huánuco: Universidad Nacional Hermilio Valdizan.
1975   *Formaciones económicas y políticas en el mundo, andino.* Líma: Instituto de Estudios Peruanos.
1985   El archipiélago vertical. *Andean ecology, and civilization.* edited by S. Masuda, I. Shimada, and C. Morris, 3–13. Tokyo: University of Tokyo Press.

Nicholas, Francis C.
1901   The aborigines of the province of Santa Marta (Colombia). *American Anthropologist* 3(4):606–649.

Nordenskiöld, Erland
1929   Les rapports entre L'art, la religion et la magie chez les Indiens Cuna et Chocó. *Journal de la Société des Américanistes n.s.* 21:141–158.
1979   *An historical, and ethnological survey of the Cuna Indians.* edited by Henry Wassén, Reprinted from 1925 edition by AMS Press, New York.

Norr,L.
1995   Interpreting dietary maize from bone stable isotopes in American tropics: the state of the art. In *Archaeology in the lowland American tropics.* edited by P.W. Stahl, 198–223. Cambridge: Cambridge University Press.

Norton, P.
1977   The Loma Alta connection. Paper presented at the 42nd Annual Meeting of the Society for American Archaeology, New Orleans.
1982   Preliminary observations on Loma Alta, an early Valdivia midden in Guayas Province, Ecuador. In *Primer Simposio de Correlaciones Antropológicas Andino—Mesoamericano.* edited by J.G. Marcos, and

P. Norton, 101–119. Guayaquil: Escuela Superior
Politecnica del Litoral.

Nuñez- Regueiro, V., M.R.A. Tartusi, and J. Valdés

1985   Efecto de la contaminación por carbon inerte en la
        datación radio-carbónica del sitio Z-102, Rancho
        Peludo, Venezuela. *Acta Científica Venezolana* 36:384–
        400.

Oberem, Udo

1976   El accesso a recursos naturales de diferentes
        ecologias an la sierra ecuatoriana (siglo XVI). In
        *Organizacion social y complementaridad economica
        en los Andes centrales*, edited by Jorge A. Flores Ochoa.
        Actes, Fourty-second International Congress of
        Americanists, vol. 4, 51–64. Paris.

1980   *Los Quijos*. Colección Pendoneros 16. Otavalo-
        Ecuador: Instituto Otavaleño de Antropología.

1981   El acceso a recursos naturales de diferentes ecologias
        en la Sierra Ecuatoriana (siglo XVI). In
        Contribuciones a la etnohistoria Ecuatoriana, edited
        by S. Moreno Y. y U. Oberem, 45–71. Otavalo, Ecuador:
        Istituto Otavaleño de Antropología.

Ohnuki-Tierney, Emiko

1984   *The Ainu of the northwest coast of Southern Sakhalin.*
        Prospect Heights, Illinois: Waveland Press.

Oliver, J.R.

1989   The Archaeological, linguistic, and ethnohistorical
        evidence for the expansion of Arawakan into north-
        western Venezuela, and northeastern Colombia. Ph.D.
        Dissertation, Dept. of Anthropology, University of
        Illinois at Urbana-Champaign.

Osborn, Ann

1990   Eat, and be eaten: Animals in U'wa (Tunebo) oral
        tradition. In *Signifying animals*, edited by Roy Willis,
        140–157. London: Unwin Hyman.

Oviedo y Valdés, Gonzalo Fernández de,

1849-1853 *Historia general y natural de las Indias, islas y
        tierra firme del Mar Océano*. Imprenta de la Real
        Academia de Historia. 4 vols (I:1849, II:1852, III:1853,
        IV:1855). Madrid.

Oyuela Caycedo, Augusto

1986a   De los Tairona a los Kogi: Una interpretación del
        cambio cultura. *Boletín Museo del Oro* 17:32–43.
        Bogotá.

1986b   Contribución a la periodización cultural en el litoral
        del Parque Tairona. *Boletín de Arqueológia* 1(2):24–28.

1986c   Excavación de un basurero en Ciudad Perdida. *Boletín
        de Arqueológia* 1(1):28–37.

1987a   Aspectos culturales de las secuencias locales y
        regionales en los Tairona. In *Chiefdoms in the
        Americas*, edited by Robert D. Drennan, and Carlos A.
        Uribe, 213–228. Lanham, MD: University Press of
        America.

1987b   Gaira: Introducción a la ecología y arqueología del
        litoral de la Sierra Nevada de Santa Marta. *Boletín
        Museo del Oro* 19:35–55. Bogotá.

1987c   Dos sitios arqueológicos con cerámica de fibra
        vegetal en la serranía de San Jacinto (Departamento
        de Bolívar). *Boletín de Arqueología* 2 (1):5–26.

1989   Investigaciones arqueologicas en la region baja del
        rio Gaira, Departamento del Magdalena. Ms. on file.
        Fundacion de Investigaciones Arqueologicas del
        Banco de la Republica, Bogotá.

1990   Las redes de caminos prehispanicas en la Sierra
        Nevada de Santa Marta. In *Ingenierías Prehispánicas*,
        edited by Santiago Mora, 47–72. Bogotá: Instituto
        Colombiano de Antropologia, and Fondo Electrico
        Nacional (FEN).

1991   Ideology, and structure of gender spaces: The case of
        the Kaggaba Indians. In *Gender archaeology*, edited by
        Dale Walde, and Noreen D. Willows, 327–335. Proceed-
        ings of the 22nd Annual Conference of the Archaeo-
        logical Association of the University of Calgary.
        University of Calgary, Canada.

1993   Sedentism, food production, and pottery origins in
        the tropics: San Jacinto 1; A case study in the Sabana
        de Bolivar, Serranía de San Jacinto, Colombia. Ph.D.
        dissertation, Department of Anthropology, University
        of Pittsburgh.

1995   Rocks vs clay: The evolution of pottery technology in
        the case of San Jacinto 1, Colombia. In *The emergence
        of pottery*, edited by W.K. Barnett, and J.W. Hoopes,
        133–144. Washington DC: Smithsonian Institution
        Press.

1996   The study of collector variability in the transition to
        sedentary food producers in Northern Colombia.
        Journal of World Prehistory 10(1):49–92.

N.D.   Seasonality in the tropical lowlands of northwest
        South America: The Case of San Jacinto 1, Colombia.
        In *Seasonality, and sedentism*, edited by Ofer Bar-
        Yosef, and Thomas R. Rocek. Peabody Museum,
        Harvard University.

Oyuela-Caycedo, A., and C. Rodriguez Ramirez

1990   Shell midden formation: The case of northwestern
        South America. Paper presented at the Sixth Interna-
        tional Conference of the International Council for
        Archaeozoology, Smithsonian Institution, April 23,
        1990. Washington D.C.

Palmatary, Helen C.

1960   The archaeology of the lower Tapajos Valley, Brazil.
        Transactions of the American Philosophical Society
        N.S. 50:1–243.

Parducci, Resfa

1966   Sellos zoomorfos de Manabí (Ecuador). *Cuadernos de
        Historia y Arqueología* 11–12 (28–29):123–128.

Parker Pearson, Michael

1982   Mortuary practices, society, and ideology: An
        ethnoarchaeological study. In *Symbolic, and structural
        archaeology*, edited by Ian Hodder, 99–113. Cam-
        bridge: Cambridge University Press.

Parsons, Elsie Clews

1945   *Peguche, Canton of Otavalo, Province of Imbabura,
        Ecuador: A study of Andean Indians*. Chicago:
        University of Chicago Press.

Parsons, James J.

1980   Europeanization of the savanna lands of northern
        South America. In *Human ecology in savanna
        environments*, edited by David R. Harris, 267–289.
        NY:Academic Press.

Patiño Castaño, D.

1988   *Asentamientos prehispánicos en la Costa Pacífica
        Caucana*. Santa Fe de Bogotá: Banco de la República.

Paulsen, Allison C.

1974   The thorny oyster, and the voice of god: *Spondylus*,
        and *Strombus* in Andean prehistory. *American
        Antiquity* 39:597–607.

Pearsall, Deborah M.

1988   An overview of formative period subsistence in
        Ecuador: Paleoethnobotanical data, and perspectives.
        In *Diet, and subsistence: Current archaeological
        perspectives*, Edited by B.V. Kennedy, and G.M.
        LeMoine, 149–158. Calgary: The Archaeological
        Association of the University of Calgary.

1980   Pachamachay ethnobotanical report: Plant utiliza-
        tion at a hunting base camp. In *Prehistoric hunters of the
        high Andes*, edited by John W. Rick, 191–231. NY:
        Academic Press.

1989   *Paleoethnobotany: A handbook of procedures*. New
        York: Academic Press, Inc.

1992   The origins of plant cultivation in South America. In
        The origins of agriculture, edited by C. Wesley Cowan,
        and Patty Jo Watson, 173–205. Washington DC:
        Smithsonian Institution.

Pearsall, D. M., and D. R. Piperno

1990   Antiquity of maize cultivation in Ecuador: Summary,
        and reevaluation of the evidence. *American Antiquity*
        55 (2):324–337.

Pedrarias de Avila

1993   Memoria que da pedrarias sobre la provisión a Vasco
        Nuñez de Balboa de la gobernación y adelantamiento.
        1510. In C. Jopling (editor), *Indios y Negros en
        Panamá en los Siglos XVI y XVII: Selecciones de los
        Documentos del 'Archivo General de Indias'*. South
        Woodstock, VT: CRC Press.

Peebles, Christopher S.

1978   Determinants of settlement size, and location in the
        Moundville phase. In *Mississippian settlement
        patterns*, edited by Bruce D. Smith, 369–416. New York:
        Academic Press.

1979   *Excavations at Moundville: 1905–1951*. Ann
        Arbor:University of Michigan Press.

1981   Archaeological research at Moundville: 1840–1980.
        Southeastern Archaeological Conference Bulletin
        24:77–81.

1983a   Paradise lost, strayed, and stolen: Prehistoric social
        revolution in the Southeast. Paper presented at the
        Annual Meeting, Southern Anthropological Society,
        Baton Rouge.

1983b   Moundville: Late prehistoric sociopolitical organiza-
        tion in the southeastern United States. In *The
        development of political organization in native North
        America*, edited by Elisabeth Tooker, 183–198.
        Washington, DC: The American Ethnological Society.

Peebles, Christopher S., and Susan M. Kus

1977   Some archaeological correlates of ranked societies.
        American Antiquity 42(3):421–449.

Peebles, C.S., M.J. Schoeninger, V.P. Steponaitis, and C.M.
Scarry

1981   A precious bequest: Contemporary research with the
        WPA-CCC collections from Moundville, Alabama. In
        The Research Potential of Anthropological Museum
        Collections, edited by A.M. Cantwell, J.B. Griffin, and
        N.A. Rothschild. *Annals of the New York Academy of
        Sciences* 376:433–447.

Pérez-Arbelaez, E.

1978   *Plantas utiles de Colombia*. Bogotá: Litografía Arco.

Pérez de Barradas

1937   *Arqueología y antropología precolombinas de
        Tierradentro*. Bogotá: Ministerio de Educación
        Nacional, Imprenta Nacional.

1943a   *Arqueología Agustiniana: Excavaciones arqueológicas
        realizadas de Marzo a Diciembre 1937*. Bogotá:
        Imprenta Nacional.

1943b   *Colombia de norte a sur*. Madrid: Ministerio de
        Asuntos Exteriores.

1954   *Orfebrería prehispanica de Colombia. Estilo Calima*. 2
        vols. Bogotá: Museo del Oro.

Peyton, Bernard

1980   Ecology, distribution, and food habits of spectacled
        bears, *Tremarctos ornatus*, in Peru. *Journal of
        Mammalogy* 61:639–652.

Pickersgill, Barbara, and Charles B. Heiser, Jr.

1977   Origins, and distribution of plants domesticated in
        the New World tropics. In *Origins of agriculture*,
        edited by Charles A. Reed, 803–835. The Hague:
        Mouton Publishers.

Pinder, David, Izumi Shimada, and David Gregory

1979   The nearest-neighbor statistic: Archaeological
        application, and new developments. *American*

Antiquity 44(3):430–445.

Pineda, Roberto

1945   Material arqueológico de la zona Calima. *Boletín de Arqueología* 1:491–518.

Pineda, Victor Manuel

1991   Vías, transportes, comunicaciones. In *Historia de la Cultura Material en la América Equinoccial.*, Tomo III. Bogotá: Instituto Caro y Cuervo, Biblioteca Ezequiel Uricoechea.

Piperno, D. R.

1988   Primer informe sobre los fitolitos de las plantas del OGSE-80 y la evidencia del cultivo de maiz en el Ecuador. In *La prehistoria temprana de la península de Santa Elena, Ecuador: Cultura Las Vegas*, edited by K.E. Stothert, 203–214. Miscelánea Antropológica Ecuatoriana, Serie Monográfica 10. Guayaquil: Museos del Banco Central del Ecuador.

1994a   On the emergence of agriculture in the New World. *Current Anthropology* 35(5):637–643.

1994b   Phytolith, and carbon evidence for prehistoric slash, and burn agriculture in the Darién rainforest of Panama. *The Holocene* 4:321–25.

Piperno, D., M. B. Bush, and P. A. Colinvaux

1991   Paleoecological perspectives on human adaptation in Central Panama. 2. The Holocene. *Geoarchaeology* 6:227–50.

Plazas, Clemencia, and Ana María Falchetti,

1985   Cultural patterns in the prehispanic goldwork of Colombia. In *The Art of Precolumbian Gold,* edited by Julio Jones, 146–159. London: Weidenfeld, and Nicholson.

Porras, Pedro

1973   *El Encanto—La Puna: Un sitio insular de la fase Valdivia asociada a un conchero anular.* Guayaquil: Ediciones Huancavilca.

Powell, Mary Lucas

1988   *Status, and wealth in prehistory: A case study of the Moundville chiefdom.* Washington, DC: Smithsonian Institution Press.

Pratt, Jo Ann F.

1995   Determining the function of one of the New World's earliest pottery assemblages: The case of San Jacinto, Colombia. Master's thesis, Department of Anthropology, University of Pittsburgh, Pittsburgh, PA.

Pressman, Jon F.

1991   Feathers of blood, and fire: The mythological origins of avian coloration. In *The gift of birds: Featherwork of Native South American peoples*, edited by Ruben E. Reina, and Kenneth M. Kensinger. Philadelphia: University Museum, University of Pennsylvania.

Preuss, K.T.

1931   *Arte monumental prehistórico: Excavaciones hechas en el Alto Magdalena y San Agustín (Colombia). Comparación arqueológica con las manifestaciones artísticas de las demás civilizaciones Americanas.* Bogotá: Escuela Salesiana de Tipografía y Fotograbado.

1967   *Forschungsreise zu den Kágaba-Indianern de Sierra Nevada de Santa Marta in Kolombien.* St. Gabriel-Mödling, Part 1: Travel Impressions, Transladed by Marianne Moerman. Originally published 1926, and 1927, Human Relations Area Files.

Quattrin, Dale W.

1995   Verticality, and social complexity: What does the archaeological record say? Paper presented at the 60th Annual Meeting of the Society for American Archaeology, Minneapolis, May 3–7.

Ranere, A. J., and P. Hansell

1978   Early subsistence patterns along the Pacific Coast of Central Panama. In *Prehistoric coastal adaptations*, edited by B.Stark, and B. Voorhies, 43–59. New York: Academic Press.

Ranere, Anthony

1992   Implements of change in the Holocene environments of Panama. In *Archaeology, and environment in Latin America.* edited by O. Ortiz-Troncoso, and T. van der Hammen. 25–44. Amsterdam:Instituut voor pre-en protohistorische archeologie Albert egges van Giffen.

Ranere, A., and Cooke, R.

1991   Stone tools, and cultural boundaries in prehistoric Panama: an Initial Assessment. Ms. on file Smithsonian Tropical Research Institute, Panama.

Rappaport, Joanne

1990   *Politics of memory: Native historical interpretation in the Colonial Andes.* Cambridge: Cambridge University Press.

Rappaport, Roy A.

1971   The sacred in human evolution. *Annual Review of Ecology, and Systematics* 2:23–44.

1976   Adaptation, and maladaptation in social systems. In *The Ethical basis of economic freedom*, edited by Ivan Hill, 39–79. Chapel Hill: American Viewpoint, Inc.

1979   *Ecology, meaning, and religion.* Richmond, California: North Atlantic Books.

Raymond, J. Scott

1988   Subsistence patterns during the Early Formative in the Valdivia Valley, Ecuador. In *Diet, and subsistence: Current archaeological perspectives*, edited by B.V. Kennedy, and G.M. LeMoine 159–164. Calgary: Archaeological Association of the University of Calgary.

1989   Early Formative societies in the tropical lowlands of Western Ecuador, A View from the Valdivia Valley. Paper presented at the Circum-Pacific Prehistory

Conference, Seattle.

1993 Ceremonialism in the Early Formative of Ecuador. In El Mundo ceremonial Andino, edited by Luis Millones, and Yoshio Onuki, 25–43. *Senri Ethnological Studies*, vol. 37. Osaka: National Museum of Ethnology.

Raymond, J. S., J. Marcos, and D.W. Lathrap

1980 Evidence of Early Formative settlement in the Guayas Basin, Ecuador. *Current Anthropology* 21(5):700–701.

Raymond, J.S., A. Oyuela-Caycedo, and P. Carmichael

1994 Una comparación de la ceramica temprana de Ecuador y Colombia. In *Technología y organización de la producción ceramica Prehispanica en Los Andes*, edited by I. Shimada, 33–52. Lima: Pontificia Universidad Católica del Perú, Fondo Editorial.

Recasens, J., and V. Oppenheim

1945 Análisis tipológicos de materiales cerámicos y líticos procedentes del Chocó. *Revista del Instituto Etnológico Nacional* 1:351–394. Bogotá.

Reclus, E.

1881 *Voyage á la Sierra-Nevada de Sainte Marthe.* París: Librairie Hachette & Cie.

Redmond, Elsa, and Charles S. Spencer

1994 The cacicazgo: An indigenous design. In *Caciques, and their people: A Volume in honor of Ronald Spores*, edited by Joyce Marcus, and Judith Francis Zeitlin. 189–225. Anthropological Papers, Museum of Anthropology no. 89. Ann Arbor: Univeristy of Michigan.

Reichel-Dolmatoff, Gerardo

1942 La cueva funeraria de La Paz. *Boletín de Arqueología* 2(6):403–412.

1944 La cultura material de los indios Guahibo. *Revista del Instituto Etnológico Nacional* 1(2):437–506. Bogotá.

1949 Aspectos económicos entre los indios de la Sierra Nevada de Santa Marta. *Boletín de Arqueología* 2(5/6):573–580.

1950 Los Kogi: Una tribu indígena de la Sierra Nevada de Santa Marta, Colombia, Tomo I. *Revista del Instituto Etnológico Nacional* 4(1/2). Bogotá.

1951a *Los Kogi: Una tribu indígena de la Sierra Nevada de Santa Marta, Colombia, Tomo 2.* Bogotá: Editorial Iqueima.

1951b *Datos histórico-culturales sobre las tribus de la antigua Gobernación de Santa Marta.* Bogotá: Banco de la República.

1953 Contactos y cambios culturales en la Sierra Nevada de Santa Marta. *Revista Colombiana de Antropología* 1(1)15–122.

1954a A preliminary study of space, and time perspective in northern Colombia. *American Antiquity* 19(4)352–365.

1954b Investigaciones arqueológicas en la Sierra Nevada de Santa Marta, partes 1 y 2. *Revista Colombiana de Antropología* 2(2):145–206.

1954c Investigaciones arqueológicas en la Sierra Nevada de Santa Marta, parte 3. Sitios de contacto español en Pueblito. *Revista Colombiana de Antropología* 3:139–170.

1955 Excavaciones en los Conchales de la Costa de Barlovento. *Revista Colombiana de Antropología* 4:247–272.

1961a The agricultural basis of the sub-Andean chiefdoms of Colombia. In *The evolution of horticultural systems in native South America: Causes, and consequences*, edited by Johannes Wilber, Caracas: *Antropológica* (Sociedad de Ciencias Naturales de La Salle. Supplement 2:83–89.

1961b Anthropomorphic figurines from Colombia: their magic, and art. In *Essays in pre-Columbian art, and archaeology*, edited by Samuel K. Lothrop, 229–241. Cambridge: Harvard University Press.

1962 Una nueva fecha de carbono-14 de Colombia. *Revista Colombiana de Antropología* 11:331–332.

1965a *Excavaciones arqueológicas en Puerto Hormiga (Departamento de Bolivar). Antropología* 2, Ediciones de la Universidad de los Andes. Bogotá: Editorial Tercer Mundo.

1965b *Colombia: Ancient peoples, and places.* London: Thames, and Hudson.

1971 *Amazonian Cosmos: The sexual, and religious symbolism of the Tukano Indians.* Chicago, and London: University of Chicago Press.

1972a *San Agustín: a culture of Colombia.* New York, and Washington, DC: Praeger.

1972b The feline motif in prehistoric San Agustín sculpture. In *The cult of the feline*, edited by Elizabeth P. Benson, 51–68. Washington, DC:Dumbarton Oaks Research Library, and Collections.

1972c The cultural context of an aboriginal hallucinogen: Banisteriopsis Caapi. In *Flesh of the gods: The ritual use of hallucinogens*, edited by Peter T. Furst, 84–113. New York: Praeger Publishers, Inc.

1974 Funerary customs, and religious symbolism among the Kogi. In *Native South Americans: Ethology of the least-known continent*, edited by Patricia J. Lyon, 289–301. Boston, and Toronto: Little, Brown & Company.

1975a *The shaman, and the jaguar: A study of narcotic drugs among the indians of Colombia.* Philadelphia: Temple University Press.

1975b Templos Kogi: Introducción al simbolismo y a la astronomía del espacio sagrado. *Revista Colombiana de Antropología* 19:199–245.

1975c *Contribuciones al conocimiento de la estratigrafía cerámica de San Agustín, Colombia.* Bogotá: Biblioteca

Banco Popular.

1976a   Cosmology as ecological analysis: A view from the rain forest. *Man* 11:307–318.

1976b   Training for the priesthood among the Kogi of Colombia. In *Enculturation in Latin America: an anthology*, edited by Johannes Wilbert, 265–288. Los Angeles: Latin American Center, University of California.

1977   Templos Kogi: Introducción al simbolismo y a la astronomía del espacio sagrado. *Revista Colombiana de Antropología* 19:199–246.

1978a   *Beyond the Milky Way: Hallucinatory imagery of the Tukano indians.* UCLA Latin American Studies 42. Los Angeles: Latin American Center, University of California.

1978b   Desana animal categories, food restrictions, and the concept of color energies. *Journal of Latin American Lore* 4(2):243-291.

1978c   The loom of life: A Kogi principle of integration. *Journal of Latin American Lore* 4(1):5–27.

1978d   Colombia indígena: Período prehispánico. In *Manual de historia de Colombia.* 1:35–115. Bogotá: Instituto Colombiano de Cultura.

1979   Desana shaman's rock crystals, and the hexagonal universe. *Journal of Latin American Lore* 5(1):117–128.

1982a   Cultural change, and environmental awareness: A case study of the Sierra Nevada de Santa Marta. *Mountain Research, and Development* 2(3):289–298.

1982b   Astronomical models of social behavior among some indians of Colombia. In *Ethnoastronomy, and archaeastronomy in the American tropics,* edited by Anthony F. Aveni, and Gary Urton. *Annals of the New York Academy of Sciences* 385:165–181.

1984   Some Kogi models of the beyond. *Journal of Latin American Lore* 10(1):63–85.

1985a   *Monsú: Un sitio arqueológico.* Bogotá: Biblioteca Banco Popular, Textos Universitarios.

1985b   *Basketry as metaphor: Arts, and crafts of the Desana indians of the northwest Amazon.* Occasional Papers 5 of the Museum of Cultural History. Los Angeles: University of California.

1985c   *Los Kogi. Una tribu de la Sierra Nevada de Santa Marta.* 2 vols. Bogotá: Procultura Nueva Biblioteca Colombiana de Cultura.

1986   *Arqueología de Colombia: Un texto introductorio.* Bogotá: Presidencia de la República, Fundación Segunda Expedición Botánica.

1987   The great mother, and the Kogi universe: A concise overview. *Journal of Latin American Lore* 13(1):73–113.

1988   *Goldwork, and shamanism: An iconographic study of the Gold Museum.* Medellín: Editorial Colina.

1990   *The sacred mountain of Colombia's Kogi indians.* Iconography of Religions, section IX, South America; fasc. 2. New York: E.J. Brill.

1991a   *Los Ika: Sierra Nevada de Santa Marta, Colombia: Notas etnográficas 1946–1966.* Bogotá: Centro Editorial, Universidad Nacional de Colombia.

1991b   *Indians of Colombia: Experience, and cognition.* Bogotá: Villegas Editores.

1992   Short-cuts in the Tukano rain forest of symbols. Paper presented at the X Symposio Internacional, Asociación de Literaturas Indígenas Latinoamericanas (LAILA/AILA). Old San Juan, Puerto Rico.

Reichel-Dolmatoff, G., and Alicia Dussán de Reichel

1951   Investigaciones arqueológicas en el departamento de Magdalena, Colombia (Parte I y II). *Boletín de Arqueología* 3(1–6):1–334.

1953   Investigaciones arqueológicas en el departamento del Magdalena: 1946-1950; Parte III *Arqueología del Bajo Magdalena: Divulgaciones Etnólogicas* 3(4):1–96.

1955   Investigaciones arqueológicas en la Sierra Nevada de Santa Marta; Parte 4, Sitios de Habitación del Período Tairona II, en Pueblito. *Revista Colombiana de Antropología* 4:191–245.

1961   Investigaciones arqueológicas en la Costa Pacífica de Colombia. I. El Sitio Cupica. *Revista Colombiana de Antropología* 10:237–330.

1962   Investigaciones arqueológicas en la Costa Pacífica de Colombia. II. Una Secuencia Cultural del Bajo Río San Juan. *Revista Colombiana de Antropología* 11:9–72.

Restrepo Tirado, Ernesto

1943   Nueva Salamanca de la Ramada. *Boletín de Historia y Antiguedades* 30(347):859–862.

1975   *Historia de la Provincia de Santa Marta.* Bogotá: Colcultura.

Robledo, Emilio

1954   Migraciones oceánicas en el poblamiento de Colombia. *Boletín del Instituto de Antropología Universidad de Antioquia* 1(3):215–234.

Rodríguez, Carlos A.

1992   *Tras las huellas del hombre prehispánico y su cultura en el valle del Cauca.* Cali: INCIVA.

Rodriguez, Camilo

1988   Agricultores prehispánicos de la Hoya del Quindío. *Boletín de Arqueología* 3(1):25–33.

1991   *Patrones de asentamiento de los agricultores prehispánicos de El Limón, Municipio de Chaparral (Tolima).* Bogotá: Banco de la República.

Romero, Fray Francisco.

1955   *Llanto sagrado de la America Meridional.* Originally published 1693. Edited by Gabriel Giraldo Jaramill. Bogotá.

Romoli, K.

1976   El Alto Chocó en el siglo XVI. Las gentes. *Revista Colombiana de Antropología* 20:25–53.

1987   *Los de la Lengua de Cueva: los grupos indígenas del Istmo Oriental en la epoca de la conquista Española.* Bogotá: Instituto Colombiano de Antropología, and Instituto Colombiano de Cultura.

Roosevelt, A. C., M. Lima da Costa, C. Lopez Machado, M. Michab, N. Mercier, H. Valladas, J. Feathers, W. Barnett, M. Imazio da Silveira, A. Henderson, J. Sliva, B. Chernoff, D. S. Reese, J. A. Holman, N. Toth, and K. Schick.

1996   Paleoindian cave dwellers in the Amazon: The Peopling of the Americas. *Science* 272:373–384.

Rouse, I., and J. M. Cruxent

1963   *Venezuelan archaeology.* New Haven: Yale University Press.

Rowe, John H.

1946   Inca culture at the time of the Spanish Conquest. In *Handbook of South American Culture*, edited by Julian H. Steward, Bureau of American Ethnology, Bulletin 143, vol. 2:183–330. Washington, DC.

1950   The Idibáez: Unknown Indians of the Chocó coast. *Kroeber Anthropological Society Papers* 1:34–44.

Rozo Gauta, José

1978   *Los Muiscas. Organización social y régimen político.* Bogotá: Fondo Editorial Sudamérica.

Sahlins, Marshall

1963   Poor man, rich man, big man, chief: Political types in Melanesia, and Polynesia. In *Comparative Studies in Society, and History* 5(3):285–303.

Salavata, Domingo

1983   Interview by A. Oyuela-Caycedo, December 19.

Salgado, H.

1986   *Asentamientos prehispánicos en el noroccidente del valle del Cauca.* Santa Fé de Bogotá: Banco de la República.

1989   *Medio ambiente y asentamientos humanos prehispánicos en el Calima Medio.* Cali: Instituto Vallecaucano de Investigaciones Científicas.

Salgado, H., C. Rodríguez, and V. Bashilov

1993   *La vivienda orehispánica Calima.* Cali: INCIVA.

Salgado, Héctor, and David Michael Stemper

1995   *Cambios en alfarería y agricultura en el centro del Litoral Pacífico Colombiano durante los dos ultimos milenios.* Bogotá: Banco de la República.

Salomon, Frank

1986   *Native lords of Quito in the age of the Incas: The political economy of North Andean chiefdoms.* New York: Cambridge University Press.

1995   The beautiful grandparents: Andean ancestor shrines, and mortuary ritual as seen through Colonial records.

In *Tombs for the living: Andean mortuary practices,* edited by Tom Dillehay, 315–353. Washington, DC: Dumbarton Oak Research.

Sanchez Herrera, L.A.

1995   *Análisis estilístico de dos componentes cerámicos de Cerro Juan Díaz: Su relación con el surgimiento de las sociedades cacicales en Panamá.* Práctica dirigida presentada ante la Escuela de Antropología y Sociología para optar al Grado de Licenciado en Antropología con Enfasis en Arqueología. San José: Universidad de Costa Rica, Facultad de Ciencias Sociales, Escuela de Antropología y Sociología.

Sanoja, M.

1970   *La fase Zancudo. Investigaciones arqueológicas en el Lago de Maracaibo.* Caracas: Instituto de Investigaciones Económicas y Sociales, U.C.V.

Sanoja, Mario, and Iraida Vargas

1974   *Antiguos modos de producción y formación económico social Venezolanos.* Caracas: Monte Avila Editores.

Santos Granero, Fernando

1986   Power, ideology, and the ritual of production in lowland South America. *Man* 21:657–679.

Santos Vecino, G.

1989   Las etnias indígenas prehispánicas y de la conquista en la región del Golfo de Urabá. *Boletín de Antropología, Universidad de Antioquia* 6(22).

Sarmiento, Guillermo

1984   *The ecology of neotropical savannas.* Cambridge, MA: Harvard University Press.

Sauer, C.O.

1966   *The early Spanish Main.* Berkeley: University of California Press.

Saville, Marshall H.

1910   *The antiquities of Manabí, Ecuador. Final report.* Contributions to South American Archaeology, vol. 2. New York: The George G. Heye Foundation.

Saxe, Arthur A.

1970   Social dimensions of mortuary practices in a Mesolithic population from Wadi Halfa, Sudan. Ph.D. dissertation, Department of Anthropology, University of Michigan, Ann Arbor.

Schávelzon, J.

1981   Notas sobre las cerámicas Valdivia tardías de Manabí. *Arqueología y Arquitectura del Ecuador Prehispánico,* 121–126. Universidad Nacional Autonoma de México, México.

Schultes, Richard Evans, and Robert F. Raffauf

1990   *The healing forest: Medicinal, and toxic plants of the northwest Amazonia.* Portland: Dioscorides Press.

Schwarz, F.A.

1987   Prehistoric settlement patterns in the Valdivia Valley, Southwest Coastal Ecuador. Master's Thesis, Department of Archaeology, Univesity of Calgary, Calgary, Canada.

Schwarz, F.A., and J.S. Raymond
1996   Formative settlement patterns in the Valdivia Valley, Southwest Coastal Ecuador. *Journal of Field Archaelogy* 23(2):205–224.

Serje de la Ossa, Margarita.
1984   Organización urbana en Ciudad Perdida. *Cuadernos de Arquitectura Escala* no 9. Bogotá.

Servant, Michel, Jean Maley, Bruno Turcq, Maria-Lucia Absy, Patrice Brenac, Marc Fournier, and Marie-Pierre Ledru
1993   Tropical forest changes during the Late Quaternary in African, and South American lowlands. *Global, and Planetary Change* 7:25–40.

Shanks, Michael, and Christopher Tilley
1982   Ideology, symbolic power, and ritual communication: A reinterpretation of Neolithic mortuary practices. In *Symbolic, and Structural Archaeology*, edited by Ian Hodder, 129–154. Cambridge: Cambridge University Press.

Sharon, Douglas
1976   Distribution of the Mesa in Latin America. *Journal of Latin American Lore* 2(1):71–96.

Shepard, Paul, and Barry Sanders
1985   *The sacred paw: The bear in nature, myth, and literature.* New York: Viking Press.

Sievers, Wilhelm
1986   Los Indigenas Arhuacos en la Sierra Nevada de Santa Marta. Originally published 1886. *Boletin Museo del Oro* 16:3–15.

Simón, Fray Pedro.
1882   *Noticias historiales de las conquistas de Tierra Firme en las Indias Occidentales.* Bogotá: Imprenta de Medardo Rivas.
1981   *Noticias historiales de la conquìsta de Tierra Fìrme en las Indias Occidentales.* 6 vols. Originally published 1625. Bogotá: Biblioteca Banco Popular.

Simons, Frederick. A. A.
1879   Notes on the topography of the Sierra Nevada de Santa Marta. *Proceedings of the Royal Geographical Society* 1:689–694.
1881   On the Sierra Nevada de Santa Marta, and its watershed (State of Magdalena, U.S. of Colombia). *Proceedings of the Royal Geographical Society* 3:705–723, 768.

Smith, Bruce D.
1992   Prehistoric plant husbandry in eastern North America. In *The origins of agriculture*, edited by C. Wesley Cowan, and Patty Jo Watson, 101–119. Washington: Smithsonian Institution Press.
1995   *The emergence of agriculture.* New York: Scientific

American Library.

Solomon, Frank.
1986   Vertical politics on the Inka frontier. In *Anthropological history of Andean polities.* edited by John V. Murra, Nathan Wachtel, and Jacques Revel, 89–118. Cambridge: Cambridge University Press.

Sotomayor, María Lucía, and Uribe, María Victoria
1987   *Estatuaria del Macizo Colombiano.* Bogotá: Instituto Colombiano de Antropología.

Spencer, Charles S.
1987   Rethinking the chiefdom. In *Chiefdoms in the Americas*, edited by R.D. Drennan, and C.A. Uribe, 369–390. New York: University Press of America.

Stahl, Peter W.
1984   Tropical forest cosmology: The cultural context of the Early Valdivia occupations at Loma Alta. Ph.D dissertation, Department of Anthropology, University of Illinois, Urbana.
1985a   Native American cosmology in archaeological interpretation: Tropical forest cosmology, and the Early Valdivia phase at Loma Alta. In *Status, structure, and stratification: Current archaeological reconstructions*, edited by Marc Thompson, Maria Teresa Garcia, and Francois Kense, 31–37. Calgary: Archaeological Association, University of Calgary.
1985b   The hallucinogenic basis of Early Valdivia phase ceramic bowl iconography. *Journal of Psychoactive Drugs* 17(2):105–123.
1986   Hallucinatory imagery, and the origin of Early South American figurine art. *World Archaeology* 18(1):134–150.
1994   Qualitative assessment of archaeofaunal taxa from the Jama Valley. In *Regional Archaeology in Northern Ecuador, Volume 1: Environment, cultural chronology, and prehistoric subsistence in the Jama River Valley*, edited by James A. Zeidler, and Deborah M. Pearsall, 185–199. University of Pittsburgh, Memoirs in Latin American Archaeology no. 8, Pittsburgh.
1995   Differential preservation histories affecting the mammalian zooarchaeological record from the forested neotropical lowlands. In *Archaeology in the lowland American tropics: Current analytical methods, and recent applications*, edited by Peter W. Stahl, 154–180. Cambridge: Cambridge University Press.

Staller, John Edward
1994   Late Valdivia occupations in southern coastal El Oro Province, Ecuador: Excavations at the Early Formative Period (3500-1500 BC) Site of La Emerenciana. Ph.D dissertation, Department of Anthropology, Southern Methodist University, Dallas.

Stemper, David M.
1993   *The persistence of prehispanic chiefdoms on the Río*

Daule, Coastal Ecuador. University of Pittsburgh Memoirs in Latin American Archaeology no. 7. Pittsburgh, and Quito: University of Pittsburgh, and Ediciones Libri Mundi.

Steponaitis, Vincas P.

1978   Locational theory, and complex chiefdoms: A Mississippian example. In *Mississippian settlement patterns*, edited by Bruce D. Smith, 417–453. New York: Academic Press.

1983a   *Ceramics, chronology, and community patterns: An archaeological study at Moundville*. New York: Academic Press.

1983b   The Smithsonian Institution's investigations at Moundville in 1869, and 1882. *Midcontinental Journal of Archaeology* 8:127–160.

Steward, J.H., and L. Faron

1959   *The native peoples of South America*. New York: McGraw Hill.

Steward, Julian H., and Alfred Metraux

1948   Tribes of the Peruvian, and Ecuadorian Montaña. In *Handbook of South American Indians,* edited by Julian H. Steward, Bureau of American Ethnology, Bulletin 143, vol. 3:535–656. Washington, DC.

Stirling, M.W., and M. Stirling

1964   The archaeology of Taboga, Urabá, and Taboguilla islands of Panama. *Smithsonian Institution Bureau of American Ethnology Bulletin* 191:285–348.

Stothert, Karen E.

1985   The preceramic Las Vegas culture of coastal Ecuador. *American Antiquity* 50(3):613–637.

1988   *La prehistoria temprana de la península de Santa Elena: Cultura Las Vegas*. Miscelanea Antropológica Ecuatoriana No 10. Guayaquil: Museos del Banco Central del Ecuador.

Stout, David B.

1945   The Cuna. In *Handbook of South American Indians*, edited by Julian H. Steward, Bureau of American Ethnology, Bullentin 143, vol.4:257–268. Washington DC.

1948   The Chocó. In *Handbook of South American Indians*, edited by Julian H. Steward, Bureau of American Ethnology, Bulletin 143, vol. 4:1–41. Washington, DC.

Stuiver, M., and B. Becker

1993   High-precision decadal calibration of the radiocarbon time scale, AD 1950–6000 BC. *Radiocarbon* 35:35–65.

Taft, Mary M.

1991   Ceramic distribution patterns in the Valle de la Plata, Colombia. Ph.D. dissertation, Department of Anthropology, University of Pittsburgh.

1993   Part Two: Patterns of ceramic production, and distribution. In *Prehispanic chiefdoms in the Valle de la Plata, Volume 2: Ceramics–chronology, and craft production*, edited by R.D. Drennan, M.M. Taft, and C.A. Uribe, 105–172. University of Pittsburgh Memoirs in Latin American Archaeology no. 5. Pittsburgh, and Santa Fe de Bogotá: University of Pittsburgh, and Universidad de los Andes.

Tarble, K.

1982   *Comparación estilística de Dos colecciones cerámicas del noroeste de Venezuela: Una nueva metodología*. Caracas: Ernesto Armitano Editor.

1993   Criterios para la ubicación de los asentamientos prehispánicos en el area de Barraguán, Edo. Bolívar. In *Contribuciones a la Arqueología Regional de Venezuela*, edited by Francisco Fernández, and Rafael Gassón, 139–164. Caracas: Fondo Editorial Acta Científica Venezolana.

Tartusi, M., A. Niño, and V. Nuñez-Regueiro

1984   Relaciones entre el area Occidental de la Cuenca del Lago de Maracaibo con las areas vecinas. In *Relaciones Prehispánicas de Venezuela*, edited by E. Wagner, 67–88. Caracas: Fondo Editorial Acta Científica Venezolana.

Taussig, Michael

1980   Folk healing, and the structure of conquest in southwest Colombia. *Journal of Latin American Lore* 6:217–278.

1987   *Shamanism, colonialism, and the wild man*. Chicago: University of Chicago Press.

1993   *Mimesis, and alterity*. New York: Routledge.

Tello Cifuentes, Hernán

1981   *Geología de algunos sitios arqueológicos*. Bogotá: Banco de la República.

Tindale, Norman B.

1977   Adaptive significance of the Panara or grass seed culture of Australia. In *Stone tools as cultural markers*, edited by R. V. Wright, 345–349. Canberra: Australian Institute of Aboriginal Studies.

Torres de Araúz, R.

1975   *Darién, etnoecología de una región histórica*. Panamá: INAC.

Torroni, A., T.G. Schurr, M.F. Cabell, M.D. Brown, J.V. Neel, M. Larsen, D.G. Smith, C.M. Vullo, and D.C. Wallace

1993   Asian affinities, and continental radiation of the four founding Native American mtDNAs. *American Journal of Human Genetics* 53:563–590.

Tovar Pinzón, Hermes, ed.

1988   *No Hay Caciques Ni Señores*. Barcelona: Ediciones Sendai.

Tovar Pinzón, Hermes

1980   *La formación social Chibcha*. Cooperativa de Profesores de la Universidad Nacional de Colombia. Bogotá.

N.D.   *Relaciones y visitas a los Andes: Siglo XVI*, Tomo II, Región del Caribe. Bogotá: Colcultura.

Trimborn, Hermann
1949   *Señorío y barbarie en el Valle del Cauca*. Madrid: Instituto Gonzalo Fernández de Oviedo.

Trombold, Charles D., ed.
1991   *Ancient road networks, and settlement hierarchies in the New World*. Cambridge: Cambridge University Press.

Ubelaker, Douglas R.
1995   Letter to Zeidler, 21 February 1995.

Upham, Steadman
1987   A theoretical consideration of middle range societies. In *Archaeological reconstruction, and chiefdoms in the Americas,* edited by R. Drennan, and C. Uribe, 345–368. New York: University Press of America.

Uribe, M. A.
1988   Introducción a la orfebrería de San Pedro de Urabá, una región del noroccidente colombiano. *Boletín Museo del Oro* 20:35–54.

Uribe Tobón, Carlos A.
1990   Nosotros los hermanos mayores: continuidad y cambio entre los Kággaba de la Sierra Nevada de Santa Marta, Colombia. Ph.D dissertation, University of Pittsburgh, Pittsburgh, PA.
1993   La etnografía de la Sierra Nevada de Santa Marta y tierras bajas adyacentes. In *Geografía humana de Colombia: Noroeste indígena*, edited by Carlos A. Uribe Tobón, vol. 2:8–214. Bogotá: Instituto Colombiano de Cultura Hispánica.

Urton, Gary
1985   Animal metaphors, and the life cycle in an Andean community. In *Animal myths, and metaphors in South America,* edited by Gary Urton, 251–284. Salt Lake City: University of Utah Press.

van der Hammen, Thomas
1974   The Pleistocene changes of vegetation, and climate in tropical South America. *Journal of Biogeography* 1:3–26.
1983   The paleoecology, and paleogeography of savannas. In *Ecosystems of the world: Tropical savannas*, edited by Francois Bourliere, vol. 13:19–35. Amsterdam: Elsevier Scientific Publishing Company.
1984   Datos sobre la historia de clima, vegetación y glaciación de la Sierra Nevada de Santa Marta. In *La Sierra Nevada de Santa Marta (Colombia) transecto buritaca—La Cumbre*, edited by Thomas van der Hammen, and Pedro M. Ruiz, 561–573. Berlin: J. Cramer.
1988   Cambios medioambientales y la extinción del mastodonte en el Norte de los Andes. In *Revista de Antropología* 2 (2):27-33.

1992   *Historia, ecología y vegetación*. Bogotá: Corporación Colombiana para la Amazonia.

van der Hammen, T., J. F. Duivenvoorden, J. M. Lips, L. E. Urrego, and N. Espejo
1991   Fluctuaciones de nivel del agua del río y de la velocidad de sedimentación durante los ultimos 13000 años en el area del Medio Caquetá (Amazonia Colombiana). *Colombia Amazonica* 5(1):91–118.

van der Hammen, T., and O. Ortiz-Troncoso
1992   Arqueología y medio ambiente en Suramérica septentrional. In *Archaeology, and environment in Latin America*, edited by O. Ortiz-Troncoso, and T. van der Hammen, 9–24. Amsterdam: Instituut voor Pre-en Protohistorische Archeologie Albert egges van Giffen.

van der Hammen T., and Pedro T. Ruiz. ed.
1986   *Studies on tropical Andean ecosistem: Trancecto buritaca–la Cumbre*. Berlin-Stutgart: Cramer.

van der Merwe, N., J. Lee-Thorp, and J. S. Raymond
1993   Light stable isotopes, and the subsistence base of Formative cultures at Valdivia, Ecuador. In *Prehistoric human bone: Archaeology at the molecular level,* edited by J. Lambert, and Gisela Grupe, 63–97. Berlin: Springer-Verlag.

van Gelder, Richard G.
1990   The spectacled bear. *Collier's Encyclopedia*, vol. 3:733. New York: Macmillan.

van Rosen, Beatrice
1990   Mammals. *Collier's Encyclopedia*, vol. 15, 294–316. New York: MacMillan.

Vanzolini, P.E.
1973   Paleoclimates, relief, and species multiplication in equatorial forests. In *Tropical forest ecosystems in Africa, and South America: A comparative review*, edited by B. Meggers, Ayensu, and Duckworth 255–258. Washington: Smithsonian Institution.

Vargas, Iraida.
1985   *Gens*, Vol. 1, No 2.

Vargas, Patricia
1990   Los Emberãs y los Cunas en frontera con el imperio Español. *Boletín del Museo del Oro* 29:75–100.
1993   *Los Emberá y los Cuna: Impacto y reacción ante la ocupación Española, siglos XVI y XVII.* Bogotá: CEREC/Instituto Colombiano de Antropología.

Vila, Marco Aurelio
1968   *Aspectos geográficos del estado de Lara.* Caracas: Corporación Venezolana de Fomento.

Villamarín, Juan
1972   Encomenderos, and Indians in the formation of Colonial society in the Sabana de Bogotá, Colombia 1937 to 1740. Dissertation Information Service. Ann Arbor, Michigan.

Villamarín, Juan, and Judith Villamarín

1975   Kinship, and inheritance among the Sabana de Bogotá Chibcha at the time of the Spanish Conquest. *Ethnology* 14:173–179.

Wagner, E.

1967   *The prehistory, and ethnohistory of the Carache Area in western Venezuela.* Yale University Publication in Anthropology no. 71. New Haven: Yale University.

1978a   Recent research in Venezuelan prehistory. In *Archaeological essays in honor of Irving B. Rouse*, edited by Robert C. Dunnell, and Edwin S. Hall, Jr. 319–342. The Hague: Mouton Publishers.

1978b   La prehistoria de la cuenca de Maracaibo. In *Unidad y variedad ensayos en homenaje a J. M. Cruxent*, edited by E. Wagner y A. Zucchi, 367–375. Caracas: Ediciones CEA-IVIC.

1992   Diversidad cultural y ambiental en el occidente de Venezuela. In *Archaeology, and environmental in Latin America*, edited by Omar R. Ortíz-Troncoso, and Thomas van der Hammen, 207–221. Amsterdam: Institut-voor Pre. Protohistorische Archeologie Albert, Eggs van Liffen.

1993   La prehistoria de la Cordillera de Mérida. In *El Cuaternario de la Cordillera de Mérida Andes Venezolanos*, edited by Carlos Schubert, and Leonel Vivas, 271–291. Mérida: Universidad de Los Andes, Fundación Polar.

Wagner, E., and K. Tarble de Ruíz

1975   Lagunillas: A new Archaeological phase for the Lake Maracaibo Basin, Venezuela. *Journal of Field Archaeology* 2(1–2):105–118.

Walker, Ernest P., et al.

1975   *Mammals of the world.* Third edition, vol. 2. Baltimore: Johns Hopkins University Press.

Walsh, R. P. D.

1981   The nature of climatic seasonality. In *Climatic seasonality in the tropics*, edited by Robert Chambers, Richard Longhurst and Arnold Pacey, 11–29. London: Frances Printer Ltd.

Wason, Paul K.

1994   *The archaeology of rank.* Cambridge: Cambridge University Press.

Wassén, Henry

1935   Notes on southern groups of Chocó Indians in Colombia. *Ethnological Studies* 1:35–182.

1940   An analogy between a South American, and oceanic myth motif, and negro influence in the Darién. *Etnologiska Studier* 10:69–79. Göteborg.

1949   Contributions to Cuna ethnography. *Etnologiska Studier* 16:7–139. Göteborg.

1955   Algunos datos del comercio precolombino en Colombia. *Revista Colombiana de Antropología* 4:87–109.

1976   Un estudio arqueológico en la Cordillera Occidental de Colombia. *Cespedesia* 5(17–18):9–38.

Wassén, Henry, ed.

1938   *An historical, and ethnological survey of the Cuna Indians.* Comparative Ethnographical Studies, 10. Göteborg.

Watson, P. J.

1976   In pursuit of prehistoric subsistence. A comparative account of some contemporary flotation techniques. *Midcontinental Journal of Archaeology* 1:77–100.

Weinhardt, Diana

1993   The spectacled bear. In *Bears: Majestic creatures of the wild*, edited by Ian Stirling, 134–139. PA: Rodale Press.

Welch, Paul D.

1991   *Moundville's economy.* Tuscaloosa: University of Alabama Press.

West, R.C.

1957   *The Pacific lowlands of Colombia: A Negroid area of the American tropics.* Baton Rouge: Louisiana State University Press.

Wetterstrom, W.

1993   Foraging, and farming in Egypt: The transition from hunting, and gathering to horticulture in the Nile Valley. In *The Archaeology of Africa: Food, metals, and towns*, edited by Thurstan Shaw, Paul Sinclair, Bassey Andah, and Alex Okpoko, 165–226. New York: Routledge.

Whiffen, Thomas

1915   *The north-west Amazons: Notes of some months spent among cannibal tribes.* New York: Duffield.

Whitten, Norman

1976   *Sacha Runa: Ethnicity, and adaptation of Ecuadorian jungle Quichua.* Urbana: University of Illinois Press.

Wilbert, Johannes

1974   *The thread of life: Symbolism of miniature art from Ecuador.* Studies in Pre-Columbian Art, and Archaeology no. 12. Washington DC: Dumbarton Oaks Research Library, and Collections.

1975   Eschatology in a participatory universe: Destinies of the soul among the Warao Indians of Venezuela. In *Death, and the afterlife in pre-Columbian America*, edited by Elizabeth P. Benson, 163–189. Washington, DC: Dumbarton Oaks Research Library, and Collection.

Willey, Gordon R.

1958   Estimated correlations, and dating of South, and Central American culture sequences. *American Antiquity* 23(4):353–378.

1971   *An introduction to American archaeology*, vol. 2: South America. Englewood Cliffs, New Jersey: Prentice-Hall.

1984   A summary of the archaeology of lower Central America. In *The archaeology of lower Central America*, edited by F.W. Lange, and D.Z. Stone, 341–378. Albuquerque: School of American Research-University of New Mexico Press.

Willey, G.R., and C. R. McGimsey III

1954   *The Monagrillo culture of Panama*. Papers of the
       Peabody Museum of Archaeology, and Ethnology,
       Harvard University, vol. XLIX, no. 2. Cambridge.

Wilson, David J.

1992   Modeling the role of ideology in societal adaptation.
       In *Ideology, and precolumbian civilization*, edited by
       Arthur A. Demarest, and G. W. Conrad, 37–64. Santa
       Fe, New Mexico: School of American Research Press.

Winter, Marcus C., and Jane W. Pires-Ferreira

1976   Distribution of obsidian among households in two
       Oaxacan villages. In *The early Mesoamerican village*,
       edited by K.V. Flannery, 306-311. New York, Academic
       Press.

Winterhalder, Bruce

1990   Open field, common pot: Harvest variability, and risk
       avoidance in agricultural, and foraging societies. In
       *Risk, and uncertainty in tribal, and peasant econo-
       mies*, edited by Elizabeth Cashdan, pp. 67–87. Boulder,
       CO: Westview Press.

1986   Diet choice, risk, and food sharing in a stochastic
       environment. *Journal of Anthropological Archaeology*
       5(4):369–392.

Wolford, Jack A.

1994   Some problems of theory, and method in lithic
       studies: Ecuador, Colombia, and Venezuela. In *History
       of Latin American archaeology*, edited by Augusto
       Oyuela-Caycedo, 155–172. Hampshire: Avebury.

Yepes, Benjamín

1982   *La estatuaria múrui-muinane. Simbolismo de la Gente
       "Huitoto"de la Amazonía Colombiana*. Bogotá: Banco
       de la República.

Zeidler, James A.

1977/78 Primitive exchange, prehistoric trade, and the
       problem of a Mesoamerican-South American
       connection. *Journal of the Steward Anthropological
       Society* 9 (1/2):7–39.

1984   Social space in Valdivia society: Community pattern-
       ing, and domestic structure at Real Alto, 3000–2000 BC.
       Ph.D dissertation, Department of Anthropology,
       University of Illinois, Urbana.

1986   La Evolución local de asentamientos Formativos en el
       Litoral Ecuatoriano: El caso de Real Alto. In
       Arqueología de la costa Ecuatoriana: Nuevos enfoques,
       Edited by J. G. Marcos, vol. 1:85–127. Quito:
       Corporación Editora Nacional.

1988   Feline imagery, stone mortars, and Formative period
       interaction spheres in the northern Andean area.
       Journal of Latin American Lore 14:243–283.

1991   Maritime exchange in the Early Formative period of
       coastal Ecuador: Geopolitical origins of uneven

development. *Research in Economic Anthropology*
       13:247–268.

1992   Cosmology, and community plan in Early Formative
       Ecuador. Paper Presented at the 91st Annual Meeting
       of the American Anthropological Association, San
       Francisco, December 2.

1994a Archaeological testing in the Middle Jama Valley. In
       *Regional archaeology in Northern Ecuador, volume 1:
       Environment, cultural chronology, and prehistoric
       subsistence in the Jama River Valley*, edited by James
       A. Zeidler, and Deborah M. Pearsall, 71-98. University
       of Pittsburgh, Memoirs in Latin American Archaeol-
       ogy no. 8, Pittsburgh.

1994b Archaeological testing in the Lower Jama Valley. In
       *Regional archaeology in Northern Ecuador, Volume 1:
       Environment, cultural chronology, and prehistoric
       subsistence in the Jama River Valley*, edited by James
       A. Zeidler, and Deborah M. Pearsall, 99-110. University
       of Pittsburgh, Memoirs in Latin American Archaeol-
       ogy no. 8, Pittsburgh.

1995   Archaeological survey, and site discovery in the
       forested neotropics. In *Archaeology in the lowland
       American tropics: Current analytical methods, and
       recent applications*, edited by Peter W. Stahl, 7–41.
       Cambridge: Cambridge University Press.

Zeidler, J. A., and D. M. Pearsall ed.

1994   *Regional archaeology in Northern Ecuador, Volume 1:
       Environment, cultural chronology, and prehistoric
       subsistence in the Jama River Valley*. University of
       Pittsburgh, Memoirs in Latin American Archaeology
       no. 8, Pittsburgh.

Zeidler, James A., Caitlin E. Buck, and Clive D. Litton

1996   The integration of archaeological phase information,
       and radiocarbon results from the Jama River Valley,
       Ecuador: A Bayesian Approach. *Latin American
       Antiquity*. In press.

Zevallos M., Carlos

1971   *La agricultura en el Formativo temprano del Ecuador
       (Cultura Valdivia)*. Guayquil: Editorial Casa de la
       Cultura Ecuatoriana.

Zevallos M., Carlos, and Olaf Holm

1960a Excavaciones arqueológicas en San Pablo. *Ciencia y
       Naturaleza* 3(2–3):62–95.

1960b *Excavaciones arqueológicas en San Pablo: Informe
       Preliminar*. Nucleo del Guayas, Guayaquil: Editorial
       Casa de la Cultura Ecuatoriana.

Zuidema, R. Tom

1985   The lion in the city: Royal symbols of transition in
       Cuzco. In *Animal myths, and metaphors in South
       America*, edited by Gary Urton, 183–250. Salt Lake
       City: University of Utah Press.

Contributors

Jeffrey P. Blick
Lawson State Community College, Birmingham

Ana Maria Boada Rivas
University of Pittsburgh

Renee M. Bonzani
IMANI, Universidad Nacional de Colombia

Marianne Cardale Schrimpff
Fundación ProCalima, Bogotá

Richard Cooke
Smithsonian Tropical Research Institute, Panama

Warren DeBoer
Queens College, City University of New York

Peter T. Furst
University of Pennsylvania

Mary W. Helms
University of North Carolina at Greensboro

Carlos López
Temple University, Philadelphia

Peter Stahl
State University of New York at Binghamton

Marie J. Sutliff
Escuela Superior Politécnica del Litoral, Guayaquil

Erika Wagner
Instituto Venezolano de Investigaciones Científicas, Caracas

James A. Zeidler
University of Illinois at Urbana-Champaign